DECODING THE RABBIS

A Thirteenth-Century Commentary
on the Aggadah

MARC SAPERSTEIN

HARVARD UNIVERSITY PRESS
Cambridge, Massachusetts
London, England
1980

Library of Congress Cataloging in Publication Data

Saperstein, Marc.
    Decoding the Rabbis.

    (Harvard Judaic monographs; 3)
    Includes bibliographical references and indexes.
    1.   Isaac ben Jedaiah, 13th cent.   2.   Aggada—
History and criticism.   I.   Title.   II.   Series.
BM516.5.I823S26   296.1'27606   80-13166
ISBN 0-674-19445-4

For My Parents

PREFACE

THIS BOOK IS ABOUT the work of a thirteenth-century Provençal author named R. Isaac ben Yedaiah. The reader who turns to any of the standard reference books for background information about R. Isaac will be disappointed. No one of such a name is to be found in the Jewish encyclopedias or in the general histories of Hebrew literature or even in the monumental bibliographic studies of the *Wissenschaft des Judentums*. I am suggesting that a new figure in the history of Jewish culture has been discovered, the importance of whose work is by no means belied by the fact that his traces were all but lost in subsequent Hebrew literature.

What follows, therefore, is not merely an analysis of manuscript material, much of which has never before been carefully read or adequately described. It is also a reclamation of an author ill treated by the vagaries of history. Medieval scribes were probably reluctant to begin copying works of such prodigious length as his commentaries. There is also at least the possibility of a conscious decision by scribes and other Jewish writers to avoid R. Isaac's work because it contained controversial or provocative material. Whatever the reason, all that remain are unique manuscripts of two small portions of the originals. And this extant material has been attributed to the wrong author. Though R. Isaac did not believe that the souls of the departed have knowledge of what transpires in our sublunar realm, we might assume that the discovery and proper accreditation of at least part of his lifework would not displease him.

If one purpose of this book is to reclaim an individual author, the second major purpose is to delineate upon the broad canvas of Jewish cultural history the area of his major interest and efforts. The history of interpretation of the aggadah has yet to be generally recognized as a subject worthy of systematic study. While many scholars have begun to apply various analytical tools to the aggadah itself, there has been relatively little investigation of the ways in which Jews throughout the ages have interpreted the aggadah in response to changing intellectual assumptions, new historical pressures, the intrinsic challenge of the material itself, and the demands of an educated community for novel insights into familiar texts. Many of the most important works of aggadic exegesis remain in manuscript; these must be published and studied before any general survey—even for a single geographical area such as southern France—may be safely attempted. I hope that my monograph will demonstrate the importance of this exegetical genre, not so much for the insights it may bring into the original meaning of the Talmudic material as for the light it throws upon the medieval Jewish mind, drawing upon an ancient and venerable literature to contend with the challenges of new intellectual movements, the lures of powerful daughter religions, the agonies of external oppression and inner social strife. This study of Isaac ben Yedaiah's commentaries is, therefore, not a work of pure history or philosophy or literature. It is rather an attempt to follow two major documents, one of them hitherto unknown, wherever the texts themselves lead and to extract from these documents their full significance for our understanding of the Jew and his culture in medieval Europe.

It is always a pleasant responsibility to acknowledge help and to express gratitude where it is due. Most of my research into published material was done in the Hebraica and Judaica Collections of Harvard's Widener Library, where Dr. Charles Berlin was always ready to solve bibliographical problems after I had become stymied. The staff of the Institute for the Microfilming of Hebrew Manuscripts in Jerusalem, where the unpublished Hebrew treasures of the great European libraries are made available in less time than it takes to fill out a requisition card, was extremely helpful and courteous when I worked there during the summers of 1975 and 1979. I am grateful to the Biblioteca Real de San Lorenzo de El Escorial of Madrid for sending me copies of pages in the Aggadot Commentary that do not appear in the Jerusalem microfilm and for answering specific queries about that manuscript; and to Dr. Menahem Schmelzer of the library of the Jewish Theological Seminary of America, whose suggestion provided the key to the discovery of R. Isaac ben Yedaiah.

I cannot sufficiently express my gratitude to the Danforth Foundation for the financial support and general encouragement made available through a Kent Fellowship during three years of my graduate work. Grants from the Memorial Foundation for Jewish Culture and Harvard's Center for Jewish Studies enabled me to pursue indispensable manuscript research in Jerusalem. I feel a deep sense of indebtedness to the members of Temple Beth David in Canton, Massachusetts, where I have served as part-time rabbi during the past six years. They have never allowed me to remain immersed in the thirteenth century for too long; they have often called me down from the rarefied heights of medieval philosophical thought and summoned me up from the drudgery of footnotes into the cauldron of human life with its immediate needs and painful problems. But they have never made demands that interfered with my academic work, and they have made me feel that this work was important to them as well as to me.

I acknowledge with gratitude the help of many friends, colleagues, and teachers. Beth Finkelstein graciously typed all the notes in a form suitable for the printer. Dr. Bernard Cooperman has provided me with countless opportunities to discuss my work and test my ideas. Professor Herbert Davidson of UCLA and Professor Yosef Dan, Dr. Jacob Elbaum, and Dr. Colette Sirat, all of Jerusalem, made helpful suggestions and corrections based on their reading of my work in part or in its entirety. Professor Yosef Hayim Yerushalmi made many valuable comments, especially on the messianic material; my debt to him for what I have learned during the course of my graduate studies at Harvard goes far beyond the confines of this book. Professor Isadore Twersky guided every stage in the preparation of my doctoral dissertation and its transformation into a book, from the choice of subject to the final touches. He has never sought to intrude by imposing his own conclusions, but he has always been available to keep me from swerving too wide of the mark. Were it not for his careful reading and his erudite criticism, there would be many more errors, oversights, and imprecise formulations than those that the reader will still undoubtedly find.

I conclude with that most important circle of all: the members of my family. My wife's parents, Sylvia Shapiro and Dr. Robert Shapiro, and my brother, Rabbi David Saperstein, have been constant sources of encouragement and support. My own parents, Marcia Saperstein and Rabbi Harold Saperstein, have given me so much and taught me so much throughout the years that even this book, lovingly dedicated to them, can be only a token repayment of my debt. Finally, my wife, Roberta, and my daughters, Sara and Adina: without you, this might have been completed a little earlier. But without you, my life would have been a pale and empty shadow of what it is today.

M.S.

CONTENTS

DECODING THE RABBIS

I

THE AGGADAH:
PROBLEM AND CHALLENGE

ON THE FACE OF IT, nothing could be more alien to the nature of systematic religious philosophy than the aggadah of the classical rabbinic literature.[1] By the tenth century, when a far more logically rigorous and coherent style of exposition had come into vogue, the aggadah was rapidly becoming a source of confusion, consternation, and embarrassment for many Jews. A growing corpus of literature, produced both outside and within rabbinic Judaism, portrayed various aggadic utterances as trivial, foolish, irrational, or absurd.

This attack was spearheaded by the Karaites, adherents of a Jewish sectarian movement that challenged the authority of the Talmud and its official Babylonian expositors. Probing the Talmud for weakness, they found the aggadah to be a particularly vulnerable spot through which their barbs could penetrate to the heart of rabbinic hegemony. The Karaite Jacob al-Kirkisani expresses abhorrence of certain Talmudic statements concerning God, complaining that the rabbis "attribute to Him [human] likeness and corporeality, and describe Him with most shameful descriptions . . . This, as well as other tales and acts, mentioned by them in the Talmud and their other writings, does not suit [even] one of the [earthly] creatures, much less the Creator." He is outraged by the designation of the angel Metatron as "the minor YHWH" and by the aphorism "His name is as the name of his Master," and he derides other aggadot with biting sarcasm.[2] Al-Kirkisani's Karaite colleague Salmon ben Yeruham similarly mocks selected Talmudic and extra-Talmudic statements concerning God and the figure of Metatron. One of his reactions is poignantly prophetic: "If the Gentiles hear of these great abominations which we have recounted, they will stone us, mock us, scorn us."[3] In the eleventh century, such matters would indeed come to Gentile ears.

There is a vicious attack upon the aggadah of the Talmud in the polemical literature of Islam. The Spanish encyclopedist and theologian Ahmad ibn Hazm quotes a passage that seems to be a hybrid of two aggadot, both familiar from Karaite diatribes: the story in which R. Ishmael enters a ruin and hears God moaning like a dove over the destruction of the Temple that He caused (*Berakhot*, 3a)[4] and the story in which R. Ishmael enters the Holy of Holies and hears God ask him to bless Him (*Ber.*, 7a). Ibn Hazm's remarks differ in tone from the Karaite attacks: they are filled with blatant animosity and rancor, personal vituperation and abuse. He heaps sarcasm and scorn upon Ishmael and all who consider him to be a pious scholar worthy of respect. At the same time, he proffers, in rudimentary form, a logical analysis of the aggadah, especially the statement that God feels remorse because of the destruction of the Temple. Whereas the Karaites were usually content to cite a statement and then to dismiss it out of hand as obviously erroneous, ibn Hazm takes a longer passage, breaks it down into its component parts, and attempts to demonstrate how it reflects in various ways the outlook of the infidel.

He continues his attack by focusing on angelic figures who, he alleges, are raised to the level of divinity by rabbanite Jews:

> They say, "On the night of Yom Kippur—the tenth day of Tishri, that is, the month of October—Metatron stands up, tears out his hair, and weeps slowly, saying 'Woe is me, for I have destroyed my house and made my sons and daughters orphans, my form is bent over, I cannot raise myself erect until I rebuild my house and bring my sons and daughters back to it.' Then he repeats these words anew." The word "Metatron" means, "the small God." God be exalted above their unbelief! . . .
> Once I engaged one of the Jews in conversation about this. He said to me, "Metatron is one of the angels." "But," I answered, "how is this possible? Can an angel say, 'Woe is me, for I have destroyed my house' and so forth? Has anyone other than God Himself done this?" If the Jews had tried to object that God delegated to this angel the execution of this task, I would have rejoined that this would be an impossible absurdity, that an angel should feel remorse over that which he carries out at the instruction of God, and for having rendered obedience to God. This would have been blasphemy on the part of the angel if he had felt this at all, not to mention that such an open expression by the angel would not merit the applause given to it. All of this is nothing more than a fabrication by them, through which they persist in their stiff-necked character. The more enlightened among them are divided into two categories. One maintains that Metatron is God Himself, by which they belittle God, scorn Him, and leave Him afflicted with deficiencies. The other maintains that Metatron is another god, different from the exalted God.[5]

It is probably impossible to determine whether or not this discussion is based on an authentic text placing in Metatron's mouth the words attributed to God in *Berakhot*, 3a. But in any case, ibn Hazm's criticism underscores the general problem of angelic figures in the aggadah, and it points to Jews who recognized it as a problem and attempted to grapple with it.

A few sentences later, after another round of invective against the Jews, ibn Hazm turns to his coreligionists and stresses the contrast between the two faiths. "But you, thank God for the great kindness that He has rendered us through Islam, this luminous religion, which reason explains as true, and through the Book of revelation sent by Him as pure light and glistening truths. Let us beseech God to strengthen us in that which He has bestowed upon us in His kindness, so that we may encounter Him as believers, not as those who will be objects of wrath because of their error."[6] Exploited for polemical purposes, the aggadot of the rabbinic literature greatly facilitated the portrayal of Islam as the religion of reason and Judaism as the religion of foolish superstitions and blasphemous untruth.

Detailed knowledge of the aggadot was introduced into medieval Christian literature by Petrus Alfonsi, a Spanish Jew who converted to Christianity in the first decade of the twelfth century and spent the rest of his life in England. Following his apostasy, he wrote a polemical work against the religion he had abandoned in the form of dialogues between "Peter," his name as a Christian, and "Moses," his name as a Jew.[7] The first chapter of these Dialogues is devoted, in large part, to a critique of the aggadah. Many of the passages cited speak about God, and they are introduced by the charge that "your sages . . . assert that God has body and form, and attribute to His ineffable majesty such things as are inconsistent with any manner of reason." Here is part of his discussion of the assertion that God prays:

> Tell me, Moses [the adversary in the dialogue], when God prays, whom does He address? Himself or another? If another, then one whom He addresses is more powerful than He. If He addresses Himself, He is either capable of that for which He prays or incapable. If incapable, He addresses Himself in vain. If capable, either He wants it or He does not want it. If He does not want it, He prays for nothing. If, however, He does want it, there is no need for Him to pray. Do you see, therefore, Moses, how far all this type of thing is from true theology? For if it is indeed true that God weeps for you, roars like a lion, beats the sky with His feet, sighs in the manner of doves, moves His head and cries "Woe is Me" out of excessive grief; that He furthermore strikes His feet in His grief, claps His hands and every day prays that He may pity you—what then stands in the way of your being set free from your captivity? To believe this about God is blasphemy.[8]

Alfonsi, applying dialectical tools made available by the philosophical tradition, is reducing aggadic statements to absurdity in accordance with the major thrust of his work: to show that Christianity and not Judaism

fits the rationality of the philosopher. He also discusses a number of aggadot relating to Biblical personalities and rabbinic figures, employing
arguments from common sense to show that they ought not to be taken
seriously or that they contradict the Bible itself.[9] He concludes that "the
words of your sages seem to be nothing other than the words of jesters in
schools for children, or of weavers in the streets of the women." Then, in
the following sentence, the rapier strikes home: "Do you judge that the
law of such men is to be accepted or their authority to be confirmed?"[10]
The attack on the aggadah leads to an attack on the authority of the sages
as guardians of the halakha. This was a challenge that Judaism could not
ignore.

A generation after Alfonsi's *Dialogues*, Peter the Venerable, abbot of
Cluny and a towering figure in twelfth-century Christendom, turned to
the aggadah in the fifth section of his *Tractate* "against the inveterate
obstinacy of the Jews."[11] Many of the aggadot discussed in the *Dialogues*
reappear in the *Tractate*, but in tone, Peter the Venerable is far closer to
ibn Hazm. His is the voice not of a patient instructor but of a raging
demagogue. He does not converse with the Jews, and he rarely reasons
with them; he mocks them, insults them, reviles them, heaps upon them
torrents of scorn and abuse, all because of "the absurd and utterly foolish
fables" of the Talmud.

One example will suffice to represent Peter's approach. The Karaite
al-Kirkisani had criticized two aggadot from *Baba Metzia* with a somewhat parallel theme: they involve a difference of opinion between God
and the sages on a halakhic matter, one concerning R. Eliezer b. Hyrcanos
(*BM*, 59a-b) and the other Rabba bar Nahmani (*BM*, 86a). Peter the Venerable grafts the ending of the first onto a greatly expanded text of the
second, making a composite story with a hero called Nehemias. As his
analysis proceeds, the arrangement of forces becomes clear: God is the
source of the Holy Scripture; the Jews produced the Talmud. The diver-
gences between the Talmud and the Bible therefore show the Jews to be in
rebellion against God. No better statement of this alignment could be
made than that which appears in the Talmud itself, where the sages defy
the Almighty in the interpretation of the law and insist on their own way.
This defiance is exploited by Peter with consummate sarcasm:

> But it is not enough that God is condemned by the judgment of
> Nehemiah; He must be condemned by His own confession. "When
> this statement was made, God blushed and, not daring to say any-
> thing against the opinion of such a man, replied laughingly, 'NAZA
> HUNI BENAI' [sic], that is, my children have defeated me." What
> remains? Defeated by the judgment of man, defeated by the sign of
> shame [His blush], defeated by His own declaration, why does God
> tarry on the throne of omnipotence? God has been deposed by the

Jews, overthrown by the Jews! Not omnipotent, not omniscient, He is tested by His superiors the Jews, who are wiser than He!

The comment continues ominously:

I know that these mad or demonic words are not to be refuted by authority or reason, but are eminently worthy of being spat upon with derision and execration. But since these words are believed, spoken and written by you, O nation that is doomed and deserving of doom, who can remain silent? Who can restrain his hands, let alone his words? For 1100 years now, you have groaned under the feet of those whom you detest above all else, the Christians, and you have been made the laughingstock not only of them but also of the Saracens and at the same time of all nations and demons. Who of us could restrain his hands from your blood, were it not for the command of that God who has cast you away and chosen us, speaking through your prophet: "Slay them not."[12]

That the aggadah of the Talmud implies limitations on God's power and knowledge is a claim that had been made often enough before. That the aggadah of the Talmud exposes the rabbis in a conscious distortion and defiance of God's will was a novel and vexing accusation, especially when this defiance was associated with the devil, placed into the framework of Christian theology as a counterpart to God's rejection of the Jewish people, and accompanied by a thinly veiled threat. The thrust of such claims, as one scholar has noted, was "to undermine the *modus vivendi* between tolerated Judaism and tolerant Christianity."[13]

The dangers inherent in Peter the Venerable's animadversions on the aggadah were manifest a century later in the so-called Disputation of Paris, when the Talmud was brought before the recently established papal Inquisition and denounced by the apostate Nicholas Donin.[14] Familiar from Karaite or earlier Christian sources are the aggadic passages expressing the overriding importance of the oral law and the sages who expound it, the "blasphemous" assertions about God, the "errors," "foolishness," "turpid and filthy stories," and the stories "too preposterous to believe."[15] But what turned out to be most dangerous to the Jews were new categories of charges made against the aggadot of the Talmud —that they included "blasphemies against the Christians" and "blasphemies against the humanity of Christ." Included in this category is the accusation that Jews curse the clergy of the Church, the king, and all other Christians three times each day in a blessing considered to be extremely important, known as *birkat ha-minim.*[16] The Jewish leaders called upon to defend the Talmud were forced to explain embarrassing aggadic statements under conditions hardly conducive to rational discourse. The question had shifted from whether Judaism was an irrational religion to

whether the Talmud should be tolerated; the problem of the aggadah had
become bound up with the very survival of the books in which it was
contained.[17]

So far, I have examined only hostile sources—Karaite, Muslim, and
Christian—from beyond the pale of rabbinic Judaism. However, sources
emanating from the community of those ideologically committed to the
Talmud and its companion rabbinic works suggest that rabbanite Jews
too were sensitive to the intellectual problems raised by the aggadah.
General references to Jews who mocked and scorned this type of rabbinic
utterance are legion.[18] More important, discussions of specific statements
reveal the perplexity they engendered. The literature of the geonim is
filled with questions seeking authoritative guidance in understanding
problematic passages. Puzzled and confused, Jews asked about familiar
aggadot that seemed incompatible with a philosophical conception of
God[19] or about a lack of clarity in the simple meaning of an aggadic statement[20] or about apparent internal contradictions[21] or conflicts between
an aggadic pronouncement and the current practice of Jews[22] or about
aggadot opposed to ethical sensibilities, reason, the laws of nature, or
common sense.[23]

Similar problems continued to trouble Jews in the centuries following
the geonic period. Judah Halevi devoted a chapter of the *Kuzari* to various categories of perplexing aggadic statements, concluding by con-
fessing his inability to understand some of them.[24] Moses Maimonides
discusses dozens of aggadot that seem to contradict basic principles of
Judaism as he understood it. He concedes that on the face of it, the statement "The Holy One, blessed be He, has nothing in His world but the
four ells of halakha" (*Ber.*, 8a), seems "very far from the truth—as if the
four ells of halakha were the only quality desired, and all the other disciplines and beliefs were to be cast away."[25] Similarly, the assertion that
Hezekiah suppressed a "book of remedies" and that the sages agreed with
him (*Pesahim*, 56a) appears to indicate that the study of medicine was
forbidden as implying lack of faith in God.[26] Other aggadot apparently
teach that the reward for fulfilling the Torah consists of physical benefits
either in the Garden of Eden or in a messianic age when changes in the
order of nature will improve the standard of living; or that the world was
created from preexistent matter; or that some commandments serve no
externally useful purpose and have no reason other than the fact they
were commanded; or that human fate is inexorably preordained.[27]

Unlike the Karaite, Muslim, and Christian polemicists, Maimonides
does not ridicule or dismiss such aggadot. Yet they create problems that
he cannot ignore. He discusses these passages because he knows that any
Jew reading his work will think of the rabbinic pronouncements as a
counterexample. Unless they can be explained away, they will undermine

the foundations of his exposition. In all of these examples, the aggadah appears as a potential source of trouble that must be neutralized. Whether the purpose was to resist attacks from without or to resolve tensions from within, some kind of coherent response to the problems of the aggadah was obviously needed.

Some Jews reacted to these pressures by affirming the simple meaning (*peshat*) of the aggadot all the more strongly. While it is not always possible to establish whether one who maintains the peshat is fully conscious or blithely unaware of the difficulties it entails, we know that throughout the period under discussion, and especially in northern Europe, there were Jews who insisted on accepting even the most troubling aggadic utterances as sacrosanct and who were therefore unwilling to dismiss them or to tamper with their meaning.[28] The comments of Rashi and the Tosafists provide grounds to argue that these scholars were not particularly troubled even by blatantly anthropomorphic statements in the aggadah, and that those in the mainstream of Ashkenazic culture, at least before the thirteenth century, accepted these aggadot in their literal sense. The Ashkenazic commentators disregard many of the passages that delighted anti-Jewish polemicists and dismayed Arabic-speaking rabbanite Jews.[29] Where they do explicate problematic aggadot, it is almost always to explain an unclear word or phrase or to reconcile a conflict between well-known aggadic statements rather than to explore the underlying idea or to give an interpretation at variance with the peshat.[30] Nothing in their commentaries indicates that these Jews rejected the plain sense of such statements.

R. Moses Taku, a thirteenth-century German Talmudist, appears to be a somewhat anachronistic representative of what was once the mainstream of Ashkenazic tradition in his fierce commitment to the plain meaning of the aggadot. By his time, such a commitment could not be tacitly assumed; it had to be vociferously defended. Taku insisted on the peshat, though he was fully cognizant of the problems it raised in the minds of others. In order to prove his contention that God has an "image," he cites a dozen aggadic statements that attribute corporeal qualities to God. He is not at all embarrassed by the exploits attributed to Sandalfon or by the name "the minor YHWH" given to Metatron. He views the simple sense of the aggadah as a source of truth second only to the Bible itself. Any divergence from the peshat of the aggadah to accommodate it to another body of thought is heresy: "We must not abandon the language of the Torah and the words of our rabbis to seize new ideas that have recently appeared." Or, as he put it even more forcefully,

> after these words of truth, the words of the Torah and of our rabbis, the tannaim and the amoraim, is it right to listen to one who comes

to deny the true and the certain and to introduce unfounded innovations through alarming and reckless verbal artifices? Even if he would make the sun stand in the middle of the sky for us, and even if Joshua b. Nun and Elijah the prophet would come, who would listen to him?[31]

The surviving work of Moses Taku shows that, at least in northern Europe, clinging tenaciously to the plain meaning of the aggadot despite the consequences was a position not held solely by the ignorant. It could be defiantly maintained by a respected and distinguished scholar. For those who championed this view, the words of the sages, inspired by the *ruah ha-kodesh*, must be accepted as they are. If God had not wanted them to be understood in this way, they would not have been so written.

By the thirteenth century, however, Taku appears lonely and isolated in the upper echelons of Jewish intellectual life. Long before this, others had attempted to resolve the problems raised by various aggadot in ways that recognized these problems as legitimate and serious. One such technique may have been simply to change the text of expressions that were particularly troubling. This is a large and complicated subject, and the full extent of such changes will never be known because of the paucity of pre-thirteenth-century manuscript material. Saul Lieberman has argued convincingly that Jewish scribes began to change the readings of rabbinic texts and to omit expressions that had caused difficulty at the hands of Christian adversaries to such an extent that the original texts were no longer recognized as authentic by fifteenth-century Jewish scholars. For example, there is abundant textual evidence that the original reading of the statement attributed to God in *Berakhot*, 3a, was "*Woe to Me* that I destroyed My house and burned My temple and exiled My children." The omission of the Hebrew word for "to me" eliminated the idea that God has been hurt by His own action.[32] There is also good reason to think that the epithet "the minor *YHWH*" associated with Metatron appeared in the original text of *Sanhedrin* and was later purposely removed from the manuscripts.[33] Obviously, not all of the problematic aggadot were susceptible to such a simple solution.

Another approach to the problems raised by various aggadic statements was to deny their authority. This response can be seen on different levels. It could be applied to books of a particularly troubling nature, such as the notorious *Shi'ur Komah*, attributed to R. Ishmael. While some Jewish leaders, such as Sherira and Hai Gaon, Abraham ibn Ezra, and Eleazar Rokeah of Worms sought to defend its authenticity, Saadia Gaon raised the possibility that the attribution to R. Ishmael might be spurious. Maimonides, asked about the work near the end of his life, denounced it sharply and recommended that it be suppressed as idolatrous, for "a being with body and dimensions is certainly not the true God."[34] The distinction could be drawn more broadly between the aggadot of the Talmud and those of all other works. Hai Gaon argued that "everything written in the Talmud is more correct than what is not included in it," for had it not contained some worthwhile truth, it would not have been incorporated into the Talmud. One is therefore obliged to make every possible effort to understand the Talmudic aggadah correctly, while an aggadic statement from a non-Talmudic source requires no such exertion and may simply be ignored if it seems inappropriate. From a very different set of assumptions, Moses Taku formulated a similar principle: "If a man sees something astounding in the books outside [the Talmud], he should not worry about it, since it is not explicitly stated in the aggadot of our Talmud, for upon *them* we rely." Like Hai, he maintains that not all sources of the aggadah are of equal authority; the Talmud is the touchstone for judging everything else.[35]

What about problematic aggadot in the Talmud itself? Some took the position that not all statements in the Talmud need be accepted as binding, for some might reflect the opinion of an individual that was rejected by the sages as a whole. This would make them analogous to the dissenting views of individuals on halakhic questions—opinions preserved for the record but lacking any authoritative status.[36] Maimonides emphasized the nonbinding nature of idiosyncratic opinions in his letter on astrology to the rabbis of southern France:

> I know that you may search and find sayings of some individual sages in the Talmud and Midrashim whose words appear to maintain that at the moment of a man's birth, the stars will cause such and such to happen to him. Do not regard this as a difficulty, for it is not fitting for a man to abandon the prevailing law and raise again the counterarguments and replies [that preceded its enactment]. Similarly it is not proper to abandon matters of reason that have already been verified by proofs, shake loose of them, and depend on the words of a single one of the sages from whom possibly the matter was hidden.[37]

According to this view, individual statements of aggadah could indeed be in error.

Some went farther, dismissing entire categories of aggadic statements as nonauthoritative. The medicines and cures recommended by the Talmudic sages were repudiated by Hai Gaon as reflecting a state of knowledge more primitive than that of his own time; intelligent Jews should, therefore, receive their prescriptions from contemporary physicians and not from the pages of the gemara.[38] According to Maimonides' son, R. Abraham, not all rabbinic interpretations of Biblical verses should be considered to be genuine traditions; many such homiletical interpretations were intended to give the kind of pleasure produced by poetry, and they should not be confused with basic principles of the faith.[39]

Perhaps the most far-reaching attempt to repudiate the authoritativeness of certain aggadot was the insistence that all be subjected to the test of rationality. Hai Gaon maintained that, if after making a serious effort to discover the truth of a Talmudic aggadah it still seems to be false, one is not obligated to accept it but may treat it like those legal opinions rejected by the halakha. R. Samuel b. Hofni's position was more extreme; he is quoted as saying bluntly, "If the words of the sages contradict reason, we are not obligated to accept them."[40] The geonic literature is filled with pejorative epithets for specific statements under discussion: "mere words," "opinions," "approximate estimation," "like idle chatter," "hyperbole and a figure of speech."[41] From this piecemeal rejection, the next step would be the blanket refusal to consider as authoritative and binding the aggadah as a whole.

This position was based on a statement of the Palestinian Talmud, "We do not draw authoritative conclusions from the aggadot" (Yerushalmi Peah, 2:6). The geonim seized upon it, reiterated it in slightly different formulations ("We do not rely upon the aggadot," "We do not raise questions from the aggadot"), and developed it into an important defense when confronted with the problems noted above. Saadia Gaon may have been the first to use it in this context. R. Sherira Gaon wrote: "These statements which stem from Biblical verses and are called midrash and aggadah are approximate estimations [umdanah]; some of them are so . . . and many of them are not so . . . Therefore, we do not rely on aggadic utterances; that portion of their words which is confirmed by reason and the Biblical text is correct." His son, R. Hai, argued similarly: "Aggadic sayings are not like authentic tradition. Rather, each sage expounded as it occurred to him, as if to say, 'Perhaps,' or 'One might say,' and not as something definite. Therefore, we do not rely on them."[42] Spanish scholars continued this geonic tradition; it is found in the general introduction to the Talmud attributed to Samuel ha-Nagid and even in Maimonides, in whose work the aggadah played an extremely important role.[43]

These were internal Jewish texts, written in a Muslim environment. In the thirteenth century, placed on the defensive by external attack, leading Jews of Christian Europe publicly stated the principle that the aggadah is not binding. In Paris, forced to defend embarrassing statements from the Talmud before the Inquisition, R. Yehiel proclaimed: "I believe in all the laws and ordinances written [in these books] . . . but there are also in them aggadic statements intended to attract a person to understand their language . . . With regard to this category, I am not compelled to answer you. If you want, you may believe them, if you do not want, you do not believe them."[44] A generation later in Barcelona, Nachmanides resorted to a similar distinction between the obligatory Biblical and halakhic material and the optional aggadic utterance, explaining to his Christian audience the notion of midrash as homily:

Further, there is a third kind of writing which we have [in addition to Bible and Talmud, or, halakha] called *midrash*, that is to say, sermonic literature of the sort that would be produced if the bishop here should stand up and deliver a sermon, which someone in the audience who likes it should write down. To a document of this sort, should any of us extend belief, then well and good, but if he refuses to do so no one will do him any harm. Furthermore, this literature is given by us the title *aggadah*, which is the equivalent of *razionamiento* in the vernacular, that is to say that it is purely conversational in character.[45]

The sermon of a bishop is to be taken seriously, but it does not have the force of official dogma, from which no dissent is tolerated. So it is in the case of the aggadah. The fact that it issues from the sages means that it should not be lightly dismissed. But acceptance or rejection of any aggadic statement is, in the final analysis, optional. Such a statement is not automatically binding but must be judged independently, according to its content.

This principle solved one problem while at the same time creating another. Not all Jews were prepared to accept the neat division of the rabbinic literature into that which was binding (halakha) and that which was not (aggadah). The two categories of material are interspersed in the Talmud with no clear lines of demarcation; the discussion in the gemara flows from one to the other and back without pause. Moreover, in many cases, the same individuals issue halakhic rulings and aggadic opinions. If their statements are authoritative in one realm, why should they not be so in the other? On the other hand, if their aggadic pronouncements are judged to be merely their personal opinion and not a genuine tradition that all Jews are obliged to accept, might not this be the case also with regard to the halakha that they teach? If they could say something foolish or erroneous or absurd about God Himself, might they not err in their reasoning about the intricacies of Jewish law? And if the neat division between halakha and aggadah raised such questions in the minds of Jews, it was even less likely to be understood and accepted by the Christians against whom they were arguing. When Nachmanides affirmed that he did not accept as authoritative a statement cited by Pablo Christiani, his opponent shouted triumphantly, "See! He denies their own [sacred] writings."[46] For these reasons, even those who took the position denying the binding nature of the aggadah were reluctant to leave it at that. Almost invariably, they supplemented this disclaimer with a different technique for resolving their problem—a new manner of interpretation.

Such interpretation seeks not so much to elucidate the original meaning of the text as to discover new meaning in order to resolve tensions and difficulties. It is a classic response to certain cultural and historical conditions.[47] Typically, in the first place, the text is of sufficient authority that it cannot be casually dismissed. Second, a new world view provides a compelling set of ideas that appear to be in radical conflict with the simple meaning of the original text. Under such circumstances, a typology of positions is predictable. Some will turn their backs with disdain on the new world view, adhering to the authority of the ancient text. At the other pole, there will be those whose commitment to the new world view is so powerful that it shatters the authority of the text, which they then ignore or even explicitly repudiate in a dramatic break from tradition. In the middle will be those who retain their commitment to both the ancient text and the new thought system.[48] They may do this through a kind of intellectual schizophrenia, which recognizes conflicts but either does not attempt to or is unable to reconcile them.[49] More productively, they may resort to interpretation in order to demonstrate that the conflict between ancient text and new truth is only apparent, the result of an imperfect comprehension of the text; that the new idea is actually consistent with, implicit in, or even the ultimate meaning of the long-familiar but inadequately understood words.[50]

The aggadot conferring anthropomorphic qualities upon God were explained through several new principles of interpretation, which could be applied to the Bible as well as the aggadah. Hai Gaon, asked about a graphically corporealist statement in which God sheds tears, strikes His hands together, sighs, kicks the firmament, and squeezes His legs under the Throne of Glory (*Ber.*, 59a), moves from the familiar statement rejecting the authority of the aggadah to a new canon of interpretation:

> This statement is aggadah. Concerning it and all that are similar to it, the rabbis said, "We do not rely on the aggadah." *The way to interpret them* is to make clear at the outset that both according to reason and according to the words of the sages, there is no doubt that God cannot be compared to any creature, and that no laughter, weeping, sighing, tears, or distress apply to Him. When this statement is explained, it becomes known that all rabbinical statements similar to it were said not in accordance with their apparent meaning, but as analogies and comparisons with things known to us by the senses. Just as *the Torah spoke in the language of men* when the prophets used such metaphoric expressions as the "eye of God," the "hand of God" . . . so in the case of aggadic statements.[51]

A theological axiom has become the standard against which the aggadah is measured; those statements that do not conform to the standard are not totally dismissed but are interpreted. According to this approach, neither prophets nor sages intended their assertions about God to be understood literally; they used graphic language because this is the only way the average human being can understand the abstract notion being expressed. This use of the phrase "the Torah spoke in the language of men" to emphasize the need for metaphoric interpretation of statements about God became a cornerstone of Spanish philosophical exegesis.[52]

Visions of God were also interpreted in a way that resolved their conflict with accepted notions about the deity. Different approaches were set forth. Saadia Gaon, responding to the strictures of the Karaite Salmon b. Yeruham concerning R. Ishmael's encounter with "Akatriel, the Lord of Hosts" in the Holy of Holies (Ber., 7a), explains that both prophets and sages saw a created light known as the kavod, intended specifically for the purpose of communicating with outstanding men.[53] A second way of interpreting the visions of God in Bible and aggadah was to make them into purely psychic phenomena occurring in the mind of the beholder and having no objective reality perceivable by anyone else. This is the way R. Hananel deals with the assertions about God's tefillin (Ber., 6a, 7a): "The meaning is that the Holy One, blessed be He reveals His glory to His faithful who revere Him through intellectual understanding . . . The 'seeing' that is mentioned is the seeing of the mind, not the seeing of the eye . . . Moses 'saw' and understood the knot and the [Hebrew letter shin] of the tefillin."[54] Some writers, including Judah Halevi and possibly R. Hananel himself, wavered between the interpretations based on the created form and the psychic vision.[55] Maimonides opted for the psychological approach, even for such Biblical events as the appearance of strangers to Abraham and the nocturnal wrestling of Jacob.[56] But whatever answer they gave, it followed a recognition that aggadot in which God appeared could not be accepted in accordance with their plain sense and, therefore, required interpretation.

Interpretation was often used to resolve difficulties other than anthropomorphisms in the aggadah. Discussing the disintegration of the body after the separation of the soul, Saadia Gaon cites the rabbinic statement "Vermin are as painful to the dead as a needle to the flesh of a living person" (Ber., 18b). This notion was obviously problematic to Saadia, for it seems to assert that physical pain can be felt even after death, whereas such pain is incompatible both with the lifeless body and with the immaterial soul. He resolves the problem through interpretation. The disintegration of the body causes pain to the soul, just as it is painful for a man to see a house in which he once lived destroyed, with briars and thorns growing inside it. The pain of which the statement speaks is not physical pain but the pain that comes from unpleasant knowledge.[57] The graphic language of the aggadah is reduced to mere hyperbole, and the new interpretation makes it possible for Saadia to fit the statement into his overall scheme without difficulty.

Judah Halevi, discussing the various problems raised by the aggadot, points out that some sayings "appear senseless on the face of them, but their meaning becomes apparent after but a little reflection." His example is the statement "Seven things were created before the world was created: Paradise, the Torah, the just, Israel, the Throne of Glory, Jerusalem, and the Messiah, the son of David" (*Pes.*, 54a). The problem here is obvious. To speak of material things existing before the universe was created ex nihilo is a contradiction, and the very notion of priority in time before the existence of the heavenly bodies is fraught with difficulty. Halevi explains the statement by referring to the philosophical adage "The primary thought includes the ultimate deed." Before a person actually begins to build an edifice, he first plans that which is most important—the ultimate purpose his building will serve. In this way, it can be said, figuratively speaking, that these seven things, which were the objects of divine wisdom in creating the world, were "created" before the world.[58]

Moses Maimonides was asked by Obadiah the Proselyte about the statement "All is in the hands of Heaven except for the fear of Heaven" (*Ber.*, 33b). The first part of this statement seems to imply a deterministic view, in which God ordains human actions outside of one specific realm. This view conflicts with the principle that man is free to choose, which Maimonides considered to be crucial to all of Jewish thought. Once again, the difficulty is eluded through interpretation. "Fear of heaven" is understood to include the entire realm of human actions, while the "all" that is in the "hands of Heaven" has nothing to do with man but refers to the realms of animal life and vegetation, of the stars and the spheres, which proceed according to laws established by God at the time of Creation. Having used this interpretation to resolve the particular problem, Maimonides enunciates a general approach to such aggadot:

> When one finds a verse from the prophets or a statement of the sages which conflicts with a basic principle, or contradicts an important matter, he must delve deeply with his power of reason until he understands the words of the prophet or sage. If they turn out to be consistent with the matter explicit in the Torah, fine; if not, he must say, "I do not understand the words of this prophet or the words of this sage."[59]

The "basic principles" of Judaism against which aggadic statements are to be measured are, of course, those which Maimonides has distilled as the essence of his philosophical exposition of Jewish faith. One could hardly expect a clearer formulation of the need for interpretation, or silence, when the aggadah appears to conflict with them.

Although all of the interpretations cited so far abandon the simple meaning of the aggadah in order to resolve problems inherent in that meaning, none of these interpretations is allegorical. Much has been written on the use of allegorical interpretation to dissipate the tension between ancient text and new intellectual commitment, especially with regard to the work of Philo.[60] But the word has been used in an insufficiently precise manner by scholars writing about medieval Jewish exegesis, a confusion abetted by the promiscuous use of the word *mashal* in medieval works and the absence of a technical term for "allegory" in medieval Hebrew.[61] This is an area in which distinctions are important; the interpretation that treats Biblical text or aggadic utterance as allegory may be fundamentally different from the interpretation that treats them as metaphor or as symbol. The word "allegory" has a specific meaning in literary criticism, and its use should be restricted to refer to the representation of an abstract concept by a concrete image somehow related to it.[62] The potential value of this approach as a means of dealing with embarrassing or difficult statements without dismissing them as the eccentric opinions of individuals is obvious.

To what extent was allegorical interpretation actually used by medieval Jewish thinkers to resolve problems in the aggadah? It is somewhat surprising to find few examples of problematic aggadot interpreted allegorically in the works of pre-thirteenth-century thinkers. The tendency to use techniques of interpretation other than allegory can be seen in Maimonides' treatment of an aggadah that implies a change in the order of nature with the advent of the messianic age: "In the future, the land of Israel will bring forth ready baked rolls and fine woolen garments" (*Shabbat*, 30b). An allegorical interpretation of this statement is not difficult to imagine. It could be maintained, for example, that "ready baked rolls refers to ethical perfection and "fine woolen garments" to intellectual perfection, and that a life of freedom in the land of Israel with its fine climate and atmosphere will enable all Jews to attain these goals. This interpretation would have been consistent with Maimonides' view of the messianic age, and it would have removed the problem inherent in the statement. But Maimonides does not treat the aggadah as allegory; he treats it as hyperbolic, figurative language, meaning simply that a minimum of labor will produce all that men need to fill their material needs.[63] It may be stated as a working generalization that among the geonim and the Spanish scholars, allegorical interpretation was not a common approach to problematic statements of the aggadah.

Up to this point, I have treated the aggadah as an intellectual problem and interpretation of the aggadah as an attempt to solve this problem. But there was another use for interpretation as well. Rather than merely neutralize the harmful effect of problematic aggadot, the author could interpret the aggadah in such a way as to make it into a mouthpiece for the fundamental truths of a new system of thought. In this manner, doctrines that the historian might consider to be novel are shown to be the teachings of the sages, the true meaning of their statements when properly understood. If this interpretation is made effectively and convincingly, the aggadah not only ceases to be an embarrassment; it becomes transformed into a powerful ideological weapon of the new world view.

Such an approach to the aggadah was used by the early Kabbalists in southern France, who introduced strikingly novel doctrines into the mainstream of medieval Jewish thought, but whose self-image derived from the claim that they were transmitting venerable traditions. Gershom Scholem's analysis of *Sefer ha-Bahir*, the enigmatic focal point for the origins of the Kabbala, teaches us about the kabbalistic use of aggadic literature:

> We are dealing with a late exegesis, which reinterprets on the basis of a medieval mentality some of the most ancient texts, already sanctioned by authority, and which gives them a symbolic character . . . In *Sefer ha-Bahir*, we already encounter interpretations of this kind relating to the Talmudic aggadah. In many passages, this is noticeable not only for images drawn from the aggadic literature of the Talmud or Midrash, where their meaning and function is entirely exoteric, but which are transposed here to a mystical realm, where the new statement often gains a quality of strangeness, an air of difficulty far more pronounced than that which served as the pretext for the comment. It is especially noticeable when actual quotations from the Talmud are treated this way, in the manner of ancient materials. [This approach] is possible only in an era when, for the pious consciousness of large areas, the aggadah could already claim the authority of a sacred text, and at a time when, for other circles, the very extravagance of its assertions were a cause of perplexity . . . In the ancient aggadic literature, we do not have a single example of the reinterpretation as esoteric mystery of discourse that the aggadists took in very concrete ways. In contrast, during the Middle Ages, this was the custom, whether by the philosophers, finding in it esoteric allusions to their particular views, or by the mystics, appropriating it for their own use.[64]

Scholem illustrates this point with the kabbalistic explication of R. Judah's remark that Abraham had a daughter named *Bakol* (*Baba Batra*, 16b). *Sefer ha-Bahir* makes "bakol" into a designation for the *shekhinah*, the last of the *sefirot*, symbolized by a beautiful vase containing precious gems (the other divine powers), given by God to Abraham as a "daughter."[65] The author of the *Bahir* has been led to the aggadah not by the need to explain a difficulty that it raises but rather by the desire to find in it hints of the new teachings being expounded.

In the first half of the thirteenth century, Kabbalists began collecting aggadic material that they believed expressed in an esoteric manner the secrets of their doctrine. Especially noteworthy is the Commentary on the Aggadot by R. Azriel of Gerona. Discussing the passage about God's wearing tefillin, R. Azriel explains the symbolism of the phylactery containing four compartments which is placed on the head. The first compartment, holding the verses beginning "Sanctify to Me every firstborn" (Exod. 13:1-10), is the sefirah called "the beginning of wisdom." The second, with the verses commanding the teaching and explaining of the Exodus (Exod. 13:11-16), is the sefirah "understanding." The third, containing the injunctions "Hear O Israel" and "You shall love the Lord" (Deut. 6:4-9), is the sefirah "love of mercy." The fourth, containing the paragraph "If you obey," with its threat of punishment for disobedience (Deut. 11.13-21), is the sefirah "strict justice." The fifth sefirah, called "strength," is the "left hand of God," and this is the meaning of the statement in the aggadah under discussion: "the word 'strength' [in Isaiah 62:8, the proof text] can mean only tefillin." For this reason, it is placed on the left hand. In Exodus 13:16, "It will be as a sign on your hand," the word for "your hand" (yadkhah) has an extraneous letter heh at the end; since heh is the fifth letter of the Hebrew alphabet, this is additional proof that the phylactery placed on the hand is the fifth sefirah. The "knot of the tefillin," seen by Moses when God revealed His back (Exod. 33:24), is the lower five sefirot.[66]

This interpretation does resolve the most obvious problems of the aggadah, making it clear that God does not put on phylacteries of leather and parchment. But this is not the purpose of the comment. For a Jewish philosopher or a Christian polemicist troubled by the aggadah, the explanation would create as many problems as it solved. The purpose is rather, as the author states, to teach "the meaning [ta'am] of the phylacteries" according to the Kabbalistic doctrine. The tefillin that God wears are none other than the sefirot. The tefillin that Jews are commanded to wear are not mere reminders of an abstract thought but a symbol of the sefirot, representing in concrete fashion a reality that is ultimately beyond human comprehension. By performing the commandment to put on phylacteries in the proper manner at the proper time, the Jew helps ensure that the flow of divine beneficence from the infinite, unknown God through the sefirot to the human realm will occur without obstacle. In this manner, an aggadah that was a source of embarrassment becomes a weapon of propaganda on behalf of the views to which the commentator is committed.[67]

It has sometimes been maintained that in contrast with the Kabbalists, Jewish philosophers viewed the aggadah as little more than an embarrassing problem, "a stumbling block rather than . . . a precious heritage."[68] Such a generalization is inaccurate. Maimonides, the dominant figure among the philosophers, showed how the aggadah could be integrated into the exposition of this new system of Judaism to give it roots in the sacred texts of the past without resorting either to allegorical interpretation or to esoteric mysteries. Sometimes, little reinterpretation of the texts was required.[69] More often, however, Maimonides' use of an aggadah in his exposition entails the reinterpretation of a key term or the transposition of a nonphilosophical concept into a new philosophical key. Rather than rehearse well-known examples of aggadot used by Maimonides to support his philosophical doctrine,[70] I shall illustrate this technique by examining closely a single chapter in the *Guide for the Perplexed*, chapter 51 of part III.

The first aggadic passage appears after the famous parable of the castle has been explained in general terms. The various positions in relation to the castle are then linked with the mastery of different disciplines from the educational curriculum: "My son, so long as you are engaged in studying the mathematical sciences and logic, you belong to those who go round about the palace in search of the gate. Thus our sages, speaking figuratively, said, 'Ben-Zoma is still outside.' " The laconic nature of this proof text makes several assumptions. First, the reader must be able to identify the phrase as belonging to an aggadic passage in *Hagigah*, 15a:

Once R. Joshua b. Hanania was standing on a step of the Temple Mount, and Ben Zoma saw him and did not stand up before him. So [R. Joshua] said to him: "Whence and whither, Ben Zoma?" He replied, "I was gazing between the upper and lower waters, and there is only a bare three fingers [breadth] between them, for it is said, 'And the spirit of God hovered over the face of the waters'—like a dove which hovers over her young without touching [them]." Thereupon R. Joshua said to his disciples, "Ben Zoma is still outside."

Ben Zoma's error shows that he has misunderstood Genesis 1:2, which pertains to *ma'aseh bereshit*, the work of Creation. The reader must be familiar with Maimonides' own identification of this rabbinic term with the Greek discipline of physics, and he must draw the conclusion that Ben Zoma has not yet mastered the study of physics. Furthermore, he must know the fixed order of progression in the philosophical curriculum, according to which logic and the mathematical sciences precede physics. Then it becomes clear why Ben Zoma represents those whose education has not extended beyond the preliminary subjects. R. Joshua's remark, "Ben Zoma is still outside," is understood, following the metaphor of the castle that Maimonides is explicating, to mean that Ben Zoma has not attained the most rudimentary knowledge of God. Only if the reader knows all this is it clear how the few words from the Talmud cited by Maimonides support his assertion. For a reader with the proper background, the aggadic proof text is relevant and cogent.

The second reference to the rabbinic literature appears in Maimonides' discussion of the central topic of this chapter: the ultimate service of God, which is undistracted concentration of one's thought upon God alone. As a prerequisite to this service, one must attain the fullest possible knowledge of God, for without correct knowledge, the object of thought will be not God but a figment of the imagination. The ultimate religious achievement is to go a step beyond the love of God, which Maimonides identifies with intellectual apprehension:

> The Torah has made it clear that this ultimate worship to which we have drawn attention in this chapter can be achieved only after the achievement of intellectual apprehension. It says, "To love the Lord your God, and to serve Him with all your heart and with all your soul" [Deut. 11:13]. Now we have made it clear several times that love is proportionate to apprehension. After love comes this worship, to which attention has also been drawn by the sages, who said, "This is the service of the heart." In my opinion, it consists of concentrating one's thought on the first intelligible and devoting oneself exclusively to this insofar as is possible.

The phrase "service of the heart" is actually used by the rabbis in deriving the obligation of standardized prayer from the Torah (*Ta'anit*, 2a). Maimonides himself uses the phrase this way at the beginning of *Hilkhot Tefillah* in the *Mishneh Torah*. Here it is removed from its original context, treated as if it were pure aggadah, reinterpreted to mean not standardized prayer but something akin to Bahya's "duties of the heart," and integrated into the presentation of Maimonides' philosophical-religious ideal.

As Maimonides continues to discuss this ideal of exclusive concentration on God, a third aggadic citation is employed. Even the philosopher, possessed of true knowledge concerning the Almighty, breaks the bond between himself and God when he directs his thoughts to matters of the world such as business or food. "The pious were therefore very strict about the times in which they did not think about God, and they warned about this, saying 'Do not make your mind empty of God.' " Here too, reinterpretation allows the aggadah to be integrated into the argument. The statement occurs in *Shabbat*, 149a, in conjunction with Leviticus 19:3, "Do not turn unto idols" (*al tifnu el ha-elilim*). Rashi's comment shows that he read the rabbinic phrase as *al tifnu el mi-da'atkhem*, "Do not turn unto that which is merely the creation of your own mind." Maimonides reads the words with a different pointing: *al tefannu ēl mi-da'atkhem*, "Do not make your mind empty of God." The original context, which deals with the prohibition of looking at the image of an idol, is forgotten, and the phrase becomes another building block in the explication of the goal of human existence.

Finally, near the conclusion of the chapter, Maimonides speaks about the attainment of this goal near the end of life, when the powers of the body are weakened:

For the more the physical powers are weakened and the fire of the passions subdued, the stronger is the intellect, the greater its light, the purer its apprehensions and the pleasure in what it apprehends. Finally, when the perfect man reaches the end of his days, this apprehension grows enormously, and so does the concommitant joy and the passionate love for that which is apprehended, until the soul is separated from the body in a moment of intense pleasure. The sages alluded to this matter in relation to the death of Moses, Aaron, and Miriam, saying that all three died with a kiss: "And Moses, the servant of the Lord, died there in the land of Moab at the mouth of the Lord' [Deut. 34:4]—this teaches that he died with a kiss" [BB, 17a] . . . The meaning in all three cases is that they died with the pleasure of that intellectual apprehension from intense and passionate love. In this statement, the sages were drawn after the manner of the famous metaphor in the Song of Songs, wherein that intellectual apprehension that comes with the intensification of love for God is called a "kiss," as it says, "Let him kiss me with the kisses of his mouth" [Song 1:2].

This aggadah might be considered in the same category as those that troubled the geonim and their followers, the ascription of human features to God. But the interpretation does not merely neutralize an embarrassing anthropomorphism; like the other aggadot cited in this chapter, it furthers and strengthens the author's argument.

In all four cases, Maimonides, the medieval religious philosopher, is able to speak through the words of the sages, and the aggadic utterances, appropriately reinterpreted, become expressions of a world view that the rabbis would hardly have recognized as their own. It is impressive how easily this appears to be done, how naturally the aggadah is mustered for the service of the philosopher, how pliant it becomes in the hands of the master dialectician. Maimonides showed how the aggadah could serve as an effective weapon in the battle for the allegiance of Jewish minds.[71] What he left undone was the arduous task of applying these prodigious powers of interpretation to the entire corpus of aggadic discourse.[72]

II

ISAAC BEN YEDAIAH
AND THE SAGES

History did not deal kindly with the writings of R. Isaac b. Yedaiah. He wrote at least three major works, of which relatively little has been preserved. His commentary on the Torah (or possibly a book of homilies based on the weekly pericope) has apparently been totally lost. Probably 80 percent of his monumental Commentary on the Aggadot of the Talmud is no longer extant, and an even greater percentage of his Commentary on the Midrash Rabbah seems not to have survived. What does remain from the commentaries on the aggadot and the Midrash Rabbah has been universally but erroneously attributed to a different author, the well-known poet, moralist, and philosopher Yedaiah ha-Penini Bedersi.[1] Only small portions of these works are available in print.[2]

The unique manuscript of the extant Commentary on the Aggadot of the Talmud (to be referred to as CAT) is found in the Escorial Library of Madrid (Hebrew MS G.IV.3).[3] It is 163 folios in length and contains comments on statements from *Avot* and on selected passages, most but not all aggadic in nature, from tractates *Sanhedrin, Avodah Zarah, Shevu'ot, Makkot,* and *Horayot* from the order *Nezikin.* These pages contain dozens of cross-references to the author's own comments on other Talmudic tractates, directing the reader to explications of *Berakhot, Shabbat, Erubin, Pesahim, Yoma, Rosh Hashana, Ta'anit, Megillah, Hagigah, Ketubot, Sotah, Baba Batra,* and *Hullin.* Several extensive quotations from the commentary on *Berakhot* appear in Jacob ibn Habib's *Ein Ya'akov* on that tractate.[4] It is very possible that R. Isaac wrote a commentary on all the tractates of the Babylonian Talmud, even though no specific references to the other tractates are to be found in the extant material. A reasonable estimate would be that the original work was between seven hundred and one thousand folios in length.

The extant Commentary on the Midrash Rabbah also survives in a unique manuscript (to be referred to as CMR), found in the library of the

Jewish Theological Seminary of America (Hebrew MS 5028).[5] One hundred folios long, it discusses midrashic statements from the beginning and end of *Leviticus Rabbah* and from chapter 1 through the beginning of chapter 13 of *Numbers Rabbah*. Like CAT, it is obviously a small part of a much larger work. Not only does it begin and end in the middle of comments, but it contains specific cross-references to comments on *Genesis Rabbah*, chapter 6, *Genesis Rabbah*, chapter 39, *Genesis Rabbah*, chapter 99, *Leviticus Rabbah*, chapter 1. If the whole of the Midrash Rabbah was interpreted as extensively as the first twelve chapters of *Numbers Rabbah*—and it is hard to imagine why this material should be intrinsically more worthy of detailed examination than the rest—the original work may have been ten times the size of the surviving manuscript, or one thousand folios. Probably dating from the third quarter of the thirteenth century, it would appear to be the earliest known commentary on the Midrash Rabbah as a whole.[6]

The fragmentary nature of these two works is indeed lamentable. Many of the most problematic aggadot of the Talmud, which we have seen recurring in both Jewish and non-Jewish sources, appear in tractates for which no commentary is extant, and we therefore do not know how R. Isaac responded to the difficulties in these passages. Furthermore, we would expect to find at the beginning of both works an introduction in which the author explains his purpose and describes his approach. In the absence of such material, the purpose, the methodological assumptions, and the techniques of interpretation must be inductively reconstructed from that which has been preserved. By analyzing R. Isaac's conception of the aggadah and his method in interpreting it, it will be possible to appreciate his work as a response to the twofold nature of the aggadah discussed in the previous chapter: the aggadah as problem and embarrassment because of its apparent conflict with the assumptions of a new world view, and the aggadah as challenge and opportunity for expounding this world view as an integral part of traditional Judaism.

Assumptions

While no single statement in the extant commentaries expresses a full theory of aggadic discourse, brief, almost incidental remarks scattered through the comments point to some of the assumptions with which R. Isaac is working. First, there is the assumption that the material itself is weighty and important, that the sages do not make trivial, tedious remarks. This assumption itself is not new; what is new is that in the hands of R. Isaac, it becomes the basis for extensive commentaries on material that had not traditionally been chosen for systematic exegesis. For example, a midrash on Psalm 91:6, "Nor of the destruction [*ketev*] that wasteth at noonday," states, "It is a demon, who has no power in shade or in sun, but in the area between shade and sun . . ." (*Num. R.*, 12:3). R. Isaac, referring the reader to a comment about *Ketev Meriri*, in his Composition on the Babylonian Talmud (*Hibbur ha-Talmud Bavli*),[7] notes that in this midrash the sages "added some things that seem to every reader at first glance to be tedious, but I will judge the speakers in a favorable light, for they did not speak empty words; their hearts overflowed with good content." He then interprets the statement.[8] The assumption that the words of the sages are pregnant with important meaning provides much of the motivation for taking these words so seriously.

A second assumption is that there is no intrinsic difference between the material in the Babylonian Talmud and that in the midrashim. The relationship between Talmud and Midrash is analogous to the relationship between different tractates of the Talmud. Both works are of equal authority; R. Isaac did not consider the Babylonian Talmud to be the touchstone against which other aggadic sources had to be judged. This judgment can be seen wherever a statement by the "Babylonians," a term used consistently to refer to those sages whose words are recorded in the Babylonian Talmud, differs from one by the "sages of the land of Israel," meaning those quoted in the Midrash Rabbah. For example, "At the time Solomon built the Temple, he formed all kinds of trees of gold . . ." (*Numbers Rabbah*, 12:4) is compared with its parallel in the Bavli (*Yoma*, 39b). Again the comment is introduced with the phrase, "I have interpreted it in the *Hibbur ha-Talmud Bavli*, Tractate *Yoma*." R. Isaac claims that his interpretation eliminates all absurdities that may seem to be implied by the statement. But in the Talmud, the text continues, "When the Gentiles entered the Temple," while in the Midrash it reads, "When Menasseh placed an image in the Temple." R. Isaac argues that the difference is significant, representing divergent points of view, and he explains first the statement of the Babylonians and then that of the Palestinian sages. This difference is allowed to stand without resolution, as if the commentator were explicating contrasting opinions of two rabbis in the same aggadic passage.[9]

Another comparison reveals that the statement of the Palestinian sages is superior to its Talmudic parallel. The text is *Numbers Rabbah*, 12:8: "The golden clasps in the Tabernacle looked like stars fixed in the sky." R. Isaac comments:

> I have explained it in the *Hibbur ha-Talmud Bavli*. But here they supplemented the words of the Babylonians by saying "fixed," which the Babylonians did not say. For you have already discovered that the Babylonian sages were perplexed about this matter: whether the star is fixed in the sphere or whether the star revolves by itself and the sphere is fixed and unmoving. They did not possess the full

truth of astronomical science in their days. Therefore, they discussed the matter with Gentile sages to find out the truth according to those who observed the stars scientifically, learning that they were fixed in the revolving sphere. Eventually, the Jews conceded to the Gentiles, unashamed that they had been vanquished, for they knew that the truth would ultimately benefit them. But the sages of the land of Israel were not like this, for they knew the truth about God's creation. Nothing relating to the "paths of the firmament" was concealed from their intellect. They did not need to learn this from the sages of other nations, from magician, stargazer or astronomer. In order to teach this to all who understand their words, they said here "fixed," confirming the fact that each star is fixed in the sphere and does not move except through the movement of the sphere, as the movement of the part in the whole. In their wisdom, they understood this.[10]

The addition of a single word reveals the scientific enlightenment of the Palestinian sages over that of their Babylonian colleagues. More often, however, when parallel statements have slightly different formulations in the Talmud and Midrash, their meaning is said to be the same.[11] On the whole, it is the similarity of doctrine in these two works, rather than the occasional divergence, that is stressed.

The most important assumption about the aggadah is its twofold level of meaning, exoteric and esoteric, manifest and hidden. This premise, its roots deep in the history of Biblical and aggadic interpretation,[12] underlies the majority of comments in these works. It is stated as a general principle many times. A representative example is the following introduction to an allegorical interpretation of "the well through the merit of Miriam" (Num. R., 1:2):

> All of their words here come on two levels—manifest and hidden [nigleh ve-nistar]—for they [the sages] looked at Moses and the other prophets who prophesied to the people, each of whom spoke on two levels, as commanded by God, to conceal the meaning from those unprepared to comprehend the undeniable truth of their words. Thus the sages too spoke in an esoteric manner, with the rhetoric of riddle.[13]

These few lines bring together a number of conventional yet significant themes. First, the model of twofold communication is the Bible. When the sages concealed deeper meaning in apparently simple words, they were not innovating; they were imitating the divinely inspired utterances of Moses and the prophets. The approach to interpreting the aggadah, therefore, is essentially the same as that used for Biblical material; the same code language is applied to both Biblical and aggadic statements. Second, the full meaning lies hidden. It is the function of the commentator to penetrate to this deeper level and expound the insights it provides.

Finally, the purpose of this mode of communication is to conceal the full truth from those inadequately prepared to comprehend it. As both prophets and sages addressed the entire people, they could not speak directly in philosophical language; they had to communicate in a manner that only the select few would fully understand.

This last point about the purpose for concealing the true meaning is repeated many times in the commentaries. The sages use a certain expression "so that the ignorant among the people will not understand their words, but only the select few."[14] They add details not actually relevant to the true meaning "in order to make the allegory realistic and to conceal it from one who is constitutionally unprepared to accept their words in the esoteric manner."[15] Sometimes a Biblical verse may be cited as apparent support (asmakhta) precisely "in order to conceal the matter and hide the meaning."[16] The sages are not above stating something patently false on its manifest level in order to make it more appealing to the masses. An example of this tactic can be seen in the comment on the first statement of *Avot*, "And Joshua [transmitted Torah] to the elders and the elders to the prophets." R. Isaac understands the statement as referring to the transmission of the esoteric knowledge of God to the chosen few who are intellectually capable of apprehending it. The order of transmission is in descending levels of intellectual perfection, from Moses to the enlightened men of each age ("men of the Great Assembly"), never including the masses. According to this scheme, the prophets should come before the elders, for the level of perfection in a prophet is much higher than in the "wise man." Nevertheless, the rabbis placed elders before prophets because they were speaking "according to the opinion of the masses of Jews, who think that prophecy can rest upon an ignorant and foolish man." This is an error, according to R. Isaac, for philosophical enlightenment is a prerequisite for prophecy. Yet the rabbis formulated this statement in accordance with a popular belief that they themselves knew to be wrong.[17]

A second example of the way this assumption is applied can be seen in the statement of *Sanhedrin*, 59b that the ministering angels roasted meat for Adam, and the meat descended from heaven. Here too the sages spoke

according to the opinion of the multitude, the masses of the Torah who believe in everything impossible. They think that Adam ate meat and drank wine preserved from the six days of Creation on the day when he was created and stood in Eden, the garden of God. They think that this is true of him, that it is not impossible for it to be so. The sages spoke according to their opinion [the opinion of the masses], intending to conceal the true matter from the multitude who are unable to comprehend it at first glance and who will believe nothing other than this.

The philosophical truth as stated at the beginning of the comment is that
Adam was at first entirely intellectual in nature, similar to the incorporeal intelligences of the highest realm of being. He therefore had no need
at all for eating and drinking.[18] But this doctrine is beyond the capacity
of the masses to comprehend. In order to conceal it from them as effectively as possible, the sages formulated their teaching in terms that seem
to negate it.

Most striking is the comment on the midrash mentioned above: "It is a
demon, who holds sway neither in the shade nor in the sun, but in the
area between shade and sun. His head is like that of a calf, and a horn
grows out from his forehead, and he rolls like a pitcher, and no one who
sees him survives, whether it be man or beast . . ." (Num. R., 12:3). After
explaining how these phrases actually refer to the harmful effects of heat
and cold in summer and winter, R. Isaac continues:

> The rest of the words spoken here at such length about demons,
> imps, and evil spirits, are intended to conceal [the true content] from
> the impoverished commoners, who believe that demons are spiritual
> beings, invisible to the eye, like the ministering angels; that they
> come to everyone in the dark of night; that one lies on the bed of the
> person he has possessed; that he does not appear at daybreak to that
> person, but only in the heat of the day, at noon, do they become
> visible; that nights are their special time—hidden in men's homes at
> midnight while they sleep peacefully.
>
> The sages spoke about demons in an esoteric manner according to
> this opinion of the masses, who accept the reality of something
> which does not exist and which cannot possibly exist by the laws of
> nature, but who cannot suddenly abandon this perplexity so preva-
> lent among them. They did so in order that the masses would accept
> their words at face value and be in mortal fear for the wrong reason,
> because of the "demons." Perhaps they would then come to fear for
> the right reason, understanding ultimately that generations had in-
> herited a lie and come to naught. Lifting their intellectual sight up-
> ward, each one individually would fear the Lord.
>
> The elite among them tried hard to reveal their secret about de-
> mons to all, but they could not because of the wrath of the masses of
> Jews [hamonei ha-Torah], who made ready to pelt them with stones
> if they should deny the existence of demons, for these demons were
> etched into the tablets of their hearts. Thus the sages spoke about
> demons esoterically, so that the fools would retain their presump-
> tion about everything the demons intend, continuing to accept
> them, though their hope in them will lead to despair, while the en-
> lightened will become radiant as they pass over these words to their
> hidden content. The secret of the Lord is for them that fear Him.[19]

The problem vexing R. Isaac is clear. The statement about demons can be
explained easily enough as metaphor or personification. But why did the

sages, in concealing their true message, choose a linguistic camouflage that could only reinforce preposterous and ultimately harmful beliefs among the masses? The answer is that the sages realized their attempts to make the masses confront the hard truth—that demons simply do not exist—were counterproductive, destroying respect for the rabbis rather than enlightening the multitude. They therefore resorted to a kind of ruse, using the language of popular belief, and thereby temporarily confirming the masses in their error in order to convey their message to the intellectual elite. The literal level of the aggadah not only conceals meaning from the masses; in a sense it panders to them. It would be hard to find a more dramatic expression of the tension between the two levels of discourse in any discussion of the aggadah.[20]

One final assumption relates to the sages' use of code language to express the truths of religious philosophy. For example, the words "woman" and "wife" are often interpreted as referring to the physical component of the human being. After interpreting several aggadic statements in this manner, R. Isaac concludes:

> As for the other things which [the sages] said at such length about one's wife, all of them follow this same good meaning, over and again. From these statements which we have explained, you can extract the meanings of the others, for all of them are linked together and have the same meaning, so that citing and explaining them would serve no purpose.[21]

R. Isaac assumes that the rabbis repeat themselves, saying the same thing in different words, expressing one message in a variety of ways. Therefore, the commentator need not explicate every statement of the aggadah, for this would be unduly repetitious. Having provided the key to the code, he can trust the responsible reader to use it on his own. Apparently, one of the purposes of R. Isaac's commentaries was precisely to give the reader the tools with which he could properly understand the aggadot by himself.[22]

Exploration of the Peshat

Despite the insistence that rabbinic statements are to be understood on two levels, not all comments are concerned with both meanings. A significant number deal with the simple meaning of the dictum, what others would call the peshat, although this term is not regularly used by R. Isaac.[23] Pronouncements of halakhic significance, for example, are usually, although not always, discussed in accordance with their simple meaning. In addition, the Tractate *Avot* is not treated as a repository of cryptic teaching and hidden doctrine. This is not to deny that R. Isaac occasionally uses the rabbis for purposes they hardly would have recognized. In the very first statement of *Avot*, "Moses received Torah from Sinai and transmitted it to Joshua," "Torah" is understood to refer to the philosophical knowledge of God and the angels, and "transmit" (*masar*) is taken to refer specifically to esoteric material that should be restricted to the initiated elite.[24] But even if most medieval and modern readers would not have considered this the peshat of the statement, R. Isaac apparently did. He reformulates and expands the pronouncements of this tractate from the perspective of a philosopher, but he does not make them into parables or allegories. The explanation of advice such as "Make for yourself a master and get for yourself a colleague," "Keep far from the evil neighbor and do not consort with the wicked," "Do not make yourself known to the ruling power," is founded in worldly experience and common sense. We are told of the advantages of contact with teacher and fellow student, the dangers of being influenced by bad companions, the perils of court life.[25] Only in a few instances is there unwillingness to adhere to the obvious meaning of the words.[26]

In these two categories—halakha and *Avot*—the peshat is ordinarily respected; it is difficult to generalize about other statements. R. Isaac often focuses on individual words, stating what he considers to be their lexical meaning in order to elucidate a Biblical verse or an aggadic dictum. On rare occasions, he will even translate the word into his native language. Commenting on a statement about "the danger of *alukah* " (*Avodah Zarah*, 12b) he begins, "The alukah is a creature that grows in the water, called in the secular tongue '*i rutgei*." This is a precise transcription of the langue d'oc word *iroutge*, meaning "leech."[27] Far more often, he merely repeats the philological insights of Maimonides in the *Guide* (without referring to his source), using the same meaning and the same Biblical illustration but going a step further by applying this meaning to the aggadah. This is done for common words such as *ēl* and *elohim*, *mal'akh*, *adam*, *lev*, *panim*, *regel*, and *ruah*.[28]

The distinction between apparent synonyms may be elucidated. The word *navon* may imply acumen used for evil purposes, as in Proverbs 1:5,[29] and *hakham* implies outstanding skill in any craft, even in making beautiful idols (Isa. 40:20). But while both of these terms are extended in use for evil as well as good, *maskil* is used only for one who has actualized his intellect by apprehending noncorporeal things. It is for this reason that Psalm 119:99, used as a proof text in *Avot*, 4:1, employs the word *hiskalti*.[30] Similarly, the word *nasi*, as used in Ezekiel 37:25, is not a synonym for *melekh*; it is a title higher than melekh, implying that the individual is himself exalted in personal status, not one who merely inherited the throne and now depends on the counsel of other wise men.[31]

The underlying meaning of an important abstraction may be explored. While *kadosh* is used to refer to the separation of the intellect from material things,[32] the basic meaning of the root is related to the idea of preparation. The word kedeisha, as in Deuteronomy 23:18, implies a whoring woman prepared for every man; kiddushin means that the woman is prepared for her husband and forbidden to all others; the land of Israel is called mekudeshet (Num. R., 7:8) because, through the purity of its air, it prepares its inhabitants for intellectual apprehension.[33] A common expression may be given a slightly different nuance. Thus, the term am haaretz is used in rabbinic writings to refer to those who know the proper conduct within a social setting. They may act in accordance with the Torah and provide a firm basis for society, but they are not a model for emulation because their lack of intellectual achievement results in a failure to attain eternal life.[34]

Some words are interpreted in a rather unusual way, although R. Isaac still seems to feel that he is working on the level of the peshat. Proverbs 29:4 states, "A king by justice builds up the land, but ish terumot destroys it." The phrase "ish terumot" is understood by the commentators to apply either to haughtiness of character (Rashi) or to oppressive exaction of "gifts" (ibn Ezra, Ralbag). R. Isaac, using the rabbinic definition of "terumah" as one part in fifty, interprets the second part of the verse to mean that a king who perverts justice by punishing only one out of fifty guilty persons, allowing the others to go free because of bribes, destroys his dominion; he is then only a commoner (ish), not a true king.[35] The interpretation of the word yesh in Proverbs 8:21 as "eternal existence after nonbeing" is not original. But the application of this meaning to Deuteronomy 13:4 and to Exodus 17:7, and the association of Proverbs 8:21 with Psalm 76:12—"They will bring a shai to the God-fearing man" —through the assertion that "yesh" and "shai" have the same meaning of "eternal blessing"[36] is rather ingeniously novel. Yet the commentator makes no claim to exploring a level of meaning deeper than the surface.

A similar approach is used with the word sham, encountered in Ezekiel's vision: "[the hand of the Lord] was upon him sham" (Ezek. 1:3). We are informed that "sham" "is a word applied to something associated with a recondite matter, hidden from view." In Genesis 21:17, ba-asher hu sham means "wherever he may be hidden or lost." Job 3:19, "The small and the great are sham," refers to the unknown place, not perceivable by the senses, where the souls of the dead are found. And Ezekiel 48:35, "The name of the city shall be 'The Lord is shamah,' " means that God is concealed in every room of the city, which stands for the entire realm of being.[37] With this interpretation of "sham," most readers would probably judge that the border between the simple meaning and a philosophical homily has been crossed.

There are also attempts to deal with entire aggadic statements on the level of their simple meaning. On rare occasions, R. Isaac will explicate

the homiletical reading of a Biblical verse (*derash*) that lies at the heart of
an aggadic passage. For example, " 'He brings out the prisoners *ba-
kosharot*' " (Ps. 68:7); "He brings them out from their houses as prisoners, and unites them against their will [in marriage] ba-kosharot—if they
are unsuccessful, they weep [*bokhim*], if they are successful, they sing
[*meshorerim*]" (*Num. R.*, 3:6). R. Isaac explains that the sages divided
the word *ba-kosharot* into *bakhu* and *sharot*.[38] This insight is certainly
not original; it is explicit in the gemara of *Sanhedrin*, 22a,[39] and it is
unclear why the commentator felt it necessary to explain this particular
derash. The rest of the comment deals similarly with the simple meaning
of the statement, describing in a rather compelling manner the misery of
a bad marriage and the joys of a good one. This interpretation contrasts
with others, both in CAT and CMR, in which the marriage between man
and woman is viewed as an allegorical expression for the relationship
between intellect and body.

Exegesis of the simple meaning can be seen in the comment on " 'I will
give your rains in their times'—on the nights of Shabbat" (*Lev. R.*, 35:
10). A similar statement appears in *Ta'anit*, 23a, though this includes
Tuesday and Friday nights; Rashi explains that on these nights people are
accustomed not to go out because of their fear of demons. R. Isaac, in
contrast, tells why Friday-night rains are a blessing to Jews in simple,
mundane terms that fit the realities of agricultural life. Friday night,
when no one is at work, is the most opportune time for rain to fall. On
the following day, Saturday, when the men are observing Sabbath rest,
the wet fields will be gradually dried by the winds, so that on Sunday
morning, everyone will be able to return to work as normal. In this way,
no workday is lost. Without this providential provision of God, rains
will fall randomly throughout the week, and farmers will often be unable
to labor in the wet fields. The resulting harvest will be smaller.[40] Again,
this interpretation contrasts with the usual allegorical interpretation of
rain as intellectual perception of God, which could have fit the context
quite well.

A comment reflecting a combination of peshat and allegory refers to
the midrash that states, "In this world, rains are a sign of trouble for
everyone . . . but in the future, God will make them a blessing" (*Lev. R.*,
35:12). The gloss seems almost trivial, stating obvious reasons why rains
are a source of inconvenience for merchants travelling by land, voyagers
by sea, farmers who cannot work, and the wealthy, who get their feet
and clothing soiled in the mud. But the second part of the statement is
interpreted allegorically as referring to the intellectual apprehension of
God bestowed upon the soul after it is separated from the body.[41] Apparently, R. Isaac's reluctance to recognize a permanent change in the natural order to accompany messianic times led him to allegorize the second

part of the statement; but the difficulty of fitting the first part into the allegory impelled him to explicate its peshat.

Other aggadic pronouncements are given simple explanations that make them more credible and convincing. "He who wants a corpse not to stink should turn it over on its face" (AZ, 20b). The reason for this, we are told, is that the stench in a dead body is caused by the air that enters it. By turning it on its face and preventing air from entering, the reason for the stench is removed, and the body will remain cool for a period of time.[42] "One is jealous of every man except for his son and his disciple: his son from Solomon and his disciple from Moses" (Sanh., 105b). The gemara validates the generalization by referring to Biblical models and verses; R. Isaac explains why it is in the nature of man to be envious of his competitors who excel him and why this does not apply to a man's son or to his disciple.[43] Exemplification by individual cases is replaced by explanation based on rudimentary psychology applicable to all.

The gemara tells of an incident in which R. Gamliel's female neighbor, who had lost her son, wept so loudly at night that Gamliel, hearing her, wept bitterly as well. In the morning, his students realized what had happened and removed her from the neighborhood (Sanh., 104b). R. Isaac deals with the questions this incident might raise in the reader's mind: why Gamliel wept, why this situation was a bad one, why Gamliel himself did not move to a new abode.[44] Other examples of this kind of comment could be added: why effective leadership can be maintained with one leader but is undermined when two share authority (Sanh., 8a), why a leader must first set himself right before he can expect others to obey him (Sanh., 18a), why the choice of a good adviser is important (Sanh., 76b), why Aaron's predilection for compromise "turned many away from iniquity" (Sanh., 6b).[45] All of these comments accept the rabbinic statement at its face value. They go beyond the simplest type of exegesis, which limits itself to explication of meaning, explaining difficult words, obscure syntax, and so forth. R. Isaac attempts to reconstruct the thinking that lies behind the rabbinic dictum, to demonstrate not only what it means but why it is true. But in these comments, there is no indication that any deeper, hidden meaning exists.

Sometimes, without claiming to explore an esoteric level of meaning, R. Isaac substitutes a new peshat for that of the sages. Several examples will establish a continuum of interpretations in which the plain meaning of the rabbinic dictum is transformed to an ever-greater degree. "The sword and the book were given from heaven wrapped together. The Holy One, blessed be He, said to them, 'If you keep what is written in this book, you will be saved from the sword, if not, the sword will kill you'" (Lev. R., 35:6). The comment is straightforward: the sages are using concrete imagery (mashal, here a metonymy) to express the idea that each human being is given a set of standards for proper conduct toward other people. If he chooses to live by these standards ("fulfils the words of the book"), he will not die before his time, for he will guard himself against spilling innocent blood, and there will be no enemies waiting to take his life in vengeance. This interpretation is not literal; it recognizes that no sword actually descended from heaven wrapped up with a book. But the statement was never intended to be taken literally. R. Isaac explains "book" and "sword" as emblems for the life of ethical behavior and the life of violence, and shows how life lived by the book logically and naturally guards a person from meeting a violent end. Despite the subtle transference of this statement from the realm of providential action affecting the entire people of Israel to the realm of natural causation affecting any individual, the interpretation does not distort the intention of the sages in any significant way.[46]

Anthropomorphic assertions about God consistently inspire nonliteral exegesis. One example will suffice: God "sits and teaches schoolchildren" (AZ, 3b). The use of the proof text (Isa., 28:9), as noted by Rashi, indicates that the pupils here are children who died young, but R. Isaac refocuses the statement and applies it to all children. God gives infants in the womb and in the cradle the natural endowments that will enable them to attain knowledge and acquire perfection when they are old enough to do so. The help of the father and the teacher is not enough; the child needs also the innate proclivity, which comes from God. This explanation, which follows an emphatic reminder that the preceding remark about God's sadness after the destruction of the Temple is not to be taken literally, transforms a graphic anthropomorphism into an acceptable scientific doctrine, again without doing violence to the language of the original.[47]

Often a single word interpreted in a philosophical sense gives an entirely new flavor to a passage. For example, "Whoever utters song every day in this world shall be privileged to do so in the next world." (Sanh., 91b). Obviously not just any song is intended here; the proof text (Ps. 84:5) shows that a song of praise to God is meant. R. Isaac, true to the philosophical tradition, is uneasy about praise based on the affirmation of positive attributes. For him, the only proper and acceptable "song" is the knowledge of God attained through philosophical investigation, repudiating all attributes inconsistent with the pure concept of oneness. The statement therefore promises that whoever "sings" this song of true intellectual apprehension during his life will sing it uninterrupted after his intellect is separated from the body at death. By extending the meaning of "song," the commentator makes the aggadah express a philosophical truth without radically altering its basic intention.[48]

The same is true of another statement relating to the Hereafter, this one speaking not of reward but of punishment: "Those who allow themselves liberties with servant women in this world will be hanged by the scalps of their heads in the future world" (*Num. R.*, 10:1). The first part is explained according to its plain meaning; it refers to men who have sexual relations with their servant women while their wives are ritually impure.[49] This excessive indulgence will vex the minds of these men with shameful matters, which will prevent them from fulfilling the potential in their soul by acquiring true knowledge. "Scalp" refers to the brain, the seat of the intellect, which is thereby diminished. Being "hanged by the scalp of their heads" is simply a graphic way of saying that at the time of death, the intellects of such men will be inadequately prepared for apprehension of God. A very physical punishment is transformed in accordance with the philosophical view that the ultimate punishment after death is for the soul to be annihilated, and thereby deprived of experiencing direct knowledge of its Creator.[50] And the causal relationship between crime and punishment, which the midrash finds in its understanding of a Biblical verse (Ps. 68:22), is fully rationalized and explicated.[51]

In none of the interpretations cited so far can it be said that R. Isaac has tortured the plain meaning of the aggadah, even where he has departed from it. But sometimes the interpretation of a single word in a philosophical sense, while still nonallegorical, brings us far away from the peshat. Consider the statement "Nothing unclean [ritually impure] descends from heaven" (*Sanh.*, 59b). The context in the gemara shows clearly that this pronouncement concerns meat that has actually descended from the sky. R. Isaac, ignoring this context, asserts that "uncleanness" is used metaphorically (*hush'al*) for uncleanness of soul, manifest in disgraceful ethical qualities and false beliefs. These do not "descend from heaven," in that they are not bestowed by God. A man who finds himself impure in this way should know that he is not fulfilling God's intention, for God made man capable of doing good and gaining true enlightenment.[52] Given this interpretation of the key word *tum'ah*, an interpretation that R. Isaac applies to Torah commandments as well, the new reading is carried by the words of the statement. But the doctrine expressed, while unexceptionable in itself, makes no sense in the larger context of the passage where it occurs.[53]

Similarly, "The Holy One, blessed be He, does nothing except by consulting with the heavenly household" (*Sanh.*, 38b) is, we are told, an allusion to the "intermediate beings" necessary for the continued existence of the world. Now the identification of the angels of rabbinic discourse with the intelligences of medieval cosmology was a natural and commonplace transformation.[54] The interpretation alters the thrust of the statement not so much by redefining "heavenly household" as by reversing the significance of the consultation. It is not that God turns to others for advice but that the intermediate beings cannot act by themselves. Although God invested them with authority at the time of Creation, He remains supreme, and they are unable to do anything unless God consults with them. In the rabbinic statement, God acts after receiving counsel from the heavenly family; here the heavenly family acts in order to carry out the will of the Creator.[55]

One final example will demonstrate how an interpretation dealing with the manifest level of the aggadah can still go far beyond the peshat. In Job 38:15, "The light of the wicked shall be withheld from them," the letter *ayin* in *resha'im* is suspended, as if the word were also to be read *rashim* ("poor"). The sages ask, "Why is the ayin of resha'im suspended? Once a man becomes poor below, he has become poor above" (*Sanh.*, 103b). Rashi explains that when a man has become poor in friends, disliked and hated by his fellow men, it is a sign that he is hated on high. R. Samuel Edels, in support of Rashi's interpretation, cites Proverbs 19:7 to corroborate this meaning of the word *rash* ("All the brethren of the poor [*rash*] who hate him"). R. Isaac's interpretation is quite different:

> The sages called *rash* one who is impoverished in mind. They teach that such a man will be ensnared by his iniquities and do that which is evil in God's sight throughout his life. He will not fear for his soul during the time apportioned for his physical existence— seventy years, the number of the letter ayin. These days will be void, and his life in the flesh will be suspended before him, doing him no good . . . Therefore he will be lost and suffer total destruction with the body; he will no longer be able to set right the perversions of his soul, as the sages said, "There is no atonement for the dead," which we have explained in its place.
>
> In order to show this, the letter ayin, which equals the number seventy, was suspended. Moreover, this is to show that all this happened to him because his eye [ayin] was blind so that he was drawn completely after his corporeal element. He cast his Creator behind his back; his mind never envisaged knowledge and wisdom, never apprehended God in the way intended for it. Because he remained "impoverished" throughout his physical life, he will perish without knowledge, and be carried to the grave naked and barefoot, with buttocks uncovered, just as he entered the world impoverished when he was born.[56]

The transference of the meaning of "poor" from Rashi's "poor in friends" to "impoverished in knowledge" is not at all surprising. What is striking here is the treatment of the letter *ayin*. In Rashi's interpretation, the identity of the suspended letter is unimportant; its only function is to make the difference between the words for "evil" and "poor." Here, the ayin is of the essence. Through the use of the numerical equivalent of the letter to represent the seventy years of the human life span,[57] R. Isaac rather ingeniously links the suspended letter of Job with the climactic curse of Deuteronomy 28:66: "Your life shall hang [in doubt] before you." And then, as if he felt this did not exhaust the full meaning of the statement, he links the semantic meaning of the letter ayin, "eye", with Ecclesiastes 1:16, "My heart has *seen* much wisdom and knowledge," taking the suspended "eye" as an image of intellectual blindness. A rather simple aggadah has become the text for a homiletical tour de force.

Repudiation of the Peshat

In none of these comments does the author recognize that he may have gone beyond the confines of the peshat. There are many other comments in which he openly proclaims that he is addressing not the peshat but a meaning on the hidden, esoteric level. In some such cases, the plain meaning is simply ignored as obvious or unimportant; in others, the plain meaning is explicitly repudiated. After giving his own interpretation of the passage, R. Isaac states that it may not be understood the way it appears at first glance, and explains why this is so. In these comments, R. Isaac's own approach to the aggadah emerges in high relief. By analyzing the various reasons that impel him to abandon the apparent, simple meaning of a rabbinic pronouncement, we can develop a working hypothesis about assumptions that may have been made explicit in a general introductory description of his work.

First, the simple meaning is repudiated when it conflicts with the natural order as perceived through science and empirical observation. This may apply to a verse from the Bible, such as Ecclesiastes 10:2, "The heart of a wise man is on his right," which must not be understood literally because it is "known according to nature" that the fleshly heart of a fool has exactly the same location in the body as the heart of a genius.[58] The rabbinic interpretation of a Biblical verse is held to the same standard. "What is *va-yisharnah ha-parot* [I Sam. 6:12]? That they [the cows] turned their faces toward the ark and sang a song [*shirah*]" (AZ, 24b). It should not occur to anyone, says R. Isaac, that the sages actually thought the cows sang a song, "for it is impossible for any living creature to speak except for man, to whom God gave intellect, but the other creatures do not have intellect or understanding."[59] Rashi, commenting on the Biblical verse, refers to the derash in *Avodah Zarah* and then gives the meaning of the verse *le-fi peshuto*. R. Isaac argues that even the derash cannot mean what it seems to mean because of the implied conflict with the laws of nature.

Another statement from the Midrash dealing with the same Biblical event is treated in a similar manner. "It was taught in the name of R. Meir, 'The wagons and cows which the Philistines sent for sacrifice exist to this time: they did not develop a blemish, nor grow old, nor become afflicted with an organic disease, nor become broken' " (*Num. R.*, 12:18). R. Isaac insists that the sages were not asserting something impossible. It is known that the wood in a wagon must begin to rot, and its iron must necessarily decompose, so that a wagon "cannot last for a thousand generations." Similarly, any cow will die when its limbs become fragile and broken. Furthermore, the Biblical story itself indicates that the Levites and the people took the wood of the wagon and used it to burn the cows as an offering (I Sam. 6:14). The simple meaning of the midrash would contradict this story by implying that the nature of the wagon and the animals was somehow changed so that they did not burn when they were thrown into the fire. Therefore, the statement must be understood solely on the level of its hidden content.[60] A Talmudic dictum about animal species raises a comparable problem: "There are three whose strength increases as they get older, and these are the fish, the snake, and the pig" (*AZ*, 30b). Despite the apparent meaning, the sages did not intend to "deny the nature of lower beings with respect to these three species" by asserting that they are essentially different from all others. It is known that the nature of all generated and corrupted beings, including the three mentioned, is to grow weaker in old age. Since this cannot be negated, interpretation is necessary.[61]

The refusal to countenance the simple meaning of rabbinic statements when they clearly conflict with the natural order is obviously relevant to the doctrine of miracles. Although R. Isaac insists that God has the power to intervene and change the natural order, he also reveals a strong tendency, characteristic of the philosophical tradition in medieval Judaism, to minimize this kind of intervention, especially where it is not mandated by a clear Biblical text. This is exemplified in a discussion of a midrash on II Samuel 6:12, "The Lord has blessed the house of Obed-Edom," which states that the blessing consisted of grandchildren in abundance, each of the wives of his eight sons bearing two children a month for each of the three months that the ark remained on his property, making forty-eight grandchildren in all (*Num. R.*, 4:20). After giving an allegorical interpretation of the passage, R. Isaac discards the obvious meaning in his familiar manner.

> Let it not occur to anyone that, in accordance with the manifest meaning [*le-fi ha-nigleh*], Obed-Edom's daughters-in-law bore forty-eight children during this period, each one bearing six children at the rate of two per month, making a total of forty-eight. For a woman who is intimate with a man and conceives cannot possibly bear a son or a daughter who will live, unless the months of gestation are com-

pleted, and she gives birth after seven [months] or 272 or 273 [days]. Then the child may live. But such a thing could not happen to a fetus during the brief period that the ark was at that home, unless it occurred miraculously, through a change in the necessary nature of a woman on the day of birth. However, such a miracle was unknown in ancient times. Among all the miracles wrought by God in the new land, no such thing about a woman is written in any text. And Obed-Edom was not better than the Patriarchs, such that he should be shown a sign and wonder which had never occurred before. Therefore, the creation of these male children in the house of Obed occurred to him according to the cryptic meaning of the words . . . And this follows what the Babylonians said: "In the future, women will give birth each day," for this woman who they assert will give birth every day without rising from her labor is not what the words seem to indicate [einah ke-mashma'ah], for no man has ever known her, as we have explained in the Hibbur ha-Talmud Bavli, Tractate Shabbat.[62]

Here too, the esoteric meaning does not merely supplement the peshat but replaces it entirely. The simple meaning of the statement is ruled out of order because it violently overturns the natural pattern of conception, gestation, and birth in the human species. While such a dramatic departure from nature is theoretically possible for God to arrange, R. Isaac argues that the sages could not have intended to affirm such a miracle, for this would have been unprecedented, and there is no reason why Obed-Edom should have been singled out for such a unique honor. Where no miracle is even hinted in the Biblical text, R. Isaac is reluctant to posit one in order to maintain the peshat of the midrash, especially when he has an esoteric interpretation readily at hand.

A similar approach can be seen in relation to the statement of the Talmud, "If one feels pain in his head, let him engage in words of Torah . . ." (Erubin, 54a). Again, R. Isaac's remarks are worth quoting at length.

They spoke here in an esoteric manner, with figurative language and riddles, for if the manifest content of these words is of the essence, without a hidden meaning, all of these words are tedious and irrational. If the perfect man has a pain in his head, how can he concentrate on his learning; if he has taken to bed, how can he lift his head to engage in Torah; if his eyes have grown dim so that he cannot see light, how can he read from that book, which he cannot even see? . . . Furthermore, they say things here that are impossible, testifying that some of the people who are afflicted with boils are cured through the Torah. And as for the blind . . . who can restore his eyes to his head if the eye, gouged out of his head, has been thrown onto a dungheap and eaten by a worm or mole or mouse, which then excretes it in a filthy place. And as for the lame who limps upon his thigh, who can restore him to health so that he can walk upright on his legs? Such a man would be called an expert physician and a skillful craftsman! But no one like this, Jew or Gentile, has ever existed. For all this is impossible in the nature of reality. If it might occur to one out of a thousand as a miracle, no such miracle is written in the sacred text. Rather, they spoke these divine words in the manner of riddle . . . as we have explained in the *Hibbur ha-Talmud Bavli*, Tractate *Erubin*, in a true interpretation following this: fine, acceptable, consistent with reason, repudiating all that is absurd . . .[63]

The first objection to the statement is that it simply does not make much sense; one who is suffering from a severe headache is in no condition to study Torah, so that the suggested remedy is unrealistic and implausible.[64] But the more serious problem is the apparent assertion that permanent afflictions can be healed through the Torah. Since such afflictions are beyond the capacity of medical knowledge to cure, there can be no causal relationship between the study of Torah and the return to normal except for a miraculous intervention by God. While such an occurrence is theoretically possible, there is no evidence for it in the Bible, and the sages could not have given general advice based on the remote possibility that an unprecedented miracle might occur. Their meaning must therefore be understood in a different manner.

The examples cited so far show that R. Isaac tends to reject the simple meaning of a rabbinic statement when it conflicts with the teachings of science about the natural order and when there is no compelling reason to assume that a miracle has taken place. But this is not the only basis for repudiating the peshat. Some rabbinic dicta seem to conflict not necessarily with the laws of nature but with the common experience and empirical observation of most human beings. For example, "R. Elazar said, 'Every house in which the words of Torah are not heard at night is consumed by fire' " (*Sanh.*, 92a). R. Isaac insists that these words should not be understood to refer to a house made of wood and stone and a fire that literally destroys these materials, "for we have surely seen houses of ignorant men, on whose lips the words of Torah are never heard, that are filled with all good things and secure against fear." There are other reasons why the manifest meaning is unacceptable: the emphasis on night does not make sense, as we are commanded to meditate on Torah both day and night, and the rabbis themselves said that "the reward for the commandments is not in this world," which implies that the punishment for their abrogation is not in our world either. But this inconsistency with Biblical verse and other aggadah does not seem as compelling as what we see all around us. On its simplest level, the statement does not ring true to reality, and it must therefore be interpreted as esoteric doctrine.[65]

The same is true for aggadot mentioning children. Many rabbinic

statements indicate that numerous children, especially sons, are a reward
for good behavior. R. Isaac is unhappy with the apparent meaning of
these statements. In the passage already discussed about the children
born to Obed-Edom while the ark rested on his property, he points out
that a multitude of sons might be a curse rather than a blessing if they are
foolish or rebellious. This is yet another proof that the statement must
not be understood according to the peshat.[66] A different midrash maintains that "the glory of the Holy One, blessed be He, arises from the
males, and about them David said [Ps. 127:3], 'Children are a heritage
of the Lord, the fruit of the womb is a reward'—these are males" (Num.
R., 3:8). R. Isaac contends that David was not speaking about sons and
daughters, for there are sons who are stupid and evil, whose parents feel
it would have been better if they had never been born. In fact, he asserts
that it is a matter of some consternation for those who have endeavored
to perfect themselves that a wise man may have a dolt for a son and a
good-for-nothing father may spawn a genius.[67] The disappointment
caused by children seems to have hung heavily over R. Isaac.

Perhaps the most poignant instance of rejecting the simple meaning
about children because it contravenes common experience is found in the
interpretation of "A woman who keeps herself modestly in retirement
has worthy sons" (Num. R., 1:3).

> These words do not come in accordance with their manifest meaning
> . . . You can find right now many women who keep themselves
> modestly in retirement from all men, and even to their husbands in
> the bedrooms of their homes they do not display their genitals, yet
> they give birth to unworthy sons, who speak shamefully to their
> mothers and do not refrain from spitting in their father's face, utterly
> scorning him. The modesty of the mother does not help with these
> sons. And just as such women can be found today, so it was in ear-
> lier ages, for there is nothing new about our own time, or about any
> other age up to now; things were the same in days of old. Further-
> more, you can find dissolute women who give birth to a wise son for
> his father, a source of great joy, so that his mother can rejoice
> among her neighbors with happiness and singing because of her son.
> Therefore, the sages spoke in an esoteric manner as we have ex-
> plained.[68]

R. Isaac apparently assumes that each reader of his commentary will con-
cur with the argument because he will know personally of such cases.
Faced with the irrefutable evidence of modest women bearing unworthy
sons and dissolute mothers producing scholars, the only way to defend
the peshat of the rabbis is to insist that ancient times were qualitatively
different from the present, that it is the imperfection of the moderns that
has made the statement no longer applicable. This argument R. Isaac re-

soundingly refuses to countenance. He insists that his own experience of reality is no different from that of ancient times, so that what is true when he writes was true when the statement was originally uttered. The simple meaning is so inaccurate as to be impossible.

The peshat of an aggadah is also abandoned when it would contradict basic theological or religious assumptions. We must not understand literally a statement such as "The *shekhinah* is in the east," for this would imply a boundary to God. The sages did not intend "to assert erroneously about Him that He is present in the east but not in the west or other directions. Heaven forbid! For the true God is present in every place, in all four directions, as we have explained in its place in the *Hibbur ha-Talmud Bavli.*"[69] The omnipresence of God is bound up with His incorporeality. R. Isaac hardly feels it necessary to point out that phrases attributing to God parts of the human body or physical actions, such as sitting, must not be understood literally; this goes without saying.[70] He is more concerned with reminding his readers that anthropopathic statements about God's joy and sadness were intended to be read "in the manner of analogy," "in metaphoric style," "according to human language."[71] Even to assert that God is impressed by the physical properties of the human being would be inconsistent with His absolute detachment from matter. R. Yohanan's injunction to seat in the Sanhedrin only those who are *ba'alei komah* and *ba'alei mar'eh* (*Sanh.*, 17a) cannot be taken literally, for God does not choose men because of their physical qualities, nor does He look at the beauty of their body or face.[72]

Other theological doctrines serve as touchstones for judging the aggadah. One of the sages said that God "arched the mountain [Sinai] over them like a tank and said, 'If you accept the Torah, fine; if not, there will be your grave' " (*AZ*, 2b et al.). But, says the commentator, "it should not occur to anyone that [the sages] thought or meant that God forced the people to accept the Torah by making them fear that He would bury them there beneath the mountain unless they accepted it, as it appears from the manifest content [*nigleh*] of their words." From the beginning of Creation, God gave to every person "the ability to make his deeds good or evil, and to choose from possible alternatives whichever they want without any compulsion." Since the apparent meaning of the statement contradicts the doctrine of human free choice, the peshat must be abandoned.[73] A statement that gives the tribe of Zebulon priority over Issachar because Zebulon engaged in business affairs and gave of its earnings to the other (*Lev. R.*, 25:2) is said to be "impossible" on its face. The sages could not have meant that whoever gives material support to a scholar is given a reward greater than that given to the scholar himself, who strives day and night to find God and to publicize the truth of His existence.[74] This is impossible not because it contradicts any principle of nature but because it is in blatant conflict with an entire theory of human perfection, the ultimate good, and the final reward from God.

As we have seen with the statement about eligibility for the Sanhedrin, passages with halakhic import are judged by many of the same criteria as are purely aggadic dicta. A midrashic statement about the ceremony of breaking the heifer's neck (*Num. R.*, 9:17) leads R. Isaac to remark that he has found a parallel statement in the Yerushalmi of *Peah*, chapter 6 (19c): "When Rav went down there, he said, 'I am the Ben Azzai of this place.' One scholar came and asked him, 'What about two men killed lying one on top of the other?' He said, 'The ceremony of breaking the neck is not performed.' 'Why?' 'The bottom one because it is concealed, and the top one because it is floating' [not lying on the ground]. When [the scholar] came up here, he came before [Ben Azzai] and said, 'Is it right?' [Ben Azzai] said, 'It is written, "If there is found . . ." not "If there *are* found . . ." [Deut. 21:1].' " According to the apparent meaning of this passage, the commandment about the heifer applies specifically to a single corpse found lying on the ground, but if the corpse is found hanging from a tree or covered with earth, or if two corpses are found one on top of the other, the ceremony is not applicable, and God's will is that the murderer be allowed to go free. But if this were true, the words would be insulting to God, for they would imply that His commandments are arbitrary and result in injustice. This, of course, is untrue. God is just, and His commandments serve a beneficial purpose. The passage must, therefore, be interpreted in a way that does not lead to this apparent conclusion.[75]

Another statement of halakhic nature in which the peshat is abandoned because of religious assumptions is from *Yoma*, 53b: "One who prays must take three steps backward, and after that give greeting."

> People thought erroneously that these words are to be understood according to their simple meaning [*ki-feshatan*], and they go backward three steps after they complete their prayer, which is pure in their own eyes, as if it were intended by God that they go backward rather than forward. Thus the entire people walks backward rebelliously three times each day, following its uncircumcized heart, a heart of flesh too impenetrable and dull to know the truths of the living God . . . For how can one who does these things ascend to his Father, how can one please his Master by walking backward these three steps after his prayer? Did He not tell him and warn him about his eyes—whether eyes of the flesh or eyes of the intellect—to "look right on" [Prov. 4:25] in all matters for his own good? For they are the "agents of sin" if they look from afar . . .[76]

Unfortunately, the precise nature of R. Isaac's objection to the literal performance of this injunction is not as fully delineated here as it must have been in the commentary on *Yoma,* to which he refers the reader enthusiastically. All that emerges clearly from this passage is that the spectacle of Jews actually walking backward as they finish their prayer is unseemly and improper for the service of God. This assumption about the proper attitude and conduct in worship is enough to turn the author not only against the peshat of a Talmudic statement but against the prevailing practice of his people.

A final example of the conflict between the simple meaning of a rabbinic pronouncement and general religious assumptions can be seen in the treatment of two messianic statements. The first is from *Sanhedrin,* 98a: "R. Joshua ben Levi met Elijah and R. Simeon ben Yohai standing at the entrance of the Garden of Eden. He said to them, 'When will the Messiah come?' They replied, 'When this master here desires it.' "[77] After giving his allegorical interpretation, R. Isaac writes:

> And it appears from their words that they have spoken not openly but cryptically, in the manner we have explained. For how could the messianic king come by means of that sage [R. Joshua b. Levi] if his generation was totally guilty? And if the keys to bring [the Messiah] whenever he wanted were given over into his hands, how is it that he did not pray his pure prayer concerning [the Messiah], for he would not have withheld good from those to whom it was due. And how is it that [the Messiah] has been late in coming, and still has not come? Rather, they spoke in the manner which we have explained, and in no other.[78]

A literal interpretation would have placed inordinate powers in the hands of R. Joshua b. Levi, and it would have made his failure to exercise these powers incomprehensible. The simple meaning of the statement is therefore dismissed.

The second passage is from the same section of *Sanhedrin* (98b): "Ula said, 'Let him [the Messiah] come, but let *me* not see him.' R. Joseph said, 'Let him come, and let me see him, and I will sit in the shadow of his donkey.' "[79] Again, after the allegorical interpretation, the comment continues:

> It should not occur to anyone that the sages, may their memory be a blessing, have spoken here about the messianic king, a king of flesh and blood, for whose saving help we eagerly await, and that they sincerely prayed that he should not come in their lifetime. Heaven forbid that they did this! For the prophets have already designated good for the people at the time of his coming, that he will bring them back to the purified land . . . How could they have prayed that he not come during their lives, that they would not see the joy [resulting] from him, but shamefully remain throughout the duration of the exile in servitude. Heaven forbid! Rather, they spoke in an esoteric manner . . .[80]

Here too, the simple meaning is repudiated in order to safeguard the purity of the messianic hope. Where Jewish writers had eagerly seized upon every word that could possibly provide a hint of the Messiah's coming, sometimes finding hidden allusions to messianic events in passages that apparently had little to do with this subject, R. Isaac is arguing that statements openly about the Messiah are not at all what they seem to be but hide a totally different message.

The simple meaning of an aggadah may also be rejected when it conflicts with the commentator's understanding of the Bible. In *Sanhedrin*, 100b, Rabbi Judah says, "Under no circumstances should a man have many friends within his house, as it is said, 'There are friends that one hath to his own hurt' " (Prov. 18:24). R. Isaac insists that the sages did not intend here "to prevent a man from having many friends who like him—heaven forbid!—as is apparent [*nigleh*] from their words. For *they would be going against the intention of the Torah* if the apparent meaning of their words was of the essence." The Torah teaches as general principles that we should love our fellow human beings and help our good friends in time of need. Therefore the sages "did not mean to teach according to the manifest content, but esoterically, in the manner we have explained—none other than this."[81]

On Exodus 29:9, "And thou shalt gird them with girdles . . . and they shall have the priesthood by a perpetual statute," the Talmud comments: "While their vestments are upon them, their priesthood is upon them, but if their vestments are not upon them, their priesthood is not upon them, and they are as aliens" (*Sanh.*, 83b). After interpreting the passage in his own manner, R. Isaac reminds his reader once again that the sages "did not intend to teach according to the manifest content of their words, that whenever the priests are not wearing their vestments, they are as aliens for all matters concerning the priesthood. Heaven forbid! For they wear their precious vestments only during the Temple service; when they eat, and at other times of the day, they do not wear these vestments, yet they eat of the *terumah* . . ."[82] Just as R. Isaac rejects the idea that the physical appearance of a man determines his fitness to sit in the Sanhedrin, so he recoils before the notion that clothing, even the priestly vestments, can change a man's status in God's sight, that the mere act of dressing in these garments bestows the quality of priesthood, and that the removal of the garments transforms a man from priest to alien. In order to combat this notion and to substitute an appropriate philosophical teaching, he argues that a literal reading of the statement leads to an obvious conflict with Torah law.[83]

To summarize, R. Isaac's criteria for rejecting the simple meaning of a rabbinic dictum are varied, including conflict with the laws of nature, with common experience, with principles of faith, and with the Bible, and they should be assessed in the context of other attempts by Jewish philosophers to formulate standards for abandoning the peshat of Bible or aggadah.[84] The interplay of several such criteria can be seen in his treatment of two categories of statements for which he regularly abandons the apparent simple meaning for an esoteric one. The first category concerns gold, silver, and other forms of wealth. Several such statements can be considered as a group. *Avot*, 4:9, asserts that "Whoever fulfills the Torah out of poverty will eventually fulfill it out of wealth." This, according to R. Isaac, refers to the true wealth of high status in God's sight; it cannot mean the "imaginary" wealth of money or material possessions. For a person wealthy in possessions is bothered by others to engage in business transactions, so that his mind is distracted and his time diverted from achieving his ultimate goal.[85] Similarly, R. Eliezer said, "Every man who has knowledge will eventually become wealthy" (*Sanh.*, 92a). Here too, the wealth mentioned is the spiritual wealth of eternal life. The rabbis did not promise imaginary wealth to the man of understanding, for this would be the opposite of their intent. "You do not find sages and enlightened men who strive to know their Creator desiring this type of wealth, consisting of imaginary good, for whoever strives to fill his barns with this will find it brings him harm rather than benefit." This justification for rejecting the obvious meaning of "wealth" is supported by a new interpretation of a phrase from Ecclesiastes 9:11, which itself does violence to the peshat. "Wealth is not to men of understanding" is read not as a cynical complaint but as an assertion that the elite who strive to know God have no desire to become wealthy in the common meaning of the term.[86]

Statements dealing with wealth in the context of Jewish history and destiny are treated in a similar manner. "I said, 'I will redeem them with money in the world . . .' " (*AZ*, 4a). After giving his own interpretation of the passage, R. Isaac continues, almost predictably:

> And we cannot say in accordance with the manifest content of their words that He, may He be blessed, redeemed the people from its enemy through a large amount of money paid so that they would let the people go free, for . . . the people left Egypt, its first exile, without payment of any price . . . , and as for this present long exile, the prophet has promised in God's own word that 'Ye shall be redeemed without money' [Isa. 52:3]. If so, this redemption mentioned here is one of the individual soul, in the manner that we have explained, none other than this."[87]

Here Biblical narrative and prophecy compel the commentator to spurn the simple meaning of the statement. But even where a Biblical prophecy speaks of precious metals, as in Isaiah 60:17, "For brass I will bring gold," the manifest meaning is repudiated. For what good would result from the accumulation of wealth in men's homes, asks the author. Such wealth is only cause for rebellion and turning away from God.

> And furthermore, this promise of the prophet to the entire people [if understood according to the peshat] can never be fulfilled, for the poor will never disappear from among the people to the end of time . . . The nature of reality requires that there be among the human species both rich and poor . . . ; it is impossible for things to be different except through a miracle, and no such sign or wonder has ever occurred to the entire people together, it is not written in the sacred texts . . . , it never happened before, and it will not occur in the future, for "there is nothing new."[88]

We have here a recapitulation of familiar themes. The peshat is in conflict with a Biblical verse (Deut. 15:11), with theoretical assumptions about material wealth and human perfection, and with the "nature of reality," although here not natural science but social theory is at issue. While it is possible to posit a miracle to resolve the last contradiction, there is no precedent, and therefore no reason to assume that the statement is predicated on such a miracle. Such an assumption would violate another Biblical verse (Eccles. 1:9) and the theological premise that the messianic age will introduce no change in the natural order. For all of these reasons, "gold" must be interpreted to mean not gold literally but something else.

The second category of statements relates to women and wives. R. Isaac refuses to accept the simple meaning of many such remarks, offering a variety of different justifications. "The world of a man whose wife dies during his life darkens upon him" (Sanh., 22a). This cannot refer to a good and beloved wife who dies, for the way of men is to forget the dead and to take another wife in place of the departed; therefore, "They did not speak in accordance with the manifest content of these words but in an esoteric manner."[89] There is nothing either impossible or repugnant about the simple meaning here. The problem is that it does not conform to experience. A comparable argument is made with regard to the statement "Only with one's first wife does he find gratification" (Sanh., 22a). Again, "They did not speak according to the manifest content of these words, dwelling at length upon a 'wife' in the basic meaning of that word [isha ke-mashma'ah]." For the relationship between a man and his wife depends not on the order of their marriage but on the nature and temperament of the two individuals. According to its plain meaning, the statement simply does not ring true.[90]

But after rejecting the peshat on this basis, R. Isaac turns to a different point: "If a man speaks to his wife such words of irreverence and mirth about sexual intercourse while he is with her, why should the sages speak of this—whether a man is gratified with his wife or whether violent passion seizes him. Heaven forbid that they should speak of such tedious matters, which would be disgraceful were a common man to say them, and engage in such trivial conversation. Rather, they spoke in an esoteric manner."[91] Here we have a new element. The entire subject matter of the peshat is ruled out of court as incompatible with the high seriousness and purpose of rabbinic discourse. A similar argument is made in CMR about a number of Talmudic statements concerning women: "All these words are tedious; they should not rise to the lips of a man of wisdom and understanding, for it would be disgraceful for him to make such a disgusting utterance: praising a woman for her great beauty."[92]

Specificially in relation to the statement that "a women is unformed matter and her husband makes her a vessel" (Sanh., 22b), R. Isaac recoils before his understanding of the peshat that the husband makes his wife a vessel by taking her virginity in the act of intercourse. "They did not speak crude jests! Heaven forbid that they spoke such words of irreverence, rising to laugh and make fun! For their purpose in speaking was for the sake of heaven: to shun that which is repulsive and the like. If these words are as their simple meaning indicates [ki-feshatan], they have not shunned anything, for these are shameful words to say."[93] R. Isaac's assumptions about the purpose of the aggadah and the dignity of rabbinic discourse, together with his assumptions about women and sex (see chapter IV, section 2), lead him to repudiate an entire category of statements for which the peshat is often not even intrinsically implausible. The final criterion for rejecting the peshat is the commentator's own somewhat subjective sense of propriety.[94]

III

CRYPTIC MEANINGS
IN THE AGGADAH

THE ESOTERIC CONTENT of the aggadah exists both where the peshat is maintained as one of two levels and where the peshat is explicitly rejected for reasons noted in the previous chapter. The most common technique of discovering arcane meanings is to assert that the sages, following the method of the prophets, used concrete entities such as fire, water, bird, woman, cloud, and so forth to represent more abstract concepts. "It is the way of the prophets to represent exalted things, which no eye has ever seen, through visible images."[1] If both prophets and sages spoke in a kind of code language, the task of the commentator is to decode their statements, to translate them back into the more abstract language of philosophical discourse. By collating all such examples of decoding in R. Isaac's commentaries, we might reconstruct his key to the code.

As the material is examined from this perspective, several principles come into focus. First, the two works reveal almost total consistency in their understanding of the cryptic language in Bible, Talmud, and Midrash. Second, the commentator's thesis that the sages followed the model of the Biblical authors is exemplified in the actual deciphering of the code. When a code word from aggadah or midrash is explained, it is invariably linked with a similar use of that word in the Bible, unless it is a word that does not appear in the Bible at all. Finally, it is worth noting that the code is not entirely arbitrary. When prophets or sages wanted to speak about a philosophical matter in an esoteric way—whether it was incorporeal angels, heavenly spheres, primal matter, the elements, the intellect, the faculties of the soul, or the human body and its impulses— their selection of images or terms to represent these concepts was not random or capricious. This would have made their code incomprehensible or hopelessly ambiguous, defeating the purpose of their two-level communication. There must be some connection between the concept and the image or emblem that appears in literary discourse. This connection,

47

which enables the cognoscenti to crack the code, is generally elucidated by the commentator.[2]

Some of the interpretations are allegorical, some are not; it is important to distinguish between them. If the river emerging from Eden and dividing into four represents primal matter being differentiated into the four elements, if Jonah setting out on the sea is the human intellect in quest of metaphysical knowledge through the realm of creation, if a man's "wife" is really his body with its impulses and his "children" are faculties of the soul, this is clearly allegorical interpretation. On the other hand, when God's "right hand" is explained as referring to the supreme Angel and His "left hand" as the highest sphere, or when "night" is interpreted as the span of a human life, we are in the realm not of allegory but of metaphor, metonymy, or other tropes. These distinctions are not always recognized by R. Isaac. He identifies the code language of esoteric discourse by certain key words, expressing the method by which he understands the prophets and sages to have disguised their meaning: *himshilu* (usually related to allegory, but having the basic meaning of "analogy"), *hish'ilu* (usually related to metaphor, but having the basic meaning of "extension"),[3] and sometimes just the general term *kar'u*. But these words are not used in a fully rigorous manner; at times they may be interchangeable,[4] and they express a range of different tropes. The proper translation is determined by the context.

The Universe

As we scan the realm of being refracted through the code words of prophet and sage, we note that, in R. Isaac's view, the Creator is never represented allegorically. He suggests no code word for God; when the aggadah speaks about God, it does so directly, although using figurative language which must not be understood literally. This is significant because both Bible and rabbinic literature provide so many metaphors traditionally associated with God—king, father, shepherd, husband, lover. An allegoristically oriented commentator could easily have taken rabbinic statements about kings, fathers, or husbands and made them into allegories about the Holy One. R. Isaac never does this. Where "king" or "husband" is part of the code, the term is applied to the ethical realm concerning the human being, not to the religious realm concerning the Deity.[5]

Directly beneath God in the hierarchy of being is the supreme incorporeal Angel (literally, "the Angel Detached from Matter"), a doctrine of central importance to R. Isaac (see chapter IV). This supreme Angel—the source of the soul, the instrument of revelation, and the means of divine manifestation to human beings—is represented in a number of ways. Most common is the allegorical representation of the Angel as fire. The image is first established by reference to Biblical usage: "It is well known to those who understand the words of the prophets that they spoke allegorically [himshilu] about the incorporeal Angel as burning fire, for he refines the inner man, figuratively speaking [al derekh mashal], just as silver is refined [by fire], and he actualizes the thoughts of the human mind just as gold is tested until it is purified and purged."[6] Support for this generalization is found in Exodus 3:2, "The angel of the Lord appeared to him in a flame of fire"; Deuteronomy 4:24, "The Lord thy God is a devouring fire"; Isaiah 6:6, "Then flew unto me one of the seraphim with a glowing stone"; and II Kings 2:11, "There appeared a chariot of fire and horses of fire."[7]

This identification of fire with the Angel is then used to explain various rabbinic pronouncements. Concerning the "strange fire" offered by Nadab and Abihu (Lev. 10:1), the Talmud reports, "Two threads of fire issued from the Holy of Holies, branching off into four, and two entered the nostrils of each one and burned them" (Sanh., 52a). R. Isaac identifies the sin of Nadab and Abihu as the heretical belief in dualism. The "strange fire" is the Angel, which they believe to have full control over human affairs, thereby denying God's providence. The "threads of fire" dividing and then entering the nostrils represent the Angel as conceived by the confused intellect that accepts a dualistic world view.[8] "When Israel were on their journeys, two sparks of fire would emerge from the two staves of the ark to strike their enemies" (Num. R., 5:1) refers to purification of the intellect through the two cherubim of the tabernacle, which confirm the Angel's existence so that all obstacles to intellectual apprehension ("the enemies"), including the physical impulses, are subdued.[9] "The Holy One, blessed be He, showed Moses on high red fire, green fire, black fire, and white fire" (Num. R., 12:8) means that as red is the color most pleasing to the human eye, so the red fire signifies the Angel, the cause of those angels below him, whose existence is taught by the tabernacle.[10] "The Torah was given in three things, in fire . . ." (Num. R., 1:7) means simply that the Torah was given by means of the Angel.[11]

A second allegorical representation of the Angel is the bird:

The prophets used the full-feathered bird as an allegorical image of the Angel that appears to man from heaven. Just as the bird that flies into the heavens grows distant from the physical eyes and disappears as it goes to a far-off land, so the Angel appears to man when he purifies his intellect and does not turn to his corporeal elements— then it appears to man wherever he is, at home or abroad, teaching him how to do what is right so that his soul may envisage the light of the King's face. But whenever he uses his corporeal element to prepare his daily provisions, then the King departs from him, and he will not see Him any more until his mind returns to intellectual endeavor. Then He will reappear to him.[12]

This image is used to explain the midrash that states: "The tabernacle is equal in importance to the world . . . It is written of the fifth day, 'Let fowl fly above the earth,' and of the tabernacle, 'The cherubim shall spread out their wings . . .' " (Num. R., 12:13). Explaining in philosophical terms the series of correspondences between the tabernacle and the realm of Creation, R. Isaac comes to the birds, created on the fifth day to confirm the fact of the Angel's existence. The whereabouts of this Angel is not known before the fifth day, as it is needed only then, to serve as the source for the human soul, which is required for the sixth day's work.[13] In the tabernacle, the Angel's existence is confirmed by the cherubim. The comment solidifies the connection established by the midrash between bird and cherub, as both become concrete images for the supreme incorporeal Angel.

Other code words for the Angel, such as the "right hand" of God[14] and the "Throne of Glory,"[15] are drawn from the realm of theological discourse in the Bible and aggadah. This is no longer allegory but rather the interpretation of one problematic term by another with which the author feels more comfortable. An especially fertile source of code words is the tradition of rabbinic angelology. The expression "ministering angels" itself can have this specialized meaning, as it does in the statement " 'You shall not make with me' [Exod. 20:20]: You shall not make something like the image of those attendants who serve before Me on high, such as the ofanim, the sacred hayyot, the serafim, and the ministering angels" (AZ, 43b). The supreme Angel is "the last of all [the ultimate or highest] in status and rank: it serves God by appearing to man to guide him in the 'way to the dwelling of light.' "[16] Michael is one of the names for this Angel, as in "He set about His throne four angels: Michael, Gabriel, Uriel, and Raphael, Michael at His right . . ." (Num. R., 2:10), and "Even Michael, even Gabriel were afraid of Moses . . ." (Num. R., 11:3). This Michael, the most distinguished of all caused beings, calls out, "Who is Like God" (mi ka-el), for God is the cause even of the most exalted Angel.[17]

The most important name for the Angel in rabbinic literature is Metatron. We have seen that statements about Metatron appear prominently in Karaite, Muslim, and Christian attacks on the aggadah. R. Isaac deals with some of these issues while discussing the Talmudic statements "That is Metatron, whose name is like that of his Master" (Sanh., 38b) and "If you choose, say it was Metatron" (AZ, 3b). The significance of the name is explained in the following comment:

They called him Metatron, for this name applies to any emissary, sent for any purpose. Since he is the Angel of the Lord, sent by Him to human beings, they called him Metatron, for he performs God's task in perfecting man to the point where man attains that goal desired of him.[18]

This passage assumes that the name Metatron is derived from the word *metator*, which can indeed mean "messenger." The derivation is mentioned in *Sefer ha-Arukh* and in the writings of German Pietists and Kabbalists.[19] The association of both names, Michael and Metatron, with the supreme incorporeal Angel seems to reflect the historical fact that many of the functions ascribed in earlier sources to Michael were later associated with Metatron, so that the two figures were more or less assimilated into one.[20]

Some of the terms used to indicate the supreme Angel may also represent the entire realm of incorporeal beings. This is true of the word "birds," as in the statement "In connection with the Torah, it is written, 'It is hid from the eyes of all living, and from the birds of the heavens it is kept secret' [Job 28:21]" (*Shevu'ot*, 5a). "Torah" here means philosophical knowledge of God; Job called "birds of the heavens" the immaterial angels, "as you will find that the prophets attributed to them wings and the ability to fly." The statement means that even the angels, untroubled by the obstacles to intellectual apprehension inherent in matter, are not vouchsafed full and perfect knowledge of God.[21] Similarly, the term "Throne of Glory" may refer to the general category of incorporeal angels. "Precious in God's sight was the construction of the ark even as that of the Throne of Glory in heaven" (*Num. R.*, 4:13).

> They called the angels God's "Throne of Glory" because they publicize in heaven the existence of God . . . the One exalted over them . . . just as all who enter a palace can learn from the throne the identity of the king. When he sits on his throne in the royal palace, with all his courtiers and servants standing around the throne set aside exclusively for him, all will recognize who it is that rules over the people. Even so the angel is the "throne" to his God, confirming the fact of God's existence to those who do not know Him.

The statement, as interpreted, does not mean that the ark is actually as important as the angels but that the ark represents to the people of Israel the realm of the incorporeal beings.[22]

Descending along the great chain of being, we come to the realm of the heavenly bodies. Just as one Angel is supreme among the incorporeal beings beneath God, so one sphere is primary among the heavenly bodies. Referred to simply as "the sphere," this is undoubtedly the "ninth sphere . . . which rotates from east to west every day, encircling and encompassing everything else."[23] According to R. Isaac, the terms used by the rabbis to represent this sphere are analogous to those used for the Angel, but of a lower order. Whereas the "right hand" of God denotes the Angel, the "left hand" of God denotes the sphere.[24] Whereas Michael and Metatron are names used for the Angel, Gabriel is "the sphere that tells of the power [*gevurat*] of God."[25] "God said to Gabriel, 'Is your sickle sharpened?' He replied, 'Sovereign of the Universe, it has been sharpened since the six days of Creation' " (*Sanh.*, 95b). R. Isaac writes:

> "Gabriel" comes in the language of the sages to teach about the sphere, called "Gabriel" because it tells the power and might of God. It knows by itself its own deficiency: that it has no ability to do anything, large or small, of its own initiative, but only through the direction of God. The sages said here that God beckons to Gabriel, figuratively speaking, and asks him if he is prepared to fulfil the divine will by helping the chosen people. He replies, "It has been sharpened . . . ," meaning that his sword is unsheathed in his hand to do the will of his Maker whenever He desires, just as He stipulated with him when He brought him into being during the six days of Creation.[26]

The vivid and rather dramatic language of the rabbis is decoded to express the Maimonidean principle that the natural order, controlled by the highest sphere, was programmed at the time of its creation to act at certain historical moments for the benefit of Israel.[27]

Finally, whereas the Angel is signified by "Throne of Glory," the sphere is intended by the simple word "throne." The Biblical basis for this identification is Isaiah 66:1, "The heaven is my throne," as contrasted with Jeremiah 17:12, "Throne of glory, on high from the beginning," which implies a superior realm.[28] When the rabbis say, "The sanctuary corresponds to the throne, the ark to the Throne of Glory" (*Num. R.*, 4:13), the first phrase teaches that "the tabernacle and the tent in the 'royal palace' which Solomon built correspond in their craft to the realm of the spheres."[29] This distinction between "throne" and "Throne of Glory" is reflected in the *Yotzer* of the Sabbath-morning liturgy, "Purity and rectitude are before his throne, loving kindness and tender mercy are before his Throne of Glory": "They taught that every star which works to the detriment of a nation or an individual does so at the behest of the King, in order to chastise him because of his sins . . . But they attributed to the Angel mercy and forgiveness of man, for it teaches man how to find the right way in order to attain perpetual life for his soul."[30] In this interpretation, the liturgical hymn does not merely assert that both justice and mercy originate with God; it teaches that justice is implemented through the heavenly bodies, but that the instrument of mercy is higher in the realm of being.

The universe in its entirety, including the sublunar world of corruptible matter, may be represented by the sea, as in the statement, "Three things were presented as a gift to the world . . . Also passage through the high seas" (*Lev. R.*, 35:8). The comment provides a fine example of allegorical code applied to Bible and aggadah:

You have already found that the prophets represented allegorically all of reality by the sea . . . and all beings, great and small, whether beast, man, or star, by fish. Thus you find that Ezekiel, prophesying about the chariot of the living God, said "And there shall be a great multitude of fish" [47:9], intimating that he found the "fish" in the "sea" created by God of all different kinds, a thousand thousand species ministering unto Him. Also Jonah, son of Amitai, spoke cryptically . . . about the sea, intimating that he went to seek out God . . . and he found on his way a great fish who swallowed him without cause and enemies in the gate which he entered, and he did not find what his soul desired until he descended to his garden to pluck a flower . . . The Psalmist also represented the totality of existence by the wide sea, saying "therein are innumerable creeping things, living creatures both small and great" [104:25], alluding to the higher beings found in the "sea" and the creatures that are of no account and feeble which dwell in the lower realm, and teaching that they are a great and innumerable host.

The Babylonians noted the way of the prophets, and they also said, "Why is blue different from all other colors? Because blue is similar to the sea, and the sea to the firmament, and the firmament to the Throne of Glory" [*Sotah*, 17a]. For the realm of being is a throne for the King, set aside for the King of Glory. And all the statements of Rabba bar bar Hana, told to him by those who went to sea in ships—that they saw in the sea the great sea-monsters and birds and beasts—allude to this . . . And many others as well. When they said, "his ship set sail on the sea," they alluded by "ship" to the human body, which sets out to sea to inquire of God for itself and to see His marvels, until the ship is apt to be broken on the high waters. Furthermore, the Psalmist said, "There go the ships" [104:26] . . .[31]

After these provocative allusions to an allegorical interpretation of Jonah,[32] the stories of Rabba bar bar Hana,[33] and other verses, the commentator eventually returns to the statement of the midrash under consideration, explaining that God has given man permission to go to this great sea, to seek metaphysical knowledge by investigating the realm of being, but that he should not enter treacherous waters by seeking to know ultimate truths without the necessary preliminaries. One who puts out to sea without a captain or sailors or oars is in serious danger of drowning.[34]

The same code is applied to *Sanhedrin*, 108a: "R. Hisda said, 'The decree did not apply to the fish of the sea, as it is said, "All that was in the dry land died" [Gen. 7:22], but not the fish in the sea.' " Again, "they called the entire realm of being 'the sea,' figuratively speaking. The 'fish' in the sea are the four basic elements, for just as the sea is great in comparison with the tiny fish in its midst, so is the all-encompassing sphere great in comparison with the elements emanated from it." The statement teaches the eternal nature of the fundamental elements, which will not be destroyed despite the dissolution of individual things formed by their combination.[35]

A second image for the universe in its entirety is the hand of God. We have already seen the "right hand" as the Angel and the "left hand" as the sphere; here we have "hand" in general as all-inclusive. This is its meaning in *Sanhedrin*, 95b: "With what did He smite them? R. Eliezer said, 'He smote them with the hand, as it is written, "And Israel saw the great hand" [Exod. 14:31]—this is the hand destined to exact vengeance on Sennacherib.' R. Joshua said, 'He smote them with a finger, as it is written, "Then the magicians said unto Pharaoh, 'This is the finger of God' " [Exod. 8:15]—that is, the finger destined to exact venegeance on Sennacherib.' " The disagreement between the two sages is decoded as a dispute over the natural cause of the sudden and unexpected destruction of the Assyrian host. R. Eliezer "called the entire realm of being His 'hand,' for it is, figuratively speaking, God's 'hand,' through which He performs all actions, just as a craftsman performs his actions with his hands, bringing his thoughts into actuality . . ." Just as the hand is composed of five fingers, so the physical world is composed of four elements and the sphere. The proof text from Exodus about the "great hand" teaches that the plagues resulted from changes in each of the four elements: earth (becoming gnats), water (becoming blood), air (becoming pestilent), and fire (not being extinguished in the hail), and that the sphere itself was temporarily changed to afflict the Egyptians (bringing darkness). So it was in the time of Sennacherib. In contrast, R. Joshua maintains that the Assyrians died through the alteration of only one element (or "finger"), the air, which suddenly became putrid, while the other elements and the sphere remained unchanged.[36]

With the "fish" and the "fingers" in these last two images, we have arrived in the sublunar realm, which came into being when the primal matter, receiving four forms, produced the fundamental elements, and these in turn combined to produce various mixtures and compounds. This process is represented in several ways. One is read into the statement "Behemoth was created only for the sake of Jacob" (*Lev. R.*, 36:4). R. Isaac notes, "We have already pointed out in this work of ours that when they speak about Behemoth, it is not a beast walking on all fours, as would appear from its lexical meaning [*mashma'ah*]. Rather, 'behemah' is what, speaking figuratively, they called the primal matter, comparing it to a beast walking on all fours because it received four forms, each of which was an element, from which all flesh came into being." "Jacob" here is accepted at face value, but the statement is characterized as hyperbolic in nature.[37]

Another midrash decoded to express the same process is *Numbers Rabbah*, 12:8: " 'He makes peace in His high heavens' . . . The matter does not end at reconciliation between angel and angel. He makes peace even within the person of each angel, who possesses five [antagonistic] features. 'A fiery stream issued and came forth' [Dan. 2:10], and the firmament consists of water, yet neither extinguished the other." The comment merits being quoted at length:

"Angel" is a noun extended metaphorically. Its primary application is the Angel of God, incorporeal, which stands before Him to minister to Him and to bless in His name. Then it is applied metaphorically to anything that carries out the mission of Him who commands it, whatever it may be, whether a beast or a man or a bird or an inanimate object or a physical faculty, it is called "angel" because it performs its mission, doing God's work. In this manner, they called metaphorically the primal matter "angel" and said that it has five features—the four forms that it received when it was created, each form being a simple element, from which the various species came into existence, and the fifth the underlying matter, which sustains them perpetually . . .

And God in heaven makes peace within this "angel," among the parts that emerge from it, for the elemental fire emerges first, as God brings it forth from its midst, and from this source emerges the elemental water, antithetical to it, as is plainly seen from the fact that water extinguishes fire. Yet God made peace between them when He created them, enabling these two opposites to coexist simultaneously in one object, something impossible for man to accomplish . . .

This elemental fire they called "fiery stream," for so the Master of the prophets called the elements "rivers." For whatever the prophet spoke in the name of God, and was written in Scripture, was given to him by the King on two levels. The manifest level is obvious . . . But the esoteric meaning of the river which issues forth from Eden, its springs dispersed abroad, dividing into four heads [Gen. 2:10-14], is that it confirms the existence of primal matter, from which was generated the four elements and everything produced from them in all generations—man, beast, and winged bird, which will never cease to exist as separate species.

Although these rivers were called by the names of the various lands—Pishon, Gihon, Hidekel, and Parath—each name applies to the relevant element. Pishon applies to elemental fire, not blown by man, necessarily greater than the others, for it encompasses all the rest, and that which encompasses must be greater than that which is encompassed and lies in its midst. Because it is greater than the others, it is called Pishon, indicating greatness in something, as in

"their horsemen are many" [u-fashu parashav, Hab. 1:8], indicating
a great and powerful host, innumerable armies.

The name Gihon applies to elemental air, which blows as a great
strong wind until it pours upon the earth, sweeping away everything
in its path, destroying every fruit-bearing tree, making mourners out
of rampart and wall.

The name Hidekel applies to the watery element—a stream which
can be heard [mashmi'ah kol] far away as it pours down a steep de-
clivity, flowing torrents of mighty waters—just as every man of wisdom, priest and prophet, attributed a "voice" [kol] to the water, for
it is said, "Like the voice of many waters" [Ezek. 1:24].

The name Parath applies to the elemental earth, in that it grows
vegetation in the field for all, enabling them to be fruitful [u-faru]
and multiply on the earth by providing harvest and seed for the
sower. You will find that Ezekiel called the elements "streams" according to the cryptic meaning of his words, one by one, calling the
elemental earth and the elemental water "waters to the ankles" and
"waters to the knees," which move slowly. And he called elemental
air and fire "waters to the loins" and "waters to swim in"—mighty
waters, through which no man can pass [Ezek. 47:3-5].

And through the divine wisdom bestowed upon him, Solomon
spoke always on two levels, and he called the elements "rivers" in an
esoteric manner, saying, "All the rivers run into the sea, yet the sea
is not full" [Eccles. 1:7]. The manifest meaning of this is obvious . . .
But the esoteric meaning of "rivers" is that he called the entire realm
of being "the sea," and proclaimed the fact that all the "rivers" flow
into this "sea," so that its great multitude of "fish" come into being,
fourfold in nature, from under these heavens.

And this "sea" is never filled with individual beings that are
formed in it—man, beast, birds—for just as these individuals come
into existence, so they pass away, one generation going, another
coming, and the "sea" is never filled of them to eternity . . . God
made it part of the nature of each individual being to die; he cannot
endure in his identity forever, for the "sea" grows ever more stormy
over him, and seeks an occasion to kill him . . . But there is never
any lack of individual beings, for when the composition of each
individual breaks up into its component parts, each part returns to
its own element, so that the earth is restored with new generations
time after time, and no species is ever exhausted to eternity.[38]

Let us examine some of the salient features of this passage as code interpretation of Bible and Midrash.

First, there is the discussion of the word "angel," interpreted to mean
primal matter.[39] This definition is applied to the "five features" of each
angel, which are explained as signifying the underlying matter and the
four forms (elements), the basis for the diversity of the sublunar realm.
The passage is not intended as systematic cosmology, for according to

medieval scientific speculation, while fire was indeed the first element that came into being, the second was not water but air. Since the Midrash mentions the antagonism of fire and water, the element of air is temporarily overlooked. With the discussion of the term "fiery stream" in the midrashic proof text (Dan. 7:10), a new realm of pure allegory is introduced. Rivers—paradigmatically the four rivers of Genesis 2:10-14—represent the fundamental elements. This interpretation appears in the work of several philosophically oriented authors, both before and after R. Isaac: Solomon ibn Gabirol, Abraham ibn Ezra, Isaac Albalag, Levi b. Abraham, Nissim of Marseilles. It is also found in places not ordinarily associated with the allegorical approach of the philosophers: the Zohar and the commentary of Isaac Abravanel.[40] While the etymological derivations of the names, with the possible exception of Gihon, are not original, the application of these names to the respective elements may have been. Only Levi b. Abraham, writing a generation after R. Isaac, attempted a similar feat.[41]

R. Isaac's esoteric interpretation of Ezekiel 47:3-5 is not entirely clear. The prophet is led through water of increasing depth—said to represent the elements of earth, water, and air—but he finds himself unable to cross the deepest water, representing the elemental fire. Perhaps R. Isaac is referring to the intellectual apprehension of the terrestrial realm, implying that the human intellect, while still in the body, cannot fully comprehend that which is beyond fire, the first of the elements to emerge. The explanation of Ecclesiastes 1:7 is more easily intelligible and is not out of harmony with the patent meaning of the verse. The water cycle is chosen to represent the never-ending process of generation, destruction, and new generation of individual beings, while the underlying matter of which they are composed remains forever unchanged.[42]

A few more examples will complete the list of code words for the sublunar world with its four elements. The interpretation of Ecclesiastes 1:7 is complemented by a different passage explaining Ecclesiastes 1:4, which introduces the word "earth" (aretz) as another code expression for the four elements. This is not allegory but merely an all-inclusive term for the terrestrial realm understood in a specifically scientific way:

> The elements are called "earth" by the prophets and all wise men among the people, as in "He established the earth upon its foundations" [Ps. 104:5]. Similarly, the wise Solomon said, "and the earth abides forever" [Eccles. 1:4], teaching in his wisdom that the elements, once having come into existence, will never again be annihilated, for the supreme God renews the earth from them generation after generation, and no species is ever exhausted to eternity. In this manner, the sages said here that the cherubim were precious to God as representing the heaven and earth [Num. R., 4:13], for from them

[the sphere and the four elements] came into being the varied multitude of individuals, the work of God by Whose command they were created.[43]

The same interpretation of aretz as representing the four elements, linked with Ecclesiastes 1:4, is used in the comment upon the statement "I did well in preparing graves for them in the earth" (Sanh., 108a).[44]

The names of individual angels are also interpreted as representing this sublunar realm. We have already seen that Michael is the supreme Angel and Gabriel is the sphere. The other two archangels complete the cosmos: "It appears from their words that they called the elemental fire 'Uriel,' for this is God's lamp, the Lord's flame, which many waters cannot extinguish. It is a play on words, coming from 'fire.' And they called all that is actualized in the sublunar realm, coming into being from the four elements 'Raphael,' because all this is weak [rafeh], feeble, of no account, incapable of ultimately enduring." R. Isaac then explains the midrashic statement that "Raphael corresponds to Ephraim, from whom came Jeroboam" (Num. R., 2:10) as meaning that the corporeal component of Jeroboam kept him from apprehending metaphysical truths about God.[45] It is noteworthy that this explication of the name Raphael as deriving from "rafeh" meaning "weak" ignores the traditional explanation, found in this very midrash, as deriving from the root meaning "to heal."

The four elements combine with each other in various proportions to form the vast medley of individual beings that populate the terrestrial realm, each existing for a limited period of time before succumbing to dissolution. R. Isaac maintains that this process is expressed by the term "Leviathan," as in the assertion that during the fourth period of each day, God "sits and plays with Leviathan" (AZ, 3b). The entire aggadah is interpreted as describing the four stages in the human life, the last being the period of the Leviathan:

> They called the privation inherent in matter, which changes forms and assumes new forms, "Leviathan." God "plays with it," giving it power over the individual man and all similar to him, for through the changing of forms, the group as a whole is preserved . . . They called this joining [of the elements] "Leviathan," for the root of that noun is etymologically derived from "joining," as in the verse "My husband will be joined [yil-laveh] to me" [Gen. 29:34]. Here the sages have taught that God desires the perpetuation of the human species and also the other species created because of its needs. He desires that they will never disappear and cease to exist on the earth. This [Leviathan] is His emissary for this purpose, in one sense. In this way, He "plays with it," figuratively speaking, in that it does what He has commanded it. Thus the Psalmist taught when he said "Leviathan, whom you have formed to play with" [104:26], mean-

ing that it is His emissary, prepared from the outset to serve Him and act in this way at His bidding, "playing" with the terrestrial creatures by destroying the physical structure in even the best of them. For this destruction is constructive for their soul, preparing it and sustaining it for the spiritual pleasure of Eden, the garden of God.

This destruction, which turns out to be so constructive, is called by the sages "Leviathan," in the manner of the prophet who said "Leviathan the slant serpent," then repeating the same matter by saying "Leviathan the tortuous serpent" [Isa. 27:1]. The prophet used the word "Leviathan" to teach about the combination brought into being because of it, and the word "serpent" [nahash] to teach about the corruption and destruction [hash-hatah] brought into being in material things as a result. All of them followed the Master of the prophets, who used the word "serpent" at the beginning of Creation, saying, "The serpent was the cleverest of all" [Gen. 3:1], teaching that it incited Eve and caused death for all who eat from the fruit of the tree of knowledge; in every generation they die because of it.[46]

The term "Leviathan" is explained as signifying two things: the combination of the elements to form individual beings and the inherent corruptibility that results from this combination, as all such beings inevitably undergo dissolution into their component parts. The aggadic pronouncement that during the final three hours of the day God "plays with Leviathan" is decoded to mean that toward the end of life, the process of deterioration in the human body accomplishes the task intended by God for all mundane beings. The formulation "This destruction [of the body] is constructive for the soul" (ha-harisah ha-hi binyan le-nafsham) seems to be influenced by an uncharacteristically severe statement of Maimonides, who maintained in the Introduction to his Mishnah Commentary that "the well-being of the soul lies in the destruction of the body."[47]

The rest of the comment dovetails nicely with others quoted above. We have already seen R. Isaac's interpretation of Psalm 104:25 and the first part of 104:26: the sea is the realm of existence in its entirety; the sea creatures are the beings that populate the upper and lower realms; the ships are human bodies setting out to seek knowledge of God. Here we have the second part of verse 26: Leviathan, the ultimate corruptibility of the body as a composite of elements, awaits the ships at the end of their journey. Furthermore, we have seen how an allegorical interpretation of the four rivers of Eden is incorporated almost incidentally into a discussion of nahar dinur. Here too, an allegorical interpretation of the snake is suggested by the explanation of Leviathan in Isaiah 27:1, which most commentators understood quite differently as a historical allusion to the powerful kings of the Gentiles. Nahash—"snake"—is linked with the word for "destruction"—hash-hatah—so that the snake of Eden becomes the principle of ultimate dissolution inherent in the combination of the elements represented by the rivers.[48] Placing this interpretation alongside the view that Adam was created as a fully intellectual being who did not have to use his body any more than if he had been totally incorporeal, we can begin to reconstruct an allegorical interpretation of the entire Eden story.

The Human Being

The realm of the human being—his components and faculties, his ultimate goal, and the obstacles in his path—is represented by a panoply of images even more varied than those used for the universe outside man. First, there is the physical element of the human being, the body with the corporeal impulses and faculties, all of which serve generally to impede progress toward the actualization of the intellect and the attainment of eternal life. The most common allegorical representation of this corporeal element is "woman." Maimonides reported that "Plato and his predecessors called matter 'female' and form 'male' " (Guide, I, 17). He also states that Solomon represented the body by an adulteress, and that this figure is a key to a proper understanding of Proverbs (Guide, Introduction; III, 8).[49] Many Jewish writers of the thirteenth century repeated this principle and applied it to the task of Biblical exegesis.[50] It is no surprise that this type of interpretation was eventually extended to the aggadah.

R. Isaac comments in this way upon a group of statements from *Sanhedrin*, 21a-22b dealing with the relations between husband and wife. The first statement to appear is of a halakhic nature: "If even one [wife] diverts [the king's] mind, he must not marry her" (21a). The sages

> called matter [the body] "female," in the style of that wise man Solomon, following the esoteric content of his fine words. He said, "She is riotous and rebellious" [Prov. 7:11], teaching that when this "woman" is innately disposed to fulfil her will passionately, to be evil in her master's sight, and to rebel against all he ordains for her, he must constrain her as much as he can, not giving in to her panting desire by seeking after every superfluous, base pleasure. He spoke here figuratively about matter that is not good or properly disposed for a man to fulfil his true purpose. Thus the sages alluded to this
> . . .[51]

In the Maimonidean tradition, the basis for this allegory is located in the book of Proverbs, and the sages are said to follow the Biblical model. Subsequent statements from *Sanhedrin* and other sources are treated in a similar manner, emphasizing two different themes. The first, evident in the interpretation of the Proverbs verse above, is that the impulses of the body can lead to disastrous results if they are given free rein and that they must therefore be kept subservient to the intellect. "The world of a man whose wife dies during his life darkens upon him, as it is said [Job 18:6], 'The light shall be dark in his tent, and his lamp over him shall be put out' " (*Sanh.*, 22a). As Rashi points out, the sages read the verse from Job to say, "The light shall be dark *because of* his tent," and interpreted the word "tent" to mean the man's wife.[52] R. Isaac takes a further step, making the *nimshal* ("wife") into a new *mashal*. The dying wife represents the corporeal element of a human being, leading him to sin so that the man is considered to be "dead." The darkening world is the ultimate annihilation of both body and soul caused by the physical obstacles that kept him from achieving immortality. The proof text of the sages is similarly reinterpreted: tent = wife = body. Man lives in a tent, figuratively speaking, all the days of his life. Like a shepherd carrying his tent on his shoulders in search of new pasture land, so man moves, day after day, on his journey toward death. If, because of man's physical nature, the soul does not achieve light during its life in the body ("the light is dark because of his tent"), then ultimately the soul itself will perish ("his lamp will be put out"). As the new philosophical allegory, wife = body, is fused with a rabbinic metonymy (tent = wife) and a Biblical metaphor (lamp = soul, as in Proverbs 20:27), a powerful homily is produced.[53]

If one extreme is allowing the body to run rampant to the detriment of soul and intellect, the other is excessive mortification of the body. R. Isaac's criticism of this extreme is found in statements such as "He whose first wife has died is as if the Temple had been destroyed during his life," "For him who divorces the first wife, the very altar sheds tears," and "Only with one's first wife does he find gratification, as it is said [Prov. 5:18], 'Let thy fountain be blessed and have joy with the wife of thy youth' " (all *Sanh.*, 22a). In these dicta, the "first wife" or "wife of youth" represents the body of the young man, with corporeal impulses and powers at full strength. The first two statements are decoded to mean that one who causes his own premature death by excessive mortification of his body commits a great sin, for he destroys the house without which it is impossible for the soul to achieve eternal life.[54] And the third statement teaches that a man can find gratification for his soul at the end of his life only by providing for his body when he is young. The verse from Proverbs is read not as two parallel blessings but as an effect and its cause. *Yehi mekorkha barukh:* if you want your *makor* (probably the intellect, although not explicitly stated) to provide a never-ending flow of living waters (the intelligibles, which bestow eternal life upon the soul), then *ve-samah me-eshet ne'urekha*, you must provide for the body to be satisfied in its basic needs when young. This is true even though the physical powers of the youthful body are so strong that once it has been provided with necessities, it will seek more than it needs. For if the body is driven to a premature death by being denied the requirements for life, the intellect may not have developed sufficiently to guarantee immortality.[55]

We may consider more briefly some of the other code words for the human body with its impulses, the obstacles to intellectual perfection. Just as the word "tent," understood by the rabbis as "wife," is used by R. Isaac as a metaphor for the human body, so is the word "house." As I have mentioned, R. Isaac repudiates the literal meaning of "The house in which the words of the Torah are not heard at night shall be consumed by fire," because prosperous houses of ignorant men are by no means uncommon. He therefore turns to the esoteric interpretation: "We have already pointed out many times in this work of ours that the sages used the word 'house' as a metaphor [hish'ilu] for the human body, as this is the house prepared for the soul." The rest of the statement is explained accordingly: the life span of the human being is the "night,"[56] the punishment of annihilation is "fire." When the code is deciphered, the new statement reads, "Whoever does not actualize his intellect through the study of 'Torah' [philosophy] during the period of life in the body will be punished by annihilation."[57] Similarly, "One should not have a multitude of friends in his house" (Sanh., 100b) is unacceptable in its apparent meaning. But if "house" is understood as the body and "friends" as those faculties that serve the body, the advice makes good sense: a man must not allow his physical impulses to predominate but should follow only those good faculties of the soul that aid in the purification of the intellect.[58]

Other allegorical representations of the body have Biblical resonance. In his comment on Numbers Rabbah, 12:11, discussing Elijah's ascent to heaven in a storm, R. Isaac draws an analogy with Moses:

> Elijah ascended to the heights to seek that which his soul desired, searching until he found Him in a holy place. He spoke to Elijah while he was still alive in the flesh. Elijah's material component did not keep him from this glory; his corporeal nature did not stop him from gazing at his God.
>
> So did God appear to Moses within the bush: a lowly tree full of prickly thorns, the branches of which are also full of moving thorns. This is an allegorical representation of the corporeal element, which contains within it obstacles that pain the heart, even in Moses. And God from above appeared to Moses from this shrub because the great degree of preparation made his body suitable, in order that Moses might know the Most High and Awesome.
>
> Thus God appeared from the "storm" to Elijah, because of the great purity of his matter, close to that of Moses. He did not find a

single thorn or thistle on the way which he walked; his bare foot was not pained; he searched without finding enemies in the gate of the Lord. Elijah saw Him whenever he wanted from the "storm," without being misled. *And all these words—bush, storm, cloud, fog—all of them are used metaphorically for the corporeal element of man,* because it hinders the perfect man from being able to see God's goodness. His right eye is plastered over, covered by a cloud.[59]

This passage brings us into a thicket of thorny problems relating to a crucial issue in the allegorical interpretation of Bible and aggadah. I have pointed out places where R. Isaac explicitly repudiates the simple, obvious meaning of a statement, insisting that only the esoteric meaning is intended, and other places where he says, "The manifest meaning is obvious . . . and the esoteric meaning is [as follows]." What is his position here, where no clear guidelines are given? Does he believe that Moses actually saw a burning bush, that Elijah actually ascended to heaven in a whirlwind, and that bush and storm were chosen as instruments of God's communication because they were appropriate images of the human body? Or are we to understand that there was no bush and no storm at all, that these are merely allegorical representations of the body and that the two Biblical accounts are simply picturesque ways of saying that Moses and Elijah, despite the obstacles generally presented by the corporeal element of man, were vouchsafed pure visions of the Eternal One? This is by no means a trivial question; bitter battles were fought over it. Let us consider the cases individually.

The description of the burning bush must be compared with other references to the incident. R. Isaac views fire as an allegorical representation of the supreme incorporeal Angel: "It is well-known to all who possess true wisdom of the Torah that the Angel who appears to man is represented by burning fire when the prophets speak about him. Thus the Master of the prophets said, 'And the angel of the Lord appeared to him in a flame of fire.' "[60] This is not very helpful, as it contains an ambiguity similar to that in which the bush is described. Was there really a flame, or is fire merely a literary image chosen to represent the effect of the Angel? Fortunately, the interpretation of Exodus 3:5 in a different context is more explicit. When God tells Moses to "take off your shoes from upon your feet," He is informing him that he must "remove all internal obstacles to the two faculties which must necessarily be strong in every prophet"—the imagination and the intellect. Had the comment ended here, the same ambiguity would have remained. But R. Isaac continues, *"And on the manifest level,* He taught him that he should take off his shoe and act with respect toward the place where he stood because of the future, when the glory of the Lord would descend to give the Torah of truth to the chosen people on that spot. Thus He disclosed to him that it was holy ground because the Jews were destined to receive the Torah there, and he should therefore not walk there in shoes that he had worn in filthy and contaminated places."[61] This clarifies several points: Moses did actually take off his shoes (as well as remove the obstacles to prophecy), and he was actually standing in a particular geographical location as indicated by the plain meaning of the Biblical text. The historicity of the incident as narrated is maintained, and the ambiguity of the other passages should probably be resolved by the conclusion that Moses did indeed see a burning bush.[62] It is consistent with the author's outlook that the place in which Moses stood is described as holy not because of the metaphysical presence of the Angel there at that moment but because of the event destined to occur there in the future.[63]

With regard to Elijah, the matter is less clear, and the ambiguity may be intentional. Here too the code use of fire is relevant. One example of the allegorical representation of the Angel by fire is II Kings 2:11: " 'And behold! a chariot of fire, and horses of fire which came between the two of them,' teaching that on the day he was taken, the angels of God were revealed to him going forth from the fire out of his sight, and since the Angel was represented allegorically by fire, so each of its implements was represented by fire—chariot and horsemen."[64] In a similar passage later in this commentary, R. Isaac writes, "They represented allegorically by fire all the implements in all the visions that the Angel reveals to man below on earth, [saying] that they went forth from fire, figuratively speaking; thus in the story about Elijah . . ."[65] These "implements" refer to the objects appearing in a prophetic vision. All this seems to indicate that the second chapter of II Kings should not be taken literally. God's raising of Elijah to heaven in a whirlwind may be understood to mean simply that Elijah attained an unusually pure intellectual apprehension of God while he was still alive in the flesh; the chariot of fire and horses of fire are a prophetic vision vouchsafed to Elisha by the Angel, teaching him of his master's lofty intellectual achievement.[66] This interpretation is consistent with the comment on R. Joshua b. Levi's encounter with Elijah and R. Simeon b. Yohai:

> They taught that Elijah and R. Simeon b. Yohai purified themselves during their lives so that they could stand at the King's gate to serve the Lord their Maker there, until they could reach their ultimate goal, when their souls would enter Eden, God's garden, after [separation from] matter. For it is widely known among the Jewish nation that Elijah's soul ascended to heaven, entering its resting place in the realm of God and His angels.[67]

Note that Elijah's soul is said to have ascended to heaven, not his body. R. David Kimhi denied Elijah's physical ascent into heaven by insisting that his body was consumed when it reached the sphere of fire. R. Isaac seems to have gone even further in his rationalization of this passage by implying that the entire episode was written in figurative language.[68]

The end of this comment provides a list of words used as allegorical representations of the human body: not only "bush" and "storm" but "cloud" and "fog." Similarly, in CAT, R. Isaac notes that the "cloud and darkness which the prophets say cover a man, and the fog that envelops him" represent the forces that prevent a human being from apprehending the true reality of God.[69] This code is then applied to the interpretation of statements such as "Moses, who entered into the midst of the cloud, which is the 'covert of the Most High' " (Num. R., 12:3). "The cloud that covers the perfect man and keeps him from the glory of gazing at God whenever he wants, limiting this to infrequent occasions, is his corporeal element, composed of opposites that contend with each other throughout his life, and all his impulses, which seek superfluous things, never becoming quiescent, day or night." But despite the fact that Moses was in a "cloud," the matter composing his body had been purified to such an extent that it did not prevent him from attaining a unique intellectual apprehension of the Deity.[70]

The special term for a human body naturally constituted so as to interfere minimally with the intellectual process is "clouds of glory," as in "It was due to the merit of Aaron that I set clouds of glory about you" (Num. R., 1:2). "I have already stated . . . that they called 'clouds of glory' those bodies made of pure matter, and thereby suitable for the apprehension of every intelligible, having no improper physical faculty, entirely capable of aiding the intellectual faculty . . . Yet although they are good and ready to help, they are nevertheless called 'clouds' because they separate man from God." The midrash decoded tells us that the influence of Aaron inspired the people to live good lives, cultivating fine ethical qualities by following the mean, and acquiring for themselves a purity of nature and temperament that they did not have before or after.[71]

The body and its perils are also represented allegorically by various animals. In conjunction with the interpretation of "Leviathan," R. Isaac interpreted the serpent of Eden as an allegorical representation of the corruptibility and destruction that necessarily result from the combination of elements in the terrestrial realm. In a less metaphysical, more ethical sense, "serpent" can stand for the destructive impulses of man's corporeal element. "The Master of the prophets began to use the word 'serpent' for that impulse of the human heart which is 'evil toward him from his youth' [Gen. 8:21], ready to lead him astray, seeking his death, if the man heeds it . . . And the other prophets and every sage among the people regarded the example of Moses, and called this a 'serpent' as he did." A statement such as "Before they moved from that place, a serpent came and bit him [the murderer whose crime had not been witnessed in accordance with proper standards of evidence] and he died" (Sanh., 37b) is not to be understood as if the animal mentioned could just as well have been any other wild creature. The fact that it was a serpent teaches that just as the man committed murder because he heeded his evil impulse, so this crime will be the cause of his death.[72] Similarly, in the midrashic assertion that one of the "clouds of glory" preceded the Israelites in the wilderness and struck down the snakes and the scorpions (Num. R., 1:2), there is an allegorical expression of the fact that the physical impulse toward evil, purified through the leadership and example of Aaron, in turn began to quell those physical faculties and drives that originally aided it in destroying the life of the soul.[73]

Still another image for the harmful physical faculties can be seen in the comment on the statement "There is a demon that flies through the air like a bird" (Num. R., 12:3):

> They called here every internal human impulse that is perverse and askew "a demon flying in the air" . . . calling it this in a figurative manner because it is a faculty of the body, unseen by the eye. The bird flies away into the distance, disappearing from sight, roaming far away from men over sea and land, so that those who see it have no idea whither it is going and ask, "Where is it?" So every physical faculty "flies" in man, for it is invisible to the eye . . . and a man does not feel that it is smiting him mortally. This is their way, to call these faculties "demon," as you will find that the Babylonians represented allegorically every physical faculty harmful to man by a flying bird, and said, "Every bird that flew over him was immediately burned" [Sukkah, 28a], teaching about the superior wisdom of Jonathan b. Uzziel . . . Not that this righteous man, the foundation of the earth, would burn every winged and feathery bird that flew in the air over his academy when the bird had not wronged him—heaven forbid!— but rather that he refined and purified every physical faculty that harmed him . . .[74]

While the allegorical interpretation of the aggadah about Jonathan b. Uzziel solves two problems in the literal meaning of that text—precisely why the birds were burned and why it is considered praiseworthy for a scholar to bring about the death of innocent creatures—the code word itself is at first somewhat surprising. For we have seen that "bird" is used as an image for the Angel, for the same reason cited here: it disappears from sight in the distance. The use of the code word for two totally different meanings warns us that no simple key can automatically be applied to all statements.

Biblical names are also used as code words for the body and its obstacles to intellectual apprehension. The point of departure is the midrash

"Moses said to the Israelites, 'Why should you be afraid of the sons of Anak?' " (*Num. R.*, 5:1):

> Here they called the old, foolish king who rules over the impulses of man from his youth "Anak," for he is awesome, haughty like cedars in his nefarious work. And they called all those evildoers who serve in the house "sons of Anak," in that they do his will, hero-ically helping the cause of evil . . .
> Similarly, you find that the destroying angel has many names ap-plied to him according to his deeds. They called him "Canaanite" because he has in his hands deceitful scales which love to defraud, acting with utmost treachery toward all who trust him, no matter who. And they called him "Zephonite" to teach that he is a faculty hidden [*tzafun*] in the midst of the body, lurking in the cellar every night to steal away the heart . . .[75]

The characteristically metaphoric language and the use of terms such as "old, foolish king" (Eccles. 4:13, understood by the rabbis as the *yetzer ha-ra*) and "destroying angel" almost obfuscate the fact that R. Isaac is still speaking about the same physical impulses that hinder the intellect.

The clearest and most compelling explanation of a Biblical code name is the last, Zephonite (Joel 2:20), already identified by the rabbis as "the impulse to evil, which remains hidden in man's heart" (*Suk.*, 52a). The hidden character of this impulse, emphasized by R. Isaac in elucidating the image of flying demon and bird, is here applied to the Biblical term. The use of "Canaanite" to express the deceptive and treacherous char-acter of the impulse to evil is based on the meaning of "merchant" for "Canaanite" in Zechariah 14:21: "And in that day there shall be no more a Canaanite in the house of the Lord of Hosts" (see Targum, Rashi, and ibn Ezra). This passage enables us to reconstruct what was undoubtedly R. Isaac's esoteric interpretation of the verse: near the end of the perfect man's life, the impulse toward evil is totally overcome, so that his body's impulses no longer oppose but serve the intellect. Finally, the term "Anak" is used because of its connotation of power and arrogance. One wonders whether this understanding of the Biblical "sons of Anak" (Num. 13:33) might imply that the conquest of the land of Israel was in-terpreted allegorically as the effort of the individual to overcome the obstacles to intellectual perfection. Such an interpretation is found not only among certain Jewish philosophers but also in the Zohar and in Christian sources.[76]

To this list of Biblical names should be added "Philistine." We are told that the story of Samson can be understood

> according to the esoteric content of the words of its narrator, who informs us that the Philistines hated him with consummate hatred,

lying in wait for him and pursuing him day after day, shooting at him in their attempt to kill him, so that his entire life was a bitter battle between these great enemies. But he prevailed valiantly, smiting every first-born in their camps, making many fall as corpses in battle. And one of the names used metaphorically for Satan by the prophets is "Philistine," according to his deeds, for just as the Philistine oppressed Israel, so Satan oppressed Samson and everyone similar to him in nature. But Samson prevailed over his enemy . . ."[77]

The term "Satan" itself is used in a philosophical sense, in accordance with the following definition: "It is known that 'Satan' is a *special faculty of man*, which accompanies him to accuse him, as the sages attested when they said, 'Satan, the angel [of death], and the impulse toward evil are all the same.' "[78] The story of Samson battling the Philistines is viewed, at least on one level, as an allegory of the man born with a powerful physical impulse opposing the potential for ethical and intellectual fulfillment who struggles against and ultimately overcomes that impulse.[79]

In addition to having a body with its physical impulses, the human being possesses a soul with component parts or faculties. In the Aristotelian tradition, these were generally understood as the nutritive, sensitive, imaginative, appetitive, and rational parts of the soul.[80] R. Isaac maintains that these are represented by the rabbis in various ways through their code language. First, there are statements relating to children. The Midrash declares that "The glory of the Holy One, blessed be He, is derived from the males, and about them David said, 'Sons are a heritage of the Lord; the fruit of the womb are a reward' [Ps. 127:3]—these are males, but if females come, they too are a reward" (*Num. R.*, 3:8). After rejecting the literal meaning, R. Isaac explains this passage on two levels. The manifest significance is that a good man who has sons similar to him —a relatively rare occurrence, we are told—is truly blessed. But the esoteric meaning is "better than this":

The Psalmist called the impulses of man "the fruit of the womb," for they are a reward to him if they are good and intrinsically honest, thus helping him. Every faculty in his body, whether good or bad, is the "fruit of his womb." But the male child is the "poor and wise lad," all lofty and rational in actuality, while the female alludes to the faculty of imagination which furnishes to the rational faculty images of the divine visions which appear to it. This faculty of imagination, and all that is similar to it among the various components of the soul,[81] he called "female," because it and the others make a composite of the impossible and the possible,[82] just like women, who compare one thing with another in their imagination, for their intellect is weak, and incapable of penetrating to the true essence of a matter.

These impulses of his are a man's "reward," for through them he will prosper, if they are prepared to help him attain perpetual life for his soul.[83]

The assertion that the "glory of the Holy One arises from the males" is decoded to mean that man achieves knowledge of God through his intellect, which is indispensible for the vision of the divine.

The term "children" is understood allegorically in statements such as "He who separates from his wife near her menstrual period will have male children" (Shev., 18b). "Those components of the soul that help the intellect attain the perfection intended of it, thereby bestowing immortality, are called 'children,' teaching that [if one does not allow himself to be drawn after his corporeal drives by engaging in sexual activity excessively] they will all be prepared to help actualize the intellect, so that when it is separated from the body, it will have glorious rest." In contrast, "He who does not separate from his wife near her menstrual period, even if he has sons like the sons of Aaron, they will die" teaches that those faculties naturally inclined toward good may be confounded by excessive preoccupation with the body, resulting in death for "all components of the soul" when the body perishes.[84]

The diverse aspects of the soul also appear in the comment on a midrash already discussed: "It was due to the merit of Aaron that I set clouds of glory about you" (Num. R., 1:2). The midrash continues, "How many clouds of glory encircled Israel in the wilderness? R. Hoshaia said, 'Four,' R. Josiah said, 'Five . . .' " According to R. Isaac, the first sage intended to teach about the four components of the human soul that help it achieve intellectual apprehension of God. "He did not include 'the impulse of the human heart,' for in his view it is all but impossible to transform its nature so that it will help in this task, even when it grows old, for it does not abate. But his colleague, having investigated the matter, adds the fifth to the other four, believing that it can also be prepared like the rest, so that even 'Satan' may come under the category of the good. Though at first a source of oppression for Israel, [Satan] can become a leader of others in subduing all its impulses."[85] It is unfortunate that the psychology underlying this passage is not made explicit. If R. Isaac is following the Aristotelian-Maimonidean model, then the four "clouds of glory" of the first sage would represent the nutritive, sensitive, imaginative, and rational faculties. The issue between the two sages is whether or not the appetitive faculty, identified with Satan and the impulse to evil, can be purified (made into "clouds of glory") so as to aid the quest for immortality.[86] A seemingly trivial dispute of the rabbis is transformed into a genuine problem of both rabbinic and philosophical ethical theory.

A similar theme emerges from R. Isaac's interpretation of the first two chapters of Job. Here he argues that "sons of God" refers to the various faculties of the human being, with Satan representing the "special faculty that accompanies man to accuse him." The author of Job does not affirm that "Satan came 'to present himself before the Lord' and to do His will like the other faculties (for the retentive, digestive, and excretory faculties, as well as all the others, do nothing in vain, but act as they are commanded)." Satan, however, does not act as God's emissary when he leads man astray, yet he does carry out God's purpose by arousing man to engage occasionally in sexual intercourse in order to perpetuate the species. He is therefore included among the "sons of God," although he does not present himself before the Almighty.[87]

This interpretation of the "sons of God" as human faculties is analogous to the code use of the phrase "ministering angels." R. Isaac often explicates messianic statements as allegories pertaining to the spiritual destiny of the individual: " 'For the day of vengeance is in My heart, and the year of My redemption is come' [Isa. 63:4]: R. Yohanan said, 'I have revealed it to My heart, but not to My limbs'; R. Simeon b. Lakish said, 'I have revealed it to My heart, but not to the ministering angels' " (Sanh., 99a). In R. Isaac's interpretation, "redemption" means the liberation from the material nature of the body, and "heart" refers to the intellect. The "redemption" granted to the "heart" but not to the limbs is the gift of perpetual life; the intellect can acquire it, but the physical impulses are destined to perish as if they had never been. R. Simeon b. Lakish says much the same thing:

> He called "ministering angels" the parts of the soul that help the intellect attain perfection, which it cannot attain without the beneficial assistance of these helpers, such as the imaginative faculty, which helps the rational faculty by forming images for its rational apprehensions. He taught that this and the other parts of the soul and the impulses in general will be destroyed with the death of the man who bears them, each one decomposing separately, not one escaping, except for the intellect, which remains after death as a blessing.[88]

The doctrines of medieval psychology are found in the most unexpected places.[89]

The body and its impulses, together with all the components of the soul save one, are destined to oblivion; the intellect alone can achieve immortality. Perpetual life is attained through the actualization of those perfections potential in man at birth. These are represented by precious stones, as in the statement "Had not the serpent been cursed, every Israelite would have had two valuable serpents, sending one to the north and one to the south to bring him costly gems, precious stones, and pearls" (Sanh., 59b). The "serpents" are the human impulses toward good and toward evil; as we have noted, even the latter can help in achieving the ultimate goal. "The sages represented allegorically the perfections needed by the human being as stones of onyx, beryl, and jasper, figuratively speaking, for just as these precious stones are the imaginary good for man, desired because his human frailty impels him to covet them, so human perfection is a precious stone for his soul, stones to be set, which perfect it so that after the death of the corporeal element it may come to rest in honor, glory and splendor."[90]

Perfections of the soul are divided into two categories—ethical and intellectual. The process by which ethical perfection is achieved is expressed in the word "exile," according to the interpretation of the following aggadah: "R. Judah said, 'Exile atones for half of men's sins' . . . R. Yohanan said, 'Exile atones for everything' " (Sanh., 37b). R. Isaac explains that these sages, speaking cryptically, are actually disputing an issue of ethical theory. The term "sins" refers to the natural, innate qualities that lead to sin. "Exile" (galut) means a compulsory change from one place to another; therefore, it is used here to represent the transformation that results from compelling one's nature through habit to make itself permanently better, "for there is no galut more difficult than this: to exile one's body from one quality to another by changing its taste." The sages disagree as to whether a total transformation is possible. R. Judah says that only partial change can occur; R. Yohanan says that one's nature can be constrained so that there will no longer be any proclivity toward sin.[91] By reading "sin" as metonymy, the effect substituted for the cause, and by stretching (or contorting) the maning of "exile" to apply to the internal life, R. Isaac shifts the statement from the realm of religious doctrine to the realm of ethical theory. The deeper significance of the debate pertains not to atonement for sins already committed but to the inner struggle to overcome the tendency toward sin.

A rather elliptical reference to ethical perfection comes in a discussion of the period of life between ages twenty and forty, by the end of which time this perfection should have been achieved: "The sages attested that R. Akiba and many similar men who followed him remained until they were forty years old as shepherds, metaphorically speaking, asserting figuratively that [such individuals] achieved great perfection in the human ethical qualities."[92] There is no further explanation of the image, but it is not difficult to reconstruct the thought behind it. As a good shepherd is able to control his flock, which docilely follows his lead, so one who has reached ethical perfection can control the impulses that might lead to aberrations in his personality or conduct. The application to Akiba's life is suggestive. Does R. Isaac believe that Akiba was actually a shepherd, or does he imply that the assertion is to be understood solely on the allegorical level? And might this be applied also to figures of the Bible, including the statement that "Moses kept the flock of Jethro" before the vision of the bush?

"Bread" is the most common image for ethical perfection. The verse from Proverbs (12:11, 28:19), "He that tills his ground shall have plenty of bread," is interpreted to mean that a man must humble himself by preparing and cultivating his corporeal component so that he may perfect his ethical qualities.[93] The aptness of this image is explained in another context, which associates ethical perfection with the commandments that regulate interpersonal behavior: "The practical commandments, which provide for just order in the relationships between human beings, are expressed metaphorically as 'bread' in many places of the prophetic writings, in order to show that just as bread 'satisfies man's heart' when he is hungry, so proper ethical qualities satisfy the soul, preparing it by giving it a new nature that enables it to achieve what it seeks. Without these qualities, this is impossible."[94] The cultivation of good ethical attributes is indispensable for the ultimate perfection of the soul. But it is just the first stage of the process, not an end in itself, as can be seen in the interpretation of the Biblical verse, "Man does not live by bread alone" (Deut. 8:3):

> This teaches that man cannot attain perpetual life for his soul through the commandments which give him a just [social] order, but that he must fulfill the rational commandments, which bestow upon him a mind capable of comprehending truth. These are the principal commandments, and the others are secondary to them. Therefore, they [the rational commandments] are attributed to God, for they are "that which proceeds from His mouth." He desires that through them, man will bring perpetual life to his soul.[95]

The bread of ethical perfection, necessary for immortality, is not sufficient, for it alone cannot bestow eternal life.

On the other hand, ethical perfection is not to be viewed merely as a subsidiary acquisition that may be abandoned once the higher, intellectual perfection is attained. An important warning is sounded in the comment on the dictum of R. Eliezer: "He who leaves no bread on the table will never see a sign of blessing, as it is written [Job 20:21], 'There was nothing left over of his food, therefore he shall not hope for His goodness' " (Sanh., 92a).

> We have already stated in many places that the sages used "crumb" and "bread" as images for ethical qualities of man. Here they are teaching that whoever has perfected himself by acquiring the purest and most valuable qualities, and then afterward sets about perfecting his soul, must not abandon these important qualities, even if he has attained the soul's ultimate quest. He must not say, "I'll be all right, though I follow my inner impulse by giving my body every

physical pleasure. Now that I have attained the desired goal, what good to me are these ethical qualities which deny the body all that is superfluous?" Heaven forbid that he say this! For these qualities help man prepare his mind for that wisdom which brings eternal life to its possessor. This wisdom remains in him because of the ethical qualities; it cannot endure without them . . . Thus they taught, saying, "Therefore he shall not hope for His goodness," meaning that if he does not retain a piece of "bread" in his hand, he should not expect God's goodness for his soul, the vision of God's sweetness.[96]

In the hands of R. Isaac, R. Eliezer's remark becomes a powerful indictment that could be applied to various elite groups who felt that their intellectual enlightenment or their lofty spiritual status removed them from the constraints of conventional moral standards. R. Isaac insists that the bread of ethical achievement must not be allowed to disappear even after the individual has proceeded to higher quests.[97]

Ultimate intellectual perfection is achieved through the acquisition of knowledge culminating in the fullest possible apprehension of God. One set of code words dealing with this subject is drawn from the rhetoric of traditional Jewish eschatology: the "Messiah" represents the human intellect; the "days of the Messiah" refers to that period of a man's life in which the physical faculties are weakened and the intellect can reign supreme; "redemption" signifies the release of the intellect from the body.[98] A second allegorical representation of intellectual speculation leading to knowledge of God is water, flowing from the earth or falling from the heavens. The "well through the merit of Miriam" (*Num. R.*, 1:2) has this esoteric meaning: "Throughout the nation, it is widely known from the Torah that every priest and prophet spoke allegorically about the knowledge of God, for those who ponder His name, as digging a well. When one has dug a well, water flows from the bucket twice or three times a day, and the water surges up when he draws from it, never failing him in summer or in winter; he can always drink it. So it is with the supreme knowledge for all who hold fast to it . . ." The prophetess Miriam, learned in the knowledge of God, provided the "water" of knowledge to all—men, women and children alike.[99] The assertion that the "well traveled before the people in all their journeys," understood in the esoteric manner, teaches "that each person increased his great knowledge of God while traveling on his journey from childhood to youth, until in old age, God would appear to the pure of heart."[100] Again, the implications of this allegory for the interpretation of the Torah, especially the stories of the Patriarchs, are extremely suggestive.

The recondite significance of flowing water explains Jacob's blessing of Pharaoh: that "The Nile should rise *le-raglo*" [literally "to his foot"] (*Num. R.*, 12:2). The prophets represented metaphysics (*hokhmat ha-Elohim*) by flowing water; here the example given is the verse "Unto him that is thirsty, bring water!" (Isa. 21:14), which the sages themselves had interpreted allegorically as referring to knowledge of Torah (*Ta'anit*, 7a). This could not mean that people were literally thirsty for water, for they could walk over to a brook and drink without any payment. It must therefore mean that they were ignorant of metaphysical knowledge. The midrash teaches that Jacob proved to Pharaoh the existence of God with "rational proofs." His blessing, then, is that Jacob led Pharaoh little by little away from his false beliefs and caused the true knowledge of God to "rise" in him. The word "le-raglo" is understood not as "to the foot of Pharaoh" but rather "because of Jacob," for *regel* can have the meaning of "cause," as in Genesis 30:30.[101]

This meaning is also applied to the verse "And a river went out from Eden to water the garden" (Gen. 2:10). Eden is the realm of God and His incorporeal angels, where the souls of the righteous can exist after they have been separated from matter; the garden is a place where man can actualize his intellect while in the body; the river is the intellectual speculation that comes to man by means of the Angel, enabling him to gain knowledge of the upper realm.[102] This interpretation of Genesis 2:10 conflicts with the explanation of the river as the primal matter differentiated into four elements. It is the only significant instance of a glaring inconsistency in the allegorical interpretation of an important Biblical verse. Perhaps R. Isaac meant to indicate that the sages themselves had different views about the cryptic meaning of this passage.[103]

Water descending from heaven may be just as apt an image for the intellectual apprehension of God, although we are told that it is used by only "some of the prophets."[104] Explaining the assertion that the Torah was given in water (*Num. R.*, 1:7), R. Isaac mentions the verse "The heavens dropped water" (Jud. 5:4), generally understood as applying to the revelation at Sinai (see *Guide*, III, 9). This meteorological detail indicates that "God enlightened the eyes of their intellect when He sent down bounteous 'rain' to them like dew from on high which pours its moisture upon their heads." It is especially appropriate as an allegorical representation in that it teaches all who would delve into metaphysics that they must do so gradually, proceeding step by step from the proper axioms. For just as a gentle rain waters the earth and causes seed to sprout while a torrential downpour washes away both soil and seed, so one who proceeds in his quest slowly and gradually will reach his goal in the end while one who wants to know the ultimate without sufficient preparation will arrive at false conclusions and "die of thirst, but not thirst for the water of a brook."[105] As in so many other places, what begins as interpretation ends as a homiletical lesson.

The need for deliberate progress in metaphysical speculation is emphasized in relation to another midrash, "How do we know that the blessings emanate from Zion? Because it says, 'Like the dew of Hermon, that comes down upon the mountains of Zion, for there the Lord commanded the blessing, life forever' [Ps. 133:3], and it says, 'The Lord bless you out of Zion' [Ps. 134:3]" (*Num. R.*, 8:9). Again we are told that the Psalmist represented the apprehension of God by dew, but here a further reason is given: the dew, which descends at night, signifies the knowledge that the intellect can acquire while in the darkness of the body. The words "mountains of Zion" introduce an additional aspect of the code. Mountains, because of their height, are used as still another image for the realms of the spheres and of the incorporeal angels, which confirm the true existence of God, their First Cause. And "Zion" is explained by the lexical meaning of its root: "The prophets used this name metaphorically in an esoteric manner for the intellectual signification and speculation [*ha-tziyyun ve-ha-iyyun*] that is in man." The Psalmist thus teaches that the intellectual investigation of the upper realms of being (*harerei tzion*) will result in knowledge of God (dew), which will bring about true blessing for the soul.[106]

In the explanation of "Zion," etymology is exploited for the purpose of allegorical interpretation. One final image for the activity of the intellect leading to knowledge of God is also derived by this process. At the dedication of the tabernacle, each prince of the Israelites brought an ox as an offering (Num. 7:2). The significance of this ox is

> to allude to the intellectual speculation necessary for each one—that he must ponder the work of the tabernacle . . . until God appears to him from above as a result of this work. In order to allude to this speculation, the animal chosen to bear the tabernacle was not the cow but rather the firstling ox, majestic. Thus you find that the Babylonians used the ox [*shor*] as a metaphor for precise intellectual speculation, as if it were pointed with a *shuruk* [*shur*], which applies to gazing and seeing something. They said, *shor she-hikriv adam ha-rishon keren ahat be-mitzho*. This describes the power of intellectual speculation about God possessed by Adam when he was created, for he was then of an extremely elevated nature, fully intellectual like a divine being. And this speculation brought him near to God, a closeness showing his merit. The words *she-hikriv Adam* have as their subject the shor mentioned earlier: speculation brought him near to God, knowing Him and cleaving to Him. The reason why he could be brought so near to God is the horn issuing forth from his forehead, for from the forehead emerge memories in man. And because of the clarity and purity of the corporeal element in the first man, his intellect was more purified, and the light of the King's face shone resplendent upon him . . .
>
> The "horn" is used to establish the clarity and purity of the corporeal element in Adam, for thus it is applied in various places. It

says that the skin of Moses' face sent forth rays [*karan*] [Exod.
34:29], and the Babylonians said in the same manner, " 'What is
your name?' 'Karna.' 'May it be His will that a horn [*karna*] will
sprout in your eye' " [*Shab.*, 108a]. His colleague did not curse him
with a vain curse—heaven forbid! Rather, he blessed him with the
good wish that his eyes would be illumined to understand valuable
things, and the law would not be concealed from him.

This is as we explained in the *Hibbur ha-Talmud Bavli*, Tractate
Hullin, chapter *Elu Terefot*, about the *shor she-hikriv adam ha-
rishon*—how it was different from other oxen, having a horn on its
forehead which they did not, and why its horns preceded its hooves.
We explained the cryptic meaning of these assertions, for it was not
a young bull which walks on four legs. No one has revealed this hidden meaning before me, or enabled men to discover the true interpretation, which has been unknown until now.

Connected with this is the fact that the princes came with one ox
each, with no one else sharing in the ox, to teach the prince that he
stands alone in the house, speculating with his intellect upon the
"chariot" in isolation, in order to apprehend the Rider from His
chariot. Each man stands alone; no one else can help him. This is
what the Babylonians taught when they said, "Speculation about the
chariot [is not taught] to an individual" as we have explained in the
Hibbur ha-Talmud Bavli, Tractate *Hagigah*, chapter *Ein Dorshin*.[107]

Here is a web of exegesis in which the various strands joining Biblical
verses and Talmudic aggadot entwine to form a dense texture of meanings. The interpretation of Numbers 7:3 explains why the ox was chosen
and why each prince had to offer an ox of his own. The identification of
"shor" ("ox") with "shur" ("see," extended to mean intellectual apprehension)[108] forms the bridge connecting this verse with doctrines about
the purpose of the sanctuary—to inspire rational investigation of the
realm of being leading to knowledge of God—and about the nature of
such speculation, in which each individual must engage personally, not
participate vicariously. This leads to a pure allegorical interpretation of
the aggadah about Adam. Not only are code meanings substituted for the
key words, but the syntax of the entire statement is transformed: it is not
the "ox that Adam sacrificed," but the "speculation that brought Adam
close [to God]," and the "horn" is not on the forehead of the ox but on
that of Adam. Now the commentator must deal with the meaning of
"horn," which brings him, by way of the verse describing Moses' descent
from Sinai, to a radical reinterpretation of Rav's remark to Karna. In
this, as in the previous passage from the Talmud, the plain meaning is
repudiated. While the princes actually brought an ox to the tabernacle,
no ox was sacrificed by Adam; and Rav's remark was not a curse to be
understood esoterically as a blessing but simply an expression of a pious

hope for the colleague who had tested him. Finally, the reader is brought back to the point of departure, the verse from Numbers, and left with still another Talmudic statement (*Hag.*, 11b) about which he is invited to read further in the commentary on *Hagigah*. Once the code is established —in this case the esoteric meanings of "ox" and "horn"—it can lead through Bible, Talmud, and Midrash with unexpected results.

The Method and its Significance

Enough examples have been given for a full picture of how the code works. What is needed now is some general evaluation of the entire enterprise, assessing its achievement and implications. The system of code words, some of them original, most of them not, enables R. Isaac to read the statements of the sages as expressing a totally different set of doctrines. What can be said about the relationship between the newer, cryptic meaning and the older manifest one? One conclusion is that the aggadah in its esoteric reading has been drastically reduced in scope. A multiplicity of code words have the same referent. The result is that after decoding hundreds of comments about dozens of different subjects, we are left with a relatively few doctrines of religious philosophy bearing on the structure of the universe, the nature of the human being, and the quest to surmount the various obstacles to intellectual apprehension and the achievement of immortal life. Hundreds of statements are distilled into a message that could be formulated in a single paragraph, possibly even in one long and involuted sentence. The rich diversity of the aggadah is sacrificed to the constant repetition of several crucial points. These doctrines, which constitute the hidden message of the sages, are by no means technical in nature. Once expounded, they require no special preparation or rigorous philosophical training to understand.[109]

The second result of R. Isaac's decoding of the aggadah is the removal of much of its distinctively Jewish content. It is not merely that the hidden message here ignores the themes of Jewish history and destiny.[110] The Jewish content already present in the plain meaning of the aggadah disappears at the deeper level. There is an unmistakable pattern of translating words with specifically Jewish significance or resonance into concepts of universal import. For example, "exile" comes to signify the improvement of the ethical qualities, "Messiah" means the intellect, "redemption" the liberation of the intellect from the body, "Zion" intellectual speculation, "Jerusalem" the entire realm of being,[111] "Leviathan" the combination of elements into corruptible composites, and the names of various angels become the different realms of beings. Statements about the history and destiny of the Jewish people are regularly interpreted to apply to the life cycle of the individual, Jew or non-Jew. Even the words "Torah" and "Talmud" are usually understood as referring to metaphysical knowledge of the divine realm, and "Israel" becomes the philosophically educated elite.[112]

This effect of the decoding can be viewed from different perspectives. On the one hand, it may be described as a universalization of the aggadah. In R. Isaac's reading, the profound and crucially important words of the sages teach a doctrine that applies not to a specific people as bearers of a distinctive religion but to a particular class among all peoples: the philosophers, or those who would embark on the long and arduous journey toward philosophical enlightenment. This is not to say that R. Isaac fails to recognize any validity in Jewish distinctiveness; indeed, his works contain the elements of a confident polemic, both latent and open, against "the religions that pretend to be like us." What it does mean is that R. Isaac, probing the depths of the rabbinic utterances, finds material addressing the general human condition, not just the specific historical situation of the Jews.

Of course, this general philosophical doctrine is expressed not in a topically organized treatise but in massive commentaries on the rabbinic literature. If allegorization produces a de-Judaicizing of the sages' message, it also produces an importation of universal concepts and values into the Jewish lore, or what might be called a Judaicizing of the philosophical world view. The very fact that he takes the aggadah so seriously places R. Isaac in the middle ground, rather like the Jewish poets in Muslim Spain, whose insistence on the Hebrew language as the medium for their expression aroused the antagonism of both traditionalists, who objected to the Arabic content and form of the new poetry, and assimilationists, who would have preferred Hebraic culture to be abandoned altogether. To those whose outlook was circumscribed by the subjects discussed in the manifest content of the aggadot, R. Isaac insisted that the rabbis pointed to a more universal and ultimately more important agenda. To those who felt that the imperatives of philosophical enlightenment had rendered the aggadic lore antiquated and irrelevant, R. Isaac attempted to demonstrate that the entire program for the pursuit of perfection had already been mapped out by the sages.

IV

FROM EXEGESIS
TO INNOVATION

SYSTEMATIC RIGOR AND PROFUNDITY are not hallmarks of R. Isaac's literary oeuvre. Yet the lack of these qualities does not imply the absence of unusual or idiosyncratic teachings. In this chapter, we move from exegesis to innovation, concentrating on R. Isaac's own thought largely divorced from its exegetical context. While it is somewhat artificial to separate method from content in the work of a commentator, a rounded intellectual portrait requires consideration of both. The doctrines to be discussed reveal much of what is most novel and unusual about R. Isaac, as they lead into the realm of medieval philosophy and Jewish religious thought and even to the frontiers of abnormal psychology.

The Supreme Incorporeal Angel

R. Isaac refers to a supreme incorporeal Angel in dozens of comments from both CAT and CMR. This doctrine is important enough in his outlook to merit a systematic analysis against the background of medieval Jewish thought. The Angel's role in the creation of the cosmos is introduced in the commentary on *Avot:*

> It is known to the cognoscenti, those scientists expert in the highest discipline of metaphysics, that the entire cosmos is like one human being, part encompassing part, having been emanated one from the other. The realm of the Angel was emanated first at the beginning of Creation from the effluence of divine goodness. God brought it into being first and is its first cause. Then the Sphere was emanated from the effluence of the incorporeal Angel, to which it is attracted by desire. It moves in unabated circular motion in order to be as much like the Angel as possible. The four elements were caused by the Sphere, which works upon them, so that they follow its direction. Therefore, the incorporeal Angel is the cause of the entire realm of being, as an intermediary for its own First Cause.[1]

The analogy between the universe and the human being which introduces
this passage is taken directly from Maimonides' *Guide* (I, 72), but the rest
of the passage is not Maimonidean.[2] This is a doctrine of emanation,
beginning with God and ending with the elements of the sublunar realm.
While expressed here in such a general, schematic way that it is hardly
significant as a theory of cosmogony,[3] it establishes the axiom that the
first being to be emanated, and the only one emanated directly from
God, is the supreme incorporeal Angel. It is therefore an immediate effect
of the First Cause, but it becomes in turn the cause not only of the terrestrial realm but of the entire universe outside God.

Other passages of the commentaries reiterate these themes, adding
further details of the doctrine. From the perspective of the First Cause,
the order is what has been stated: Angel, Sphere, elements and compounds. But from the perspective of the human mind, which begins with
the world around it and endeavors to ascend to more spiritual heights,
the order is reversed. The changes that occur in the terrestrial realm are
the result of the motion of the Sphere.[4] If the Sphere were to stop mov-
ing, the entire sublunar realm would be destroyed.[5] But the Sphere itself
moves perpetually without rest because of its desire for the Angel, from
whose effluence it emerged.[6] Thus the elements and their compounds
point to the Sphere, and the Sphere directs the mind to the incorporeal
Angel. The Angel in turn is proof of the existence of God—its cause and
the First Cause of all being.[7]

There are other incorporeal angels or intellects as well as this special
Angel. In accordance with accepted theory, we are told that every sphere
must have its own separate intellect to cause its circular motion.[8] In some
places, R. Isaac seems to use the phrase "Angel detached from matter" to
refer to the entire realm of incorporeal beings, as in the assertion that
only the Angel, God, and the purified human soul after death are totally
spiritual in nature.[9] But elsewhere he indicates a definite hierarchy, in
which the "Angel detached from matter" is superior to all other incorporeal intelligences except for God. The rabbinic statement that God
showed Moses "red fire, green fire, black fire, white fire" (*Num. R.*, 12:8)
is interpreted to mean that Moses was enabled to envision first the "supreme Angel in rank and status," represented by red, because this is the
color most pleasing to the human eye, and then "all the other angels . . .
green or black or white, to show him that they are all caused by the red
one, that all that have white or black or green in them are the effects of
the one that emerged first."[10] In the allegorical interpretation of Jacob's
ladder, the second step represents the heavenly bodies, the third step, the
"angels of God," and the fourth step, the special Angel, which is "more
precious in God's sight than any other being, both in rank and in status."[11] Apparently, this Angel is part of a category of separate intelli-

gences and at the same time above the rest, God's "anointed, the Angel who sits first in the kingdom."[12]

More important to R. Isaac than the cosmological and metaphysical aspects of the Angel is its special relationship with the human soul. Almost all commentators have assumed that the "precious instrument" of R. Akiba's statement in *Avot*, III, "Beloved is Israel in that there was given to them a precious instrument by means of which the world was created," refers to the Torah, into which God looked before creating the world.[13] R. Isaac, with no explanations or apologies, boldly asserts that the "precious instrument" is the "rational soul" (*nafsho ha-maskelet*) of the human being. He must therefore demonstrate how it can be maintained that the world was created by means of the human soul.

There follows the passage quoted above about the Angel as the "cause of the entire realm of being." And then: "It is known that the form that cleaves to matter [the soul] is emanated from the incorporeal Angel, and it will return to it after [separating from] matter, if man has perfected it. [The soul] will then become part of the Angel . . . Thus it is a 'precious instrument from which the world was created,' for it returns to the level of the Angel after [separating from] matter, and from it is created the totality of existence; it is like one of the ministering angels, having become again eternal."[14] In other words, the Angel is both the remote cause of all being outside of God and itself and the immediate source of the rational soul. Since the soul, if perfected through the actualization of its intellectual potential while in the body, will again become part of the Angel, it can be described as the instrument through which the world was created.

A comparison of various passages expressing this same idea shows that R. Isaac was not overly concerned with terminological consistency. Here he used the words "rational soul" and "form that cleaves to matter." In a parallel passage he refers simply to the soul (*nefesh*) "which is emanated from the incorporeal Angel, to which it returns after [separation from] matter if the man has perfected it during his life."[15] In a third place, virtually the same sentence occurs, but this time with the word "intellect" (*sekhel*) in place of "soul."[16] Finally, in CMR we are told that man alone of all the creatures on earth has need for the Angel, "for from it is emanated his spirit and breath [*ruho ve-nishmato*] which cleaves to his material component and will return to it when it has separated from this matter."[17] The apparent interchangeability of "nefesh," "sekhel," "ruah," and "neshamah" reveals a realm of discourse quite different from that of more rigorous philosophy or Kabbalah.[18] For R. Isaac, only the basic idea is crucial: that the eternal aspect of the human soul, associated with intellect, has its origin and its end in the supreme incorporeal Angel.

This does not exhaust the relationship between the Angel and the human being. Paradoxically, this highest and closest to God of all the angels is the only one that appears to man.[19] Here we find R. Isaac's solution to the problem of divine manifestation, which is a major crux in the interpretation of Bible and aggadah. God does not appear directly to a prophet but only through an "emissary," the Angel, which is at the center of all prophetic visions.[20] And it is this Angel that commands the prophet, at God's instigation, to prophesy; were it not for the Angel, prophecy would be impossible.[21] The Biblical verses that speak of prophetic visions, whether mentioning an angel or alluding to God Himself, refer to the supreme incorporeal Angel; Moses' vision of the burning bush, his instructions to ascend Mt. Sinai in Exodus 24:1 and 24:12, and his request to see God's glory, Elijah's encounter with the flaming chariot and horses, and Isaiah's vision of the throne all exemplify this generalization.[22]

Prophets are not the only beneficiaries of the Angel's communication, as can be seen from this passage:

The Angel comes to the God-fearing ones, His servants the prophets. And to those wise in heart, even if they have not reached the level of prophecy, it comes to perfect their form [the soul] so that it will remain after them perpetually, not being annihilated with the destruction of the body. From the Angel are the sources of life for every rational creature who seeks that which is truly valuable, for through it one achieves rational apprehensions of God and His holy angels who stand around Him. This Angel is the source of instruction for all who seek the Lord. To the most perfect of men comes prophecy, which is impossible without the Angel, appointed by God over the human species to perfect it, by commanding at God's behest how to act toward one's neighbor with proper personal qualities, and how to believe that which is true and bestows true life. The sages spoke about this Angel, teaching that it is in God's place over the human species, for God placed the perfect in the Angel's custody, so that they would apprehend truths about Him by means of the Angel, which would show them the path in which to walk. It is set in God's place over all men.[23]

Several important themes appear here in phrases that recur often in the commentaries. The starting point is the prophet of Biblical times, but this is only an excuse to turn to a subject more important to the author: the philosopher of his own age. The Angel is indispensible in the pursuit of perfection, for it instructs men in the proper behavior toward other human beings—leading to ethical perfection—and in correct beliefs about God—leading to intellectual perfection. Specifically, it is through this Angel that man "achieves rational apprehensions of God" (*mi-mennu yasig hasagotav ha-sikhliyot mi-mennu yitbarakh*), and it is these appre-

hensions that actualize the intellect. Especially striking is the assertion
that God has given the Angel custody (*hifkid be-yado*) over those human
beings who seek perfection of soul, so that it stands in place of God for
the human species.[24]

The Angel's effect on human beings in their pursuit of perfection is reiterated on many occasions in slightly different formulations. The Angel
appears to the soul to actualize and perfect it, examining and purifying
the human heart of all false beliefs; it appears to the man who strives to
purify his intellect, sent on a mission by God to show him the right way;
it appears to man in order to perfect him and direct him in the conduct
that leads to the perpetuation of the soul.[25] In these passages, R. Isaac is
speaking not of actual prophetic visions but of metaphorical appearances
to the inquiring mind of the philosopher.

This is linked with yet another theme relating to the Angel's function:
its role in the giving of the Torah. Here some care must be exercised in
the treatment of the Hebrew word "torah." There are places where the
word is not intended to refer to the document containing the revelation
of Sinai but is used more generally in the sense of "divine instruction"; an
example is the long passage cited immediately above, where the phrase
mi-mennu tetze torah is based on a Biblical phrase (Isaiah 2:3) in which
the noun has this meaning.[26] This would then be merely a different expression of the role already discussed: the Angel as instrument of moral
and intellectual enlightenment in the individual. Where we find the assertion "through it [the Angel] the torah was given to human beings,"[27] the
same ambiguity exists, as it does in the proclamation that torah is impossible without this special Angel, so that in its absence, man would have
no torah.[28] Here too, the best translation is probably "instruction,"
meaning that the Angel is necessary for the attainment of human knowledge.

But there are other passages in which this function of the Angel is set in
the historical context of the Sinaitic revelation. Discussing Exodus 15:26,
R. Isaac states that after the Exodus, the Israelites were sick with false
beliefs, which they had acquired in Egypt. Having compassion for Israel,
God sent His Angel to them, saying, "Go, descend, give them the true
Teaching [*torat emet*], to bring [eternal] life to the spirit of terrestrial
creatures." The Angel did this, and the eyes of the intellect were opened,
so that people no longer believed impossible things. Thus, "I am the Lord
who heals you" means "If the people accept and fulfil the Torah, they
will be saved through it from all diseases of the soul."[29] This account of
the Angel's activity is obviously the author's interpretation of the revelation at Sinai. In a different passage, discussing the verses in which Moses
is instructed to ascend Mt. Sinai and receive the tablets, we are again
introduced to the Angel and told that "through it was given the Torah

and the commandments to mankind."[30] Or again, we have the Angel, "through whom was given law [dat] and the tablets of testimony, testimony to Israel that God is among His people, and gave them true Teaching through the Angel."[31] In these passages, the Angel is depicted not only as the promoter of all human intellectual activity but as the intermediary agent of the unique revelation at Sinai.

We should also recall that the Angel is identified with the names Metatron and Michael (see chapter III). It is symbolized for the people of Israel by the cherubim in the sanctuary. In this regard, R. Isaac fails to be absolutely consistent. Sometimes one cherub is said to represent the Angel; sometimes both cherubim are given this significance; sometimes the cherubim are explained as teaching about the entire realm of incorporeal angels.[32] In one passage, it is not the cherubim but the ark cover (kaporet) that represents the Angel, while the cherubim are said to symbolize the concepts of cause and effect, from which the existence of God is known.[33] The assumption underlying all these interpretations is that the Israelites were required to learn of the existence and nature of the supreme incorporeal Angel, and that the means of their instruction was the sanctuary.

This was intended to keep the people from falling into two heretical errors of belief. The first is the categorical denial of the Angel's existence. Such denial can be expressed as a thoroughgoing atheism, proclaiming that there is nothing above the Sphere, no God and no incorporeal Angel, and that the affairs of the world are determined entirely by the stars.[34] Or it may merely deny the existence of the Angel while allowing God to exist in exalted remoteness. This latter theory implies that "there is no Torah from heaven" and that God leaves human beings to their own destiny on earth, there being no divine providence below the moon.[35] But if the first heresy is to negate the activity of the Angel in the sublunar realm, the second is to exaggerate it and to assign to the Angel excessive powers. This is the belief in two authorities attributed by R. Isaac to Nadab and Abihu: "Each authority rules over its own portion, with no overlap between the two realms." According to this view, God is concerned solely with the more exalted beings and abandons mankind to the power of the Angel.[36] The ultimate conclusion of this belief is that the Angel, rather than God, should be the object of our worship. In order to repudiate this heresy, R. Isaac insists that the glory of God must not be attributed to any created being, for the Angel has no independent power, and all its authority is a delegation from the Almighty.[37] To assert that God has placed man in the custody of the Angel (hifkid) is accurate, to assert that God has abandoned man to the power of the Angel (azav) is blasphemy.

The most plausible interpretation of R. Isaac's doctrine is that the supreme incorporeal Angel, to which he finds allusions throughout the Bible and aggadah, corresponds to that which is called by other philosophers the "active intellect," a term that never appears in the extant commentaries of R. Isaac. But to draw this analogy is by no means a simple matter. The active intellect represented here is not to be found as such in any recognizable philosophical system; it combines an assortment of functions attributed to the active intellect in different and mutually incompatible systems. Therefore, each aspect of the Angel's activity will have to be reviewed separately in order to determine the background from which it is derived.

The Angel is the first being emanated from God, the cause of the universe, and the highest of all incorporeal beings other than the Deity Himself. This is in obvious and dramatic conflict with the usual view of the active intellect in Muslim and Jewish philosophy. Virtually all medieval philosophers agreed that the active intellect was the lowest of the incorporeal intelligences and the last to come into being. To cite just a few representative statements, the philosopher in the *Kuzari* speaks of "the active intellect, which is that angel whose degree is below the angel connected with the sphere of the moon" (I, 1), and he says that "the lowest degree, nearest to us, is the active intellect, of which [the philosophers] taught that it guided the terrestrial realm" (V, 21).[38] And in the *Guide for the Perplexed*, Maimonides writes that "nine intelligences correspond to the nine spheres; the tenth intelligence is the active intellect, the last in the series of purely spiritual beings" (II, 4). This view is shared by other thinkers such as ibn Daud, Gersonides, and Albo, to name just a few.[39]

If we are to find this function of R. Isaac's Angel associated with the active intellect, it must be in a different philosophical tradition, one with a strong neo-Platonic orientation. For example, *Torot ha-Nefesh* of the "Pseudo-Bahya" states that "the first of those that are brought into being, the simplest, most exalted, and closest in relationship to the Creator, is what is called in Hebrew *shekhinah* . . . and the Torah and prophets called it 'Name' . . . and the Greeks call it 'active intellect.' "[40] Similarly, in *Keter Shem Tov*, a work by the thirteenth-century Kabbalist Abraham Axelrod of Cologne that attempts to integrate philosophical and mystical material, the active intellect is described as "the first of the creations of God, a power emanated from the simple, pure will as something eternal, which does not increase or diminish but which brings all beings from potentiality to actuality."[41] In the passage cited at the beginning of this section, R. Isaac draws from the neo-Platonic world view the exalted cosmological status of the Angel as first emanation and cause of all being outside God and then fuses it with the classic Aristotelian notion that the circular motion of the sphere is not a natural property but is caused by its desire for the incorporeal intelligence.[42]

A similar eclecticism can be seen in the passages describing the Angel's relationship with the soul. The characterization of the soul as the "form which cleaves to matter" is derived from the Aristotelian definition.[43] But the idea that the soul is emanated from the highest being outside of God implies that it is an incorporeal substance independent of the body, a doctrine far more compatible with neo-Platonic teachings.[44] The doctrine that the soul, if perfected, becomes part of the active intellect after separating from the body is ambiguous enough to fit into either system. The neo-Platonists speak of the pure spiritual substance, a stranger in the body, returning to its original source.[45] The neo-Platonic Aristotelians speak of the actualized intellect cleaving to the active intellect, which is the means through which it has attained knowledge and thereby acquired immortality.[46] The problem of whether the soul retains its individual identity after uniting with the active intellect is a serious one for both traditions;[47] R. Isaac, who asserts merely that it returns to the Angel and becomes part of it, is noncommittal here.

The role of the Angel in prophecy reflects the active intellect as an intermediate cause between God and prophet. According to the philosopher in the *Kuzari*, when the goal of full knowledge and purity of heart has been achieved, the active intellect "may cause you to prophesy, and inform you about future matters through true dreams and reliable visions" (I, 1; cf. I, 87). And Maimonides defines prophecy as "an emanation sent forth by God through the medium of the active intellect, in the first instance to man's rational faculty and then to his imaginative faculty" (*Guide*, II, 36). The centrality of the Angel to the prophetic enterprise was clearly drawn from a well-established tradition in the philosophical interpretation of Scripture concerning the active intellect.

However, it is one thing to assert, in accordance with standard Maimonidean teaching, that the active intellect works on the rational and imaginative faculties to produce figurative representations of abstract truths and quite another to assert, as does R. Isaac, that the Angel itself is what appears to the prophet in his vision or dream. It would be hard to conceive of Maimonides or any other philosopher arguing that the active intellect actually appears to the prophet, even if the appearance occurs entirely in the prophet's mind. Yet in one place, R. Isaac does reveal a Maimonidean source. He speaks of the "incorporeal Angel, which is called in their language (may they be blessed) *ishim*, because it appears to man and comes to him to perfect him."[48] This characterization is based on a well-known crux in *Hilkhot Yesodei ha-Torah*, 2:7, in which Maimonides states that the tenth and lowest level of the incorporeal angels or separate forms is "the level of form called 'ishim,' for they are the angels who speak with the prophets and appear to them in prophetic visions." The term "active intellect" is not used in this context, but the description as tenth in descending rank of angels leaves little doubt that this is the term Maimonides would have used in a more purely philosophical work.[49] The identification of the active intellect with ishim and ishim with that which appears in the prophetic vision forms the background for R. Isaac's characterization of the Angel as appearing to the prophet.[50] What is impossible to parallel in any philosophical source I know of is R. Isaac's insistence that the highest of all the separate intelligences is the only one that appears to man.

The description of the Angel's relationship with men below the level of prophecy is fully consonant with the usual understanding of the active intellect's role. We have seen that the Angel "appears" to men, in a metaphorical sense, to help them perfect their souls by showing them the right way to act toward others and enabling them to acquire rational apprehensions of God. One of the primary functions of the active intellect according to the neo-Platonic Aristotelians is to effect the transition from potentiality to actuality of thought in all human beings, "elevating the rational power level by level from ignorance to knowledge."[51] The assertion that the Angel teaches man not only true beliefs but also how to act properly with his neighbors is somewhat more problematic, for this subject is not ordinarily considered to be within the scope of the active intellect. It may reflect the Maimonidean view that political leaders and legislators are men in whom the active intellect influences only the faculty of imagination, as political and ethical behavior, bound up with the distinction between good and evil, is not a proper subject for pure reason.[52] Or it may reflect what I have listed as the final function of the Angel, as giver of the Torah, which contains both sound doctrine and directives for conduct. The theory that God did not give the Torah directly, and that without the Angel, the Torah would never have reached man, is in a sense the most extreme of all. Yet this too is not without parallel. In his commentary on Proverbs 4:3, Gersonides maintains that the "mother," in its esoteric meaning, "refers to the active intellect, through the mediation of which God transmitted the Torah to Israel, and through the mediation of which came prophecy." In short, every function attributed by R. Isaac to his supreme incorporeal Angel can be found, in one writer or another, associated with the active intellect.

R. Isaac's conception of the supreme Angel bears comparison with one other doctrine of medieval Jewish thought, that of the Kavod. This was first given an authoritative formulation by Saadia Gaon, who spoke of a form created by God from primordial light, more magnificent than the angels, called the "glory of God" or the "Angel of God."[53] Here too is a theory of a being outside of God, higher than all the other angels, which appears to the prophets. However, this Kavod is not emanated but created, and it functions in Saadia's thought exclusively as a means of revelation to the prophets. It has absolutely no essential role in the process by which the world was brought into being or by which it is governed, and little would be missing without it. Therefore, this theory in itself could not have been an important influence on R. Isaac.

The German Pietists introduced significant modifications to Saadia's concept of the Kavod. While this doctrine was never fully crystallized in a systematic form by the Pietists, it contains some new elements that parallel the teachings of R. Isaac. The primary function of the Kavod remains, as in Saadia, that of being revealed to the prophets. But in at least some streams of the esoteric writings of German Pietism, a more active role for the Kavod, corresponding to the multifaceted role of R. Isaac's Angel, is discernible. It is emanated from God, not created, and serves as part of a series of divine lights, emanated one from the other, which bridge the gap between God and the material world. From the Kavod is emanated the soul of man, and this soul continues to receive its vital influence while in the body. By acquiring intellectual qualities, the soul can ascend the ladder that leads upward from the material world, until it finally cleaves with the Kavod. And the Kavod acts as the intermediary through which divine providence is implemented in the world.[54] All of these are functions that are also associated with R. Isaac's Angel.

Finally, there is a comparable notion in the early writings of the Kabbala originating in southern France. R. Abraham b. David, the Rabad of Posquières, is reported by his grandson to have interpreted the aggadic assertion that the Holy One, blessed be He, puts on tefillin as referring to the "Prince of the [Divine] Face," Metatron. But he then went on to speak of the possibility that above this Prince of the Face is a still higher being, emanated from the supreme Cause of all causes, and it is this being that appeared to Moses and to Ezekiel. Gershom Scholem, who discusses this passage in detail, views it as the convergence of two motifs: the divine *Kavod* revealed to the prophet, now no longer created but emanated directly from the First Cause, and a new, mystical conception of Metatron, the supreme Prince of the Angels.[55] Here too, certain elements that characterize R. Isaac's doctrine are discernible, especially the assertion that the highest spiritual being beneath God, emanated directly from the First Cause, is what appeared to the prophets. It is not clear that any cosmological function is attributed to this being.

This brief survey is not to suggest any direct contact between the Pietistic or Kabbalistic teachings and the commentaries of R. Isaac but rather to indicate how philosophical doctrines can develop in somewhat parallel ways in different intellectual milieux. It is also fascinating to see how concepts that play roughly analogous roles in different systems of thought are hung on the same traditional pegs. Abraham Abulafia and Gersonides might seem to have little in common, but both considered Metatron a name for the active intellect. Furthermore, the German Pietists tended to associate or even identify Metatron with the divine

Kavod. As we have seen, R. Isaac identifies Metatron as his supreme in-corporeal Angel.[56] These are varying approaches to a critical dilemma in medieval Jewish thought: how to preserve the pure, philosophical con-cept of God while retaining the Biblical and rabbinic Deity's active in-volvement in the world. Many were able to find a solution by postulating an intermediate being, but few attributed to this being such variegated and important functions as did R. Isaac.

What conclusions can be drawn from the study of this doctrine? Most of the philosophical material in the commentaries shows the obvious im-print of Maimonides. The doctrine of the supreme Angel, however, shows R. Isaac as an eclectic, appropriating elements of different philo-sophical systems and fusing them for his own purposes.[57] What results is more a hodgepodge than a synthesis, for he made no attempt to resolve the tension between diverse teachings that are sometimes juxtaposed in the same sentence. I have already noted the absence of technical philo-sophy in these commentaries (see the end of chapter III). There are im-portant examples of popular, nontechnical works written by men who also engaged in highly specialized philosophy, works such as Anatoli's *Malmad ha-Talmidim*, Gersonides' Biblical commentaries, and the work with which R. Isaac's commentaries have been confused—Yedaiah ha-Penini's *Commentary on the Midrashim*. It is probably fair to conclude from my analysis of the Angel doctrine that R. Isaac's commentaries are not of this nature, that he was not by temperament or training a rigorous philosopher. It would be extremely surprising to discover that he com-posed independent philosophical treatises or translated Arabic philo-sophical works in addition to writing his commentaries. R. Isaac does not appear to be simplifying and popularizing for an untrained readership; he seems rather to have mustered his considerable energies for propagat-ing a discipline in which he himself was not an outstanding expert.

Women, Sex, Marriage, and Adultery

R. Isaac would not have been happy with the subject of this next sec-tion. Throughout his commentaries, he protests that discourse about the physical beauty of a woman, erotic desire, and sexual activity is by its very nature tedious, irreverent, useless, and shameful, drawing the speaker and listener into the power of sin and diverting the intellect from achieving knowledge of God. It is bad enough if a man speaks of such matters to his own wife in privacy; there can be absolutely no justifica-tion for serious scholars and sages to discuss them in public.[58] As I have pointed out, this assumption led R. Isaac to treat rabbinic statements about women and sex in the same way that the rabbis themselves treated the Song of Songs, denying that they were ever intended to be understood in accordance with their simple meaning. Nevertheless, R. Isaac makes some rather important statements about licit and illicit sexual relations. His commentaries contain forceful expressions of an extreme philosophical outlook on human sexuality, and fascinating revelations of Jewish sexual mores in thirteenth-century southern France.

On the subject of women in general, there may be found in hundreds of pages of R. Isaac's commentaries an occasional positive remark about a particular woman. Esther, for example, was a "woman with wisdom of heart," sent by God to save the Jews from Haman's evil plot.[59] Especially interesting is his discussion of Miriam in the midrashic statement that the well provided water for the Israelites because of her merit (*Num. R.*, 1:2). Miriam was a "wise prophetess" who provided the "water" of knowledge to men, women, and children alike. When she sat in her tent, the women of Israel came to her seeking ultimate knowledge of the divine realm. "Then, toward evening, when each woman returned to her own home, she wisely told her husband what she had heard from Miriam . . . Thus men and their wives entered their tents to discuss [philosophy] with each other, and in their inner chamber they would speak to each other only about intellectual matters [*inyanim sikhliyim*], rather than learning lies related to tedious subjects."[60] This tale depicts not only a woman who could teach metaphysics but women in general as purveyors of philosophical enlightenment among the entire people. It is, however, a rare exception to the general pattern, occurring only once in history. When Miriam died, the well went dry.

The other statements about women reflect the most negative assumptions of the rabbinic literature, the philosophical tradition, and the conventions of medieval belles-lettres.[61] Women are characterized by the weakness of their intellects and the power of their tongues. "Why does the Torah say 'sorceress' [Exod. 22:17]? Because the majority of women are inclined to sorcery" (*Sanh.*, 67a). R. Isaac explains this as an intellectual failing rather than as a religious transgression: "The minds of all women are weak in comparison with the mind of a man, and they therefore indulge in useless superstitions, believing everything, while a man, whose intellect is strong enough to discern between truth and falsehood, will not involve himself in such tedious matters." Therefore, the warning about sorcery is related to women, "for the Torah penetrated to the depths of their minds, realizing that they follow empty foolishness."[62] In the time of Miriam, the women may have spread philosophical truth, but the Torah reflects the fact that their natural propensity is toward superstition. This quality makes "woman" an appropriate allegorical representation of the faculties related to the imagination. It is the function of the imagination to conjoin the possible with the impossible; therefore the prophets and sages, referring to the imagination esoterically, called it "woman," for the woman's intellect is weak, and she is therefore prone to believe impossible things.[63]

The second salient quality of women is their loquaciousness. They spend their days sewing with their neighbors and gabbing about insipid matters from morning to evening, "for so it is the nature of women to talk; they cannot remain silent without a radical change [in their nature]; all day long they talk about ridiculous subjects."[64] The statement that women took for themselves nine of the ten measures of conversation which descended to the world (*Kiddushin*, 49b) is accepted literally by our commentator as indicating that "they do not have the capacity to hold back their words even for a short time."[65] This feature is used by R. Isaac to explain a *takkanah* made by R. Yose of Sephoris "that women should talk in the privy because of the danger of private meeting" (*Sanh.*, 19a). Men are not supposed to speak in the privy, even words of Torah; they should use this opportunity to reflect upon their mortality, for with regard to bodily functions such as the elimination of waste, they have no superiority over the beasts. For women, however, the case is different. It is known that they are loquacious by nature, that their power of speech is much greater than that of men. Therefore they are not required to refrain from talking, first because this would be impossible for them and second because men will hear them and refrain from entering, thereby avoiding the danger of private meeting. In this way, the commentator concludes, a negative quality of women is directed to be used for the benefit of all.[66]

The fact that women are by nature credulous and talkative does not necessarily hinder men in their pursuit of perfection, and therefore it is not critical in the structure of R. Isaac's philosophical-religious system. The case is quite different when we consider the woman as a sexual partner, for here men are directly affected. The negative evaluation of sexual intercourse, given capsule expression in Aristotle's opinion that "the sense of touch [and all the pleasures associated with it] is a disgrace to us," reached prominence in Jewish philosophical circles through a parenthetical remark in the *Guide for the Perplexed*.[67] R. Isaac refers to this statement about the "sense of touch" both in CAT and in CMR, although characteristically, he does not attribute it either to Aristotle or to Maimonides.[68] But the antipathy toward sex reflected in these commentaries is the result not of an isolated statement in an earlier philosophical work but rather of an entire set of assumptions about the material world, the body, the intellect, and the ultimate good for man.

Remarks emphasizing the harmfulness of frequent indulgence in sex recur almost as a leitmotif throughout the pages of the commentaries. Sometimes the harm to the body is stressed. The phrase *dever havvot* in Psalm 91:3 is interpreted to mean sexual licentiousness, which drains the body of its vital fluids and thereby causes an early death.[69] The physical deterioration resulting from overly frequent sex is graphically described in a passage from CMR discussing the statement from *Avot*, "The more servant women, the more licentiousness": the servant women will compete with each other to enter their master's bed, "until the man's 'fountain' is drained dry, and the fat of his flesh becomes lean, and all his impulses become progressively weaker, and all five senses are diminished . . ."[70] It is also assumed that frequent ejaculation makes the father less capable of producing healthy children. The seed will not be fully ripe if it is used every night, the father will not be able to "shoot it like an arrow," and the chances are that any children resulting from this seed will die young.[71]

But these are not the most important grounds for opposition to sexual indulgence. Physical health per se is not important; it has value only insofar as it is necessary for the cultivation of the intellect.[72] The true danger is that frequent sex addles the brain, diminishes the power of the intellect, and sidetracks a man from his pursuit of the ultimate good. This danger can be illustrated by any number of examples relating both to the history of the Israelite people and to contemporary reality. "Whenever the people is dissolute with sexual licentiousness, pursuing beautiful women and concentrating exclusively on one of them, it diminishes its brain, which is the seat of the intellect, and it has no strength to stand in the palace of the king; it will be too weary to find the living God."[73] When the people of Israel are unrestrained in their sexual conduct, it is impossible for them to attain true metaphysical knowledge. They dissipate their strength and exhaust their intellect to no avail, and the result is that they believe impossible things about God. This was the reason, according to Jeremiah, why the people did not know God in his day.[74]

R. Isaac is even more specific, speaking of individuals. A man who is with a woman "night after night, wound around her like a turkey while it is still day . . . diminishes his brain daily with the beautiful woman he loves, and by diminishing his brain, he diminishes his intellect." He will therefore come to a bad end.[75] This danger does not arise solely from forbidden sexual unions; it is a function of the sex act itself. R. Yohanan, in the name of R. Simeon b. Yohai, said, "Whoever does not separate himself from his wife near the time of her menstruation, his sons, even if they be as fine as those of Aaron, will die" (*Shev.*, 18b). R. Isaac interprets "sons" allegorically, as faculties of the soul. But what is especially important in this context is that he explains the statement as dealing not with the theme of intercourse during menstruation but with the frequency of sexual relations with one's wife: "They taught about a man who engages in this shameful matter with his wife every day. It is well known that such a man will confuse his intellect and diminish his brain, and if he confuses his intellect, all those 'male' aspects of the soul will be lost on the way; they will perish with the death of the body, so that the man will leave no blessing after him."[76] The conclusion is far reaching but inevitable. Frequent performance of the sexual act is incompatible with attaining immortality of the soul. This judgment is made not on religious grounds—that there is something sinful about sex for which the soul will be punished—but on purely scientific and philosophical grounds. By dissipating the powers of body and mind and by diverting the intellect from worthwhile knowledge, sexual activity makes it all but impossible for a man to gain that knowledge which alone can make his intellect immortal.

It might seem that these theories would lead to the position that total abstinence from sex is the ideal. This is a position no Jewish writer could seriously maintain, owing both to the content of his own tradition and to the competing ideology of the Christian Church. R. Isaac is therefore compelled to deal with the question of when and under what circumstances sexual relations are permissible. Even within the context of marriage, the key word is "infrequently."[77] His definition of one who is "restrained in sexual matters" (gadur be-ervah) is a man "who does not desire to embrace an alien bosom, and who cleaves to his own wife infrequently when he becomes heated . . ." Such a man will be able to attain ultimate knowledge of God, for his intellect will be strong.[78] Only two reasons justify sexual relations with one's wife: to perpetuate the human species and to maintain one's physical health. This view is expressed in the comment on Avot, I:17, "Whoever increases words causes sin"; as this has been published,[79] I shall quote a similar passage from the commentary on Shevuot:

> They came to teach human beings not to be drawn after their material component by using the sense of touch, for this is a disgrace to them inasmuch as they are living men. A man should not be drawn after this shameful thing even with his wife, for it confuses his intellect. He should engage in this matter only infrequently, for the perpetuation of the species or to maintain himself in health. Then his intellect will be strong . . .[80]

The proper justification for sexual relations within marriage and the proper motivation and appropriate thoughts while engaging in sex are subjects that occupied both Jewish and Christian moralists throughout the Middle Ages. Comparison of R. Isaac's formulation with other well-known treatments shows that it is dependent not on R. Abraham b. David's Sefer Ba'alei ha-Nefesh[81] or on Abraham ibn Ezra's comment on Leviticus 18:20[82] but rather on Maimonides' Hilkhot De'ot, 3:2: "When one engages in intercourse, he should not do so except to strengthen the body or to establish offspring. Therefore he should not engage in intercourse whenever he feels desire but rather whenever he knows that he needs to ejaculate semen as a technique of cure or to establish offspring." Maimonides' failure to include the obligation of the husband to fulfil the wife's conjugal rights (*onah*) is explainable by the fact that the entire section in which this statement occurs is not formulated in terms of the religious category of mitzvot; it is a purely scientific discussion of proper physical hygiene, which enables the intellect to achieve ultimate knowledge of God.[83] But while Maimonides supplements this statement with discussions of the religious dimension, including the commandment of onah,[84] R. Isaac, at least in the extant commentaries, does not. Nowhere does he consider an obligation to fulfil the desire of the wife as a valid justification for the sexual act; indeed, the woman's desire is considered to be a serious threat to a man. Indulgence in sex is condoned only when the welfare of the human race or the welfare of the individual man necessitates it.[85]

The only instance in which R. Isaac employs the religious category of mitzvah is in a provocative comment on the statement "From the day the Temple was destroyed, the taste was taken out of sexual intercourse, and it was given to sinners" (*Sanh.*, 75a).[86] This passage reveals a deep ambivalence toward the mitzvot relating to sex within marriage. It begins by describing the time when the people lived securely in their own land. Among the Jews then were those who "indulged in every kind of harmful pleasure." Because of the multitude of pleasures in superfluous things that they pursued, their bodily fluids built up to the point where they found sex pleasurable every day. So far, it seems clear that these people were bad, for the pursuit of base pleasures and superfluous things is denounced throughout the commentaries, and R. Isaac makes clear the negative effects of overly frequent indulgence. At this point, he begins to speak in terms of a Biblical commandment (Gen. 1:28), continuing, "As the sages said, 'Those at leisure, every day' [*Ketubot*, 61b]. They taught that the man who is pampered and strong can perform the commandment of being fruitful and multiplying every day, as we explained in many places in Tractate *Ketubot*." The *Ketubot* quotation is from the discussion of the mitzvah of onah; R. Isaac seems to shift his ground from the satisfaction of the wife's desire to the commandment of procreation. But even more puzzling is his attitude toward these Jews of old. Ordinarily, the performance of a commandment every day would be considered praiseworthy and admirable. Yet the entire context makes it seem as if this particular commandment should not be fulfilled so often; that the conditions that enable one to fulfil it daily are not good but bad. The commentary on *Ketubot* would undoubtedly clarify his position; its absence leaves an element of confusion unresolved. What seems to emerge is that even where the commandments of onah and procreation are considered, they do not validate overly frequent indulgence in marital sex.

This ambivalence, flowing from a tension between the author's assumptions and the text upon which he is commenting, continues to be manifest when he turns to the contemporary situation of life in *galut*. What Rashi had expressed in a few succinct words—"The strength [of Jews] diminished because of their many worries, so that the spirit does not arise in a man to be desirous of his wife"—R. Isaac fleshes out with details of some historical interest. Jews living in subjugation to the Gentiles are under great economic pressure to provide enough for their families to live and to pay the taxes exacted of them. The work necessary to furnish this income is so exhausting that at the end of a full day, the Jew is barely able to drag himself home, eat his dinner, and collapse into bed so tired that he does not even think of sexual intercourse with his wife.

Here it might seem as if R. Isaac is lamenting yet another aspect of the negative impact of galut, as in his frequent assertion that the pressures of earning a living in exile can make it all but impossible for a Jew to find leisure for the study of Torah and philosophy. But this impression is shattered by the introduction of a loaded term: "It does not enter his mind to engage in *that shameful act* [be-ma'aseh ha-meguneh ha-hu], even with his own wife, who is permitted to him, because he is so exhausted." The aggadah has been set in the context of the philosopher's negative outlook on sexuality, typified by the Aristotelian statement that "the sense of touch is a source of shame for us." Thus the commentator's evaluation of the phrase "The taste for sexual intercourse was taken away" remains unclear. At first, he seems to feel that this is a bad thing. But if sex itself is a shameful act, then perhaps R. Isaac means to suggest that this particular effect of the galut is good.

In order to resolve this ambiguity and to understand properly the rest of the comment, one must first explore R. Isaac's entire treatment of forbidden sexual relations as contrasted with marital sex. He assumes that the natural tendency of a man is to desire every beautiful woman, no matter what her relationship to him.[87] There are several rather striking descriptions of such desire. R. Isaac speaks of a man "who gazes at finelooking women and lusts for their beauty, his heart pounding because of them; all day long he cannot hold it in. When evening comes, he 'digs through houses in darkness' going for the whoring woman who pleased him in the street of the city during the day. Alone, inconspicuous, he goes at night to sleep with her, and so he will do night after night . . ."[88] Or, commenting on the Talmudic assertion about Balaam's discovery that the openings of the Israelites' houses were not directed toward each other (*BB*, 60a), R. Isaac explains that the value of this arrangement was that

while sitting in one's own house, he will not see something sexually stimulating in his friend's house through the window or the door. If he looks at a woman standing nude in front of him across from his door, he will go around all day unrestrained, his heart impelling him to lie with her that night, and he will vex his mind during that day with this evil matter. Also at night, his thought will turn to the woman as he lies on his bed, and even if he does not know her and does not draw near to her while awake, he will speak tenderly to her in his dream and immediately have an emission.[89]

The natural desire of man applies even to his own female relations. Nature does not repudiate incest; in this way we are similar to the beasts.[90]

Evaluating the various types of sexual unions, R. Isaac shows how the practical consequences of each are harmful. The man who goes to an unmarried woman night after night will wear out both his body and his mind.[91] If he is having an affair with a married woman, there is the additional risk that he will be discovered by the woman's husband, who will try to kill him. Furthermore, the offending wife will have to leave her husband's home. This is what makes adultery worse than fornication with a single woman.[92] Adultery is also worse than incest because of its consequences. In the case of adultery, the desire for vengeance on the part of the wronged husband may lead to murder and an ongoing feud, while the incest restrictions, applying to one household, are essentially a private matter.[93] Sexual relations with women of foreign nations are dangerous because a foreign woman will seduce a man to serve her own god, thus removing him from the "community of the religion of Moses."[94]

For reasons such as these, certain types of sexual relations are more dangerous than others. It is the purpose of the Torah to restrict man from indulging his natural desires to engage in the most harmful forms of intercourse. This is accomplished through the institution of marriage. Just as one who is miserly in nature can be guided back to the mean by the Torah's regulations concerning charity, so one who is "hot" in nature, lusting after beautiful women, is guided by the Torah to take a wife in accordance with Jewish law. This wife will protect him against alien women, for he will be able to cleave to her when he feels the urge.[95] The wife's role is to guard her husband from other women

so that he will abide with her satisfied, without embracing a foreign bosom; so that he will cleave to his wife and not to the wife of his friend, who drains his bodily fluids and confuses his intellect as he diminishes his brain with her, so that she "breaks his skull" [Jud. 9:53]. He who guards his own soul will stay far from such a woman; he will become one flesh with his own wife, and neither will sin before God. Thus the man and his wife will be prepared to know the living God through their pure intellect.[96]

The quality of a marriage is measured largely in terms of its success in fulfilling this function of keeping both partners from seeking extramarital outlets for their sexual drives, an action consistently presented not as sinful but as dangerous. The one lyrical description of an ideal marriage never allows the reader to forget this theme:

They are teaching that not all marriages work out well. For love and hate between a man and a woman depend on their natures. If they are equivalent in their natural endowments, they will love each other and cling to each other. She will lie against his breast when he desires her beauty, and at her word he will kiss her lips with the loving kisses of an expectant love. He will bring joy to his wife and will not betray her by embracing a foreign bosom. She too will love him deeply because of his personal qualities, and she will cling to him and kiss him and not have an adulterous union with another man.[97]

It is not merely through the institution of marriage that the Torah helps a man to restrain his natural desire for all beautiful women. Even more important is the commandment of circumcision. In fact, this is what enables the Jewish wife to fulfil her role successfully, as can be seen in the comment on *Avodah Zarah*, 25b: "A Jew's wife guards him; a gentile's wife does not guard him." After pointing out that the Torah provides for a wife exclusive to one man, who will be at home and available to him whenever he wants her, he goes on to say that if the man desires a woman forbidden to him, "his wife will guard him, and his craving for the forbidden woman will disappear, because his foreskin has been removed from him, and the power of his member has been diminished, so that he has no strength to lie with many lewd women." In contrast, the level of desire in an uncircumcized gentile, who eats foods that add to the heat of his body, is much higher than that of a Jew. Therefore, "his one wife is not able to restrain him from the other women he pursues, compelled by his nature; he does not fear to fulfil the desire of his hungering impulse."[98]

The process by which circumcision inhibits the sexual capacity of the Jewish man (for his own benefit, according to R. Isaac) is explored in graphic detail in a passage from the Midrash Rabbah Commentary. The midrash explicates the phrase "daughters of Zion": "sons distinguished by circumcision, for if they were not circumcized, they would not be able to behold the shekhinah" (*Num. R.*, 12:8). R. Isaac explains that one who is uncircumcized cannot master his impulses except in the rare and exceptional case of a man born with a naturally cold temperament. Such a man is one in a thousand, and the sages do not speak about such extraordinary circumstances.

A man uncircumcized in the flesh desires to lie with a beautiful-looking woman who speaks seductively to attract him. He vexes his mind to be with her day after day, growing weary in his attempt to fulfil his desire through lovemaking with her.

She too will court the man who is uncircumcized in the flesh and lie against his breast with great passion, for he thrusts inside her a long time because of the foreskin, which is a barrier against ejaculation in intercourse. Thus she feels pleasure and reaches an orgasm first.[99] When an uncircumcized man sleeps with her and then resolves to return to his home, she brazenly grasps him, holding on to his genitals, and says to him, "Come back, make love to me." This is because of the pleasure that she finds in intercourse with him, from the sinews of his testicles—sinew of iron—and from his ejaculation —that of a horse—which he shoots like an arrow into her womb. They are united without separating, and he makes love twice and three times in one night, yet the appetite is not filled.

And so he acts with her night after night. The sexual activity emaciates him of his bodily fat, and afflicts his flesh, and he devotes his brain entirely to women, an evil thing. His heart dies within him; between her legs he sinks and falls. He is unable to see the light of the King's face, because the eyes of his intellect are plastered over by women so that they cannot now see light.

But when a circumcized man desires the beauty of a woman, and cleaves to his wife, or to another woman comely in appearance, he will find himself performing his task quickly, emitting his seed as soon as he inserts the crown. If he lies with her once, he sleeps satisfied, and will not know her again for another seven days. This is the way the circumcized man acts time after time with the woman he loves. He has an orgasm first; he does not hold back his strength. As soon as he begins intercourse with her, he immediately comes to a climax.

She has no pleasure from him when she lies down or when she arises, and it would be better for her if he had not known her and not drawn near to her, for he arouses her passion to no avail, and she remains in a state of desire for her husband, ashamed and confounded, while the seed is still in her "reservoir." She does not have an orgasm once a year, except on rare occasions, because of the great heat and the fire burning within her. Thus he who says "I am the Lord's" will not empty his brain because of his wife or the wife of his friend. He will find grace and good favor; his heart will be strong to seek out God. He will not fear to behold that which is beyond, and when He speaks to him, he will not turn away.[100]

This passage bears discussion and analysis from several points of view. As interpretation of a midrash, it exemplifies one type of R. Isaac's comments. Here there is no interest in allegorization or exploration of an esoteric level of meaning. The rabbinic statement asserts a correlation between two phenomena—circumcision and ability to behold the shekhinah—for which the causal nexus is not at all obvious. The commentator, who understands "beholding the shekhinah" to mean the attainment of philosophical knowledge of God, explains the connection between circumcision and intellectual achievement, making the statement rational and plausible rather than arbitrary.

But if the passage is ordinary in its methodology and approach to the aggadah, it is extraordinary in the material used to support the basic argument. The author reveals an understanding of female sexuality that is impressive—and not only for his own era—in his assertions that the woman's ability to have an orgasm is directly dependent on the amount of time before the man reaches his climax; that a woman is capable of desiring two or three intense sexual experiences in one night, thus making excessive demands even on the most potent lover; that arousal of the woman without release, owing to the male's premature ejaculation, is worse than no sexual stimulation at all because of the lingering sense of frustration and disappointment; that even with a husband who is chronically premature, the woman may occasionally experience an orgasm because of pent-up desire that must be released.

What is so striking to a modern reader is that this knowledge is presented in a context of absolute indifference toward the woman's sexual fulfilment. The situation in which the woman is chronically frustrated is good, while the situation in which she is fulfilled poses the most serious possible danger: the failure by the man to achieve eternal life for his soul because of the excessive sexual demands made upon him. The woman's own spiritual destiny is ignored. The argument is not that women must tolerate a degree of sexual frustration for the sake of their own souls; rather, they must make the sacrifice that is a necessary consequence of circumcision so that their men may live eternally in the Divine presence. In this way, insights that seem so powerful and deep are turned on their head by an author who is fundamentally unsympathetic to women and to sexual pleasure. The conclusion to which they lead in his hands is that a man must be able to release his seed, on occasion, without satisfying his female partner, so that she will eventually lose interest in sexual experience as a source of pleasure; for only then can he hope to achieve success in his philosophical endeavors.

The comment points in other directions as well. It has important implications for the psychological dynamics of Jewish-Christian relations in the Middle Ages, as the categories used here—uncircumcized and circumcized—must certainly be translated according to the realities of the thirteenth century as "Christian" and "Jew." Thus, this passage provides a powerful stereotype of the Christian male as viewed by a Jewish intellectual: the Christian is a virile, potent lover greatly desired by all women, Christian and Jewish alike, because of the pleasure and satisfaction he can bestow. In contrast, the Jew is presented as a totally ineffectual lover, unable to satisfy a woman. Even if he has an affair with a Christian woman, it will not last long, for she will immediately feel desire for her husband, who is so much more competent in such matters. These stereotypes emerge in stark relief against the background of a Christian civilization in which celibacy and sexual abstinence were the highest ideal and of a Jewish tradition far more open to the legitimacy of sexual pleasure. Furthermore, there is an abundance of contemporary evidence, from both Jewish and Christian sources, indicating that sexual intermingling between Jewish men and Christian women—whether servant women or prostitutes, single or married—was more prevalent and constituted more of a problem than relations between Jewish women and Christian men.[101] There is no evidence that would validate R. Isaac's claim that Jews, because of their circumcision, were undesirable as lovers in comparison with Christians. If this passage reflects any historical reality, it would seem to prove not that Jewish men were actually spurned by gentile women but that at least some Jews tended to perceive Christian men as sexual giants.

Of course, it is possible that this passage reflects not a prevalent Jewish perception of Christian males but only the author's idiosyncratic perceptions. Indeed, his assertions about sex—about a man's seeing a beautiful, naked woman and being unable to concentrate on anything else all day until at night he goes to a prostitute or has a nocturnal emission; about a man's being so exhausted at the end of a day's work that he has absolutely no interest in making love to his wife; about consistent premature ejaculation resulting in chronic inability to satisfy any woman—would undoubtedly make interesting reading for a psychiatrist. To what extent do such passages reflect the personal experience of the author? To what extent would other contemporary Jews have concurred with these intimate descriptions of Jewish life? To what extent can the framework of philosophical assumptions that denigrate sexual prowess and glorify inadequacy be viewed as an elaborate rationalization resolving a set of personal problems that troubled the author intensely? These are questions best left to another discipline. No matter what answers may be given, the passages lose none of their importance as documents in the history of consciousness as well as the history of ideas.

Finally, the text that I have been discussing should be seen as a rather eccentric contribution to the literature of ta'amei ha-mitzvot, the rational explanation of the divine commandments. The purpose of circumcision is clearly stated: by making the Jewish man less capable of satisfying a woman, it makes him less likely to be caught up in illicit sexual relationships. The fact that a man is unable to satisfy his wife is, for the author, unimportant; this is an obligatory relationship, and he will continue to find occasional outlet with her. But the fact that a man is unable to satisfy another woman is of great moment. The affair with another man's wife will occur only if the woman wants her lover enough to face the risks involved. If the circumcized Jew attempts such an affair, it is doomed to quick failure; after one unsuccessful tryst, the woman will show no further interest. Therefore the Jew will not be diverted by such shameful matters from pursuing his true goals. In other words, circumcision is a safeguard against sexual sin, which is important not because sin itself is bad but because it is so draining.

But all this was true while the Jews were living on their own land and marital relations were more or less normal. The situation in exile is different. The Jew is forced to work so hard throughout the day that he is uninterested in his wife at night. As a result, a major safeguard against sinful behavior is lost. The burdens of exile are enough to extinguish the lesser desire for one's wife, who is permitted, but they leave unabated the stronger desire, fueled by the libidinous *yetzer*, for the foreign woman, who is forbidden:

> He will have no desire for [sexual relations with his wife] but only for a sinful act. If he finds a "foreign woman" before him, he will embrace this alien breast, and his great toil [necessary to earn a livelihood] will not prevent him from doing so, because of the impulse that causes him to sin and feeds him that which is forbidden and shameful.[102]

That desire for the forbidden is more powerful than desire for the permitted is illustrated by the Biblical verse cited in the gemara. In the phrase "Bread eaten in secret is pleasant" (Prov. 9:17), as in the phrase "She eats, and wipes her mouth" (Prov. 30:20), eating is a metaphor for any transgression pleasant to the sinner. But in Proverbs, the assertion that the furtive and the illicit are sweet represents the false enticement with which Folly ensnares the ignorant. R. Isaac, explaining the Talmud's use of the verse, makes it into a psychological verity. For the sinner, it is true that the furtive and the illicit are more pleasurable than the permitted, and even an exhausting day of labor does not extinguish the desire for this pleasure.

What, then, is the final evaluation of the phrase "The taste for sexual intercourse [with one's wife] was taken away" after the destruction of the Temple? The sexual act may be shameful in itself, but it is obviously far less shameful and less threatening when performed for a worthwhile purpose in a licit context than when it is secret and sinful as well as degrading. The fact that life in exile makes it more difficult for Jews to have sexual relations with their wives than in the quieter era when Jews lived on their own land is not necessarily bad from the author's philosophical point of view. But it is bad in that it undermines the strongest impediment to submitting to the far more powerful desire for illicit relations.

Most of the writings about sexual licentiousness in this period refer to the highest levels of Jewish society—the wealthy and the powerful. If this text can be used as historical evidence and not merely a projection of R. Isaac's personal problems, it may indicate that the poor, burdened with long hours of hard physical work, were just as likely to seek this kind of diversion.

The Messiah

The aggadot and midrashim relating to the Messiah and the messianic age posed special problems for Jewish exegesis. Internally, they challenged those who tried to calculate the date of the expected arrival and those who felt impelled to synthesize a full and consistent messianic doctrine from the welter of seemingly incompatible statements. Externally, they served as weapons for Christian polemicists attempting to attack the basic tenets of Judaism from the sources of Judaism itself.[103] R. Isaac's treatment of these messianic passages must be seen against this background. Applying philosophical assumptions to traditional texts, he eventually reaches conclusions as extreme in their own way as those of any medieval Jewish writer.

The discussion of the Messiah's nature and personality yields few surprises. R. Isaac insists that the Messiah is a human being, nothing more, often using the rabbinic phrase *melekh basar ve-dam*, intended to specify a mortal monarch in contrast with God. The most common characterization in the commentaries is "the messianic king, a king of flesh and blood, whose saving help we eagerly await."[104] He is not essentially different from other kings of Israel, such as Saul, David, and Solomon. As he is composed of the same elements that constitute every other human being, his life span will be of normal length, and his son and subsequently his grandson will succeed him.[105]

Of course, there are differences between the Messiah and the average Israelite king. This is indicated by the title "nasi", as in Ezekiel 37:25: "And David, My servant, shall be their nasi forever." R. Isaac insists that the title nasi denotes higher status, implying greater wisdom, than does the title "melekh," ("king"). A fool can inherit the throne after the death of his father, and he can rule effectively through the advice of wise counselors, but a nasi is dependent on no one else. In the case of the Messiah, others will come from afar to seek his wisdom. His intellectual powers will be manifest especially in his ability to judge cases in which the truth is hidden from sight.[106]

Comparison of the Messiah's personal stature with that of other outstanding Biblical figures is revealing. "Rav said, 'The world was created solely for the sake of David.' Samuel said, 'For Moses.' R. Yohanan said,

'For the Messiah' " (*Sanh.*, 98b). This dispute remains unresolved in the gemara, but R. Isaac interprets each successive statement as refuting the previous one by pointing to a man of greater stature, reversing the statements of Samuel and R. Yohanan, so that the progression is David, Messiah, Moses. After discussing the greatness of David, he explains why the Messiah surpasses the founder of the royal line. After all, David, born with a powerful natural impulse, pursued women sinfully. Through idle thoughts and indulgence of the body, he wasted time that could have been used for the cultivation of his intellect. In contrast, the Messiah will have no such natural impediments to the attainment of perfection. He will not sin in deed or even in thought. Isaiah 11:3 is interpreted to mean that even the scent (suggestion) of sin will be absent.[107]

Yet not even the Messiah will reach the stature of Moses, who was superior to all other prophets and kings because the special purity of his corporeal component compelled him to use his body only on relatively rare occasions, and thereby enabled him to attain a unique intellectual apprehension of God. The verse "There has not arisen a prophet since in Israel like unto Moses" (Deut. 34:10) proclaims this uniqueness unambiguously. According to Jewish belief, R. Isaac argues, even the Messiah will fail to reach the pinnacle of human perfection that Moses alone attained.[108]

One significant passage describes activities of the Messiah that go far beyond the fulfilment of traditional messianic functions.

As for their saying that they found him sitting at the gate of Rome, having proved that he will indeed come, they went on to teach *how* he will remove the [Jewish] people from the midst of all the nations. He will go to Rome, fortified by his wisdom. For that which its adherents consider to be the new religion given to you [Christians] has its stake driven in Rome, as is well known. There, in his palace, dwells the Pope, who rules and presides over all who follow the faith. And the cardinals, his advisers, surround him, wisely strengthening every breach in the religion day after day. Each year, many notables and summoned leaders come there faithfully to greet [the Pope]. Whatever he decrees to the gentile kings who are adherents of the faith, not one of them will disobey him, nor will they speak after he has spoken; whatever he seals with his bull cannot be reversed, whether it apply to a nation or to an individual alike.

The sages wanted to teach that when the messianic king comes on God's mission to redeem the people from its enemies, he will come in Rome before the greatest of all the gentile kings of flesh and blood [the Pope], just as the master of the prophets came before that great king, Pharaoh, and all his ministers and servants . . . He asked the king for the people [of Israel], according to the word of God who had chosen them. But that king did not believe his words nor desire to hear him until he performed awesome signs and great trials at God's command. Then the eyes of the blind were opened, and the king believed in the living God and in Moses, His servant, and he sent forth the people from his land.

Even so, the messianic king. He will go to Rome, and request their supreme leader and his advisers to write to the kings under his hegemony, and seal it with his bull, that they must restore to him the people [of Israel], according to the word of God who sent him for this purpose, for he is the Messiah of which God promised the people they must not despair, for he would certainly come at the end of days; the eyes of all Israel are upon him, and they eagerly await his saving help. But they [the Pope and his advisers] will not believe him until he performs powerful signs and unmistakable portents in the sight of all present. Then will the Pope know and recognize that he is an emissary of the true God, and he will send his legate to all the kings, near and far, [informing them] that the Jews are about to go forth from slavery to freedom, and that they must let every Jew go by himself, freely, demanding no money, for a redeemer has come to Zion.[109]

Speculation about how the Messiah would accomplish the task of leading the Jewish people out of exile engendered a large literature, much of it apocalyptic in nature. Events such as the Islamic conquests in the seventh century, the Mongol invasions in the thirteenth, and the fall of Constantinople in the fifteenth, were viewed as the backdrop for eschatological confrontations of world powers from which redemption would emerge. Set against the epic conflict of huge armies and the massive movements of peoples, the messianic figure or figures appear as semimythical types, accomplishing their goals on a stage strewn with mountains of corpses and washed with torrents of blood.[110]

The philosophical tradition in medieval Judaism tended to take a more sober view of the messianic advent, a view that did not depend on cataclysmic historical events. The question of how the task was to be accomplished at a time when Jews were scattered in dozens of independent kingdoms became rather more difficult to answer and was often ignored.[111] R. Isaac seems to have concluded that the simplest and most logical approach, one that would avoid the positing of either world wars or cumbersome negotiations between the Messiah and each individual monarch, would be to have the Messiah confront one central ruler of Christendom. In a different period, this might have been the emperor. Now, cued by the rabbis' enigmatic link of the Messiah with Rome, R. Isaac opts for the Pope.

The depiction of the encounter between Messiah and pontiff is fraught with high drama. The Messiah comes to Rome not as the head of a great military force but armed only with the power of his own intellect and of

God, as Whose emissary he serves. Standing in the papal palace before the Pope and his advisers the cardinals, he introduces himself and requests that the Pope order the kings of Christendom to let his people go. Not unnaturally, the Curia is at first skeptical, but all doubts are dissolved by miracles that the Messiah performs. The Pope then sends his bull to the Christian kings through a special legate, instructing these kings to let their Jews go forth freely, in fulfillment of the prophetic words. At a time when royal expulsion of Jews from Christian territories was becoming increasingly common, the scenario is by no means absurd.

An obvious parallel to this passage is found in Nachmanides' account of his disputation in Barcelona:

> The Messiah . . . will come and command the Pope and all the kings of the nations in the name of God, "Let my people go that they may serve Me." He will perform among them many great signs and wonders, and he will not fear them at all, and will stand in their city, Rome, until he destroys it.[112]

Nachmanides points to a source only for the last statement. On the previous page of his account, he writes, "I did not want to tell them what it says in an aggadah: that the Messiah will stand in Rome until he destroys it." The aggadah to which he was referring is not known. This one apocalyptic element in Nachmanides' doctrine is conspicuously absent from R. Isaac's.

The basic themes of R. Isaac's description can be found in this brief statement of the Ramban: the confrontation between Messiah and pope, the implicit parallel between the Messiah and Moses, the performance by the Messiah of signs and wonders. But in R. Isaac's commentary, what is a vague and nebulous prophecy in the Ramban has the dramatic vividness of an actual event. R. Isaac evokes a sense of immediacy through the details of his mise en scène. It is not only the Pope but, realistically, the cardinal advisers whom the Messiah must convince. The papal edict must be accompanied by the special seal (the *bullum*, by which term the letters were called); the Messiah is aware of this procedure and specifically includes it in his request. The bull is promulgated by means of the papal legate, who bears it to the kings of Christendom. Furthermore, the clearly delineated sequence of events makes the entire episode more believable. In Nachmanides, the Messiah simply "commands the Pope and all the kings," but the mechanism for this command remains vague. In R. Isaac, he makes his request of the Pope, allowing the Pope to command the kings through the usual channels. The signs and wonders then fulfil the logical function of convincing the skeptics that the man standing before them is indeed God's emissary. In short, unlike the Messiah of Nachmanides, R. Isaac's Messiah appears as a real person functioning in a concrete historical situation. Given the assumption that the Messiah, through God's power, will be able to perform signs and wonders, there is nothing inherently implausible about the account.

This historical setting for R. Isaac's interpretation of the Messiah at the gates of Rome raises the important question of when the messianic age is to begin. There is no calculation of a date in his extant writings. In the explicitly polemical passage just discussed, he concludes one part of his argument with the assertion that "[the Messiah's] time is near; he will surely come, and not delay" (Hab. 2:3).[113] But except for this one phrase, originally intended for Christian rather than Jewish ears, no sense of immediacy or urgency is discernible in these writings. Most Talmudic statements dealing with the chronology of the messianic age are interpreted not historically but allegorically. Where the commentator does accept the historicity of a statement, he transforms it in other ways.

"R. Hanina said, 'Four hundred years after the destruction of the Temple, if someone says to you, "Buy this field worth one thousand dinars for one dinar," do not buy it' " (AZ, 9b). This statement was obviously intended to express the imminence of redemption, as Rashi explains, "For it is the beginning of redemption, and you will be gathered to the holy mountain for your ancestral patrimony, so why should you waste your dinar?" R. Isaac's comment is strikingly different:

> When the people went into exile, the land was left for other people who fought over it and attempted to seize it. Many nations came to battle over it, year after year, cutting down all its produce at harvest time, uprooting everything planted at the time of vintage, destroying every fruit-bearing tree and despoiling every vineyard, without showing compassion for the land by cultivating it and protecting it . . . For God's curse is upon that land; every enemy and foe has come upon it, one a year, to devastate its trees, and impudent conquerors have come upon it and profaned it . . . I do not know how to interpret the number [four hundred] except that the sages were teaching that the land has been subject to every devastation and punishment since the day the people were exiled from it because of their great sin.[114]

Without doing violence to the words of the statement, R. Isaac has totally reversed its thrust. In his reading, R. Hanina warns that it is a bad time to purchase real estate in the land of Israel, even at rock-bottom prices, not because the redemption is so near but because the land has been so ravaged and despoiled by plundering armies that even what seems like a good bargain is a bad investment. Absent here is any sense that things are going to change in the near future. The messianic content has been removed, and what is left is a dismal depiction, painted against the background of Crusader intrusions into the war-torn Holy Land, of the conditions of exile. Even when R. Isaac preaches encouragement and confidence, he brings no promise of imminent relief:

This is what has stood by our ancestors and us from the day of our people's exile. God has not abandoned this people while it is scattered and isolated among the nations. Its Father has loved it and preserved it in His shadow always, so that we shall perpetually survive [nihyeh . . . le-dorot olam] among the nations until such time as the captivity of Israel returns to the place where it may endure in peace.[115]

There is little suggestion here or elsewhere that he expects such a radical change to occur very soon.

The nature of the future messianic age, like its timing, is treated without much specificity. Once the Messiah effects the release of the Jews from the kings in whose lands they dwell, he will bring them back to the land of Israel, with its uniquely favorable atmosphere and climate.[116] For R. Isaac, as for Maimonides, there will be no essential change in the order of nature with the coming of the Messiah. Samuel's statement that the only difference between this world and the messianic age will be deliverance from the oppression of foreign governments (Ber., 34b) is not quoted in the extant commentaries, but we can infer R. Isaac's acceptance of this principle from his treatment of other rabbinic dicta. Discussing the midrash that claims that the daughters of Obed-Edom each bore two sons a month for the three months that the ark was present (Num. R., 4:20), R. Isaac insists that this is impossible for any woman, and he gives an allegorical interpretation in which the daughters represent the imagination and their children the impulses of the body. He then concludes:

And this follows what the Babylonians said, "In the future, women will give birth each day." This woman who they assert will give birth every day without rising from her bearing is not what it seems, for no man has ever known her, as we explained in the Hibbur ha-Talmud Bavli, Tractate Shabbat.[117]

The commentary on Shabbat is not extant; presumably the passage mentioned would have contained important evidence concerning the treatment of rabbinic statements about the messianic age. Even from this brief remark, we can conclude that the peshat of this statement, in obvious conflict with the order of nature, was rejected because of the assumption that the Messiah will bring about no such miraculous permanent change.

Just as revealing is the comment on a divine promise made in a messianic context, "For brass I will bring gold" (Isa. 60:17). R. Isaac insists that it cannot refer to material wealth, for such wealth leads the people to turn away from God—the opposite of the prophet's intention for the future. Secondly, the promise is directed toward the entire people, which would imply that poverty will be eradicated from the midst of Israel. But the Torah itself states that the poor will always remain in the land,

> for the nature of reality requires that there be among the human species both rich and poor . . . It is impossible for things to be different except through a miracle, and no such sign or wonder has ever occurred to the entire people together. It is not written in the sacred texts . . . , it never happened before, and it will not occur in the future, for "there is nothing new."[118]

The last statement is extremely important for R. Isaac's understanding of the messianic age. It does not exclude the possibility that miracles will again be performed as in Biblical times. But it limits these future miracles to those actually attested by the Scriptures. There is no reason to assume that any unprecedented miracles will occur in the wake of the Messiah, and rabbinic statements, or even Biblical verses to the contrary must be interpreted against their simple meaning. Specifically, social and economic divisions will remain even in the messianic era. These are inherent in society, and the natural order will not be changed. The innate conservatism of this doctrine is in obvious contrast with the messianic teachings of a work such as the *Ra'aya Mehemna*.[119] While R. Isaac insists that material wealth can turn people against God, and that excessive involvement in business affairs can be perilous for the fate of the soul, he does not feel that the unequal distribution of wealth and the disproportionate influence of the wealthy are evils to be set right in the messianic age.

The renewal of miracles in messianic times is evoked in the comment on a lengthy aggadah concerning the fate of the nations in the end of days (*AZ*, 2a-b). Responding to the statement that the sovereignty of certain nations will continue "until the Messiah comes," R. Isaac discusses the role of the stars in determining why some nations are dominant over others and how this will change with the messianic advent:

> Prophecy disappeared from the midst of the people [of Israel] on the day the Temple was destroyed. No frequent vision was beheld by His servants the prophets, through whom God worked signs and wonders and changed nature for the benefit of the chosen people in their moment of need. The sages taught here that when the messianic king comes to redeem the people from its enemies, to bring them forth from slavery to freedom, prophecy will return to them. Prophets will utter prophecies incessantly, and they will work true wonders. Nature will be changed through them at the word of the Almighty, for the needs of the people which He has chosen exclusively. Then the governing star that has helped all the other nations prior to his coming will be changed to work for their destruction.[120]

Not only will the Messiah himself be able to work miracles on behalf of God, miracles that will convince the Pope of his authenticity. But also Israel's intellectual elite will be elevated to the level of prophets, capable of performing wonders as in Biblical times. This power flows from a restoration of the original providential relationship between God and the people of Israel. Whereas now the success of the nations is determined by the stars, with the coming of the Messiah, God will again become directly involved in the historical process. The power of any star working against Israel will be either nullified or compelled to work on its behalf.

The ultimate purpose of the Messiah's achievements—the worldly victories and the material prosperity he will bring to Israel—is to lead the entire people toward the attainment of intellectual perfection. For example, the return to the land of Israel is important because there the air is purer and clearer than in any other country, enabling its inhabitants to actualize their intellects more easily: "Every one of its inhabitants will be prepared to comprehend the truths about Him, may He be blessed, the base as well as the honorable."[121] The Messiah's fundamental task is to free the people from galut so that they will no longer be burdened by the oppression of the nations but will have the leisure and liberty to achieve their intellectual goals.[122] According to this view, it is not the knowledge of God that makes possible the messianic age but the conditions of the messianic age that will enable all Jews to attain true knowledge of God. The national characteristics of redemption—the restoration of sovereignty, autonomy, dignity, those aspirations enunciated in the prayer of the Jew three times each day—are only instrumental to this final goal, which can be achieved, at least by some individuals, even without help from the Messiah.

This conclusion and its far-reaching implications can be seen in R. Isaac's comments on two important statements from chapter Helek of *Sanhedrin*. The first is attributed to Rav: "All the 'ends' have been exhausted, and the matter is dependent solely on repentance and good deeds" (*Sanh.*, 97b). As it stands in the gemara, the statement represents one perspective on the question, When will the Messiah come? It is counterbalanced by another opinion, expressed by Samuel. Rav's position is that there is now no fixed date but that "the matter," that is, the coming of the Messiah, is totally dependent on the conduct of the Jewish people. R. Isaac transmutes the meaning of the statement by reinterpreting one ambiguous term, "the matter." He interprets it as a reference not to the coming of the Messiah but to the spiritual destiny of the individual, the capacity of each soul to achieve ultimate bliss. In this reading, Rav says, since all dates calculated for the coming of the Messiah have passed, we now have no idea when he will come. But this is of secondary importance, for it is within the power of the individual to achieve the ultimate reward through his own endeavors. To believe otherwise, to make the fate of the soul in eternity depend upon the historical accident of whether it lived in the body before or after the advent of the Messiah, would be to attribute a monstrous injustice to God.[123]

The second statement is that of R. Hillel, "There is no messiah for Israel" (Sanh., 99a). This was a conundrum to many Jewish readers, for it seemed to deny the central premise of post-Biblical Jewish historiosophy: that the Messiah will come at some future date to transform the reality of contemporary Jewish existence. Here too, R. Isaac recasts the meaning of the statement by reinterpreting one crucial word. In his comment on the statement "All Israel has a share in the world to come," he argues that the name Israel as used by the rabbis refers not to the entire Jewish people, for which the terms "children of Jacob" or "house of Jacob" are employed, but to the philosophically educated elite, who strive with and cleave to God.[124] Applying the same meaning of "Israel" here, R. Isaac interprets R. Hillel as having said, "There is no messiah for the philosophers among the Jews," meaning that they have no need for the Messiah. The function of the Messiah is to end the oppression and the burdens of exile, which consume the Jew's energy and make it difficult for him to find time to actualize his intellect by attaining the fullest possible philosophical knowledge of God. For those who have already achieved this goal, the Messiah can serve no further purpose.[125]

The basis for these comments would seem to be the conclusion of the Mishneh Torah (Hil. Melakhim, 12:4-5). Maimonides makes the Messiah instrumental to the attainment of a more important goal. The messianic age is eagerly awaited not for itself but because it will establish conditions that will make it easier for all Jews to observe the commandments, study philosophy, and thereby achieve the ultimate reward of life in the world to come. This view is echoed in R. Isaac's statements: "For what will this king do for [the Jew], other than to bring him from slavery to freedom, so that he will be free to apprehend and to know God." And "what is [the Jew's] desire for this king [the Messiah], except that he will bring us out of this long exile, from beneath the burden of kings and princes . . . so that [the Jew] will then be free to know his Creator, and this will bring him to life in that world which truly endures."[126]

But R. Isaac carries the idea a crucial step further by raising a question that does not occur in Maimonides. If this is indeed the function of the Messiah, what about the individual who has already achieved full philosophical enlightenment despite the difficult conditions of exile? What need does he have for the Messiah? How will the coming of the Messiah benefit him? The answer is inescapable: he who is able to attain philosophical knowledge of God in premessianic times "has no need for the

Messiah, for there will be nothing lacking in him even if the Messiah fails to come during his life, since he finds himself fully perfect without [the Messiah]."[127] Once the fullest possible intellectual perception of God is attained, every earthly king, even the Messiah, must fade into insignificance.

A muted polemic against Christianity can be sensed in R. Isaac's insistence that it is totally within the realm of human capability to achieve salvation through repentance and philosophical attainment without any aid from the Messiah. This doctrine underlines a radical difference between the two faiths, for Christian dogma held that salvation was impossible except through the Savior and his mystical body—the Church—a teaching that posed serious intellectual problems for Roman Catholic theologians concerned about the fate of those who had lived virtuous lives and died before the Incarnation and Passion.[128] R. Isaac asserts in the strongest possible terms that any doctrine that makes salvation dependent on a historical event, denying the efficacy of an individual's own achievements, implies a God who is essentially unjust.

These passages also reflect the internal dynamics of Jewish thought, the tension between the future of the individual soul and the destiny of the people as a whole. The Messiah had traditionally been viewed as the key to the collective destiny. His coming, determined either by the actions of the entire people or by a date set long ago and independent of all human efforts, would bring redemption, at least in a political sense, to all Jews. By contrast, the fate of the soul in Eden was determined by the actions of the individual during his life in this world. While apocalyptic literature emphasized one pole and ethical literature the other, each retained its relative importance. Maimonides, by insisting that the "world to come" exists at present and is entered by the souls of the worthy immediately after death,[129] and by making the Messiah merely an instrument to facilitate attainment of life in this world to come, shifted the balance decisively in favor of individual destiny. R. Isaac follows these teachings to their logical conclusion. The traditional doctrine teaching that if every Jew were to repent and observe the commandments, or even one commandment, the Messiah would come[130] is turned on its head by R. Isaac's assertion that if every Jew were to repent and attain philosophical knowledge of God, the Messiah would be superfluous: "Would that all God's people were prophets, wise enough to know their Creator, so that they would not need any king other than our God, the King of kings of kings, the Holy One, praised be He."[131]

Of course, this is not the case, for the masses of Jews are unable to achieve this level of perfection under the conditions of the exile. If the Messiah is of no particular benefit to the elite who have fully actualized their intellect, he is necessary for these masses, as his task is to create conditions under which all can reach the level now attainable only by a select few. At the same time, it would be inaccurate to conclude that all the messianic statements of the rabbinic literature are therefore irrelevant to the elite. One of the most striking aspects of R. Isaac's treatment of the messianic statements in the Talmud is the extent to which, through the use of allegorization, he transmutes them until they speak no longer of the history and destiny of the Jewish people but of the individual philosopher's spiritual biography.

As we have seen, in several instances R. Isaac explicitly repudiates the simple meaning of messianic statements because he considers them to be inconsistent with the traditional doctrine of the Messiah. In such passages, he argues that the sages used the familiar language referring to the Messiah in order to hide their true meaning. The purpose of this technique of concealment is to guarantee that "not the ignorant but only the select few would understand,"[132] although the potentially harmful nature of the hidden content is anything but clear. Only once, in the case of the aggadah that speaks of the Messiah sitting at the gates of Rome, does R. Isaac offer an interpretation on both levels—hidden and revealed—and here he states that he was compelled to defend the manifest meaning by the exigencies of Christian disputation.[133] Otherwise, one has the impression that even where it is not explicitly stated, the esoteric interpretation supplants rather than supplements the peshat. Some statements are really about "the messianic king, a king of flesh and blood"; others, spoken "in the esoteric manner," only appear to be about the traditional Messiah but are actually about something entirely different.

A few quotations will establish the basic assumptions behind the allegorical approach to the messianic statements of the Talmud.

> The sages, may their memory be a blessing, used "son of David" here [Sanh., 97a] as a figure for the human intellect and soul . . . Just as the primary purpose for the existence of the human species is to perfect the soul while it is in the body so it can remain after the body, the true purpose for man of the messianic king (for whose saving help we eagerly await) in bringing us out of this long exile, is that we be free and prepared to achieve the desired purpose of the human race, with no enemy or adversary reducing us to servitude. We will then be good [enough] for everyone to perfect his soul without undo difficulty, so that it will not be destroyed with the destruction of the body. Therefore, they used "son of David" as a metaphor for the intellect cleaving to human matter but remaining after it [as] a blessing if one strives to perfect it during his physical life.[134]

Or, more simply:

> The sages, may their memory be a blessing, have spoken here [Sanh., 98a] through concealment, riddle, and parable [be-derekh

hester, hidah, u-mashal] about the intellect cleaving to human matter, which is called in their language "Messiah" in various places, because it is the purpose of man to anoint it to be king over all the other faculties of his body.[135]

The nature and function of the Messiah in the traditional sense, as understood by R. Isaac in accordance with this discussion, make the term an appropriate code word for the ideal of the human intellect.

Once the meaning of the basic word is established, the corresponding significance of other traditional terms follows naturally. The Messiah's donkey (*hamur*), following the well-established play on words, represents the matter of the human body (*homer*).[136] The "birth pangs of the Messiah" signify the conflict between the intellect and the impulse to do evil, which takes place within each individual soul.[137] The "days of the Messiah" refer to the period of life in which the intellect becomes strong enough to achieve the goal for which it was intended.[138] "Redemption" means the liberation of the intellect from the body as it returns to its place of origin.[139]

Even the doctrine of the two messiahs, Ephraimite and Davidic, is allegorically interpreted. In the extant writings of R. Isaac, this interpretation occurs only once, but it is introduced by the remark that he has already explained how the sages spoke in many places about the two messiahs "in the esoteric manner."[140] Nowhere in the extant writings is this doctrine discussed according to the peshat. R. Isaac argues that the word "son" is used in the expressions *Meshiah ben David* and *Meshiah ben Yosef*, as in certain Biblical phrases ("sons of the prophets" and "O ye children, hearken unto me"), to mean one who follows in the path of another. Therefore, the "Messiah son of David" represents all those who, like David, had a strong natural inclination to sin but who have confessed, returned to God, mastered their nature, and actualized their intellect, making it "anointed as king over all members of the household" (all faculties of the body). "Messiah son of Joseph," in contrast, refers to all those who are good by natural inclination, as was Joseph.

This distinction is then applied rather ingeniously to the statement "The son of David will not come except in a generation that is entirely innocent or entirely guilty" (*Sanh.*, 98a). "Generation" here means the faculties and impulses of the body. A "generation entirely innocent," like the Messiah son of Joseph, refers to a person in whom all these faculties endeavor to aid the intellect and to anoint it as king over them. A "generation entirely guilty," like the Messiah son of David, stands for the person in whom the physical faculties are aligned with the impulse to do evil, so that the intellect must struggle to overcome them every day. The statement therefore reflects the division of opinion among the sages themselves as to which of these two types is higher.[141]

The allegorical approach is used consistently by R. Isaac for Talmudic passages dealing with the chronology of the messianic age. All such passages are transposed to the human life, which is divided in accordance with the statement at hand. For example, in his comment on *Avodah Zarah,* 9a—"Six thousand years will the world exist, two thousand chaos, two thousand Torah, two thousand the days of the Messiah"—R. Isaac argues that the sages were referring to the three divisions of the human life. They used numbers in the thousands of years in order to conceal their meaning, as he says he has already explained in interpreting the statement "Six thousand years will the world exist and one [thousand] it shall be desolate (*Rosh Hashana,* 31a).[142] We are told that there are many other instances of this technique scattered throughout the Talmud.

This principle established, the correlation is relatively simple. The first two thousand years are the initial two decades of life, the period of childhood. They are called "chaos" because in them nothing constructive is achieved; all is vanity, under the domination of the physical impulses. The next era, called "Torah," is the period between ages twenty and forty. Here "Torah" means proper social behavior and ethical conduct. By the time a man reaches age twenty, he has reached physical perfection and is capable of choosing ethical good; during the next twenty years, he must develop ethical perfection by overpowering the impulses toward sin. Finally, "days of the Messiah" signifies the years after age forty, when one is prepared for the full actualization of the intellect. Just as the entire people will be free to engage in intellectual activity when the Messiah brings them out of exile, so the individual, upon reaching the age when the physical forces abate, is free to perfect his intellect so that it will be "anointed with oil" to reach the highest level.[143]

This system is applied in greater detail and with some variations in R. Isaac's explication of the "seven-year cycle [at the end of which] the son of David comes" (*Sanh.,* 97a). Here each year represents a decade of life. "In the first year, this verse will be fulfilled: 'And I will cause it to rain upon one city and cause it not to rain upon another city' " (Amos 4:7). This refers to the absence of intellect during the first ten years of life, for the prophets used the descent of dew or rain as an allegorical representation of intellectual apprehension. "In the second, the arrows of hunger will be sent forth" represents the second decade, in which the youth begins his study of Torah and commandments. There is still no rain of true comprehension, and pangs of hunger are felt as the intellect begins to strengthen itself and make its demands known. During the third decade, the body is at the peak of its strength; nature boils within, frustrating the growing desire to actualize the intellect and resulting in the "great famine." "Men, women, and children will die," meaning that all faculties of the body and the soul will be drawn after the impulse to sin. In the fourth decade there is "plenty and no plenty": the intellect begins to attain true conceptions, but these are still not consistent, and therefore the "plenty" is only partial.

The age of forty, beginning the fifth "year," or decade of life, marks a turning point. The body can no longer overpower the intellect, and so there is "great plenty" of intellectual conceptions. R. Isaac points out that the language of the aggadah, "The Torah will return to its disciples," poses a problem for his interpretation, for the word "returns" logically implies that it was there previously, yet this does not seem to fit the course of individual development in life. The solution is that the sages were referring to the innate potential for intellectual achievement, which is neglected while the physical powers are gaining strength. It is therefore appropriate to speak of Torah, or intellectual comprehension, as returning. During the sixth decade, there is a constant increase in wisdom as the intellect rules over a soul that is peaceful and serene, and God may respond with "voices" or "sounds," representing the lowest stage of prophecy. The "wars" in the seventh decade are the struggles of the perfect to abandon the flesh entirely, in order to keep it from interfering with the purest possible activity of the intellect. Finally, "at the conclusion of the septennate, the son of David will come," that is, the intellect, which has reached perfection, will leave the body in order to perceive God directly.

The end of the passage is interpreted in a similar manner. "R. Joseph demurred: 'But so many septennates have passed, yet he has not come!' " This alludes to the many individuals who endeavored throughout their lives to reach the goal of intellectual perfection, yet were unsuccessful. Abaye's response, "There were voices, there were not wars," refers to the fact that people may reach the lower levels of prophecy through the power of their imagination and intellect, but extremely few reach the ultimate goal of total mastery over their bodies. The final remark, "Moreover, have they occurred in this order?" reminds us that many die before the age of seventy, leaving the full progression incomplete.[144] In this way, the entire passage is transferred from the realm of historical, eschatological speculation to the realm of individual biography. The subject is no longer national redemption but the individual philosopher's pursuit of perfection.

The two critical points in the human life span with regard to the coming of the Messiah are at age forty and at the very end of life, age seventy. R. Isaac incorporates both of these into his schema in commenting upon the statements "[The third] two thousand is the days of the Messiah," and "At the end of the seven-year cycle, the son of David will come." He acknowledges a difference of opinion among the sages themselves in his comment on a passage quoted as follows: "R. Eliezer said, the days of the Messiah for Israel are forty years; R. Elazar b. Azariah said seventy years" (*Sanh.*, 99a). In the printed texts of the gemara, each position is supported by a proof verse (Ps. 95:10 and Isa. 23:15) which indicates that the sages are speaking about periods that *last* forty and seventy years respectively. R. Isaac ignores the proof texts and focuses exclusively on the statements, which could be interpreted to mean "The days of the Messiah for Israel [begin at] forty years or [at] seventy years."

The first position reflects the fact that there is no true intellect before one reaches age forty because the boiling of the natural impulses prevents one from attaining perfection. Beginning at age forty, with the weakening of the physical powers and the aging of the evil impulse, the intellect may be anointed king over the faculties of body and soul. The second position maintains that throughout the entire seventy-year life span, the body serves as a barrier to full intellectual comprehension of God. Only after death, when the intellect is separated from the body, can the "Messiah" truly enter his palace of perfection.[145]

One final example of the allegorical interpretation of messianic passages deals not with messianic chronology but with the actual person of the Messiah. R. Isaac's discussion of the manifest meaning of the Messiah at the gate of Rome, which he disputes with a Christian scholar, is preceded by an extensive allegorical interpretation of the aggadah in question. As is his practice, he begins with the reality of historical Rome and then applies this reality to the hidden content of the statement. It is known that Rome, representing the Christian Church, hates the Jewish people because the Jews are closer to the truth than any other nation. While the Church imitates Israel, pretending to follow the ways of the Torah, it also oppresses us, attempting to eradicate all memory of the Torah from our midst.

Therefore, the Messiah at the gate of Rome represents the intellect oppressed by the "old king," the impulse toward evil, and the natural tendency of all other faculties of the body. The intellect, like the Jewish people and its Messiah, is hated because its aspirations are fundamentally different from the desires of the body wherein it dwells. He then offers an alternative interpretation, in which "Rome" has a positive connotation, connected with the Hebrew root that expresses an exalted stature. The prophet Micah (2:3) states that "You must not walk upright" (*romah*), warning the people that they must subdue their hearts before God, for even the intellect of the perfect man cannot fully enter God's presence during life. So long as it is in the body, it must remain at the gate of the most exalted status. Only after death can it enter the actual palace of the king.[146]

As the rest of the passage is decoded, the Messiah "sitting among the poor who suffer from illness" comes to represent the intellect among the faculties of body and soul, which inevitably suffer because of bad foods, changes in weather, superfluous indulgences, and other obstacles inherent in the nature of matter. Yet there is a difference between the sickness of the intellect and that of the corporeal faculties. The poor at the gate "untie [their bandages] all at once, and rebandage them all together," meaning that the body suffers from illness, then is cured, then suffers again when another illness occurs. The Messiah "does not untie one until he has rebandaged one," for the intellect suffers from one uninterrupted sickness resulting from its very presence in the body, a sickness from which it cannot be cured until it is separated from the body at death. R. Joshua approaches the Messiah and asks when he will come, realizing that it is within his own power to bring his intellect to a state of perfection, anointing it king over all other powers of body and soul. The answer, "Today, if you hearken to His voice," implies that whenever the intellect finds itself fully actualized, it has no more need for the body and can depart. The rest of the details in the passage, according to R. Isaac, serve "to make the allegory realistic and to hide it from those who are not naturally prepared to accept their words in the manner of concealment. But the enlightened will understand the truth."[147]

Was R. Isaac the first to make the allegorical transfer of these messianic statements in the Talmud to the individual philosopher's aspirations toward perfection? I am unable to find a clear source for this mode of interpretation. All that can be said at this point is that Moses ibn Tibbon, a contemporary of R. Isaac's, appears to have been familiar with the approach.[148] A basis for comparison can be found in the writings of two well-known and rather eccentric younger contemporaries. First there is Levi b. Abraham, the bête noire of the Provençal traditionalists, whose encyclopedic and controversial work Livyat Hen was written about a generation after the Commentary on the Aggadot. Elucidating the allegorical significance of the Biblical sons of Adam, the author cites the Midrash Rabbah on Genesis 4:25, "She saw that that seed would arise from another source, namely, the king Messiah" (Gen. R., 23:5). The meaning, says Levi, is that the intellect "is spiritual, not derived from the body and its nature. They compared it in stature to the king Messiah, who is extremely lofty and exalted . . . Just as the king Messiah, may he be revealed quickly in our days, will build Jerusalem below, so the intellect when actualized will build Jerusalem on high." The association of "Messiah" and "intellect" leads him to the statement "The son of David will not come until all the souls destined for bodies are exhausted" (AZ, 5a). "This means that the acquired intellect will not sprout until the corporeal faculties turn aside . . . They called it the 'son of David' because 'Solomon' alludes to the perfected and actualized hylic intellect."

The passage continues with an allegorical interpretation of "Messiah son of Joseph," referring to the practical intellect, and "Messiah son of

David," referring to the theoretical intellect. In this light, the conundrum "There is no messiah for Israel" is interpreted to mean that "they will have no need for the 'Messiah son of Joseph,'" representing the practical, for they will already have abolished its mode and operation of thought by employing and actualizing the theoretical intellect . . . It is possible that the rabbi who disputed R. Hillel's statement [in the gemara] did not understand the esoteric meaning of his words, and he thought that according to the simple meaning the statement made no sense, and [wondered] how a saintly man could say such a thing."[149] Like R. Isaac, Levi b. Abraham uses allegorization to transpose messianic statements of the aggadah into an inner, spiritual realm. It is not at all unlikely that Levi was familiar with the commentaries of R. Isaac. Unfortunately, because of the fragmentary nature of the extant writings of both men, this connection cannot at present be demonstrated.

The second author is Abraham Abulafia, who developed an original system of speculative mysticism and may himself have nurtured messianic aspirations. In his Hebrew University lectures, Gershom Scholem wrote of Abulafia:

> Indeed, his messianic homilies are generally ambiguous, and most of his statements about the Messiah are not in the traditional sense of a redeemer who will lead his people to freedom. Their meaning is that a man may transform himself into the Messiah for himself. The secret of the Messiah is the redemption of a man by himself through supreme spiritual transformation, toward cleaving with God.[150]

While Scholem provides few illustrations from Abulafia's works, a recent doctoral dissertation by Moses Idel, devoted to the writings and teachings of Abulafia and based primarily on manuscript material, gives a somewhat more complete picture. In a chapter on Abulafia's messianic doctrine, Idel argues that there are actually two views of messianism present: the traditional notion of national redemption through the reestablishment of the Jewish kingdom and the concept of messianism as a process that occurs within the soul. The following discussion of the term "Messiah" is quoted from Abulafia's *Sefer ha-Melitz*:

> The noun "Messiah" is used for three different matters. First, "Messiah" is used for the true active intellect, as alluded to in the verse "And this is his name whereby he shall be called, The Lord is our righteousness" (Jer. 23:6). And "Messiah" is used for the man who will bring us out of exile, from under the power of the nations, through the strength that will flow abundantly to him from the active intellect. Finally, "Messiah" is used for the material intellect of the human being, which is the redeemer that brings influence to bear upon the soul and all of its higher faculties that are under the power

of the corporeal "kings" and their peoples and their degenerate faculties of lust. It is a commandment and an obligation to reveal this
matter to every enlightened man of Israel so as to bring about his
salvation.[151]

This allegorical interpretation of the term "Messiah," used by Abulafia in
conjunction with Biblical verses but not apparently for esoteric explication of aggadic passages, is indeed close to that which we have seen as the
basis for R. Isaac's interpretation of the messianic aggadot of *Sanhedrin*.
To this we may add a description of ecstatic communion with God in one
of Abulafia's published works: "After that, if he is worthy, the spirit of
the living God will pass over him, and the spirit of the Lord will rest upon
him . . . and they will seem to him as if they have anointed his entire
body, from head to toe, with the anointing oil, and he will be the anointed
[Messiah] of the Lord."[152]

Did Abulafia know the interpretations of R. Isaac, and was he influenced by them? If so, it would be a hitherto unsuspected component of
the variegated forces that produced this turbulent personality. It should
be clear, however, that while the terminology is similar, there is an important difference in approach. R. Isaac, the commentator, begins with a
series of Talmudic statements about the Messiah and transmutes them
into an expression of his philosophical doctrine. Abulafia is not an exe-
gete; his point of departure is not the ancient text but his own mystical
experience, which he expresses in traditional messianic terminology in
order to explain and to validate it. As he does not appear to use his spiritual messianism in the interpretation of rabbinic statements, no direct
influence is demonstrable. It is possible that R. Isaac, or someone else,
triggered a new association in the mind of Abulafia, an association then
developed within a totally different context; it is also possible that the
spiritualization of messianic terminology was the fruit of Abulafia's own
imagination, without any external literary stimulus.[153]

Some conclusions can now be drawn about R. Isaac's messianic doctrine as it emerges from his comments on the messianic passages of the
Talmud. Lip service is paid to the traditional doctrine of the Messiah who
will deliver the Jewish people from exile; and in his dispute with a Christian sage, R. Isaac argues vehemently that no valid interpretation of any
rabbinic passage can refute the belief that the Messiah is still to come. But
analysis of the role this doctrine plays in R. Isaac's understanding of
Judaism leads to the conclusion that it is minor indeed. The Messiah and
the changes traditionally associated with the messianic age—freedom
from the oppression of foreign governments, restoration to the land of
Israel, renewal of autonomous sovereignty, rebuilding of the Temple—
are not ends in themselves but means to a higher goal: the achievement of

perfection, philosophically understood. The Messiah will benefit the masses by creating conditions that will help them reach this goal, increasing the chances for all Jews to attain eternal life for their souls.

So far the doctrine is Maimonidean. But R. Isaac goes farther and argues that for the philosophical elite who can achieve this goal under existing conditions, the Messiah serves no purpose whatsoever. In fact for them, the entire concept of the Messiah is transformed so that it applies no longer to the realm of national history but to the individual's inner pursuit of perfection. This is the secret message of the sages. Its practical implications, at least for the select few, are clear. Messianic speculation and messianic activism are wasteful diversions. All effort should be concentrated on the cultivation and perfection of the intellect through philosophical study. It is in this direction that the true redemption lies.

V

TORAH, MITZVOT,
AND HALAKHA

THE AGGADAH is only one component of traditional Jewish literature, so any exposition of Judaism that restricts itself to the aggadah is necessarily incomplete. Perhaps for this reason, R. Isaac occasionally felt impelled to range beyond his paramount preoccupation and to express his views about the nature of the Torah, the commandments, and the halakha, topics central to any system of Jewish thought. During the thirteenth century, important new doctrines were being expounded in northern Europe by the German Pietists[1] and in southern Europe by the Kabbalists.[2] The kabbalistic teachings, in particular, were to have a profound impact on the subsequent course of Jewish history. At the same time, philosophically oriented Jews were grappling with the implications of insights bequeathed by their towering predecessors, R. Saadia Gaon and Maimonides.[3] While little that was new was added to the philosophical doctrine of Torah and mitzvot during this period, it is of interest to see basic assumptions restated, reformulated, and applied in new ways.[4] The extant works of R. Isaac provide ample support for this generalization.

The Concept of Torah

Following the well-beaten path of Jewish philosophers, R. Isaac assumes that the Torah was given by God not as an arbitrary test of man's obedience or as a means for the Jew to effect changes in the higher realm of being but as a direct benefit to those who received it. The gloss on the first statement of *Avot* explains that the giving of the Torah was a manifestation of God's providential compassion for human beings and His desire that they achieve immortality by perfecting their souls during their earthly lives. He gave them His Torah "to guide them so that they would walk in the straight path and not destroy the fabric of conduct between human beings, and so that they could perfect their souls by knowing

121

their Creator, apprehending Him without false speculation."[5] This theme, that the Torah teaches both correct conduct and true knowledge of God, is frequently reiterated. Later in CAT, he writes, "The Torah was given to human beings for the benefit of those who receive it, to direct the people always toward the good, to teach them the beneficial knowledge of what Israel should do and how it should act correctly."[6] But the ultimate purpose of the Torah is to help man "attain knowledge of the Most High and to apprehend the truth, avoiding false speculation."[7] When the word "Torah" appears in aggadic statements it almost invariably is interpreted to refer to "the unique part of [the Torah]: the knowledge of God and of His immaterial angels."[8] The equation of Torah with philosophy, or more specifically metaphysics, has important implications for the understanding of the aggadic message.

The twofold purpose of the Torah is reflected in R. Isaac's classification of the commandments. When necessary for the purpose of exegesis, a more traditional classification may be used. Interpreting the steps leading to the religious ideal in *Avodah Zarah*, 20b, "Strictness leads to zeal . . . ," R. Isaac explains that "strictness" refers to the observance of the negative commandments, while "zeal" refers to the performance of the positive commandments.[9] But these categories are not nearly so important to him as the classification based on philosophical considerations. In one place, he speaks of those commandments that benefit the body alone, those that benefit the soul alone, and those that benefit body and soul together.[10] More common is a twofold classification based on the dual purpose of the Torah itself.

This idea is introduced in the comment on the statement "Excellent is the study of Torah along with *derekh eretz*" (*Avot*, 2:2).

> They divided the commandments of the Torah into two categories. The first, prior in time, consists of those good qualities that provide proper order between people, so that no one will hurt another and the fabric of conduct between human beings will not be destroyed. These are the positive and negative commandments that lead man to choose the good and to flee from its opposite. They called this *"derekh eretz,"* for they are needed for proper social behavior, so that society might be preserved. But the unique category of the commandments, last in study and in attainment, are the rational qualities, necessary for true belief, so that men will not destructively conceive anything false or impossible in relation to God.[11]

Later in CAT, the terminology applied to this passage is made explicit: the Torah is composed of "practical commandments" (*mitzvot ma'asiyot*), which regulate the social order by teaching proper interpersonal behavior, and "rational commandments" (*mitzvot sikhliyot*), which bring to the mind an understanding of the truth.[12] In a parallel passage of CMR, a slightly different terminology is used: "They divided the command-ments into two categories. The first is the rational commandments, which come to bring man true belief about God, and the second is all the politi-cal commandments [kol mitzvah medinit], which teach people to conduct themselves equitably with their neighbors, so that they will not entangle their paths. All the commandments written in the Torah are included in these two categories, each one in its appropriate place, whether political or rational."[13]

This terminology represents a synthesis of different elements. The term "rational commandments" was given currency in Jewish thought by R. Saadia Gaon in the third chapter of his Emunot ve-De'ot. Saadia used this term, in contrast with "traditional commandments" (mitzvot shim-'iyot), to refer to commandments required by reason and merely reiter-ated by revelation. While these include the commandments to know, submit to, and serve God, the majority of such commandments regulate and establish norms for the conduct between human beings, which is pre-cisely the description of the nonrational, practical or political command-ments in R. Isaac's classification.[14] The term "rational commandments" may have been taken from Saadia, but the content of that term is clearly derived from some other source.

This source is undoubtedly Maimonides' Guide. Maimonides rejects the use of the term "rational commandments,"[15] but he provides two dis-tinctions that form the basis for R. Isaac's division. The first is the dis-tinction in Guide, I, 2, between the categories true and false, which are known through reason, and right and wrong, which are determined by convention. This distinction is applied to the Ten Commandments in Guide, II, 33: the first two utterances are intelligible to human reason, while the rest are conventional principles, which had to be revealed through prophecy. This is the background for R. Isaac's assertion that the nonrational, "practical" commandments include positive and nega-tive injunctions to "choose the good and to flee from its opposite." The second distinction, the basis of Maimonides' own classification of the commandments, is the "well-being of the body" as against the "well-being of the soul." The first is established by regulating the relations be-tween human beings, by prohibiting violent, antisocial behavior, and by cultivating ethical virtues useful in society. The second is achieved by providing correct opinions communicated to everyone according to his capacity to comprehend them (Guide, III, 27).

R. Isaac has taken Saadia's term "rational commandments" and in-vested it with new meaning by applying it to a Maimonidean category of commandments addressed to the intellect and intended to teach it true doctrine. As for the other class of commandments, for which he uses the terms "practical" and "political," the first, *mitzvot ma'asiyot*, may be a fusion of the traditional phrase *mitzvot aseh* (positive commandments) and the philosophical term *sekhel ma'asi* (practical intellect), through which, according to Maimonides, man distinguishes between proper and improper actions.[16] The second term, *mitzvot mediniyot*, is more unusual; it is probably based on Maimonides' assertion that the commandments relating in the broad sense to the well-being of the body are necessary for the stability of the state (*Guide*, III, 27).[17]

Let us look at these categories more closely. One function of the practical commandments is to foster the acquisition of good moral qualities. This is accomplished in accordance with standard Aristotelian-Maimonidean ethical theory. The Torah teaches the way of the mean, and whoever follows it will be moderate in every respect, whether in his eating habits or in his relations with women.[18] It commands the repudiation of all things superfluous, restricting people to what is necessary for maintaining health.[19] But it never restricts to excess, never becomes a burden. It does not, for example, command daily fasts, which would be a source of great affliction and possibly harm to human beings. The Torah never exceeds what is necessary to cultivate the desired dispositions.[20]

As for conduct between human beings, R. Isaac points to various principles that summarize the relevant commandments. The Ten Commandments are the "essence of the Torah, with all the others secondary to them,"[21] but the most encompassing injunction is to "love your neighbor as yourself." The statement in *Avot*, 2:4, "Make his will as your will . . . ," is interpreted in its entirety as applying not to the relationship between God and man but to the relationship between human beings: "You already understand that the Torah intends for man to love his fellow man as he loves himself, for the entire people descends from one person, and all are responsible one for the other, commanded to sustain each other in life. Here the sages warned every Israelite to love his neighbor as himself, and to nullify his will before that of the other, [acting] in accordance with the qualities of that neighbor who is good and not in accordance with his own qualities if they are the opposite of these."[22] Similarly, explaining the characterization " 'What is mine is yours and what is yours is mine'— *am ha-aretz*" (*Avot*, 5:10), R. Isaac points out that making one's own possessions available to a neighbor in time of need is appropriate for one who "speaks and acts in accordance with the Torah, . . . which focuses on this in most of its commandments, saying 'You shall love your neighbor as yourself.' It did not warn him to love another more than himself but as himself, while the other loves him also in the same manner. Thus, there will be peaceful relations between them. This is a good, moderate quality for men, and through it the fabric of society will endure."[23] Both statements from *Avot* are related to the commandment of loving one's neighbor, which is generalized to represent the entire realm of interpersonal relationships ordained by the Torah.

The negative formulation of this principle is the well-known statement of Hillel, "That which is hateful to you, do not do to your neighbor" (*Shab.*, 31a), described by R. Isaac as a "great general rule for most of the negative commandments of the Torah."[24] The practical implications of this rule can be seen in a discussion of the prohibition against taking interest from a Jew: "It is repugnant and difficult for any man to have to add 20 percent each year, or periodically, to the principal, and to give it to one who has lent him money. And just as this seems evil to the debtor, so it is commanded of his brother who extends his hand not to take interest from him, as the sages warned when they said, 'That which is hateful to you, do not unto your neighbor.' For this is a great general rule of the Torah, honored in God's sight: if one observes this rule in his conduct toward others, he will do what is good and not sin."[25] In another context, we are told that all the commandments regulating relations between human beings are summarized in Hillel's rule so that even the masses, women, and children can know them.[26] This is the basis of a stable society; all of the political commandments merely provide details to implement this general principle.

The rational commandments differ from the others in several ways. They are ultimately more important than those commandments that seek to regulate behavior, for they are the "essence, and all the others are secondary to them."[27] Indeed, the word "torah" is often interpreted as referring precisely to those commandments that lead to the knowledge of God. A second important difference is that all the practical commandments can be known through tradition. But the rational commandments must not be accepted through tradition alone; they must be internalized so that the intellect of each individual will participate in observing them.[28]

This is the meaning of the statement " 'I am' and 'You shall not have' [the first two of the Ten Commandments] we heard from the Almighty" (*Makkot*, 24a). This Talmudic statement is associated several times in CAT with the doctrine that the rational commandments must be known independently by each individual,[29] but the clearest exposition is in a passage of CMR that recapitulates much of what I have concluded so far. The midrash states, "At the instant when Israel heard at Sinai 'I am,' their souls left them. So the commandment returned to the Holy One, blessed be He . . . and He sweetened the Divine communication for them" (*Num. R.*, 10:1):

"I am" and "You shall not have," commandments inscribed on the tablets, were both rational commandments for the people, and both have the same good purpose in duplicate: to enable the people to attain true knowledge of the One who commanded it, to affirm His absolute unity and repudiate all corporeality, duality, and everything impossible for God by definition . . . They took here the utterance "I am" to represent all the rational commandments written in the Torah, and taught that the souls of the people "left them," because of this one representative rational commandment. For by sharpening their intellect through this, and by purifying their intellect of matter whenever they investigate it so as to see with full clarity, it becomes inscribed on the tablet of their heart . . . [Furthermore], they had to know the meaning with their own minds. Tradition would bring them no benefit with regard to the rational commandment; they had to apprehend by themselves the truths about God, without false speculation about Him, as the Babylonians taught when they said, " 'I am' and 'You shall not have' we heard from the Almighty." The same is true of every rational commandment written in the Torah . . .

And they said, "At that moment, He sweetened the Divine communication for them." The rest of the utterances that came from heaven were sweet for the people in that these commandments did not require mortification of the body . . . Most of the rest were political commandments which Moses received from the Highest One on the mountain, telling the Israelites to act toward each other peaceably and equitably, not to contend with each other, not to provoke strife or anger in their midst, and not to act presumptuously anymore. These commandments were sweet to receive and to hear, for through the power of their tongue, they could inquire of God to know the reason for each commandment and why God commanded it. And even when they turned to follow their material component, they could concentrate their thoughts upon these political commandments to know rationally that they were given so that no one would harm his brother.[30]

The rational commandments imply intellectual comprehension on the part of each individual, not mere acceptance of a tradition; this in turn necessitates an effort to escape the body, which serves as an obstacle to full rational apprehension. By contrast, the political commandments can be observed even by people who are not striving to transcend their bodies. While the rational commandments are ultimately more important, the political commandments, which do not make such severe demands, are more "sweet."

With regard to the performance of the political commandments, we find a theme not hitherto mentioned. While they are performed with the body, they must not be performed by the body alone. The mechanical performance of the commandments without any concentration of intellectual effort is all too common, and it leads to disastrous results:

For what benefit accrues to a man if he fulfils the words of the Torah in general and in specific detail, and fulfils the words of the Torah as understood by the early sages, without investigating, by inquiring of God why He commanded that which He spoke. In this category you will find innumerable Jews whose knowledge of Torah and commandment is limited to [mechanical] reading. They open their mouths and chirp like all the other animals, making noise without comprehension. But when someone asks them what this means and why it was commanded, they are silent confounded, unable to reply . . .[31]

In another context, the gravity of this situation is stressed with great force:

The purpose of the commandments of the Torah is for man to apprehend from them the One who commanded them. Here [Sanh., 99a] the sages came to teach that these commandments require concentration [kavvanah] if men are to derive from them knowledge of their Creator, so that He will bring them to the life of the world which endures and save their souls from death . . . But if they perform them as the "commandment of men learned by rote," without any other purpose or probing of the commandment to learn for what reason it was commanded and who is the One who commands, they will walk in darkness, to reproaches and to everlasting abhorhence.[32]

The mechanical performance of the commandments has no real effect on the fate of the soul. While R. Isaac warns against laxity and procrastination,[33] he also insists that performance must be accompanied by an intellectual effort if the ultimate goal is to be attained. This goal, the knowledge of God, can be reached through study of the commandments, as it can be reached through study of the realm of creation.[34] The rational purpose of the mitzvot leads from the commandments themselves to the One who commands.

Ta'amei Mitzvot

In analyzing R. Isaac's treatment of ta'amei mitzvot (the rational reasons for the commandments of the Torah), it is important to remember that a large proportion of his work is no longer extant. His commentary on the Torah has been lost, and we can assume that much relevant material would have been found there; indeed, referring to that work, he states that he has discussed "at length" the commandment to eat bitter herbs on Pesah in his comment on the section beginning "Come to Pharaoh."[35] The lost portions of the Aggadot Commentary and the Commentary on the Midrash Rabbah must also have contained a wealth of material on this subject, for there is no reason to suspect that what remains is not representative of the whole. Nevertheless, the extant pages enable us to examine R. Isaac's discussion of a number of commandments and to draw some conclusions about his general approach.

Any analysis of R. Isaac's rationalization of the commandments must be based on a comparison with the locus classicus for ta'amei mitzvot, the third part of Maimonides' *Guide*.[36] Except for one passage dealing with sacrifices,[37] R. Isaac does not refer directly to Maimonides in this context. Yet his treatment of certain commandments is obviously dependent on that of the Rambam, while in other cases he expands upon and develops the kernel of thought expressed in the *Guide*. In contrast, there are commandments for which R. Isaac gives a reason clearly different from that of Maimonides and still others for which he gives a reason where the master was silent.

Maimonidean Reason Accepted or Expanded

Some of the discussions reveal little originality. Following Maimonides, R. Isaac maintains that the reason why certain foods are prohibited by the Torah is that they are harmful to the body and cause disease.[38] The purpose of the Sabbath is twofold: it compels people to turn aside from the tasks necessitated by their physical and social nature and to devote one day out of seven to contemplation of God and study of His creation, and it confirms the doctrine of Creation in the minds of all.[39] The neck of the heifer is broken on the site where an unsolved murder occurred so that the owner of the field, which may no longer be cultivated, will do everything within his power to discover the murder and bring him to justice.[40] No new insight is revealed in any of these explanations; they merely reiterate reasons that would have been known to anyone familiar with the traditions of Jewish philosophy.

The discussion of the accidental homicide shows that Maimonides' rationale has been somewhat expanded. The Torah provides that the killer flee to cities of refuge and remain there until the death of the High Priest (Num. 35:25). The problem with this rule is that the punishment seems unfair, for in some cases the exile will last for many years while in others it will last for only a brief period.[41] Maimonides attempts to resolve this apparent injustice by explaining that the killer goes into exile because the anger of the "blood avenger" cools down when the cause of his rage is hidden from sight. The death of the High Priest reconciles the relatives of the slain person, "for it is a natural phenomenon that we find consolation in our misfortune when the same misfortune or a greater one has befallen another person. Amongst us no death causes more grief than that of the High Priest" (*Guide*, III, 40).

R. Isaac's treatment of this commandment is an expanded paraphrase of these few lines of the *Guide*. He makes it clear that the exile to the cities of refuge is required not for the punishment of the killer but for his protection, "so that he will not be in the presence of the blood avengers, for when they see him, their natural feelings for the relative he killed are aroused, and they passionately desire to take vengeance upon him." Divine wisdom has decreed that the killer remain in exile until the death of the High Priest,

> for when the people hear from afrar that the priest who is greater than his brothers, more distinguished than any in his family or generation, has died and been gathered to his people, then the blood avengers will be consoled over the dead man killed some years before. They will consider that man goes to his death every day, with no escape, and that if the person in question had not killed their relative in an untimely manner, his end might have come anyway, due to sickness . . . Thus they will be comforted for the one who was accidentally killed.[42]

By exploring the psychology of grief and revenge, the author tries to make explicit that which is implicit in the *Guide*.

The laws relating to the Nazirite (see Num. 6:1-21) represent an area passed over quickly by Maimonides and discussed in full detail by R. Isaac. Maimonides' explanation is rather simplistic: the Torah prevents the Nazirite from indulging in alcoholic beverages because such indulgence has been the ruination of many in ancient and in modern times (*Guide*, III, 48). He does not explain why this prohibition is not applied to the entire people, nor does he address the view that the Nazirite is a sinner because he has denied himself the enjoyment of wine (*Nazir*, 19a), nor does he discuss the other major provision—that the Nazirite is forbidden to shave his hair. R. Isaac, commenting on the relevant passages of *Numbers Rabbah*, confronts all these issues.

He begins by employing a favorite distinction between the person naturally inclined toward evil because of potent physical impulses and the person naturally inclined toward good. The institution of Naziritism is intended only for the first. Such a person needs to mortify and afflict his body by depriving himself even of that which is permitted in order to subdue the tumultuous raging of his impulses. The obvious example is Samson. By contrast, one who is naturally inclined toward good should not become a Nazirite. If he vows to afflict his body, it is bad in God's sight. The Babylonians were speaking of this type when they said, "He is called a sinner because he denied himself the enjoyment of wine." God does not want us to refrain from what is permitted and to afflict our bodies for no reaons.[43]

The prohibition against shaving the hair is similarly for the benefit of the individual. A man who displays well-groomed curly locks may be-

come vain and proud, refusing to obey his parents or to heed those who
would criticize him and point out the right way. If, however, he lets his
hair grow unkempt, thereby removing figuratively the crown of narcis-
sism from his head, his heart will be subdued and meek. By disfiguring
himself with long, shaggy hair, he will overcome his impulse toward evil.
Ultimately he will achieve the true crown of intellectual understanding
and vision of God.[44]

Maimonidean Reason Ignored and Rejected

The most interesting passages are those in which R. Isaac shows inde-
pendence from his mentor. Characteristically, he does not explain why
he rejects the Maimonidean interpretation. He simply ignores the discussion in the *Guide* and gives his own explanation as if none other existed.
For example, the general purpose stated in the *Guide* for the laws of ritual
purity and impurity is "to discourage people from entering the sanctuary
in order that their minds be impressed with the greatness of the sanctuary
and approach it with respect and reverence" (III, 35). If people were to
enter the sanctuary too frequently, its impact upon them would be weakened. Therefore, the many types of ritual impurity were promulgated.
The result was that people were not permitted to enter the sanctuary
whenever they liked but only on occasion; in this way, the feelings of
awe and reverence remained powerful (III, 47).

R. Isaac's discussion of this subject ignores the sanctuary entirely. He
maintains that "all of the impure and pure things in the Torah come to
emphasize to men that they must sanctify their souls from the impurity
and filth of matter [the body]."[45] This statement appears in a discussion
of the carcass of a pure fowl. R. Isaac, following Rashi (on Lev. 17:15
and *Shev.*, 7b), points out that this particular law of impurity is anomalous. Other impure things cause impurity by contact, but this causes impurity only when it passes through the esophagus. It is a "decree of the
Scripture," but such decrees are not arbitrary, burdensome, or meaningless; they are for human benefit. The flesh of pure fowl is known to be
tastier than any other kind of meat, but its natural coldness constitutes a
danger to human health. Therefore, the law discourages the frequent eating of fowl by decreeing that the carcass causes impurity if swallowed. In
this way, man is reminded "not to be drawn after the pleasures of the
body in general, and not to crave tasty dishes, for such pleasant food
causes him to become impure, so that he will not ultimately gain wisdom."[46] In this comment, the ground shifts subtly from the ritual-legal
sense of "impure" to the philosophical-metaphorical sense. The commandments relating to ritual impurity teach that one must not allow the
body and its impulses to render the soul impure.

Another example of ritual impurity discussed by R. Isaac is that which comes from contact with a dead body. Maimonides does not explain this as a special case; he merely points out that since this is one of the easiest ways for impurity to come about, the procedure for ending the state of impurity is difficult and prolonged (III, 47). R. Isaac states that he has explained the significance of this type of impurity "in many places in this work of ours." In the extant material, the relevant passage is the comment on the statement "Just as the [unclean] status of a dead person can never be nullified, so the status of an idolatrous offering can never be nullified" (AZ, 50a).

> The impurity which comes from contact with a corpse is for the benefit of those living in the flesh. When one sees the dead man, he will become aware of his own mortality and remember that his day will come, that he too will die just like the deceased. He will therefore guard himself against sinning and fear for his soul to the day of death. To teach this, the sages said that the impure status of the corpse can never be nullified but that it can cause impurity in a living person who touches it even many years after its death, so that man will remember that he is mortal flesh. He will not become defiled by the impurity and filth of matter but rather act throughout his life with purity of heart and with uprightness, fearing lest his soul be destroyed.[47]

Again the ritual impurity has become in one sense a reminder of the dangers lurking in the material component of man and in another sense a metaphor for those dangers.[48] By allowing himself to become contaminated by excessive contact with the moribund body, man runs the risk of bringing about the destruction of the potentially immortal soul.

The same approach is evident in the Midrash Commentary, in relation to the perennially enigmatic red heifer. Maimonides does not go into detail about this ritual, stating merely that the heifer takes onto itself the sin of defilement by contact with the dead. R. Isaac never even mentions tum'at meit in his discussion of the heifer; he seems to assume that his interpretation of this concept is known to the reader.

> The stubborn heifer, red as blood, entirely made into smoke in the Lord's sanctuary, comes once each year to purify all who are impure of soul. The heifer is totally consumed to teach the sinner, whose soul is stubborn and rebellious against the true heavenly Father, Creator of the soul, that he has turned aside from Him, that he is not heeding the reproaches of His instruction and counsel, revealed through the prophets.
>
> The heifer that the priest burns before his eyes will teach him that he will be totally consumed—in matter and form. That which remains of him after he dies will be burned with fire in the valley of the son of Hinnom, established long ago, and it will become ash. Just as

the heifer burned in his sight was stubborn and bad in the eyes of its master, so this man was stubborn before God with regard to all that He commanded him. He therefore bears his sin.[49]

Not every detail of the ritual is interpreted here, but two of the most important requirements are explained. The heifer must never have borne the yoke, because it is intended to represent the person who refuses to bear the yoke of the commandments. And it must be totally burnt—even its skin and flesh and blood—because it illustrates the ultimate destiny of such a person: total annihilation of soul as well as of body. The thrust of the interpretation is to divest the ritual of any magic power. The burning of the red heifer does not change the actual status of anyone. It has a purely representational function. Like the sound of the shofar for Maimonides, it serves as a powerful and dramatic reminder of the right and the wrong way. Whether or not the spectator heeds the message is entirely up to him. But only if he does heed it will his status of impurity be removed.

Reasons Given Where Maimonides Is Silent

Where Maimonides does not give a specific explanation for a commandment, R. Isaac sometimes fills the vacuum. For example, as we shall see, whereas Maimonides merely lists the putting on of tefillin as among the category of those acts intended to remind us continually of God and of our duty to fear and love Him (III, 44), R. Isaac contends that the structure of the phylactery placed on the head represents the three realms of existence and the Deity who is the cause of them all.[50]

In another instance, Deuteronomy 21:17 provides that the first-born son of the father is entitled to a double portion in the father's estate. This particular rule is not explained in the *Guide*, where all the laws of inheritance are lumped together under the principle that man must not "withhold good from those to whom it is due" (III, 42). R. Isaac develops an elaborate theory to explain this provision:

> The Torah verifies God's individual providence over the first-born son, in that He commanded the father to single him out, for his benefit, from the other sons born after him. God had mercy on his soul, and commanded that he be given a double portion of the father's estate, both movable and real property. For he is the first fruits of his parents' strength, having emerged first from the womb. This is a source of permanent fortitude. His entire body will be strong and sound, his intellect will be vigorous, and his heart bold to know his Creator when he grows up. He will not weary of that which his soul desires.
>
> If his father gives him his house full of gold and silver, and he finds precious substance, he will rejoice in his wealth and be pre-

pared in every way to derive from this joy intellectual knowledge of the living God. He will know God increasingly, day by day, and his life will be long. He will not burden his intellect by doing any manner of work at home or abroad; others will do this—farmers and vineyard keepers—but he will be free to dwell in his tent and to seek God to a ripe old age until, before his death, he arrives at full knowledge. For the first-born is naturally strong enough to behold God's goodness forever. His years will be pleasant, and he will live to the age of one hundred.

But the other sons are weak in constitution; their root will not grow old in the earth. They cannot complete the sacred task of attaining true knowledge of God within the short time allotted them. Most of them die young, expelled from the midst of men and snatched away before their time. Even if the father and mother in their leniency want to divide the possessions equally among all the children, and the father's heart moans to love them all, he may not bequeath to each one the same, for the King has ordained that for each portion given to the other sons, the first-born will be given two, and there is no changing this.

For this reason, God loves the first-born more than the other sons of the same father and mother. He did not choose him arbitrarily. For there is no iniquity in Him in robbing the younger brothers. It is only to prepare sustenance for the first-born, so that he may attain wisdom in the end and render strength to his King who has chosen him, for he is better prepared for this than all the other children because of his strength and fortitude.[51]

A number of assumptions underlie this explanation of the Torah's rule. It is assumed that the first-born son is constitutionally the strongest and will have the longest life expectancy.[52] It is assumed that the health of the body is a prerequisite for the ultimate perfection of the intellect, as one cannot concentrate on metaphysics while his body is wracked with pain or while pangs of hunger gnaw within.[53] It is assumed that the ascent on the ladder of knowledge, discipline after discipline, to the pinnacle of intellectual perfection is a difficult and perilous task, which can be accomplished only after many years, near the end of a full lifetime.[54] There is no attempt to demonstrate any of these premises, which form the background for the interpretation.

A further assumption is based on social theory of an elitist nature. Men are not equally endowed with the potential for achieving the ultimate goal. Those who have the proper natural endowment should not be diverted from perfecting their intellects by the burdensome requirement of providing food, clothing, or shelter for themselves and their families. The rest of the society should furnish these physical necessities so that the select few may be free to pursue what is of supreme importance.[55] There-

fore, the first-born son, innately constituted for achieving ultimate perfection, is given a double portion of inheritance and is thereby freed from
the need to worry about trivial, mundane matters.

A second passage is concerned with the taking of interest from non-
Jews.[56] There was a long-standing controversy as to whether or not this
was indeed a commandment. Most legal authorities understood the
words le-nokhri tashikh in Deuteronomy 23:21 to mean, "You may lend
at interest to an alien," conveying permission but no mandate. A few, led
by Maimonides, understood the words to mean, "You shall or must lend
at interest to an alien," expressing a religious obligation.[57] R. Isaac up-
holds the minority view, arguing simply that unless this is counted as a
commandment, there will not be enough to make the required number
(613).

Maimonides gives no reason for this commandment. R. Isaac does,
after first explaining the Talmudic restriction of the Torah precept (BM,
70b-71a, Mak., 24a). Ignoring the reason stated in the gemara,[58] R. Isaac
argues that the rabbis opposed the taking of interest for two reasons.
First, there is a natural antipathy toward the payment of interest, which
always seems unfair to the borrower. Therefore, on the basis of Hillel's
rule, "That which is hateful to you, do not do to your neighbor," described by R. Isaac as the basis of morality in all interpersonal relations,
the Jew is discouraged from taking interest. More important, the motivation for taking interest is covetousness or greed, an ethical quality repugnant because it is bound up with the accumulation of the imaginary good
of material wealth. Once this quality becomes established in the soul, the
desire for money is insatiable. If there is no Gentile who can provide the
coveted profit, the greedy Jew will take interest from another Jew, breaking a negative commandment. This explanation of the Talmudic restriction as a kind of "fence around the Torah" is stated by Rashi, but R. Isaac
places it within the framework of a developed ethical theory.[59]

At the time R. Isaac was writing, this restriction was simply not being
observed by European Jews. In many lands, the lending of money at interest to non-Jews was the basis of Jewish economic existence. R. Isaac
points out that each of the ideal qualities listed in Psalm 15 is exemplified
by a pious individual in the gemara except "He that puts not his money
out on interest," which the rabbis interpreted as referring to loans made
to non-Jews. No example is given, nor could one be found in any generation, for even the best and the wisest of Jews did not refrain from taking
interest from the Gentiles.

Jewish legal authorities were fully aware of the divergence between
contemporary reality and the Talmudic formulation, and they made
various attempts to reconcile this reality with the language of the gemara.[60] R. Isaac characteristically ignores all of those explanations in his
Aggadot Commentary and turns directly to the statement of the Torah:

Divine wisdom decreed that this be commanded to the people for their own benefit. Just as the other commandments come for the benefit of the entire people, so is this beneficial. For it was clearly known to God that the people would have to be punished by exile and that He would uproot them from their land because of their sin, and they would go to a different land, from nation to nation. And if, among the other peoples, they worked in crafts, the Torah would quickly be forgotten from Israel, for they would not have sufficient time to follow the proper ways of the Torah. They would thus be swallowed up in the midst [of their Gentile neighbors], and they would lose their way like [the Gentiles], because of the great toil necessary to provide sustenance and food for their households. But God gave them provisions for the road and good advice, that they could lend their money among the Gentiles for directly stipulated interest, so that the good among them would be free to teach the people knowledge and to show them the way to go. Thus they would be able to endure among [the nations], and the Torah would not be forgotten from their offspring to eternity.

For all the differences between this and the previous passage from the Midrash Commentary concerning the inheritance of the first-born, the underlying similarity of approach is unmistakable. In both, the purpose of the commandment is to free at least the elite among the Jews from the burdens of providing for physical necessities so that they will have sufficient leisure to master the most important teachings of the Torah, leading to knowledge of God. This argument is precisely the reverse of that in the Talmud, where Rabina maintains that the rabbis restricted the lending of money on interest to Gentiles lest this lead to greater contact and assimilation of non-Jewish patterns of behavior. R. Isaac insists that without taking interest from the Gentiles, an enterprise that enables Jews to generate income with little expenditure of time, there would be no opportunity for study, and the Jews would become assimilated into their host societies.

This assessment of the cultural implications of different economic enterprises may be unique for R. Isaac's time.[61] As a statement of ta'amei mitzvot, it is no less striking. Maimonides explained many of the commandments as reflecting the conditions and needs of a specific historical setting—that of the wilderness period in which they were given. Here the same approach is used, but the temporal framework is radically altered. R. Isaac boldly asserts that God provided in at least one commandment of the Torah for the needs of Jewish life in exile, especially in medieval Europe.

We have seen that in his discussion of the simple meaning of commandments, the rational reasons suggested by R. Isaac have some clear connection with the peshat of the Biblical verses. But there is also a doctrine of hidden reasons, relating to the esoteric level of the command-

ments. While it is a commonplace in medieval Jewish philosophical literature that the Torah as a whole has two levels, patent and concealed,
statements about the twofold nature of the commandments—such as the
assertion that the tablets were written on both their sides (Exod. 32:15)
"with the manifest and recondite expression of every commandment"
(be-nigleh ve-nistar le-khol mitzvah)⁶² —are not at all frequent, and they
deserve careful attention.

Commenting on the rabbinic interpretation of Deuteronomy 29:28 as
found in Sanhedrin, 43b, R. Isaac writes:

> It is well known among the Jewish nation that the commandments
> have a rational reason both exoterically and esoterically [ta'am be-
> nigleh u-ve-nistar]. It is not an empty thing; they were not given
> purposelessly. The esoteric reason is unknown except to the select
> few who understand and comprehend the truths about God. There-
> fore He associated those who understand the hidden content with
> Himself, and said "to the Lord our God" [Deut. 29:28], just as the
> sages said, " 'et Adonai Elohekha' [Deut. 6:13]—to include the disci-
> ples of the wise" [Pes., 22b] . . . Because they comprehend the hid-
> den meaning, He said "to the Lord our God," teaching that the ra-
> tional reason is comprehended not by the entire people but only by
> the God-fearing, the remnant whom the Lord did teach.
>
> Concerning the revealed things, He said "to us and to our chil-
> dren," meaning to the entire people, for they comprehend the mani-
> fest reason for the commandment, the base and the honorable alike.
> They said "to us and to our children," meaning that the knowledge
> and true comprehension of the commandments revert from genera-
> tion to generation and will never be forgotten by their descendents
> to eternity.⁶³

In a similar passage of the Midrash Commentary, the same point is
made: "The meaning of the Torah is well known to all who read it—that
all its words come on two levels, exoteric and esoteric, for each and every
commandment, not in accordance with the manifest meaning alone. The
benefit of this manifest meaning is obvious, but the value of the hidden
level of every commandment, superior to that which is revealed, is unknown except to the select few, the chosen among the people."⁶⁴ There
follows the same interpretation of Deuteronomy 29:28, linked with the
rabbinic derash on Deuteronomy 6:13. The legitimacy of finding and expounding the rational reasons for the commandments is never questioned, for R. Isaac maintains that these are known even to the masses of
uneducated Jews. It is only the hidden meaning of the commandments,
the esoteric reason for their observance, which is to be restricted to a limited circle of cognoscenti.

In order to evaluate this doctrine properly, we must see how it is applied. On the verse "Command the children of Israel, that they put out of the camp every leper, and every one that hath an issue, and whosoever is unclean by the dead" (Num. 5:2), the midrash states, "At the time when Israel left Egypt, the great majority had blemishes . . . when they came to the wilderness of Sinai, God said, 'Is this worthy of the Torah, that I give it to a generation of men with blemishes!?' . . . What did He do? He said to the angels that they should descend among Israel and cure them" (*Num. R.*, 7:1). After the general statement noted in the preceding paragraph, R. Isaac turns directly to the midrash at hand:

> They spoke there esoterically about the leper and about everyone with a blemish in the midst of the people when they left Egypt. *The manifest meaning of the leper is obvious.* God commanded His people to send them out from His presence; the person with an issue and the leper and the person afflicted with boils must leave the camp of Israel, because of God's compassion for His people: so that the air in the camp will not become putrid toward the cool of the day because of the leper dwelling in their midst. A plague might break out because of the unclean breath exhaled by [the sick], causing a stench in the nostrils of all, and afflicting the camp. So every leper must dwell alone, far from human settlement.
>
> *But the esoteric meaning of impurity is for the human soul that is not pure.* For the "leprosy" which broke out in Egypt and confounded the brains of this wilderness generation came to them because they lived in Egypt among a faithless people of impure lips, and the Israelites had no knowledge of the living God, being just like the Egyptians. They had no frequent vision through priest or prophet; they played the harlot with alien gods . . . But God had compassion for His people, and He sent an angel to communicate something good to the people, saying, "Go, descend, give them the true Teaching [*torat emet*], to bring [eternal] life to the spirit of terrestrial creatures—that every controversy and every affliction of each Israelite be fully healed, and their wounds be bound up . . . In this manner, all who sinned in their souls, thus rendering themselves impure, were healed . . ."[65]

R. Isaac begins with a metaphorical interpretation of a midrashic statement: the blemishes of the people who left Egypt were not physical but spiritual and intellectual imperfections—erroneous beliefs about God. The healing of these blemishes by the angels in the midrash is the revelation of the Torah by the supreme incorporeal Angel (see chapter IV, section 1); the Torah enlightened the eyes of the people so that they would no longer believe what was theologically impossible. But the interpretation does not remain within the confines of the midrash. It is introduced, as we have seen, with a general statement about the two levels of every commandment in the Torah, and it is presented as the esoteric meaning of the commandments about leprosy. Just as the "blemishes" in the midrash should be understood as spiritual imperfections, so the "leprosy" discussed in several chapters of the Torah should be understood—at least on its deepest level—not as the physical disease but as the belief in concepts that are philosophically incorrect. While retaining the manifest meaning of the commandments relating to leprosy and quickly explaining their purpose, the commentator adds another meaning that applies these commandments to wide circles of the Jewish population of his own time.[66] It is somewhat ironic that the manifest meaning, known by everyone, affects only a tiny group afflicted with a specific disease, while that which R. Isaac calls the esoteric meaning, known only by the chosen few, applies to the masses.

R. Isaac also speaks of an esoteric meaning with regard to the commandment concerning the Second Pesah. After discussing Isaiah 57:19 as an asmakhta for the statement "In the place where the penitent stand, those who are fully righteous do not stand" (Sanh., 99a), R. Isaac continues, "The master of the prophets alluded to this with regard to the Second Pesah, which he ordained for the people at God's word, applying to those unclean because of a dead body and those who went on a journey far away, according to the esoteric type of meaning. For all its pleasant words came on two levels, revealed and hidden; the revealed is well known, but the hidden comes to inform us . . . ." The interpretation which follows is that "impurity due to a dead body" refers to one who is impure because of the filth of matter, which moves inevitably toward death and destruction. Such a person is drawn after his physical component to pursue superfluous things. He therefore cannot observe the holiday of Pesah, the entire purpose of which is to repudiate superfluities. Only after he has returned to the way of the mean can he observe Pesah, for only then will he have comprehended its true purpose.[67] Here too, while retaining the well-known, manifest meaning of the commandment, R. Isaac extends it to a far broader category of Jews through its hidden meaning. Anyone with an ethical blemish (or according to the parallel passage in the Midrash Commentary, an intellectual blemish) is affected, for he cannot celebrate Pesah properly.

During the thirteenth and early fourteenth centuries, rabbinical leaders of Spain and southern France railed against the allegorical interpretations of various commandments and the resulting neglect of these commandments on the part of Jewish "philosophizers."[68] Since the extant literature contains the accusations of the opponents but only rare examples of the actual writings of those who were attacked,[69] it is difficult to assess the validity of the criticisms. One of the clearest statements of the fundamental issue at stake is found in R. Menahem Meiri's commentary on Avot, 3:14, "He who reveals aspects of the Torah not according to halakha." This phrase is interpreted to refer to those who pretend to know the secrets of the Torah and who deny the explicit content entirely, claiming that God does not intend it but that it is pure allegory referring to something else.

An example, writes Meiri, is if someone were to state that "it is not the meaning of the Torah that one should refrain from eating swine meat; rather, the Torah's prohibition of swine meat is pure allegory, meaning that men should not have disgraceful and filthy personal qualities." Such a person, if a Jew, would be called a heretic and would have no share in the world to come. "But, if he wants, he may say, 'Swine is unquestionably forbidden, and the *reason* for this prohibition is that it, and all that is similar to it [disgusting ethical qualities in man] is repugnant in God's sight,' or another reason." Meiri is not enthusiastic about this enterprise, and he points out the major pitfall of concluding erroneously that it is possible to fulfil the hidden meaning without performing the commandment itself; but in his view there is nothing essentially wrong with this second approach.[70]

The first approach mentioned by Meiri is that of traditional Christian exegesis.[71] The crucial historical question is whether Jews were indeed writing or saying this in the thirteenth century. I do not know of a single unequivocal statement made by a Jew that would reflect the position cited by Meiri as that of a heretic. R. Isaac does state that certain halakhic principles—notably that of taking three steps backward after the conclusion of prayer—should not be taken literally but are purely allegorical. However, this is certainly not the same as rejecting the simple meaning of a commandment from the Torah. His position in relation to ta'amei mitzvot is clearly the second, legitimate position: the commandments must be accepted and observed according to their obvious meaning, but there is also a deeper, hidden, more important meaning, which can and should be known to the philosopher.

Halakha

The fact that a significant number of passages in both CAT and CMR are concerned with statements of a purely halakhic nature distinguishes R. Isaac's work from other more or less contemporary commentaries which focus almost exclusively on the aggadah.[72] R. Isaac's approach to halakhic statements varies. Sometimes he merely explicates the peshat; sometimes he explicitly abandons the peshat as if the statement had no legal content. Most often, he attempts to explain the reasons underlying the various principles of Jewish law in accordance with his rational philosophic assumptions. Even the small proportion of the work that is extant represents a significant contribution to what might be called the literature of *ta'amei ha-halakhot*.[73]

In some instances, he interprets halakhic statements allegorically.

" 'He shall not multiply wives to himself; his heart shall not turn away'
[Deut. 16:17]. What is the reason behind 'He shall not multiply wives'? In
order that 'his heart shall not turn away.' Why was 'his heart shall not
turn away' explicitly stated? To teach that if even one wife distracts his
heart, he should not marry her" (Sanh., 21a). This discussion of the marital regulations for the Jewish king represents the position of R. Simeon b.
Yohai, which is ultimately rejected in favor of a different view. R. Isaac
insists that the statement is not to be understood in relation to the Jewish
king and his wives at all. Rather,

> they spoke here about the king in an esoteric manner, calling "the
> king" one who rules over his spirit and body, for he is a mighty king
> who fights day after day against the enemy that pursues him. And
> they called the matter [of the body] "female."

The statement "If even one distracts his heart, he should not marry her"
becomes advice appropriate to everyone who strives toward perfection.
If such a person finds himself drawn toward sin because of the innate
character of his body and the physical impulses, he must not foolishly
give in to this temptation. He must oppose and overcome his nature,
gradually transforming it until it aids him in the attainment of his goal.[74]
This allegorical interpretation retains the underlying theme of temptation
and diversion from high purpose while making it apply, in principle, to
everyone.

A second law pertaining to the Jewish king is also to be taken allegorically. Maimonides incorporated into his legal code the statement that
kings must be anointed by the flowing water of a spring so that their
reign may endure.[75] R. Isaac, in contrast, argues that the spring mentioned here is used as it is throughout Biblical and rabbinic literature as
an image for the wisdom that flows outward from the prophet or sage.
The statement means simply that the king must be chosen for his wisdom, as exemplified by King Solomon. The statement must not be taken
in accordance with the apparent meaning—that the presence of flowing
water determines the success of the reign—for "this would appear to
every enlightened man as mockery, delusion, and superstitious folly.
Heaven forbid that they [the sages] would indulge in such wearisome
matters!" Since the existence in the spring water of a magic power that
could affect the nature of a king's reign is impossible, then "spring" must
refer not to the place of anointing but to the proper qualities of the man
to be anointed.[76]

One might surmise that R. Isaac felt free to allegorize these statements
because they are taken from a halakhic realm that had long been inopera-
tive. But in a passage of CMR, R. Isaac presents an allegorical interpretation of a Talmudic dictum that affected Jews every day. The point of de-

parture is the assertion in the Midrash (*Num. R.*, 5:8) that the children of Kohat always faced the ark and never turned away from it, even though this meant walking backward. R. Isaac argues that the prophets used the "back" of God as a metaphor for the entire realm of creation.[77] Therefore, the statement about these Levites walking backward really means that the ark inspired them to purify their intellect by investigating the realm of Creation and thereby attaining knowledge of God.

The same meaning, he continues, is found in the Talmudic dictum (*Yoma*, 53b) "One who prays [the *Amidah*] should take three steps backward and then give greeting [or pronounce 'peace']." R. Isaac says that he has already explained this in his Talmud commentary on *Yoma*: "a true, acceptable interpretation; no one has anticipated me in interpreting the hidden content of words such as these . . . until now I have not seen it written in any book, no one has seen the light in this matter, for the eye of their intellect has been plastered over so that they cannot understand the true deep meaning of these words." As the commentary on *Yoma* is not extant, we are dependent on the brief summary of the interpretation here. After ridiculing those who take the statement literally and actually walk backward three steps, R. Isaac explains that the three steps in the statement refer not to the body but to the mind. One must direct his thoughts to find God from the three realms of being that are behind Him, for investigation of these realms leads to discovery of the One who is above them all, ruling over them as King. Actual steps backward at the end of prayer are ludicrous. It is the mind and not the body that must be moved.[78]

This passage in *Yoma* created a host of problems on various issues: With which foot does one step back first? What is the length of the steps? What if one is unable to step backward because of his location? What is the precise meaning of *yiten shalom*? When can one return to his place after stepping back? What is the reason for the entire procedure? It is unfortunate that the full comment on *Yoma* has been lost. What is most important is the long chain of halakhic authorities from the amoraic period on—geonim, rabbis from North Africa and Spain, and sages of southern France, as well as the scholars of northern Europe—all of whom viewed the three steps backward as an unquestioned obligation.[79] No such authority even considered the possibility that the three steps were not actually to be taken (although Rashba points out that in most places, there is not enough room for people to take three full steps). R. Isaac b. Yedaiah's critique seems to have emerged full grown from his head, as he implies when he emphasizes the originality of his interpretation.

Other writers did criticize excessive physical movement during worship. We might compare with the three steps backward at the conclusion of the *Amidah* the custom of turning the head in six directions upon the completion of the verse "Hear, O Israel." This practice is not explicitly mentioned in the gemara; it is attributed in *Sefer ha-Eshkol* and in *Sefer ha-Me'orot* to R. Hai Gaon, but R. Meir b. Simon reports that in the middle of the thirteenth century, the custom prevailed throughout Israel.[80] Yet Anatoli, writing at about the same time, lashed out against those who moved their heads in a mechanical way: "God's kingship does not come merely through movement of the head, in accordance with our base custom today . . . for that movement was ordained in the manner of the shaking of the *lulav:* to concentrate upon God's kingdom in heaven and on earth, in all four directions. The purpose lies in what the mind thinks. What value is there in the movement of the head while the mind is silent and at sleep? This is rather a source of great shame, a serious transgression."[81] And R. Meir himself, while stating that the custom should not be changed, reports in his *Milhemet Mitzvah* that he learned from his father of the requirement to concentrate on each one of the six directions to infinity, thereby affirming the infinite extent of God's kingdom.[82]

While this custom has no clear halakhic status, and while there is no attack against those who carry it out literally, these strictures are somewhat analogous to R. Isaac's comment, which substitutes an inner, intellectual exercise for physical movement. Nevertheless, it is clear that R. Isaac is more extreme. His interpretation of the gemara in *Yoma*, explicit in its opposition to performing the simple meaning of a rabbinic statement and adamant in its insistence that only the allegorical meaning is intended, has far-reaching implications. Except for the fact that this type of interpretation is highly unusual in these commentaries, it could serve as a fine example of what many thirteenth-century Jewish leaders in Christian Spain and southern France found so deeply disturbing.

This is not the only instance in which the meaning of a halakhic statement with practical significance was completely transformed by R. Isaac. *Shevuot*, 35a, states, "There are names which may be blotted out and names which may not be blotted out. *El, Eloah, Elohim* may not be blotted out; The Great, The Mighty, The Awesome may be blotted out." There was little question about the meaning or the binding character of this statement.[83] R. Isaac totally ignores the meaning that Maimonides had incorporated into his code and discusses the passage on a different plane: "They came to teach that whoever seeks the Lord must repudiate all positive attributes in relation to Him." For such attributes imply affectibility and the capacity for change, which is impossible in God. Therefore, adjectives such as "great," implying largeness of size, "mighty," implying going forth to war, and the like should be erased from any book written about God by one who strives toward perfection, lest such attributes confuse the mind and lead to the belief in corporeality.

In contrast, the names that need not be blotted out are those that are used metaphorically (*al tzad ha-hash'alah*) to teach about His necessary existence. The word "El" or "Elohim" indicates leadership of some kind without implying corporeality. It need not therefore be blotted out at the beginning of metaphysical investigation, but may be used metaphorically to indicate God's rulership over all things, of which He is the First Cause.[84] The focus has obviously been shifted from the realm of halakha to that of religious philosophy. By reinterpreting a single word, reading "blotted out" figuratively rather than literally, R. Isaac transforms a legal proscription governing a limited topic into a general expression of theological doctrine relevant to all.[85]

In expressing the punishment for a Jew who has sexual relations with a non-Jewish woman, the Talmud uses the phrase "They do not have *ishut*" (the status of matrimony) (*Sanh.*, 82a). Now the question of the matrimonial status of Gentile women was not a simple matter in the halakha.[86] R. Isaac circumvents the entire issue by reinterpreting the word "ishut," this time treating it literally. First, he summarizes what he says was a lengthy comment on the statement "There is no *emunah* among the nations" (*Hullin*, 133b), referring to the fact that the nations believe in the eternity of the world and deny revelation, providence, and reward and punishment for the soul, therefore concluding that it makes no difference how they act.

In *Sanhedrin*, he continues, we are told by the sages that such people, because of their false beliefs, "have no ishut [distinctively human quality], for every one of them is accounted as little and has no superiority over a beast. Just as there is no human quality in a beast or a bird or any other such creature who have no [true] belief [emunah], so there is no human quality [ishut] in these men, and they are similar to the beasts." Here the halakha itself is unaffected by the interpretation. The explanatory phrase is considered in isolation from its context in a halakhic statement, treated in conjunction with a parallel phrase from *Hullin* (which is itself given a new meaning unconnected with the context) and made to express a philosophical doctrine. Without true beliefs about God, the intellect, which alone distinguishes man from the animals, remains unactualized, so that the person is not fully human.[87]

This technique of defining a halakhic term in accordance with philosophical preconceptions can be seen in still another passage. The statement "Just as we do not bury an evil man next to a righteous man, so we do not bury a moderately evil man [*rasha kal*] next to an extremely evil man [*rasha hamur*]" (*Sanh.*, 47a) obviously requires some definition of terms. Rashi maintains that it should be understood in conjunction with the Mishnah, which states that there were two cemeteries for those executed by the court, one for those sentenced to beheading or strangulation, the other for those sentenced to stoning or burning (*Sanh.*, 46a).

The first two means of execution were for the most serious capital crimes, the second two for the less serious crimes; hence the statement of the gemara. R. Isaac ignores this mishnah and defines the terms in accordance with his own assumptions.

A moderately evil man is one who sins secretly because of his inability to overcome the natural impulses that lead him to sin. Recognizing the sovereignty of God and his own frailty, he can return to God at any moment. If indeed he does repent before his death, he will be "helped from Heaven," and ultimately gain eternal life. In contrast, the totally evil man (in the commentary, the phrase is changed from *rasha hamur* to *rasha gamur*) is one who denies the sovereignty of God, revelation of the Torah, and reward and punishment for the soul. He therefore transgresses publicly as an act of conscious rebellion, and he will not repent during his life. His soul is annihilated at death, never again to rise even at the time of the resurrection.[88] Once again, a statement with specific halakhic import has been generalized in a way that applies to all. The difference between the two categories is not the seriousness of their transgressions within the halakhic framework but their stance on the fundamental issues of religious philosophy.[89]

A final example of the translation of halakhic terms into philosophical categories concerns the qualifications for membership in the Sanhedrin, stated by R. Yohanan as follows: "Those appointed to the Sanhedrin must have *komah, hokhmah, mar'eh, ziknah,* knowledge of magic and of the seventy languages" (*Sanh.,* 17a). Maimonides, in codifying this passage, defined "hokhma" as expertise in the laws of the Torah and in some other disciplines, such as medicine, mathematics, and astronomy. The other qualities are presented not as absolute prerequisites but as desiderata, without interpretation, and in conjunction with another statement that members of the Sanhedrin should be free of physical blemish (*Sanh,* 36b). He apparently understood these terms to refer literally to physical appearance, height, and age.[90]

R. Isaac's interpretation is strikingly different. "Hokhma" refers to native intelligence, the ability to derive one idea from another. "Komah" is philosophical knowledge, found in those "who have perfected themselves and set their path aright to ascend the rungs of the ladder [of the sciences] and to perceive intellectually their Creator." "Mar'eh" is knowledge of the Torah, found in those who understand "its true meaning on two levels, the revealed and the esoteric." "Ziknah" is the ability to overcome the impulse toward evil, which can be present in some "even in their youth." Knowledge of *keshafim* is scientific knowledge of the true nature of the universe, which implies awareness of what is impossible and the ability to refute those who believe in magic. Finally, knowledge of the seventy languages refers to an understanding of the other religions, leading to the conviction that all are far from reason except for the religion revealed at Sinai, and enabling its possessor to answer those who polemicize against Judaism in the period of exile without need for a translator.[91]

Here is certainly a case of reading one's preconceived notions into the words of a text. The concepts are hung from the words by a thread: knowledge of God to "komah" because of the metaphor of ascending the ladder of the disciplines to the pinnacle of metaphysics; expertise in Torah to "mar'eh" because of the phrase *mar'im panim la-torah*, explained as referring to the two aspects (*panim*) or levels of meaning in sacred Scripture. The knowledge of foreign languages is set in a contemporary historical context—that of religious disputation in European countries and the ways in which a knowledge of Latin could be exploited by Jewish participants—which could have no relevance to the seating of the Sanhedrin. The text has become a pretext for the commentator to expound his ideal type against the background of his own age and his own set of assumptions and values.

In contrast with all the passages cited to this point, there are many that reveal a sincere attempt to explain the halakha on its own terms. For example, many Talmudic statements derive either a rule or an exception to a rule from a peculiarity of Biblical language. R. Isaac is not satisfied until he has explained rationally why the rule makes sense or why the exception was necessary. Several fine examples can be seen in the context of the laws relating to the wife suspected of adultery—the *sotah*—as discussed in the commentary on *Numbers Rabbah*.[92] Certain categories of husband and of wife are explicitly excluded from the sotah ordeal. " 'And it be hid from the eyes of her husband' (Num. 5:13)—this excludes a blind man" (*Num. R.*, 9:29). R. Isaac first states the general case: A man sees his wife acting shamelessly with another man and commands her before witnesses not to be secluded with him. The wife, scorning her husband, is then secluded with the man in question and is made to undergo the ordeal of the bitter waters. But if the husband is blind, a fundamental problem arises. He cannot see his wife flirting with handsome young men or acting lecherously among them, so he must depend upon the reports of informants, who may be irresponsible mischief makers. "Thus in this matter, the divine wisdom decreed that a blind man may not compel his wife to drink the waters on the basis of hearsay, for perhaps the informant is deceiving him." If he suspects his wife, his only recourse is to divorce her.[93]

The same approach is used to explain the categories of women ineligible for the ordeal. " 'The priest shall make the woman stand . . .' (Num. 5:18)—this teaches that if the woman is lame, she does not drink . . . 'And put in her hands . . .' (Num. 5:18)—from this we learn that if her

hand or fingers are stumped, she does not drink" (*Num. R.*, 9:33). From
"the woman shall say, 'Amen, amen' " (Num. 5:22) the dumb woman is
excluded, and from analogy with the husband, the blind woman is excluded (*Num. R.*, 9:42). Each of these exclusions is rationalized by the
commentator. The blind woman cannot see her spouse, and there is always the possibility that she was deceived by the adulterer into believing
that it was her husband with whom she was being intimate. Because of
this doubt inherent in the nature of the case, she cannot be forced to
undergo the ordeal. Similarly, the woman who is dumb cannot call out
for help if she is being forced, and she cannot tell her story to the priest.[94]
A lame woman alone with a man and not knowing that he desires her
will be unable to escape when he tries to force or seduce her; a woman
with a stumped arm will be unable to resist the attentions of a stranger
even if she wants to do so. Or, the comment continues, a different approach may be followed. Even if such women are alone with strange
men, it will probably not be for illicit purposes, as men do not desire
woman with such physical blemishes. Therefore, the suspicion of their
husbands is not enough to compel them to drink the bitter waters.[95]

In all of these cases, rabbinic law derived in an apparently arbitrary
manner from the peculiarities of Biblical diction is made plausible and
logical.[96] This approach is defended by R. Isaac in a general statement relating to the law of the sotah:

> For all the rabbinical laws concerning the sotah are consistent
> with reason. It never occurred to them that the Biblical decree about
> these two woman [lame and with stumped arm] has no rational basis
> [*ta'am*]; that since it said without qualification, "The priest shall
> make the woman stand," it permits the woman who is unable to
> stand on her feet to fornicate with the sanction of God's command-
> ment, since her husband may not compel her to drink the waters
> even if he has warned her; that she is not forbidden to her husband
> after his warning . . . Heaven forbid that they should play the harlot
> because of this, setting an example for other women to sin! For all
> the words of this enigmatic book are for the benefit of those who
> cling to it. Whosoever has been graciously endowed by God with
> knowledge and rational perception will certainly understand the
> true meaning of all these statements and all that is concealed in them
> . . . For no decrees have come to the people from heaven, no laws
> and commandments were written to be given to the nation, without
> benefit for those who perform them . . . All were given to illumine
> the way for a people walking in darkness to see the goodness of
> God.

> Thus the words of the Torah concerning the sotah were given to
> chastise women who play the harlot when married, giving birth to
> illegitimate children and leaving the husband in suspense, so that the

truth is known only to the adulterer and the adulteress. But the Torah speaks about healthy women with well-formed bodies, who are desired by all who see them . . . It does not speak about the extraordinary case of a lame or stump-armed woman who commits adultery. Such women are not included in the same category as those with healthy bodies, even if they are naturally hot blooded, for you will not find one out of a thousand of them who plays the harlot. Even if they brazenly seek out lovers, they will not find any with which to fornicate, because of their deformed appearance. When they feel passion and desire for another man, they commit lewdness with each other, or they stimulate themselves with phallic forms, each hidden in her own house. But no man has carnal knowledge of her except for her husband, for she cannot find a paramour at home or abroad. Thus, against her will, she remains sinless and she becomes angry and bitter because of her inability to find a lover.[97]

The ending of this passage, with its description of female sexual perversions and its attempt to penetrate the psychology of a frustrated woman, need not detain us here. What is important for this discussion is the approach to halakha. The assumptions are clear: the Torah and the rabbinic law are both fully rational, and their purpose can be known by those who understand them completely. Rabbinic law derived by the exegesis of the legal formulations in the Torah is not arbitrary; it is the product of making explicit the laws concealed in the Torah for the benefit of all. In this case, the fact that certain categories of women are excluded from the sotah ordeal does not mean that they have been capriciously granted license to commit adultery. They have been excluded because the nature of their special circumstances makes it inherently unlikely that they will be guilty of adultery, for reasons which the commentator fully explains. The Torah and the halakha do not deal with the extraordinary exception to this rule: the case of a deformed woman who may indeed be guilty. For the law is designed to apply rationally to the majority of cases, not the unusual one.[98] In this context, it is logical, and its beneficial nature is obvious.

Precisely the same approach to the halakhic midrash can be found in the extant portions of the Talmud commentary. The Mishnah of *Sanhedrin* states, " 'If a man have a stubborn and rebellious son . . .' (Deut. 21:18] a son, and not a daughter, a son and not a man" (*Sanh.*, 68b). Just as in the case of the sotah, R. Isaac explains the exclusion of these categories on logical grounds. The son who shows himself to have an unbalanced temperament and cannot be restrained by his father will probably become a criminal when he grows to maturity. He is therefore punished by this law in order to prevent him from committing crimes such as murder. But the daughter, who remains in the home, is far easier to control.

Even if she drinks to the point of inebriation, little harm will come of it. Since she can probably be prevented from doing harm by her father or husband, this special law is not applied to her.

Furthermore, the punishment can be meted out only while the son is under the authority of the father, not when he is legally responsible for his own acts ("a son and not a man"). Once he is of age, he can be punished only through the normal procedures of the court, with the proper testimony of witnesses, just like any other Jew. Also, a minor is excluded because he may not be able to distinguish between good and evil, and it is not certain that the deeds he commits are done intentionally.[99] Finally, the Mishnah (*Sanh.*, 71a) states that if "one of them" is stump armed, lame, mute, blind, or deaf, the son is excluded from this category, again deriving its exclusion from an analysis of the relevant verses (*Deut.* 21: 19-20). R. Isaac, who apparently understood "one of them" to refer to either the parent or the son, characteristically ignores the proof texts and explains that a son is born with physical blemishes because of the sins of the parents. Since they themselves are at fault in this case, the son may not be punished by the court under these special rules.[100]

The attempt to explain the underlying reason for a law stated without explanation in the sources is not limited to cases where the law is hermeneutically derived from a Biblical verse. In the Midrash Commentary, for example, there is an extensive discussion of the statement "They may not make two women take an oath at the same time, they may not break the necks of two calves at the same time, they may not execute two men at the same time, they may not lock up and pass final judgment on two [lepers] at the same time" (*Num. R.*, 9:17). The parallel passage of the Talmud (*Sotah*, 8a) states a general principle—"We do not perform religious duties in bundles"—and contains a specific statement with regard to the sotah, "So that one will not become proud in relation to the other." R. Isaac ignores both the general and the particular reasons given by the Talmud and sets out independently to explain each of the five prohibitions.[101]

In the case of the sotah, if two women are accused, there is a clear advantage to administering the oath and the ordeal seriatim. Assuming that both are guilty, if the first woman swears that she is innocent then drinks the water and dies, the second woman who watches this will undoubtedly confess her guilt to the priest and be saved. If, however, they both undergo the ordeal simultaneously, both will deny their guilt and die. Furthermore, there is a strong possibility that if the first woman confesses, the second woman, following her example, will also confess, while this is impossible if the oath is administered to both simultaneously.[102]

The prohibition against burning two heifers at the same time is explained in a different manner. First, the general purpose of the red heifer ritual is stated; this is, according to R. Isaac, "to purify once each year all who are impure in soul." The burning of the perfect animal teaches that the sinner will be destroyed in body and soul because he has rebelliously abandoned the way revealed through the prophets. Death will reduce the sinner to dust and ashes, as is shown by the heifer's remains. The burning of two cows simultaneously is therefore superfluous. One is sufficient to purify and subdue the hearts of the people for an entire year.[103] Similarly, with the breaking of the calf's neck, the purpose of the ritual is to publicize the identity of the murdered person so that the man on whose field the corpse is found will seek far and wide until the murderer is brought to justice. But if two corpses are discovered on the same day, there is no need to duplicate the ceremony. Once is enough to publicize the fact that murder has been committed and that the murderer must be found.[104]

The prohibition against executing two men or passing final judgment on two lepers at once is treated in yet another manner. The rule about execution is an instruction to the judges that "they must not get used to the quality of cruelty." Human beings must not be put to death like beasts going to the slaughter. In this sense, R. Isaac argues, it is like the principle of the "suffering of animals" (Shab., 128b). Jewish law does not categorically forbid the causing of pain to any animal. It is permissible to ride a horse for long periods of time, to load burdens on camels and donkeys, to plow with an ox, even though these activities may cause the animals pain; it is certainly permitted to slaughter animals for food. Rather, the "infliction of suffering on animals" is forbidden "because of the cruelty to which one becomes accustomed by making an animal suffer, resulting in the acquisition of a shameful quality in one's soul."[105] The same is true for the judges of the Sanhedrin and also for the priest who must remove the leper from the camp. The banishing of many lepers at once might well diminish the danger to the health of the remaining Israelites, but it would also certainly harm the soul of the priest by making him callous to the plight of the sick. It is for his sake that he is restricted to one such removal per day.

In short, the general principle of the gemara—"We do not perform religious duties in bundles," explained by Rashi as meaning that we must avoid the appearance of rushing to remove a cumbersome burden—is totally ignored. The five rituals mentioned in the Midrash are treated separately. The first is explained by the potential benefit to the women undergoing the ordeal, the second and third are explained by arguing that nothing further is accomplished by performing the ritual a second time, the fourth and fifth are explained by the psychological impact on the people responsible for performing the act. The purpose of the entire comment is to rationalize the halakha in each particular case.

Many halakhic principles are explained in this simple, common-sense manner. The Talmud states that of the various forms of capital punishment, stoning is the worst, as it is reserved for the most serious possible crimes of idolatry and blasphemy (*Sanh.*, 49b). R. Isaac explains why this is the worst form of execution: in burning, the person is suffocated almost immediately and does not feel the flames; in decapitation with a sharp sword by a strong man, death comes so quickly that no pain is felt; in strangulation, the breath is cut off so that the person has no real consciousness of dying.

> But he who dies by stoning dies a bitter death. His flesh pains him while he is still alive, for they throw a stone at him and strike him powerfully, causing a searing, mortal pain in his heart. The same is true of each and every stone, large or small. For he does not die as a result of one stone but only after many stones have been thrown at him. Thus he is conscious of his unnatural death.

It is because of the suffering involved in this form of execution that divine wisdom decreed it for the denial of God Himself, while sins against other human beings are punished in a less extreme manner.[106]

In another case, the Midrash tells us, "It is a halakha of Moses from Sinai that a man may make his son a Nazirite, but a woman may not make her son a Nazirite" (*Num. R.*, 10:7; cf. *Nazir*, 28b). Even though this is stated to be a tradition not derived by exegesis or logic, R. Isaac explains that the rationale behind the law is based on the contrasting natures of men and women. The father educates his son in every matter of holiness until the son is old enough to understand for himself that he has been taught the way to ultimate felicity. The son will then gratefully fulfil his obligations as a nazirite of his own accord. But if the father dies, the mother does not have the capacity to make her son a Nazirite,

> for whenever the son acts as a Nazirite at her bidding, trying to become pure from all uncleanness through asceticism, the mother, because of her love for him, will nurture something abominable for his soul by preparing tasty food for him to eat every day. This is the opposite of what is required—that he set away everything superfluous, eating his dry crust alone. But she will go wild over her son, preparing sweet foods and abhorrent meats, so that the son will be unable to fulfil his vow as a Nazirite so long as he remains at home with others. Thus he labors in vain all the days of his service; this woman and this son of hers will derive from his being a Nazirite only shame.[107]

The psychology of the mother and especially of the widow, which renders her incapable of depriving her son of good foods and other superfluities forbidden to the Nazirite, lies behind the tradition that prevents her from imposing a vow on her son in the absence of the father.

A very different kind of explanation is given for the statement "If the outer compartment [of the tefillin] does not look upon space, it is invalid" (*Sanh.*, 89a). R. Isaac says that he has already explained the significance of the tefillin in many places: their purpose is to authenticate the existence of the three realms of the created universe. The knots show that there is no void in the universe, for each sphere encompasses the one beneath it, down to the moon, which encompasses the four elements, finally reaching the element of dust, which is the earth.

> And the four cases teach about the three realms, for each one has its own case, and there is a special case for the One who brought them into existence, teaching that He is their First Cause, and they are contingent effects of Him, dependent upon Him, while He is necessary, not needing them. Therefore He has a separate case, to teach that they have no attachment to Him, and that their perpetuity is not necessary as is His, for their absence will not change Him, as He is utterly perfect with them and without them.
>
> Here the sages are teaching that there must be no more than four cases in the tefillin. If one encompasses these four cases with others on all sides so that they cannot "see the air," they are invalid: the purpose of the tefillin has not been fulfilled because they are not made properly . . . For if a person who makes tefillin adds a fifth or more cases to the original four . . . , he contradicts the heavenly household.[108]

Again there is an attempt to explain rationally what is explicitly stated to be a halakha of Moses from Sinai. The structure of the phylactery for the head is interpreted in typical philosophical style, although the interpretation itself is rather extreme, for it makes the tefillin a reminder not of divine providence and God's action in history on behalf of His people but of cosmological doctrine about God's relationship to the three realms of existence. The prohibition of the Talmud logically follows. It is no longer merely an attempt to defend the authority of rabbinic traditions in the realm of law but an attempt to buttress true philosophical belief. Tefillin with an additional case would no longer represent reality as they are intended to do, and the entire purpose of the commandment would therefore be undermined. In this way, the halakha is accepted in its simple meaning while it is also given an explanation that transfers it to an entirely different realm.

R. Isaac's attempts to rationalize halakhic material extend beyond statements accepted as normative in Jewish law. He also explains the reasoning behind statements that are eventually rejected and do not become halakha. This may be within the context of a halakhic dispute in the Talmud. An example is the dispute between Rava and Abaye about whether one who breaks a commandment in open defiance (*meshummad le-*

hakh'is) is disqualified from giving testimony (*Sanh.*, 27a). R. Isaac begins by enunciating what he considers to be the general principle explaining disqualification of witnesses in Jewish law: the sages refuse to accept testimony from anyone who reveals an ethical blemish in his personality. For example, one who demonstrates the quality of greed cannot be trusted, for the sages are afraid he will take a bribe. A person who plays at dice shows that he desires what belongs to others. He is not ashamed to deceive his colleagues, for this is part of the nature of the game. Therefore the sages fear that he will testify falsely for profit, and they disqualify him as a witness.[109]

However, in the case of the defiant sinner, there is a difference of opinion. Abaye holds that he should be disqualified because such a man rejects the basic principle of the faith (*kofer be-ikar*). Since he has removed himself from the totality of the Jewish people and shown his contempt for the Torah, it is impossible for his testimony to be accepted by Jews in matters concerning Torah law. Rava, in contrast, argues that such a man is not evil in relation to other human beings and shows no contemptible moral quality in himself. Rather, he has been led by philosophical doctrine to an overly exalted concept of God, which seems to be inconsistent with the belief in Creation. If there was once nothing, and then God created the world, a change of the divine will must have occurred. But this is impossible, for God's will is identical with His essence, and God Himself does not change. In this way, a basically good motive led the man to deny Creation and, by extension, revelation, providence, and retribution. Such a man should not be included in the category of a violent plunderer. The sages, however, side with Abaye, holding that if a man denies the principle of reward and punishment for the human soul, no matter what motives may have led him to this conclusion, he will not fear for his own soul if he gives false testimony. He must therefore not be deemed trustworthy, even if he is telling the truth.[110]

This comment is an attempt to treat not only the halakha but the *sugiah* from which it emerges in rational terms. First there is the general principle behind disqualification, reached inductively by the commentator from the specific cases mentioned in the Talmud. Then one clear case— that of the gambler—is brought to illustrate the principle. Finally, the controversy is introduced and each side explained. The sympathy underlying the discussion of Rava's position is quite clear. This position is, after all, consistent with the principle enunciated: Rava is made to argue that since there is no ethical fault, the sinner need not be disqualified. To be sure, the intellectual position of the defiant sinner is erroneous, but it is well intentioned (to preserve a pure concept of God) and grounded in a Biblical verse (Malachi 3:6). R. Isaac cannot accept this extreme philosophical position, and he uses every opportunity in his writings to combat it (for example, identifying it as the position of the *rasha gamur*); but in stating it, he displays both understanding and sympathy. The controversy between two amoraim is explained by being translated into thirteenth-century terms and superimposed by the commentator upon the contemporary controversy over the place of the extreme philosopher within the Jewish community. Rava's position—that the intellectual error should not be accounted as serious as the moral fault—is ultimately rejected, but it is certainly given a fair hearing.

Elsewhere, we find a sympathetic explanation of a position which the halakha rejects, while the accepted position is totally ignored. R. Yose said, "It is forbidden to compromise, and whoever effects a compromise is a sinner" (*Sanh.*, 6b). R. Isaac explains why the judge must not compromise between two men who come before him with a dispute:

> It is known that one of them must be wronged, for he summoned his opponent before the judge for a purpose. If, then, the judge effects a compromise between the two, he robs the poor plaintiff . . . Why should he give to the liar half of the money in question for no reason? . . . Judges were not instituted [by God] for the benefit of liars and thieves but for their bane, so that others will hear and be fearful. If the judge compromises, granting half of what a man denies owing his opponent, and someone who hears about this praises and blesses him for this compromise, he thereby insults the word of God and scorns the Divine Name.[111]

The demonstration of how compromise can undermine the entire legal system seems so compelling in this passage that the reader almost forgets that the statement of R. Yose is rejected in the Talmud. The position accepted as halakha is stated by R. Joshua b. Korha, "It is a commandment to compromise," the polar opposite of the view R. Isaac defends.[112] But this statement is not even mentioned in the commentary, and no defense of the principle of compromise is given anywhere. While explanation of the reasoning behind a nonnormative position is not unusual in Talmudic exegesis,[113] it appears that R. Isaac may be using the technique of selective comment to express his own position in opposition to judicial compromise, a position that implies a dissent from the halakhic norm.[114]

Another example, with more serious consequences, can be seen in the discussion of a halakhic midrash relating to the testing of a suspected adulteress (*Num. R.*, 9:28). The commentator first states the law that a proven adulteress is forbidden to return to her husband and that this applies if her partner in adultery was a convert to Judaism, "for he is considered as an Israelite in all matters." He then goes on to say:

> But if she—a married Jewish woman—played the harlot with a Gentile, her husband cannot make her drink the waters even if he

has warned her about having intercourse with an uncircumcized man of any Gentile nation. *For she is not forbidden to her husband because of a non-Jewish man; she may again be intimate with her husband.* For thus the divine wisdom decreed in saying "and a man lie with her carnally" (Num. 5:13), as no one is called a "man" [*ish*] except for a Jewish man. All the rest are compared to beasts in the eyes of God, as the Babylonians taught when they said, " 'And ye, My sheep, the sheep of my pasture, are men' (Ezek. 34:31)—*you* are called men [*adam*] . . ."

And this is consistent with the statement of the Babylonians, "If a a Gentile or a slave has sexual intercourse with a Jewish woman, the child is legitimate." They taught that in the case of a Jewish woman who has intercourse with an uncircumcized man, conceives, and gives birth to a baby boy or girl, the child of these two parents is not a *mamzer*, even if its mother is a married woman . . ., but if she had fornicated with any Jew and bore a child, God commanded His people from on high that "they should not come into your congregation." Since this child is, according to the Torah, fit to enter the congregation, its mother, who fornicated with a Gentile, is not forbidden to her husband; he may take her again without bearing any sin.[115]

This is, to say the least, a puzzling passage, for it states and defends a position in dramatic conflict with the halakha. Jewish law states quite clearly that a married woman who commits adultery with a non-Jew is forbidden to return to her husband,[116] although other subsidiary matters about such a relationship may have been in dispute. It is difficult to find parallels anywhere for R. Isaac's explicit statement that "she is not forbidden to her husband because of a non-Jewish man; she may again be intimate with her husband."

The two arguments with which he buttresses his position would hardly convince any halakhic authority. The first is an interpretation of Numbers 5:13, "And a man lie with her carnally." R. Isaac argues that "man" here excludes all non-Jews on the basis of the Talmudic interpretation of Ezekiel 34:31: "You [Israel] are called men, but idolators are not called men" (*Yebamot*, 61a). But the word under discussion in that passage, dealing with Ezekiel 34:31 and Numbers 19:14, is "adam," while the word in Numbers 5:13 is "ish"; the fact that R. Simeon b. Yohai does not include idolators under "adam"[117] proves nothing about the meaning of "ish" in the verse dealing with adultery. On the contrary, that verse is explicitly discussed in the gemara of *Sotah*, 26b: "The Torah says 'man' (Num. 5:13)—not a minor, and not one who is not a man. What is this meant to exclude?" Two possibilities are considered and rejected; the first is the *shahuf* (the impotent);[118] the second is the idolator or the Gentile. Both of these are repudiated, the second on the basis of a statement of

Rav Hamnuna, "Wives are warned with regard to idolators/Gentiles." The Talmud decides that the word "ish" in Numbers 5:13 does include non-Jews and was stated to exclude intercourse with an animal, which does not prohibit a wife to her husband. R. Isaac ignores this decision of the gemara.

The second argument is that since a child born from an adulterous relationship between a Jewish woman and a Gentile is legitimate,[119] the woman is therefore permitted to return to her husband. Here the matter is more complicated. The Tosafot to *Ketubot* record that according to Rabbenu Tam, "There is no death penalty for intercourse with an idolator because Scripture has declared free the seed of the idolator, as it is written, 'His issue is like the issue of horses' [Ezek. 23:20] . . . Thus Rabbenu Tam permitted a Jewish woman who apostasized and had an affair with an idolator to remain with him after he converted to Judaism, for we do not say 'once in relation to the husband, once in relation to the adulterer' with regard to intercourse with an idolator, for this is like intercourse with a beast." However, the passage continues, "This does not seem proper to R. Isaac b. Mordecai, for because of intercourse with an idolator she is forbidden to her husband . . . Therefore in relation to her husband, sexual relations with an idolator are not considered like intercourse with a beast, and this is also true in relation to the adulterer . . . The intercourse of an idolator is intercourse. And although 'Scripture has declared free his seed,' these words mean [only] that he has no legally recognized paternity, and his seed is considered like the seed of a beast."[120]

Now nothing in Rabbenu Tam's decision states that the woman who has an affair with a Gentile is permitted to her husband, and it was never understood to mean this. R. Asher, who concurs with the decision of Rabbenu Tam although he gives a different reason for it, assumes that the woman is forbidden to her husband: "But in the case of intercourse with an idolator, to whom she is forbidden in any case, we cannot apply the statement " 'And she is defiled'—once with regard to the adulterer" [*Sotah*, 20b]. Thus, *granted that she is forbidden to her husband*, the additional prohibition to the adulterer is not added because of his intercourse with her."[121] The law is stated unambiguously in the *Tur*: "Rabbenu Tam wrote that a Jewish woman . . . is permitted to the proselyte who converts with her, and so wrote my revered father the Rosh, may his memory be blessed, and *even though she is certainly forbidden to her husband, she is permitted to the idolator*."[122] And R. Joel Sirkes, commenting on this section of the *Tur*, explains why it is explicitly stated that a husband's warning can apply even to an idolator: "Apparently this comes to teach that even though a woman who has fornicated with an idolator is not forbidden to him, as above in the name of Rabbenu Tam, *nevertheless she is forbidden to her husband even if she fornicated with an idolator."*[123]

These sources show that even in accordance with the decision of Rabbenu Tam, the woman is forbidden to her husband. Following the position of R. Isaac b. Mordecai, it is all the more obvious, for he makes a clear distinction between the two categories that R. Isaac attempts to connect. For the purpose of genealogy, the seed of the Gentile has no status, and therefore a child born out of an adulterous union between Jewess and Gentile is legitimate. But for the purpose of rendering a woman defiled, sexual relations with a Gentile have the same status as intercourse with any other man: the wife is forbidden to her husband and also to the Gentile, even if he subsequently becomes a Jew. Thus, no argument can be made from the fact that the child is legitimate to the conclusion that the woman is permitted to return to her husband. While the later halakha is indecisive on the dispute between Rabbenu Tam and R. Isaac b. Mordecai, R. Joseph Karo cites a statement that "one must not rely on Rabbenu Tam, for all the sages of his generation disagreed with him."[124]

How is one to react to the defense of a position so blatantly in conflict with the halakha without even an admission that the position is unusual? It might be read merely as an explication of a difficult passage in the Midrash: " 'Speak to the children of Israel'—warning is made with respect to Israel but not with respect to Gentiles or residents." This statement appears to contradict the statement of *Sotah*, 26b, which is accepted as halakha by all authorities: "Warning is made with respect to idolators." Recent commentators on the passage have adopted two approaches to this problem. One is that the midrash means merely that the laws of warning and suspected adultery are not found among idolators. This interpretation would maintain consistency between Midrash and Talmud by assigning a different meaning to the phrase *mekann'im al yedei akum* in each case.[125] The other approach is that the midrash actually asserts that a Jew may not warn his wife against seclusion with an idolator, and that this conflicts with the statement of the gemara, which is after all only that of an individual.[126] R. Isaac seems to have taken the latter approach and tried to draw out its implications and buttress it with support from other sources. At the very least, then, this comment represents a case of the commentator explaining and defending the anomalous antihalakhic statement while ignoring the normative rule.

Yet it seems that more is at issue here. The comment is presented not as an explication of a divergent view but rather as a statement of the truth. The argument that excludes the Gentile from the word "ish" in the critical verse (Num. 5:13) is fully consistent with R. Isaac's interpretation of the statement that the Gentiles "have no *ishut*." The conclusion—that a woman may return to her husband after an affair with a Gentile—is stated so forcefully and categorically that one is left with the impression that this is what the author actually believed the halakha to be, or at least what it should be. What led him to such an idiosyncratic position is unclear. Might it have been more than a difficult statement in the Midrash and a philosophical understanding of the word "ish"? The issue is one that had immediate and profound implications for Jews in the Middle Ages. Other passages in the Midrash Commentary reveal an unusual preoccupation with the subject of Jewish women having affairs with Christians; the possibility that this halakhic position reflects a situation in which R. Isaac was personally involved is one that should not be discounted.

In one place, R. Isaac registers an explicit, although suitably qualified, dissent from the halakha. The Mishnah of *Makkot* recounts a dispute between the Sadducees and the sages over the execution of conspiring witnesses in a capital case. The Sadducees ruled that the witnesses could be put to death only if the person falsely accused had already been executed. The sages ruled that the witnesses could be put to death only between the moment when the decision of capital punishment is given against the man falsely accused and the moment he is actually killed (*Mak.*, 5b). The gemara cites a parallel *beraita:* "Beribbi says, 'If the accused has not yet been killed, the false witnesses are to be killed; if the accused has been killed, the false witnesses are not to be killed.' His father responded, 'My son, is there not even stronger reason [for the witnesses to be killed once the person falsely accused has been executed]?' He replied, 'You have taught us, Master, that court punishments are not meted out in accordance with this type of reasoning' " (*Mak.*, 5b).

R. Isaac comments on this passage:

The law relating to the false witness is utterly amazing. What did they see in this matter, and what compelled them to determine the law that the false witnesses are to be killed if the accused person has not yet been killed, while if he has been killed, the witnesses are exempt from punishment? For *this is the opposite of the Torah's purpose*, which is to hold the evil person guilty for every transgression in accordance with his deeds. If he has stolen, he must pay double the amount, and if he has killed a person, his penalty is to be put to death; but if he has not killed, he is not put to death. For this is God's purpose in these laws—to preserve the world. Human blood cannot be expiated except by the blood of him who shed it, who killed an innocent man for no reason . . .

I have not penetrated to the depths of their minds, I have not understood their purpose in going counter to the other punishments written in the Torah of Moses, the master of the prophets. But these are words of the living God, for they [the sages] understood the purpose of the Torah and attained total mastery of it. They received a novel halakha in this matter from tradition, and we must not disparage these words of theirs, for they knew the matter, even if it is hidden from everyone else. "It is not an empty thing."[127]

Here is a candid confession of total inability to make sense of a clear halakhic principle. R. Isaac states that the law of execution for the false witness is an anomaly: it runs counter to all the other punishments of the Torah, and it contradicts the general purpose of Torah criminal law. In addition to emphasizing the apparent injustice of this teaching, he points out practical problems in its implementation. In the case of accidental homicide, cities of refuge are set aside in order to protect the killer from vengeance at the hands of the surviving relatives. But here there can be no such provision. The witnesses caused the death of an innocent man intentionally, yet they are not punished; how will they be able to withstand the aggrieved kinsmen? The result will undoubtedly be further bloodshed and prolonged family feuds, which the Torah strives to prevent. In short, R. Isaac indicates that to his mind, the Sadducean position is more rational and more in keeping with the entire thrust of the Torah than is the position of the sages. Even Beribbi's father apparently believed this, for his question, "Ve-lav kal ve-homer hu?" implies that it is irrational and contrary to the Torah to allow the witnesses to go unpunished after the accused has been put to death.

After endeavoring to explain the rationality of so many halakhot, R. Isaac is confronted with a rule that he simply cannot explain, and this disturbs him deeply. His entire argument is a defense of the Sadducean position and a refutation of the sages. But he cannot leave it at this. Having gone as far as he could go in dissent from an undisputed rabbinic halakha, he ends with an act of obeisance, stating that we must accept it without question in the belief that the rabbis knew what they were doing and possessed a genuine tradition. When he is unable to fit a specific halakha into his elaborate structure of rational assumptions about the Torah and the rabbinic literature, he feels compelled to cede to authority, but he leaves the impression that his heart is not in it.[128]

VI

THE HISTORICAL
SETTING

THE COMMENTARIES ON THE AGGADOT and the Midrash Rabbah are essentially documents of medieval Jewish intellectual history. They reveal how sacred rabbinic texts were not only interpreted and explicated but also reinterpreted and transmuted in accordance with intellectual and spiritual needs arising from a world view radically different from that of the sages. But they serve another purpose as well. Scattered through the pages of these manuscripts are remarks in which the author reflects upon the contemporary Jewish scene, and some of these remarks are of considerable importance. In its evaluation of various leadership types within the Jewish community, R. Isaac's work contains some significant additions to the literature of social commentary produced by Jews in southern France and Christian Spain.

The Courtier

The comment on *Avot*, 1:10, "Do not make yourself known to the ruling power," reveals R. Isaac's perspective on the Jewish courtier. The rabbis he says, teach that one should not draw near to the court of the Gentile kings, especially in these times, when the Jews are afflicted by confiscatory taxes to be paid into the royal treasury.

If a Jew draws near to the royal court, attaining a high position before the king, those who hear that he gives counsel will suspect him, and they will slander him to cut him down to size. It is better for him not to draw near to the royal court, so that those who are overshadowed physically and financially will not suspect him. No one who frequents the royal court can be free of such suspicion, and all who hear slander will give their assent, whether it be true or false. For he himself is responsible for this harm by being close to the king, and God, may He be blessed, who knows every secret, will do to him

159

what he has done [to others]. If he has caused harm to another, recompense will come upon him without delay. Thus you find that every Jew close to the royal court loses his wealth before his death; it abandons him in the midst of his life, for the king takes it away. If it does not happen to him, it happens to his son or grandson: a judge will slander him and punish him as was due to his forbears, who grew powerful immorally in the realm. The wealth accrued is lost as their punishment, and none will be left over for their children, for all the ways of God are just . . .[1]

This analysis of the courtier's position is rather unexpected. From the rest of the commentaries, one would guess that R. Isaac might emphasize the compromises in religious observance that court life necessitates—the inability to observe all the mitzvot, and even more important, the distraction from the ultimately crucial endeavor of gaining philosophical knowledge of God and thereby acquiring immortality of the soul. Such perils are indeed stressed by other Jewish writers of the Middle Ages.[2]

R. Isaac's emphasis on a different kind of peril is based more on the assumptions of the courtier himself than on those of the preacher or the philosopher. The dynamics of court life produce the seeds of downfall from every success. He who gains access to the king will necessarily eclipse other ambitious men, whose resentment and jealousy will be focused against him. Any exercise of authority inevitably harms the interests of some, and the aggrieved parties will lend ready ears to malicious rumors and spurious accusations. The uncertainty of the courtier's position makes it undesirable. In the turbulence of court intrigue, few remain on top for long.

These problems are compounded if the courtier is a Jew. The natural resentment of the unsuccessful aspirants is intensified when they see themselves overshadowed by a Jewish rival. Furthermore, since the Jew is always in an exposed and vulnerable position, his insecurity is especially pronounced. The history of medieval Jewish courtiers bears out R. Isaac's generalization that few enjoy their position in tranquillity and die peacefully in old age, and that the few who do are unable to bequeath their success to their children. The violent death of Samuel the Nagid's son Yehosef was well known, and the precariousness of power was reconfirmed by the spectacular ascents and disastrous declines of thirteenth-century Jewish courtiers in Aragon and Castile.[3] Yet R. Isaac shows little sadness and less outrage at the fall of Jewish notables. The machinations and intrigues of the court represent for him the working out of divine providence in this world. The realities of the political arena compel the courtier to act unethically, thereby harming others, so that the forces that lead to his downfall are ultimately just retribution for his moral failings.

After discussing Jewish courtiers in general and the nature of power in the realm of human rulers, R. Isaac focuses upon his contemporaries:

In this generation, of all those who have become intimate with the authorities, I have not found a worthy model who does good in the royal court and is able to escape suspicion. Some of them have a root that bears gall: they indirectly cause damage to good men, thereby abetting evil, by informing against them at court so that they are punished by authority of the king, and their property is seized. Before today we have not heard of one man in a thousand who emerged clean, without taint. I have not seen him until now: a wholehearted, honest, and God-fearing man who has arisen in the midst of his people in this generation; a man in awe of the divine word, who acts kindly toward rich and poor and seeks the welfare of his people at court, so that during his era not a single person fell in the royal court; a man who wielded power with absolute integrity, who was "clothed in linen," and whose personal qualities were pleasing and compatible, in whose time there was peace afar and near; a man who lived by generosity, opening his hand to give bread to the hungry, covering the naked so that they had clothes to wear and a garment in which to lie down.

Here are two sharply contrasting pictures of contemporary Jewish courtiers. The negative picture reflects the corruption already described as the usual result of association with the centers of power. Such courtiers are responsible for the downfall of many good people, who are punished so that their property may be seized. The phrase used to describe this activity of the courtiers—va-yokhlu kortzei—is the Talmudic expression for informing the Gentile authorities about internal Jewish affairs, an enterprise that confronted the medieval Jewish community with one of its gravest problems. In Spain, the government backed the authority of the Jewish community to adjudicate informing as a capital offense.[4] This was not the case in southern France, and those Jews who had influence with the authorities were apparently beyond the control of their coreligionists.

In contrast, we have a rather striking depiction of the ideal courtier. Three themes emerge from this characterization. First, the courtier is able to maintain high standards of moral and religious integrity. He is not corrupted by court life but retains his fear of God and his reverence for God's word. Secondly, the courtier is not concerned solely with opportunities for personal advancement. He uses his position of influence to work for the benefit of his fellow Jews, putting in a good word for individuals in trouble. Finally, in the tradition of courtier benefactors, he is distinguished by his generosity and his willingness to help those in need. Nothing is said about the sponsoring of cultural enterprises, but presumably destitute poets might be beneficiaries of his largess.

The language of this passage is ambiguous on a crucial point: whether R. Isaac is speaking about an ideal Jewish courtier who in fact has never existed so far or whether he is describing a historical figure who, unlike the other courtiers of past or present, actually embodies these qualities. At first it seems that the author is presenting his view of the ideal after asserting that he has never found one who lives up to it. Gradually, however, one begins to sense that the ground has shifted from the ideal to the real and that the statement is meant to assert that *before now* there was never a courtier as outstanding as the one being described.

As the passage continues, it leaves no doubt that we are hearing about a real person:

> His root is spread out from the holy place, from the city of Beziers, the place of his rest, a city and mother in Israel, extremely great. He stood among the myrtles . . . He was intimately known by by all. And I was a son-in-law of this "king"; I saw the honor and prestige he received from the king, the lord of the land, who promoted him to authority over the economy of his people, so that his reputation spread afar, and according to his word, all the peoples of the land, lowly and honorable alike, were ruled. Whatever he would say to them they would do, without disobedience in any matter. When the king would lay a tax upon his entire realm so that the whole land was in a state of forced labor, the king delighted to honor him. Like Adoniram overseeing the taxes, he supervised all matters involving large sums of money. He did many such things; he lived with integrity, a just man. His heart was not raised haughtily over his neighbors as he led them gently, for even in his position of authority he was meek and humble, a friend to all his brothers, barring none. He was honorable in God's sight, standing before Him in the breach all the days of his life.
>
> Furthermore, I observed something miraculous concerning him even after his death, something we have not heard about any other man of Jewish lineage since the exile of our people. Everyone in the area—all the Christians, every dignitary of his populous city, and the entire royal court—agreed together with the officers and constables to shut the doors of every house on the day of his death so that none could enter. As one, they all came to bemoan him. The men of the place closed the doors in the market as was commanded; they were moved to follow after his bier, weeping as they walked. The earth split at the sound of their loud, uninterrupted mourning, until he was carried to burial and the grave was sealed. They did not fortify themselves with food from morning until evening; then everyone went home as a mourner, with head bared. No such honor has been done to any other man; his glory did not disappear after his death. From the way he was mourned, it is obvious that he dwells on high with those who enjoy the Divine presence, and that his resting

place is glorious, for all mourned him as one—Jew and Gentile—
with overwhelming grief appropriate to a unique individual, and
doleful lamentation was provoked by his death. This was the honor,
unparalleled before.

This passage enhances our understanding of Jewish life in southern
France as well as our knowledge about R. Isaac himself. Elements of ex-
aggeration and convention are to be expected in this type of elegaic encomium, but a number of assertions have a ring of authenticity.

In question is a Jewish dignitary connected with the royal government.
The center of his activities was the city of Beziers, one of the very few
specific geographical references in the extant works of R. Isaac.[5] The historical setting is important. Carcassonne-Beziers, as a distinct political
unit, had been ceded to the Capetian crown by Count Raymond VII of
Toulouse in the Treaty of 1229, which ended the era of the Albigensian
Crusades.[6] After this, Beziers was legally part of the royal domain. A
document of 1230 records an agreement between the bishop of Beziers
and the king regarding jurisdictional rights over the city and diocese; the
second provision of this agreement grants all rights over the Jews to the
king except for one tax traditionally owed to the bishop and canons.[7]
After Raimond Trenceval, son of the last vicomte of Beziers, failed in a
final attempt to reconquer the seneschalcy of Carcassonne,[8] all rights
formerly held by the vicomte were relinquished to the royal seneschal in
1247. Thus, by the middle of the thirteenth century, when other parts of
Languedoc were still formally free of direct royal control, Beziers was
being administered by officials of the king.

The precise nature of the Jewish courtier's position is not entirely clear
from the passage. The description is couched not in the technical language of royal bureaucracy but in rhetoric suffused with Biblical phrases
which must be recast to fit the contemporary historical setting. It was obviously a position related to the area of financial administration. The
individual is not described as a tax farmer, one who paid the king a fixed
amount for the right to collect and keep the taxes from a specified population. He appears rather to have held a position of authority within the
royal administration. It is inconceivable that a Jew from Beziers held an
office with jurisdiction over the entire kingdom of France, as some
phrases from the passage might seem to indicate. We may assume that
whatever authority he may have had, it was limited to the seneschalcy in
which he lived. This authority was apparently exercised over non-Jews as
well as Jews, and it must have involved more than the mere collecting of
taxes, as this alone would hardly explain the influence attributed to the
courtier.[9]

Turning to the description of the funeral, we find that the leaders of the

royal administration were instrumental in halting the normal business of
the city for an entire day. Popular participation in the funeral rites may
not have been quite so spontaneous as it would appear from this account,
and the degree of grief expressed by the masses is clearly exaggerated. Yet
we must take seriously R. Isaac's insistence that Christians joined Jews in
an unprecedented display of mourning for the Jewish notable. R. Isaac
seems to be sincerely impressed by this fact. The other royal officials
undoubtedly ordered the day of mourning because of the courtier's position in the administration, but for his coreligionists, he must have symbolized the heights to which a Jew could aspire.

I believe that the identity of this Jewish official can be established with
a reasonable degree of certainty. The monumental *Histoire générale de
Languedoc* contains a long note written by Auguste Molinier on the administration of Louis IX and Alfonse de Poitiers. In it, we read:

> Les sénéchaux et les viguiers possédaient tous les pouvoirs adminis-
> tratifs, mais la gestion des revenus du roi était déléguée à un officier
> spécial, dépendant d'eux et qui tenait leurs comptes. Avant 1247 cet
> officier, dans la sénéchaussée de Carcassonne, était un juif, nommé
> Astruguet, dont les actes disent *qu'il tenait l'argent, pour le roi* (*qui
> tunc tenebat pecuniam d.* [*domini*] *Regis*); d'autres actes le qualifient
> d'officier du roi (*officialis d. Regis*). C'est à lui que sont payés les
> amendes, les tailles, les aides (fouage et autres) les droits de justice,
> &c. Il se permet même parfois quelques exactions. Cette dérogation
> aux canons de l'Église, qui défendaient de donner à un israélite au-
> cune fonction publique, dut disparaître quand Louis IX commença à
> gouverner par lui-même . . .[10]

The evidence for this statement is found in the Registers of the Royal Inquisitors, containing complaints from the seneschalcy of Carcassonne-
Beziers made during the session of 1247-48.[11] The same *Astruguet judeus*
appears in at least a dozen of these complaints. Here is the text of one
characteristic deposition:

> Peter of Caux, a citizen of Beziers, maintains that the lord king
> previously ordered the seneschal of Beziers and Carcassonne to com-
> pel the men of Caux to indemnify said Peter for the damàge they had
> unjustly inflicted upon him. The seneschal, lord Hugh of Arcis, and
> his judge ordered these men of Caux to give Peter ten pounds be-
> cause of the damage inflicted upon him. Now these men have paid
> out the money in question to Astruguet the Jew, who collected for
> the lord king the judicial fees and fines of this region. Peter has often
> requested and admonished said Astruguet to hand over the money
> to him, but Astruguet has refused, giving it instead to the consuls of
> Beziers, without the knowledge or permission of Peter. Therefore,
> he petitions that said Jew be compelled to return the money in ques-

tion to him, for the Jew has given it to men to whom it does not belong. Peter therefore seeks justice.[12]

This text shows that the position of Astruguet was a rather important one. He was responsible for collecting and holding money adjudicated by the seneschal and his court, and he must have had the backing of royal police power. Furthermore, he apparently could exercise some discretion in the disposition of this money and was therefore at times the object of powerful conflicting pressures. We have no way of knowing from the complaint why the money was given to the consuls of Beziers rather than to the plaintiff. What is important is that when Peter felt he had been wronged by Astruguet, the only appeal he had against this Jewish official was to the special royal court of justice, which heard complaints against even the seneschal.

Other documents show Astruguet receiving and holding money at the orders of the seneschal (column 30), the viguier of Beziers (column 43), and judges of the court (columns 44, 103). He also disburses money to citizens at the instruction of the seneschal (column 27). Various kinds of funds were administered by him. One plaintiff claims that at the time of the invasion by "enemies of the king" (under Raimond Trenceval), the court of Beziers borrowed money from him to defend the royal cause, and that part of this money was still being held by Astruguet on behalf of the court rather than being returned (column 12). Another group, from Colombiers, argue that they had first been ordered by the viguier to defend the bridge of Vidorle "against the king of Aragon and the enemies of the king of France," but that when they appeared in battle array, they were instructed to return and to pay a sum of money to Astruguet in place of their military service (column 90).

In another case, the plaintiff was made notary of Servian, with all attendant powers, by the seneschal. "And for this concession of being notary, he gave to the lord king two hundred solidi, and one hundred solidi to the members of the court for the discharge of duties, as is known by the Jew Astruguet from whom he borrowed said money" (columns 68-69). Finally, there is a case concerning the payment of a financial obligation (tallage) to the king. The court of Beziers had seized as collateral some cows belonging to several residents who were outside the city at the time the tax was imposed and was keeping these cows until they would be redeemed by payment of the money owed. In the interim, the cows were being held by Astruguet (column 90).

In short, Astruguet, a Jewish financial official who held one of the most important positions in the royal administration of Carcassonne-Beziers, supervised many different types of accounts pertaining to the royal rule. All of this fits well the description of the activities and responsibilities of the Jewish courtier in the *Avot* Commentary.[13] The one apparent discrepancy is the extent of his popularity, but this is precisely the kind of question on which historical documents are most tendentious, and the difference can easily be explained by the nature of the sources. The registers of the Royal Inquisitors were intended to record complaints made against the royal administration. Favorable light on the king's officers is reflected only accidentally; all the officials, including the seneschals themselves, appear in unflattering hues. The *Avot* passage, ending as a kind of elegy by the son-in-law of the subject, is obviously intended to depict the courtier in the best possible way. The nature of his position and responsibilities undoubtedly made enemies for Astruguet. At the same time, the fact that a Jew could function in a position of such importance under a sovereign (Louis IX) not at all known for his beneficence toward the Jews must be viewed as testimony of his competence and integrity.

It has become something of a commonplace in modern historiography that the Jewry of thirteenth-century southern France did not have a courtier class comparable to that of Aragon and Castile, for after the Albigensian Crusade, Jews were officially excluded from administrative posts under royal rule and therefore played no prominent role in public life.[14] One individual alone is not enough to challenge this generalization. Yet the passage speaks as if Jewish courtiers in the author's generation and milieu were not extraordinarily rare. This impression is corroborated in another source: an elegy in the manuscript *Diwan* of Abraham Bedersi.[15] According to the compiler of this *Diwan* (possibly the poet's son, Yedaiah Bedersi), the elegy was occasioned by news of the death of Don Bonafos Rognet in Beziers. This gave the poet an occasion to express his grief not only for the deceased but for two other notables as well, Don Astruc des Gabbai and R. Abraham b. Solomon, who had died when the poet was too young to write an elegy. This would place their deaths in the middle of the thirteenth century. All three subjects were related to each other and to the poet. We are interested here solely in those elements of the elegy that bear comparison with the passage in the *Avot* Commentary of R. Isaac.

There is a long encomium devoted to the city of Beziers. This passage is far more extensive and detailed than the few corresponding lines in the *Avot* Commentary, and it contains some interesting material relating to the curriculum of Talmudic studies in Beziers.[16] As for the men themselves, it is not always clear which individual is being eulogized, but at least one of the subjects seems to have had a position in the royal administration: "Close to royal power [*karov le-malkhut*], he sought the welfare of his people and looked out for his own local region; people of every district could say about him, 'We have a brother in the house of the king.' " It is said that he "opened the chains of the king's prisoners, even for those who had never seen him; he did good in the midst of his people who had never seen the luminaries before." His help extended not only to Jews but to non-Jews as well, and they respected him greatly for this. Yet, while he was "honored in the sight of kings, he was extremely contemptible in his own eyes—humble and meek in spirit." All of these motifs, as well as many other conventional ones, are to be found in the passage from the *Avot* Commentary. Like R. Isaac, Abraham Bedersi refers to the Jewish dignitary being eulogized as "the king," explaining that he wrote the elegy "because the king was close/ a relative to me" (*ki karov ha-melekh elai*).

Whether or not the Don Astruc des Gabbai of Abraham Bedersi's elegy is the same as Astruguet judeus, the subject of the *Avot* passage, cannot at present be established. But the elegy provides confirmation of a particular historical milieu. Beziers at least seems to have had a circle of Jewish aristocrats associated with the royal administration. Abraham and Yedaiah Bedersi, and possibly also R. Isaac, were from a leading family of these notables. The generalization that the Jewry of southern France had no courtier class therefore has to be modified. Each region of southern France had a different political status in the middle of the thirteenth century, and each must be examined separately if an accurate picture is to emerge.

As for Astruguet himself, little more can be said at this point. Molinier states without citing evidence that Astruguet was removed from his position in 1247, when Louis IX took direct control over the region. It is tempting to find confirmation for this in the first part of the *Avot* passage, where the author describes the insecurity of the courtier's position and the ease with which he may be toppled from power. Yet this is not necessarily a legitimate conclusion. None of the Latin documents proves that Astruguet no longer held office when the special royal court was in session (1247-1248). As for the Hebrew source, it does not seem likely that the first part of the passage can refer to the deposition of Astruguet, as the author maintains that the downfall of the courtier is divine retribution for sins committed through the abuse of power. And the description of the funeral does not at all fit a man dismissed from his office by order of the king. It is therefore not impossible that Astruguet continued to hold his position even after 1247, perhaps until his death; the first record of another man holding that office dates from 1268.[17]

The Nasi

R. Isaac's views on another position of Jewish leadership are expressed in his discussion of a midrash on Numbers 3:4: "Whoever takes prece-

dence in inheritance takes precedence in the receiving of honors, provided that he acts in the way of his fathers" (*Num. R.*, 2:26). He first
points out that the universal practice of the Gentiles is to give the first-
born the major share of the inheritance and then to distribute what is left
to the remaining sons. Kings choose the first-born son to be their succes-
sor, even if he is an incompetent dolt. In order to assure the son's acceptance as future sovereign, the king gains the assent of the nobles and bestows certain signs of royalty upon the first-born.[18]

Similarly, the rabbis explain that according to the Torah, the first-born
son is to inherit the father's wealth or his position of honor even while the
father is alive, for the Torah verse shows Eleazar and Itamar ministering
as priests in the presence of Aaron, their father. But an important qualification is attached. The son must "fill the father's place in stature and
grandeur, and exceed his father's brothers in the highest wisdom." If,
however, an uncle of the first-born is shown to be more worthy of the
position, it is he who must receive it, and the first-born is left with nothing. The remarks of historical significance follow:

> This principle, based on the Torah, contradicts the practice of all
> other nations, who honor the first-born over all other children even
> if he is a fool, an ignoramus, a know-nothing. The fool who walks in
> darkness is not chosen by God to be honored, despite the opinion of
> those of our people who are wise in their own sight, who follow the
> Torah without sufficient preparation or rational insight to under-
> stand the profundity of its truth. They imitate the practices of the
> Gentiles by accepting the sons of prophets and *nesi'im* in the posi-
> tions of the fathers who had acted rightly, and calling them by the
> same title—*nasi*—even if the son pants with lust all day long so that
> he never acquires knowledge or wisdom, even if he gets up night
> after night to play with dice—for no one should heed such laughable
> vanities which make one weary to no avail.
>
> Yet such a man is called by his people "nasi" because his father
> was a nasi of God, due to his wisdom and personal stature. This is
> why the father was called a nasi of God; he was a great rabbi and
> therefore ruled over them. As for the son who followed him and
> associated with mindless men, they lie who call him "nasi," for the
> title "nasi" indicates great personal stature in a man, and if he is not
> known for his exalted stature, how can he be called "nasi?" Honor ill
> befits a fool. Even worse—they profane the Sabbath day and the
> Torah scroll because of him. When he rises on that day to read from
> the Torah, the *hazzan* of the synagogue calls him by the title "nasi"
> before the entire congregation. In this way, they blaspheme God and
> mock Him as one mocks a human being by honoring with His Torah
> one whom He hates because he did not fill the place of his parents.[19]

In order to appreciate this passage, we must briefly review the evidence about the use of the title "nasi" during the first half of the thirteenth century.

The title was still widely used among Jews in the Islamic east. In places such as Mosul and Yemen, nesi'im apparently held real political power in the Jewish community at the end of the twelfth century. The right to this title depended on the claim of descent from the royal line of King David, and some nesi'im possessed documents proving their Davidic lineage and thus validating their position. In Egypt, the highest political position in the Jewish community was that of the *nagid*, who did not claim Davidic descent, and two distinct positions—nasi and nagid—were held simultaneously by different individuals. While the nasi might be called upon to confirm the authority of the nagid, his position in Egypt was generally honorific, with little real power. His actual influence in the community was determined by his own personal stature as a scholar and as a moral figure.[20]

Problems arose when men of authentic royal lineage turned out to be disreputable in character. Several cases of dishonest nesi'im—men accused of taking bribes and other types of misconduct—are attested in the documents of the Geniza.[21] Did such a person deserve the title "nasi" and the attendant honors bestowed upon him in public ceremonies?[22] Abraham Maimonides, who as nagid of Egyptian Jewry[23] was not a disinterested observer, discussed this problem in a responsum. He noted that it was the current custom to call descendents of King David "nasi" even if they held no formal position. This, he argued, was not in accordance with Biblical usage or with the practice of the rabbis, who carefully restricted the title to the head of a yeshiva or to the king (or exilarch). The term "nasi" used to indicate lineage alone is trivial and meaningless (*leshon havai*). Halakhic statements referring to the nasi, such as "One who is banned by the nasi is banned for all Israel" (*Mo'ed Katan*, 16a), refer not to the nasi by lineage but to the nasi by personal stature and position. The judicial decision of a nasi by lineage alone is like that of any other Jew: if he is a scholar, it has the force of a scholar's opinion; if he is not, it carries no special weight because of his pedigree.[24]

The potential for abuse of the title was even more pronounced in Christian Spain, where some of the most influential Jewish families were designated nesi'im. One such family, for whom it was clearly not an empty title, was the Alconstantini. Bahye and Solomon Alconstantini were highly valued interpreters to James I, and a document of 1271 shows that this king had previously given Solomon the authority "to adjudicate all legal matters among the Jews of Saragossa and the kingdom of Aragon through his appointees, in accordance with Jewish law." This was apparently the background of a letter included in a collection of documents pertaining to the Maimonidean controversy of the 1230s, according to which the king required Nachmanides, under oath, to define for him the title of nasi in the Jewish tradition. Nachmanides claimed to have been reluctant to give a decision according to Jewish law, as he did not want to incriminate the powerful courtier families (probably Alconstantini), and he vigorously denied that he denounced them to the king. Nevertheless, he stated that "it has been our custom from time immemorial that fathers can bequeath to their sons only portions of which they are worthy," a statement which reads like a one-sentence epitome of R. Isaac's passage. It is clear that Nachmanides opposed the concept of hereditary position, or in the specific case at hand, the Alconstantini family's claim to all positions of authority over Aragonese Jewry based on their title of nasi.[25]

Another source provides us with greater knowledge about the position of nasi in Aragon and about the opposition to the holders of this title. This group of letters, written by ardent supporters of the nasi's authority, recounts a movement of rebellion against the nesi'im of Barcelona. Several nesi'im are mentioned: R. Sheshet b. Benveniste, the great courtier, defender of Maimonides and patron of the arts, who died in 1209; R. Todros b. Kalonymos, who died shortly before the first letter was written; R. Shealti'el, also apparently deceased at the time of writing; and R. Makhir b. Sheshet, the author of the first letter and the current nasi. The leader of the opposition was Samuel Benveniste, and at least six of his supporters are also named.[26]

Here is evidence of a major internal revolt, seriously challenging the authority of the nesi'im as leaders of the Jewish community. Both Aragon and southern France were embroiled in the resulting conflict. Even the royal family was involved. Samuel Benveniste is admitted by his enemies to have had influence with the queen of Aragon. Indeed, he asked her to request the Jewish community of Montpellier to release him from the ban imposed against him, or if that failed, to instruct her personal emissary in that city to remove the ban.[27]

The faction of Samuel Benveniste is accused of many things. Some are general, indicating refusal to accept the authority of the nasi: "Men arose in Barcelona and spoke insolently against the nasi"; "They arose in Barcelona . . . to profane the perpetual covenant: they did not pay due respect to the city's elders, or properly honor its nesi'im and sages . . . they denied God and their king, the exalted prince and honored nasi R. Makhir . . ." Other accusations are more specific. A dramatic insult to the nasi Todros occurred in the synagogue. The anti-nasi faction chose one of their number, Shealti'el b. Reuben, and gave him a position of honor "which his fathers and his fathers' fathers had not attained" by adding a special bench for him on the bimah and by calling him to read from the

Torah in the presence of the nasi. Then, when the nasi was preparing to leave the synagogue with the other communal dignitaries in his accustomed manner, the rebellious group compounded its effrontery by hurrying to leave first. Even after the death of R. Todros, his opponents continued their defiant behavior, refusing to follow his bier to its resting place and saying, "Was this not a punishment for the nasi?" Finally, they "delayed the prayer" in the synagogue during the period of mourning for R. Todros, presumably to complain about his actions and his character.

In response to the polemical letter of the current nasi, R. Makhir b. Sheshet, a group of distinguished rabbis from southern France, including R. David Kimhi, issued a ban against this "rebel" group. Those proscribed were enjoined against "casting aspersions upon the Torah scroll that the great nasi R. Shealti'el consecrated or challenging anything else upon which the nesi'im and their fathers based their authority, or the pertinent documents which they received from the king," including the document that confirmed the authority of the nasi R. Sheshet b. Benveniste. The purpose of the rabbis in issuing the ban and in ordaining the proper punishments and penances for the rebels was "to restore honor of the Torah to its former level, and to establish the prerogative of rulership in its proper place."[28] The rabbis clearly viewed a challenge to the authority of the nesi'im as a threat to the basic fabric of Jewish life.

These sources would seem to reflect severe communal tensions during the first decades of the thirteenth century. In cities such as Barcelona, influential Jewish families used the title "nasi." Documents attesting to the validity of their use of this title were signed by respected leaders of the Jewish community, and bearers of the title were often confirmed in their authority over the Jewish community by the king. In the tradition of honors due a Jewish king or exilarch,[29] ceremonial expressions of tribute were established by the community for these nesi'im, especially in the synagogue and at public religious functions. At the same time, opposition to the leadership of the nesi'im was expressed in various ways: by challenging the validity of the documents that affirmed their claim to the title, by personal attacks on the worthiness of the individual in question, and by refusal to participate in the honors traditionally accorded to the nasi. The opponents vied with the nesi'im for the support of the royal court, which would ultimately determine who would prevail. The nesi'im found support not only from the king but from wide circles of the rabbinical leadership in Christian Spain and southern France.

R. Isaac, writing perhaps a generation later, gives the impression that the aristocratic leadership structure was still fairly well entrenched, but he shows little concern for the fact that leading rabbis of southern France had once issued a solemn ban against anyone voicing a challenge to the authority of the nesi'im. Where R. Abraham Maimonides simply stated that the title "nasi" is idle nonsense when used to refer to genealogy alone, and Nachmanides gave only his conclusion—that according to Jewish custom, fathers should bequeath to their sons only that which they merit—R. Isaac provides a reasoned critique of the hereditary transfer of all positions of authority, and particularly the title "nasi."

First, he argues that the term "nasi" necessarily implies great personal stature and high individual achievements. He does not refer to its use in rabbinic literature, as does Abraham Maimonides; rather, he bases his conclusion on the etymology of the word itself, coming from a root which means "to lift up" or "exalt." It is instructive to compare a passage in the Aggadah Commentary, in which R. Isaac contrasts the title "nasi" with the title "melekh":

> The prophet [Ezekiel 34:24] called him "nasi" because his stature is greater than that of a king, for this title indicates unsurpassed wisdom, stature, and greatness all bound together, far more than does the title "king." When a king has been chosen by the people, his son will rule in his place after him, even if he is unworthy of ruling . . . If he then becomes a foolish, undistinguished king, lacking wisdom or understanding, he cannot rule by himself, but he will depend on knowledgeable men and experts to show him whatever is too difficult for him . . . But the nasi has no need for another to teach him what to do, for he is wise and discerning, a great prince in Israel.[30]

While the title "king" implies nothing about the individual except that his father was king before him, the title "nasi" may be properly used only of one who is himself exalted in his personal qualities.

The Midrash Commentary introduces another element into the polemic against abuse of the title by identifying such abuse with "the ways of the Gentiles." The universal practice of non-Jews is to follow strictly the rule of primogeniture: the first-born inherits the major portion of the father's wealth and succeeds to his title and position of authority no matter what kind of person he may be. In contrast, the teaching of Judaism, expressed in the Torah and the midrashic statement under consideration, accepts primogeniture in principle but modifies it in a way that drastically restricts its implementation: the first-born son must continue in the way of the father to be eligible for his inheritance. If the first-born is less qualified than one of the father's brothers to succeed the father, it is that uncle who succeeds, and the first-born has no valid claim. Therefore, those who insist on automatic inheritance of titles such as nasi reveal their ignorance of the Torah and "follow the practices of the Gentiles" rather than the true teachings of their own faith.

The denunciation of the nasi's supporters as profaning the Sabbath day and the Torah scroll is a powerful counterattack against the accusations in the *Minhat Kena'ot* text. There, the rebels were accused of insulting the nasi by calling someone else to the Torah while the nasi was present in the synagogue. Here we have the opposing claim: That it is sacrilege to call a man to the Torah by the title "nasi" if that man is ignorant and immoral. The supporters of the nasi accused the rebels of denying God by questioning the authority of this office.[31] R. Isaac accuses these supporters of "cursing and mocking God" by honoring with the sancta of the faith a man repugnant in God's sight.

Who precisely were these supporters of the nesi'im whom R. Isaac belittles as "wise in their own sight?" We have seen that the nasi Makhir b. Sheshet, the reigning Jewish authority in Barcelona at the time, addressed his letter to the "sages of Provence," and that a group of rabbis—probably from Narbonne, as R. David Kimhi is included—replied by expressing absolute support for the authority of the nesi'im and specifically for R. Makhir. In addition, there were briefer replies from rabbis in Montpellier and in Beziers supporting the ban against the rebels. There were undoubtedly still rabbis within R. Isaac's own community who felt that any challenge to the authority of the nesi'im threatened the stability of Jewish life.

By this time, Beziers was no longer juridically linked with Aragon, and the situation in Barcelona would not have been of primary concern. But the position of nasi was highly significant in southern France itself. Without entering into the problems relating to the origins and early history of this title there,[32] we may note its status in the late twelfth and early thirteenth centuries. Benjamin of Tudela wrote of

> Narbonne, an ancient center of Torah, from which learning spread to all countries. There are great sages in it, and at their head is Rabbi Kalonymos, son of the great R. Todros, entitled "nasi" by virtue of his Davidic descent. He has estates and lands [granted him] by the governor of the city, of which no one can forcibly deprive him.[33]

That the nasi in Narbonne held land in a publicly recognized manner different from that of other Jews is confirmed by a document of 1217, in which the Viscount Aymeri stated that the right to allodial holdings of land free from tax-paying status was reserved exclusively to the "king of the Jews."[34] The names of Kalonymos b. Todros and Todros b. Kalonymos, sometimes accompanied by the Latin designation "king of the Jews," appear on Latin documents concerning property rights dating from 1195 through 1252.[35] The names "the nasi Kalonymos of Narbonne" and "the nasi R. Meshullam son of the honored nasi R. Kalonymos" appear in letters pertaining to the Maimonidean controversy of the early 1230s.[36] In short, the nesi'im of Narbonne played a leading role in the political, economic, and cultural life of the Jewish community at the time R. Isaac was writing. It stands to reason that their power and prestige inspired much of the outrage against those who had challenged the authority of the nesi'im in Barcelona.

R. Isaac b. Yedaiah was apparently from an influential family in Beziers. Yet the nature of this influence was quite different from that of the nesi'im. As we have seen, he was related by marriage to one of the leading royal officials in the seneschalcy of Carcassonne-Beziers. This Jew, Astruguet, reached his position of power not because he was born into a family of noble lineage but because of his personal qualities of financial acumen and integrity. Juxtaposing the passage on the courtier with this passage on the nasi, we sense the tension between two different claims to influence within the Jewish community. Both were dependent upon the support of the Christian king, but one was hereditary, the other personal and individual in nature. Perhaps because of his own family ties, perhaps because of ideological reasons apparent throughout his work, R. Isaac allied himself against hereditary positions and on the side of a new type of royal official, whose claim to authority, independent of lineage, was based entirely on individual capabilities and talents.

The Rabbi

The Commentary on the Aggadot reveals the author's evaluation of current rabbinic leadership. As in the case of the courtier, R. Isaac sets some highly critical remarks against a character sketch of one individual whom he portrays as an ideal of the type. The negative passages should be seen in the context of other contemporary attacks on the Talmudic scholar. The description of R. Meshullam as a rabbinic ideal must be analyzed in some detail, as it can now be placed for the first time in its proper historical setting.

Rabbis and Talmudists are the targets of a two-pronged polemic. First, there is an attack on the intellectual limitations of those who restrict their studies exclusively to the halakhic content of the Talmud. R. Isaac assumes, as did all adherents of a philosophical approach to Judaism, that the ultimate purpose of man is to actualize his intellect by acquiring supreme knowledge—the knowledge of God. This is possible only through the study of philosophy, leading to an understanding of metaphysics. Therefore, those who study halakha to the exclusion of philosophy fail to fulfill a fundamental religious duty.

This type of critique can be seen in the comment on a passage from *Sanhedrin*, 106b: "In the years of Rab Judah, all study was confined to *Nezikin*, whilst we study a great deal more;[37] and when Judah came to the law 'If a woman preserves vegetables in a pot,' he observed, 'I see here the disputation of Rav and Samuel'; whilst we have studied *Ukzin* at thirteen sessions. Yet Judah merely took off one shoe, and the rain came down, whilst we cry out but there is none to heed us. It is because the Holy One, blessed be He, requires the heart." The statement of the gemara is intended to pose a paradox. In the generation of R. Judah, the study of halakha was far more restricted than at present, and one might therefore expect the merit of the contemporary sages to be greater. Yet R. Judah was of greater stature and more favorable in God's sight than any sage currently alive. Why? Because his motives were more pure, and God "requires the heart."

R. Isaac's interpretation gives the passage a totally new meaning:

> The sages are teaching here about those who engage in the discipline of Talmud exclusively and do not concern themselves with any other branch of knowledge. Such a person, who has not mastered another discipline and has not engaged in research enabling one to gain knowledge of God and to cleave to Him, has not fulfilled the true purpose intended by Him.
>
> In order to make this point, they taught that the pious men of early times [hasidim rishonim, here referring to R. Judah], the finest and most scrupulous of our sages, did not put all their effort into the study of Talmud alone, even though this is an exalted and honorable subject. Rather, they engaged in this discipline for part of the day. When they came to a complicated matter relating to the laws of plagues and tents, they did not allow themselves to be drawn into these subjects by posing innumerable problems and answers. Rather, they said of such matters, "I see here the disputation of Rav and Samuel," thus cutting the discussion short. Afterward, they would concern themselves with entering the pardes, attaining true knowledge of their Creator, so that they would not believe anything false or impossible about Him. In this way, they sharpened and purified their intellect of all impediments, for this is what is expected of man insofar as he is a human being capable of attaining true life.[38]

In this reading, R. Judah's failure to study obscure and abstruse halakhot does not make his stature paradoxical; it is the key to his greatness. He did not exhaust his time on relatively trivial matters. By contrast, the later sages who studied the legal minutiae of Tractate Ukzin realized that they had no time left to master what is ultimately important. The proper translation of the passage, according to this comment, would read not, "Yet R. Judah merely took off one shoe . . . ," but, "Therefore, R. Judah merely took off one shoe, and the rain came down," for his special powers were the consequence of restricting the time spent in studying the halakha.

The rest of the passage is interpreted allegorically to complete this thought. Removing the shoe represents eliminating the physical obstacles and impediments to pure intellectual understanding. The falling of rain is, as often in Biblical and rabbinic literature, a figure for the divine effluence (*shefa*) which descends upon the philosopher. This interpretation is rather ingeniously counterposed with God's instructions to Moses at the bush to remove *both* shoes. Prophecy requires the cultivation of both intellect and imagination,[39] and Moses had to remove the impediments to both. Now in exile, prophecy is impossible, but we can still remove one shoe and know God through the intellect of the philosopher. The scholars who spend all their time on the intricacies of halakha have shackled minds; they wear both "shoes," and they cry out in futility, for they are ignorant of the knowledge God wants us to attain.

The same idea is expressed in the comment on R. Jeremiah's interpretation of Lamentations 3:6: " 'He has made me to dwell in dark places, as those that have been long dead'—said R. Jeremiah, 'This is the Talmud of Babylonia' " (*Sanh.*, 24a). This statement was generally interpreted to refer not to the book called the Babylonian Talmud but to the Babylonian mode of study, which, for one reason or another, was claimed to be inferior to that of the sages in the land of Israel.[40] By applying the statement to the literary work, the object of such intense veneration and exhaustive study in his time, R. Isaac reaches a striking conclusion.

He explains that those who follow the sages of Babylonia limit their study exclusively to the discipline of halakha according to the Babylonian Talmud. Therefore, they do not study the other, philosophical disciplines, which would enable them to derive knowledge of God from the realm of Creation through rational proofs and to refute on logical grounds erroneous beliefs such as dualism and corporeality. Because of their neglect of philosophical studies, some of these Talmudists actually harbor corporealist conceptions of God. The statement means that anyone who studies the halakha of the Babylonian Talmud exclusively walks in the dark. Although it is a valuable and important subject, it is intended to serve only as a preparatory stage to the study of the "true branch of learning," which alone can provide the fullest possible knowledge of God.

The assertion that halakhic study alone is incomplete and inadequate is buttressed by arguments based on models from the Jewish past. From the Bible, R. Isaac mentions David, Solomon, and the prophets, claiming that they obviously did not restrict themselves to the study of halakha. Verses that speak of Solomon's wisdom (*hokhma*), such as I Kings 5:11, 26, must refer to philosophical and not halakhic knowledge, for why would the Queen of Sheba journey to Jerusalem to test Solomon's expertise in Jewish law? The rabbinic era furnishes a model from among the sages of Palestine. This is R. Akiva, who was praised for entering the pardes and attaining that philosophical knowledge of God which is the goal and purpose of human existence. According to R. Isaac, the Jerusalem Talmud contains many proofs that the Palestinian sages were learned in physics and metaphysics.[41]

Of course, the objects of these attacks saw things quite differently. Their own ideology, and their critique of philosophical study as a wasteful and potentially hazardous diversion from the only legitimate subject of Jewish study, is well known from the literature of the *Kulturkampf* over the role of philosophy in Judaism. The passages cited above fit into a long tradition of counterattack against an educational curriculum that produced rabbis who were experts in Talmudic dialectics but ignorant of everything else. Bahya ibn Pakuda has a learned scholar berate a disciple for inquiring about an obscure detail of the divorce law before he has even begun to master the philosophical foundations of the Jewish faith. Maimonides places the halakhic expert who has not independently investigated the foundations of belief outside the palatial abode of the King. Shem Tov Falaquera depicts the "Believer," who considers anything other than the study of Torah to be an idle waste of time, as a narrow-minded, doctrinaire, intolerant pedant from whom the "Seeker" has absolutely nothing to learn. Joseph ibn Kaspi compares the expert in Jewish law to the master of any other craft to whom one may turn for a special need but whose knowledge is far less valuable than the philosopher's knowledge of the existence and unity of God.[42] The Talmudist ignorant of philosophy was a constant target for the philosophically oriented Jews of Spain and southern France. R. Isaac's innovation lay in basing his critique of Talmudism on novel interpretations of the Talmud itself.

A second thrust to the critique of Talmudists in thirteenth-century literature was directed not at their intellectual narrowness but at their ethical perversity, their materialism, their excessive involvement in worldly affairs. R. Isaac turns to this theme while discussing the statement, "The *torah* of Doeg the Edomite was merely from his lips outward" (*Sanh.*, 106b). He explains that Doeg ignored some of the teachings of the Torah, for "he did not read from the Torah with good intentions—of transforming that which he read into a good action—but rather in order that he might be called 'rabbi' because of it, and be honored by those who saw him."

And his imprint is still noticeable in our own time among some of those who engage in the discipline of Talmudic study, meditating upon it day and night without holding their peace. Yet they destroy the fabric of social behavior far more than do poor, ignorant Jews. For they deny whatever their comrades lend to them out of the goodness of their hearts in an hour of need. And when a matter involving them comes before a judge, whose function it is to save men from the power of their oppressors by implementing justice, these Talmudists know how to make deceitful claims before him, so that unless the matter is known to a third party, the judge is unable to restore what has been stolen. For the judge may rule only on the basis of the evidence; he cannot rule on the basis of plausible reasons or intuition. These Talmudists do not fear for their souls even if they have in their homes things stolen from the poor. Although they may meditate on the Torah day in and day out, they do not fulfil its good teachings. They teach themselves to speak lies; they learn nothing from the Torah except how to lord it over their neighbors; they will not see God.[43]

The text about Doeg has obviously served as a pretext for denouncing the hypocrisy of contemporary Talmudists. Study of the halakha is bad enough when it prevents one from studying philosophy; it is even worse when the expert fails to live and to act in accordance with its imperatives and worst of all when he uses his mastery of the halakha to subvert the very values it is intended to support. There is a recognition here that a case adjudicated technically in accordance with Jewish law may not always produce a just result, that a judge may be handcuffed by a clever and deceitful defendant who uses his Talmudic learning to make the claim most beneficial to his cause, even if it is untrue. The passage implies that such practices were not uncommon. The greed of the Talmudists is also central to R. Isaac's criticism of R. Meshullam's disciples. After the death of the master, the students returned to their homes, "drawn after profit, toiling to grow rich and to fill their homes with silver and gold . . . thus the bundle came apart, for every man went in pursuit of his own profit."[44] This is rather general as a piece of historical evidence, but it confirms R. Isaac's hostility toward certain rabbis and Talmudists for being too deeply engrossed in the acquisition of material wealth.

This type of condemnation also has a tradition. An anonymous poem, apparently from the thirteenth century, excoriates the rabbis of its time:

> Their eyes and their hearts look only to ill-gain,
> Their purpose is exclusively to devise crafty schemes—
> To lend money at high interest to Gentiles,
> To accumulate wealth through perverse strategems.

Isaac ibn Sahula, in *Meshal ha-Kadmoni*, rails against the hypocrisy of the rabbinic leader who feigns religiosity when "his intention is really to deceive men through his actions, to make widows the object of his plunder, to fill his secret storehouse with treasure stolen from the poor, leaving the destitute groaning. The purpose of his piety is 'to catch the poor by drawing him up in his net' (Ps. 10:9)." Kalonymos ibn Kalonymos lashes out against rabbis who exploit their learning for material gain—by demanding a fee for every word of instruction that issues from their mouths, by claiming exemption from the taxes borne by the rest of the community, and worst of all, by giving judicial opinions that they know to be incorrect because money has secretly changed hands.[45] Various historical developments—the emergence of a professional rabbinical class, royal policies that placed significant economic opportunities within the reach of men recognized by their communities as religious leaders, the generally increasing economic pressure which impelled men to take advantage of these opportunities—seem to have created a group of rabbinic leaders who aroused powerful resentment in sensitive souls.

By contrast with these negative evaluations, R. Isaac portrays his own teacher, R. Meshullam, as the ideal Talmudist and rabbi.[46] R. Isaac's critique of contemporary rabbis and Talmudists focused on two issues: their ignorance of philosophy resulting from a narrow interest in the halakha and their unethical behavior linked with greed for material wealth. R. Meshullam is shown to be different in both respects. First, we are told that in his school were "learned scholars with reputations in every discipline and branch of knowledge." Furthermore, his disciples learned from him both "the disputations of Abaye and Rava" and "the work of the chariot and the wheel of the wagon" (ma'aseh merkavah veofan agalah). This particular school clearly did not restrict discourse to halakhic dialectics alone. As R. Meshullam was an opponent of the incipient Kabbala in southern France,[47] we may conclude that "ma'aseh merkavah" in this passage has the meaning given to it by Maimonides: the philosophical discipline of metaphysics.[48] This would certainly be consistent with the assumptions and values of R. Meshullam's disciple, R. Isaac himself.

As for the second thrust of the attack against the Talmudists—that they used their expertise for the unethical pursuit of material gain—we are told that R. Meshullam taught his students without charging any fee. This is an important detail in the history of the professional rabbinate. Maimonides' opposition to the acceptance of money for the teaching of Torah is well know.[49] At the same time, the movement toward professionalism is evident in the sources of the thirteenth century, and one fourteenth-century figure argued that if the position of the Rambam were to be followed, there would not be a single teacher of Torah in his day.[50] Our passage furnishes evidence of one scholar who apparently resisted this trend and adhered to the Maimonidean ideal. Unlike Maimonides, however, R. Meshullam did not have a profession from which he earned his livelihood; we are told that others engaged in the needs of the community, "but he occupied himself exclusively with that which God desires, meditating upon His Torah day and night." This might be understood to imply that he was independently wealthy and therefore did not rely upon the fees of his students or a salary from the community in order to live. Again, most of his disciples apparently did not continue this tradition.

R. Isaac was obviously impressed by his mentor's forcefulness and strength of character. R. Meshullam is depicted as the unquestioned leader of southern French Jewry in his age: "The entire people hearkened unto him for its own good, and the eyes of that generation were opened." For those who willfully defied him by choosing the wrong way, he had no patience. He would become inflamed with anger and zeal, denouncing the rebellious student and expelling him from the academy until such time as the student recanted. But if R. Meshullam was remembered as a zealous disciplinarian, for the seriously committed student, he was an incomparable pedagogue. His technique of instruction is described in some detail. First, he would deliver a lecture on some Talmudic subject. His students would sit silently until he finished speaking, while "he explained to them all the necessary profundity of the halakha." The lecture would concern "the *sugiah*, objections and their resolutions, and additional points which he himself thought up—mounds of material on the tip of every letter." The content of these lectures was so difficult that R. Isaac, who was fifteen years old when he entered this academy, frankly confesses his inability to comprehend the material without a prodigious effort to prepare in advance, and even then he did not absorb it all at first. After the lecture, there would be an opportunity for questions about anything the student had not understood. The rabbi would answer each question, explaining the material with painstaking care two or three times until it was clear. If the student did not ask, it was his own fault that he remained ignorant. R. Isaac was clearly impressed with the patience and the concern for effective pedagogy evinced by his model.[51]

As for R. Meshullam's own scholarship, he is praised as being without peer in his generation all the way to France.[52] Two qualities are singled out as especially worthy of praise. First was the completeness of his knowledge of the halakha: he was expert "in the totality of the oral law, in every restriction and precaution which emerges from it; he could determine what was obscure from what was clear, and no mystery was too difficult for him." The second quality was the degree to which he had internalized this knowledge. "He did not even look at the book or its commentary, for his wisdom served him and accompanied him wherever he was, entering with him even to the bathhouse. If the Torah of truth which was in his mouth had been forgotten from Israel, he could have written it for himself by memory . . . Not a single halakha was hidden from him, and he did not need to teach others from books, for the source of his understanding was within." This freedom from reliance upon the written word was an important theme in the intellectual tradition of southern France.[53] For R. Isaac, R. Meshullam was the exemplar.

The assumption that this passage was written by Yedaiah ha-Penini created insurmountable chronological difficulties.[54] The discovery that the commentary is the work not of Yedaiah but of R. Isaac, who wrote not long after the middle of the thirteenth century, makes most problems vanish. Other passages in the commentaries indicate that the author was at least forty years old when he wrote them.[55] Therefore, his entrance into the academy of R. Meshullam can be dated at least twenty-five years before the commentary was written, perhaps between 1230 and 1235, the period when Nachmanides wrote his epistle to Meshullam and the scholars of Beziers. At this time, a generation after Rabad of Posquières and R. Zerahiah ha-Levi, R. Meshullam might well have been viewed by his disciple as the outstanding Talmudist in southern France.[56]

The one outstanding difficulty in interpreting the passage concerns the destruction of the city mentioned in it. After describing the effective discipline maintained by the leaders of the Jewish community in the past, especially through the use of excommunication and social ostracism, R. Isaac continues:

> At the time when this city was destroyed, with all its spoil, when its splendor sank, and its multitudes, I saw the wicked buried [peacefully], while no-good scoundrels came out of the holes in which they hid themselves until then. The wild ones of our people abounded, the wrong-doers continually afflicted people as they once did before the community was founded. Violence proliferated among hypocrites who caused enmity between brothers; they cut themselves up in the manner of ancient times, striking each other wickedly, for they saw no figure of authority around. The young would act insolently against the aged and wise, the immature frolicked abroad, for those who ruled over the people had died, and those who did right were forgotten in this city and elsewhere. Everyone would do what seemed appropriate to himself, not knowing what was right, and sinning continually everywhere.
>
> After the city was taken and given over into the hand of the enemy, into the hand of the cruel lord, and houses full of all good things were plundered, travelers no longer knew where to find a benefactor who could do them kindness and justice, for he perverted his path. Whosoever was left living is duty bound to mourn and bewail once a year, lamenting a doleful lament for the destruction of the city—a miniature Jerusalem—a princess among the provinces, from whose ranks came "kings" and "governors"—the city that was the perfection of beauty, filled with destruction. For so long as it stood on its hill, on its own place, the name of the city was "the Lord is there." There was no breach, no one going out in the streets of the city turned away from the right path, but all the people of the land believed in the Lord and leaned upon God.
>
> In the days when the Judges ruled, there was a great but humble man . . .

There follows the description of R. Meshullam.

Neubauer, who first published this passage, suggested hesitantly that this section referred to the destruction of Beziers by Simon de Montfort's army during the Albigensian Crusade of 1209.[57] This is certainly problematic if the passage was written by Yedaiah no earlier than 1300, for the author gives the impression that the event occurred within his memory, or at least at a time when he could have heard about it as a small child. But no destruction of Beziers is known to have taken place during the second half of the thirteenth century. The proposals of other scholars to substitute a different city, sometimes in conjunction with a different R. Meshullam, are mere conjectures, none of which is convincing. Now that the passage can be placed sometime around the year 1260, written by a man at least in his forties, the identification of the destruction alluded to here with the famous sack of Beziers in 1209 is more plausible, as the author would be referring to an event not far removed from his early childhood.

However, this hypothesis is still not entirely satisfactory. The passage provides a clear picture of the way R. Isaac views the previous decades in the history of Beziers' Jewry: first there was a period of strong rabbinic leadership, close control over dissident behavior, and effective discipline, followed by the destruction, associated with a breakdown of authority in the Jewish community, and a resulting decline in the general standards of behavior. The author claims to have seen this happen. R. Meshullam would seem to belong to the earlier period of effective leadership, having lived "in the days when the Judges ruled." But if the destruction occurred in 1209, the heyday of R. Meshullam's academy in Beziers would have come later. To read the passage as if R. Meshullam restored the leadership that disappeared with the destruction is to twist its obvious meaning.

Furthermore, the actual language of the description does not entirely fit the events of 1209, even as they would have been recalled many years later. The sack of Beziers by Simon de Montfort's army culminated in a savage massacre of the civilian population, with total casualties estimated by contemporary witnesses in the area of twenty thousand.[58] The passage does not mention anyone's being killed. It speaks about "destruction," the plunder of wealth, and the transfer of the city to the power of the enemy, a cruel lord. It should also be noted that there is no clear reference to Beziers as a totality, encompassing Christians and Jews. The author seems to be interested only in the Jewish community of Beziers. This is the "miniature Jerusalem"; this is the community he describes as being destroyed.

It is possible, therefore, that the entire passage should be read as depicting not the physical destruction of a city in war but rather a breakdown in the leadership, cohesiveness, and inner discipline of the Jewish community in Beziers. Such a collapse would have come in the wake of the following historical circumstances: the incorporation of Beziers into the royal domain ("after the city was taken and given over into the hand of the enemy, into the hand of a cruel lord"); the aggressive anti-Jewish legislation of Louis IX, attacking the foundations of Jewish economic life, including the actual confiscation of funds and debts[59] ("houses full of all good things were plundered"); the end of the renowned academy of R. Meshullam, which attracted Jewish students to Beziers from afar, following the death of the master. This interpretation, which places the "destruction" sometime in the 1240s, would make chronological and historical sense of these lines that otherwise remain an enigma.

Other Jewish Types

Having looked carefully at the material relating to three leadership types—courtier, nasi, and rabbi—we may survey some other groups of thirteenth-century Jews more quickly. R. Isaac discourses on the proper role for Jewish preachers while discussing the statement "Whoever reads one Biblical verse in its proper time brings good to the world, as it is said, 'And a word in its season, how good it is!' "[60] This prescription, he maintains, is addressed to those who preach publicly at occasions such as feasts of religious obligation. Their proper function is to bring some spiritual benefit to the listeners, for example by instructing them not to eat or drink excessively, as it is a disgrace for human beings to destroy their souls in this way. The verse from Proverbs brought as an asmakhta teaches that the words spoken by a wise man should fit the circumstances of delivery:

> Not in the manner of all the preachers now in our time, who speak not on a subject pertaining to the specific occasion but rather about aggadot which seem strange to their turbid and coarse intellects. For they do not understand the profundity and true meaning of the sages in these aggadic sayings—"It is not an empty thing." It would be better for such a speaker to stop up his mouth and be silent. Then he might be considered wise, for he would not mutilate their words, which are pleasant and correct to him who understands.[61]

This passage, unfortunately so brief and general, is significant both in its allusion to Jewish preachers in the middle of the thirteenth century and in its implications for the author's own purpose in his work. Very little sermonic material has come down to us from the thirteenth century, for most sermons, preached in the vernacular, were not written in a permanent form. A major exception is Jacob Anatoli's *Malmad ha-Talmidim*. The introduction to this work describes the author's public preaching career—how he began with sermons at weddings and then came to preach regularly in the synagogue on Shabbat until he was stopped by the opposition of some of his colleagues.[62] Thus, both the practice of preaching at wedding feasts and the opposition to certain types of sermons is corroborated by Anatoli. It is unlikely, however, that sermons such as those of Anatoli himself were the object of R. Isaac's criticism. Those sermons that have been preserved deal with themes appropriate to the occasion, and they treat the aggadot in a manner not markedly different from that of R. Isaac.[63]

If Anatoli and his philosophically oriented disciples were condemned for filling their sermons with allegorical interpretations of Bible and aggadah,[64] other preachers were being castigated for taking the aggadot too literally. Maimonides led the attack, mincing no words in his denunciation of these literalist homileticians:

> The worst offenders are preachers who preach and expound to the masses what they themselves do not understand. Would that they keep silent about what they do not know, as it is written, "If only they would be utterly silent, it would be accounted to them as wisdom." Or they might at least say, "We do not understand what our sages intended in this statement, and we do not know how to explain it." But they believe they do understand, and they vigorously expound to the people what they think rather than what the sages really said. They therefore give lectures to the people on the tractate Berakhot and on this present chapter [Helek] and other texts, expounding them word-for-word according to their literal meaning.[65]

It would appear that R. Isaac's diatribe is aimed at a similar group, for his assertion that the preachers do not understand the true, profound meaning of the sages and his rhetorical use of Job 13:5 are quite close to the Maimonidean passage. Somewhat puzzling is his statement that the preachers use "aggadot which seem strange to their turbid and coarse intellects" (haggadot ha-nir'ot shel dofi le-fi sevaratam ha-akhurah ve-ha-gasah), for Maimonides is speaking about men to whom these aggadot did not seem strange at all. Why would a preacher who accepted the aggadot on their surface level alone and considered them to be bizarre and problematic choose to use them as the basis of his sermons for wedding feasts and other such occasions? Indeed, this phrase seems to apply more to the second category in Maimonides' typology of attitudes toward the aggadah: those who read the aggadot literally and deny any deeper, hidden meaning, holding them up to contempt and scorn. But while there are many references in contemporary literature to those who mocked and derided the extralegal utterances of the sages,[66] there is no indication that they did so in the context of sermons delivered at a feast of religious obligation.

A possible solution to this quandary may be found in one of the six categories of rabbinic statements as formulated by Hillel of Verona: divrei bedihutah, words of humor, intended to refresh the mind that is weary after study. He argues that such statements conceal no profound, cryptic message and are to be read in accordance with their obvious meaning. They are, nevertheless, not trivial or inconsequential, as they serve an important purpose.[67] R. Isaac vehemently rejects the notion that the sages indulged in such good-natured banter, insisting that all statements appearing to be of this nature must be understood on an esoteric level.[68] It is not difficult to imagine a preacher at a wedding feast, who felt that his function was primarily to amuse or entertain the guests, referring with levity and humor to certain aggadot that are indeed alien to the serious discourse of the philosopher.[69] It is also not difficult to imagine R. Isaac railing at such a practice and denouncing such preachers for using rabbinic quotations that, in his view, they did not begin to understand.

We have seen reference to Jews who hold philosophical doctrines so extreme that they deny such basic teachings of the Torah as Creation, resurrection, individual providence and retribution, and even the revelation of the Torah from heaven. While R. Isaac finds such a position unmistakably erroneous, he feels compelled to explain rather sympathetically how these errors may arise out of the best of intentions.[70] At the other extreme are Jews who are totally ignorant of philosophy. These he divides into two categories, following a statement from the Midrash: "One thousand enter Scripture and a hundred of them exit, one hundred enter Mishnah and ten of them exit, ten enter Talmud and one exits at a time." The first group, we are told, consists of those who "study" the Torah and prophets without understanding their true meaning and without knowing the reasons for the commandments. "Innumerable" Jews are like this, knowing only how to read the Torah mechanically, chirping like animals bereft of reason. If asked about the meaning of what they read, they are confounded and are unable to respond. The second group consists of the Talmudists who strive to master the oral law but have no knowledge of philosophy or the esoteric meaning of each commandment.[71]

Ignorance of philosophy is responsible for blatantly erroneous beliefs about God. One such falsehood is the corporealist notion described in a passage of the Midrash Commentary. Discussing the commandments relating to the tabernacle and the ark, R. Isaac concludes that these are intended

to refute the idea of the faithless "Sadducees" who say that God is [composed of] a matter which is finer, purer, and more transparent than the matter of any shining star. The sun and moon are as nothing before it, for His radiant light surpasses theirs . . . [Those who believe this] want to magnify Him, but it is merely vain words, for they are guilty of attributing to God a material nature. They remain without a true God, for philosophy teaches that such a thing does not exist. What wisdom do [these corporealists] have?[72]

Attacks by Jewish philosophers against the masses who conceived of God in physical or anthropomorphic terms are legion; references to a developed theory of divine corporealism, such as in this passage, are far more rare.

The Jews who held to this theory are identified here only by the vague term "Sadducees." Elsewhere, R. Isaac speaks of false beliefs as rampant especially among the Jews of France. He explains this phenomenon using a theory of geography and climate that characterizes the inhabitants of the north as being naturally disposed to be coarse in body and mind, a doctrine attributed to the "Babylonians [sages of the Babylonian Talmud] on the basis of scientific investigation." The theory is presented to explain the arrangement of tribes around the sanctuary in the wilderness and then applied to the contemporary scene.

As you find in our own time that the entire Diaspora community which was exiled and traveled through the earth until it reached France, located in the north, consists of coarse-brained men, without exception. They believe impossible things in every area, base and honorable alike, without shame. Even in matters of faith, the majority of our people are perplexed and ignorant; they are drawn after vanities and waste themselves upon their incorrect beliefs. So they live throughout their lives. For owing to the extreme coarseness of their material component, they do not know wherein they have stumbled. And if there is among them one person who has attained true knowledge of the Most High and reproaches his people at the gate, saying that there are those who believe incorrect things about God, and showing them the true way in which to proceed, he takes his life in his hands. They gather in opposition against him to stone him with rocks, so that he must flee and hide . . .[73]

The first part of this passage probably refers to the superstitions, especially the beliefs in demons and magic, which were rife among the Jews of northern France and Germany,[74] and which R. Isaac criticizes in other parts of his work. The prevalence of incorrect beliefs about God is a more serious accusation.

At issue here is not the true intellectual history of northern French Jewry in the thirteenth century but how the French Jews were perceived by philosophically oriented Jews of the south. This passage rather dramatically reinforces the picture that emerges from a letter written by the scholars of Narbonne during the Maimonidean conflict of the 1230s. While recognizing the greatness of the French rabbis in Talmudic studies, the authors of this letter refer with biting sarcasm and scorn to the naive and ignorant credulity of their northern colleagues with regard to beliefs.

Such a view apparently reflected an attitude prevalent in thirteenth-century southern France.[75]

In this context, another passage concerning the Jews of France should be mentioned. Again the comment begins with the motif of four directions, linked with a midrash on a verse from the Song of Songs (4:16, "Awake, O north wind") dealing with the return from exile (see Isaiah 43:6). In the course of his discussion, R. Isaac again emphasizes the perversity of the north:

> As you will find that the prophet [Jeremiah] prophesied to them in the name of God concerning the northern side, that from there evil will break forth and come to them, for that direction is set to oppose them and always liable to harm them. This applies all the way to France, where the people has lived throughout its history despised and despoiled. The king and the nobles have dealt ill with us and with our ancestors in every generation. Their hand is still stretched out to do evil, and they have the ability to do so, for their sovereign power continues. From these [French kings], the kings who rule in the land of Edom see and do likewise.[76]

Writing in southern France in the middle of the thirteenth century, R. Isaac still considers "France" to be a separate kingdom to the north. On the other hand, he implies that he too is subject to the oppressive policies of the French kings, as would fit the situation in regions of Languedoc recently incorporated under royal jurisdiction. The reaction of southern French Jews to the policies of Louis IX was forcefully articulated by R. Meir b. Simon.[77] The passage from R. Isaac probably reflects the same reality. The seriousness of the situation is underscored by the final sentence expressing the fear that other kings of Christendom may be following the example of the French monarchs in implementing anti-Jewish measures.

A final group in the spectrum of contemporary Jewish society is the apostates. The point of departure is a statement in *Avodah Zarah*, 26b, which mentions four categories of dissident Jews: *minim, meshummadim, mesurot,* and *epikorsim.* The comment[78] focuses on the categories meshummadim and minim. R. Isaac first summarizes a definition that he gave in his commentary on *Berakhot:* the *meshummad le-hakh'is* (literally, one who apostatizes in order to provoke, in a spirit of defiance) has a natural innate tendency toward good, but he overcomes this tendency through an act of rebellious will and chooses to sin. This sinfulness is primarily intellectual in nature, for the meshummad is characterized by his false beliefs about God, especially his denial of individual providence, retribution, and relevation. Here we have moved into the contemporary context, the Talmudic category identified with a group of extreme philosophers within the Jewish community. The halakhic status of a meshummad is then stated: he is considered to have removed himself from the benefits of being a Jew, to the extent that the commandment to return a lost object and the prohibition of taking interest no longer apply to him.[79] The one qualification of this rule is that the meshummad le-hakh'is is still considered a Jew in the realm of marriage law, so that his wife cannot remarry without a Jewish divorce, or *get*.[80]

As the comment continues, it shifts focus. R. Isaac insists that the terms "min" and "meshummad le-hakh'is" are essentially the same, or more precisely, that the "min" ("heretic") is merely a "min" ("subcategory") under the general category of "meshummad le-hakh'is." This is a new departure, for the "min" had always been considered a separate category both in definition[81] and in halakhic status. While a Torah scroll written by a min was to be burned, one written by a meshummad le-hakh'is was merely to be suppressed.[82] R. Isaac, in stating this halakha, fuses the two principles, maintaining that a scroll written by a Jew after he has become a meshummad le-hakh'is is to be burned.

The insistence that the two terms are synonymous appears even more forcefully in the ensuing discussion of the *Birkat ha-Minim*. The first phrase of this benediction, "May there be no hope for the meshummadim, and may the minim be instantaneously destroyed," is treated as if it is Biblical parallelism, asserting the same thing in different words:

> We cannot say that the meshummad le-hakh'is and the min are two matters which cannot be combined together, and that the sages prayed that the meshummad would no longer have any hope but would remain in a state of sin throughout his life. Heaven forbid that they would pray such a prayer, which contradicts our religion . . . Their prayer was pure; they prayed about the meshummad le-hakh'is, who is a min drawn after false belief and entrenched in it as one of the heretics, having become part of them—they prayed about both that they would be instantaneously destroyed and singled out from the community of the Diaspora for evil. For they are bad for Israel, and they try to make the Jews stumble from the path far more than does any Gentile, and they hate the Jews to the utmost. You find that the sages repeated this thought about them, saying, "And may all the enemies of your people Israel be speedily cut down," for this is from the prayer they ordained about them. They are the enemies, the enemies of God . . . All who follow the Torah and are called by the name Israel pray this prayer about them, so that every man will fear for his soul and not be drawn after these sins.

From the context, it appears that R. Isaac is no longer speaking about those who hold to extreme philosophical beliefs opposed to the principles of all religion but about those who had actually converted to Christianity. The aggressive vindictiveness of such apostates against their former coreligionists was becoming an increasingly distasteful fact of Jewish life in the thirteenth century, and it inspired many similar outbursts.[83]

This discussion of the *Birkat ha-Minim* is significant against the background of the Disputation of Paris, held in 1240. No Jew who lived through this event could have forgotten its traumatic repercussions. During the course of the Disputation, according to the account of R. Yehiel of Paris, the apostate Nicholas Donin read before the assemblage the *Birkat ha-Minim* with his explanation of the critical terms: " 'For the meshummadim may there be no hope'—these are the deniers who come to the shade of the Gentiles—'and let all the minim be instantaneously destroyed'—these are the priests who are disciples of Jesus the Nazarene." R. Yehiel tried to argue that this misrepresented the Jewish prayer, for the word "minim" referred to "those who believe in the Law of Moses but not in the Talmud," that is, Sadducees and Karaites. But Donin countered with the fact that Rashi, in commenting on several Talmudic passages including the one from *Avodah Zarah*, stated that "minim" referred to idolatrous priests. Rashi's comment may have been the reason why copies of the Talmud were ultimately burned together with their commentaries.[84]

Aware of the potential danger in this prayer, R. Isaac is anxious to show that the word "minim," in the blessing and in the Talmud, does not mean what Rashi said it did. But unlike R. Yehiel, he argues simply that the troublesome word is synonymous with "meshummadim." In his reading, the entire blessing refers to one category of people, the apostates from Judaism, who are cursed because of the harm they have caused the Jewish people. His interpretation is both a rebuttal of the charge that Jews asked for God's malediction against true Christians and an intensification of the attack upon the apostates such as Donin himself.

Contemporary Practices

In addition to the characterizations and evaluations of various groups in contemporary Jewish society, there are several passages that speak about Jewish practices. R. Isaac points out the apparent paradox in Rava's statement "Those other men are fools, who stand in the presence of a Torah scroll but do not stand in the presence of a great man, for while it is written in the Torah 'Forty stripes he shall give him,' the sages came along and reduced them by one" (*Mak.*, 22b). The Torah is the source and cause of Israel's holiness; how then can it be said that one who studies the Torah is more distinguished than the Torah itself? He then continues:

And you find that it is a matter of convention among the other nations, and the Christians who pattern themselves after us, that if a man happens across a Torah scroll, even a prince and a great man, a governor and ruler, he will stand before it when he sees it from a distance, and if he is riding, he will descend from his chariot. Nothing will prevent him, even if he is a notable of royal lineage. Furthermore, it is a conventional practice among them that when a new king arises in the land, the Jews of his entire kingdom—if it is very large, in every city and province—will go out to welcome him, carrying the Torah in their hands. The greatest among them carries the scroll in his bosom, and the priests and the people follow behind it. If the Jews do not act voluntarily in this matter, they will go summoned by the king and his courtiers, for the king desires for his glory that this honor be done to him, more than any wealth. He will send his emissary to them, and they will bring [the Torah scroll] outside to him, for this honor is very precious in his sight. When he sees the Torah scroll, he descends from his chariot, he and his retinue. Not one remains who does not descend before its splendid holiness.[85]

While the importance ascribed to the Torah in the eyes of the Christian rulers is obviously exaggerated, the passage does reflect a historical reality. The ceremonial procession of Jews bearing their Torah scrolls in honor of a non-Jewish ruler is a well-known medieval phenomenon, although it can be documented more fully from Christian than from Jewish sources. It was an established practice in Rome, dating from the twelfth century, that newly elected popes would be ceremonially greeted by leaders of the Jewish community carrying the scrolls of the Law. The popes generally accepted the scroll and responded with the formula, "We praise and revere the sacred Law, but we condemn your religious practice and your interpretation." Sometimes they would drop it or cast it behind their back as an indication of the Christian doctrine that the Law as observed by the Jews is a thing of the past. A contemporary account of the inauguration of Boniface VII in 1295 states, "[Judea] Christo gravidam legem plenamque sub umbra exhibuit Moysi. Veneratus et ille figuram hanc post terga dedit" ("Judea presented the Law of Moses, pregnant and darkly filled with Christ; he [the pope] venerated the form of the Law, then handed it behind him"). This ceremony came to be viewed by the Jews as a humiliating ordeal and not the expression of honor for the Torah that R. Isaac describes.[86]

An interesting parallel from a fourteenth-century Jewish source can be found in a work of the Provençal scholar Joseph ibn Kaspi. This passage, which purportedly records a question posed to the author by a bishop of southern France, implies that it was the Jews who demanded that deference be shown to their Torah scrolls by Christian dignitaries and that Christians did not fully understand this ritual:

Once an honored bishop of our country who was an expert in the Scriptures asked me: "Why do you require that kings and popes and bishops give honor to the Book of the Torah of Moses when you bring it before you upon entering a city, in the same way as we bring out our crosses? And what is the reason that we are required to do honor to the Book of the Torah of Moses that is in your possession? Actually, we acknowledge the necessity for all of us to give honor and respect to the Book of the Torah of Moses and after it to all the Books of Scripture that were written by the prophets who continued after the Torah of Moses. But this Torah, as well as the rest of your Scriptures, is in our possession just as it is in yours; and if our kings and our leaders desire to bring out the Book of the Torah of Moses or all of Scripture, we will take [ours] out since we have these books just as you do. Is it because the Books of the Torah of Moses are in the Hebrew language and written in Hebrew letters that they have a preponderance of holiness and excellence over our books which are taken directly from each of yours and put into the Latin language and written in Latin letters?"[87]

As in the passage of R. Isaac, a ceremony obviously intended to express obeisance on the part of Jews is interpreted here as a sign of honor to the Jewish faith.

Other passages deal with internal practices. We have already discussed the vituperative attack upon those Jews who understand a statement of the gemara literally and actually take three steps backward as they finish part of their liturgy.[88] A different criticism of contemporary liturgical practice can be found in a comment on the aggadah about Eliezer b. Dordaya and the courtesan (AZ, 17a). Passing over the first part of this earthy exemplum, R. Isaac focuses on Eliezer's appeals to the mountains and to the heavenly bodies to "beseech for mercy on my behalf." The thrust of the comment is that no intermediary can be expected to intercede between God and man, for everything that man might enlist as an intermediary is, like himself, a creation of the Almighty. Not intercession but sincere repentance on the part of the sinner is required.

> If a man is guilty before God and deserves punishment for his sins, no intermediary will help to keep God from punishing him and bringing him to justice. But if he does not deserve to be punished because his sins are few, he may find favor before his Lord, and his words will be heard without an intermediary and will be read before the King.
> Some of the masses of Jews have already erred in this matter by placing an intermediary between themselves and God to make atonement before Him, as if this were required by God. Far be it from God to demand of a human being that he place an intermediary between them. Rather, he must confess alone before Him about his sin, with no third party mixing in to make supplication on behalf of the sinner. If he implores, God will forgive his sin and make atonement for it.

For this came to them from the serpent's root and a perverted belief which nearly tends toward the belief in dualism. This occurred
previously in Israel, and its trace is still noticeable among our people, when they arise at night for the morning watch during the ten
days that occur each year from Rosh Hashana to Yom Kippur, pray-
ing the words "Introducers of mercy . . ." and thereby imploring
intermediaries to pray on their behalf. This is a great perversion,
which leads to the belief in dualism, for God does not need any intermediary. He is the source of all power, and He has given to human beings the power to know Him and to return to Him whenever
they want without any intermediary . . .

Furthermore, these fools do not know enough to repudiate that
which is actually impossible (although theoretically possible). For
they think that those who have already died—those Jews who were
good and upright in their hearts—will pray after they are no longer
in the flesh on behalf of those who are still alive. But it is known that
those who have died the death of the flesh see only with their spiritual eyes and only visions of God at that time . . .[89]

R. Isaac's opposition to the concept of mediation between man and
God, and specifically to the use of the phrase "introducers of mercy"
(*makhnisei rahamim*) in the penitential prayers used on the ten days of
repentance, fits into a long tradition, beginning before him and continuing centuries after his death.[90] Here is a passage from the *Malmad ha-
Talmidim* of Jacob Anatoli:

The practice in some places to say "Introducers of mercy, bring
mercy upon us etc." is not a good one. Let your deeds bring you
near, for it is not appropriate to entreat either angels or anyone else,
lest one accept them as God. The proof for this is that in the prayer
of Moses our teacher, in the prayer of the other prophets, and in the
liturgy of the men of the Great Assembly, we find mention *only* of
God, may He be exalted.[91]

And Meir b. Simon addresses the same issue in his *Milhemet Mitzvah*:

In most places it is customary *not* to say "Introducers of mercy . . . ,"
and in those places where it is customary to say it, we must affirm
that it was never the intention of the sages to beseech the angels to
ask for mercy upon them, God forbid! . . . If anyone should maintain that this is said actually referring to angels of mercy, and that it
entails nothing heretical, such a notion should be absolutely repudiated, for it will cause people to err by following one or more of the
angels. A person will think that it is enough to pray and cry out to
an angel, imploring it to pray in turn to God [on his behalf]. Furthermore, he will think that the angel's prayer is more acceptable than
his own, to an ever greater degree.[92]

Opposition to this particular liturgical passage addressed to the angels should be seen in the broader context of concern by Jewish leaders over deviations in worship among adherents of new intellectual streams: Moses Taku's attack on the German Pietists for addressing their prayers to the *Kavod*, and the denunciation of the Kabbalists by men such as R. Meir b. Simon, R. Isaac b. Sheshet, and the author of *Alilot Devarim*, for addressing prayers to the sefirot.[93]

R. Isaac's contribution to this tradition is his association of the prayer addressed to intermediary angels with the belief in dualism. This accusation is left vague, and it is not entirely clear what he means. This does not seem to be the dualism that views the world as divided between good and evil powers. A passage from Anatoli's *Malmad* serves as an instructive contrast:

> . . . like the thought of some men about Satan. They believe that he is a unique spiritual being, with sovereignty to do evil in the world. Far be it from us to believe such a thing! For this is connected with the belief of the Dualists, who believe that there are two gods, one good and one evil . . .[94]

This is an obvious reference to the gnostic type of dualism which the Church fought to exterminate in southern France at the beginning of the thirteenth century. The context of R. Isaac's discussion suggests that he is referring to orthodox rather than heretical Christian doctrine. The argument implied is that the appeal to angels as intermediaries in the process of repentance leads ultimately to the Christian doctrine that atonement is impossible except through the Christ, which is in turn bound up with the doctrine of God as Father and Son.[95] As we have seen, R. Isaac argues that the Jewish concept of the Messiah differs radically from the Christian concept in that for Jews, the Messiah is not necessary for the attainment of salvation. Here he points to the difference in the concept of God, affirming that for Jews, God is accessible to anyone who seeks Him, so that there is no need for any go-between, whether angel or Son.

If the pitfalls of Christian theology lead R. Isaac to denounce those who beseech the angels to appeal to God on behalf of the penitent, teachings about the intercessory role of the saints impel him to ridicule the ignorant, who believe that the righteous dead will pray to God on behalf of the living.[96] We are told that the dead have no awareness of what occurs here in the sublunar world;[97] their concern is exclusively with the apprehension of God, their ultimate reward. We therefore cannot hope for help from the dead, any more than we can depend on the mountains or the heavenly bodies or the angels. If so, it is obvious that seeking atonement through another human being is to no avail. In the emphatic denial of intermediaries between the individual sinner and God, there is also an oblique attack on the doctrine of confession to priests, which had been made obligatory by the Fourth Lateran Council in 1215.

Anti-Christian Polemics

This brings us to the general subject of anti-Christian polemic in the commentaries. Many passages reflect in passing the ongoing religious argument between Christians and Jews. One of the requirements for membership in the Sanhedrin was knowledge of the seventy languages of the world. R. Isaac explains that these Jewish leaders were required to "know about the religions of all the other nations—that all, except the religion given to the people of God's choice on Mt. Sinai, are far from rational . . . The nations in whose midst we are exiled are jealous of the Torah and those who cling to it, and they attack us because of it. Therefore the sages said that members of the Sanhedrin must know and speak all the languages of the nations from the time of our exile in their midst . . . so that they will not need a translator to reply to those who taunt them."[98] This assertion reflects the increasing pressure upon Jews during the thirteenth century to enter religious disputations, and R. Isaac's opinion concerning the usefulness of a knowledge of Latin for engaging in such debates.[99]

Christian doctrines are often repudiated in the commentaries without always being explicitly identified. The arguments that the Torah is not a burden for the people, that all its commandments bring benefit and never harm, and that the sages followed the pattern of the Torah in never burdening Jews with unnecessary restrictions and prohibitions counter the central thrust in the Pauline critique of Judaism: that the demands of the Torah make it impossible to gain salvation through good works.[100] The emphatic assertion that the glory due to God must not be bestowed upon any created being, for no other being, even a man capable of working miracles, has any independent power, and the insistence that the phrase "Son of Man" in Ezekiel implies nothing more than a human being are repudiations of dogma concerning the nature of the Christ.[101] R. Isaac uncompromisingly rejects the doctrine of Purgatory in the statement

> There is no intermediate place between the Garden of Eden and Gehinnom—if one has lived a good life, he will go to Eden, the garden of the Lord, and if he has not, he will go to its opposite, to eternal destruction . . . but there is no intermediate between this and that, for they are opposites by privation; if one has no good in him, he will necessarily fall into evil, not finding anything in between as a resting place for his soul to save it from its death . . . There is no special place for the in-between man.[102]

The explanation of Christian antipathy toward the Jews, alluded to in the comment concerning the Sanhedrin, is rather poignant. It appears again in the following passage:

It is known that the dominion of Rome oppresses all Jews because they encompass the truth more than any other nation or people, all of whom walk in darkness. Pretending to be like us in following the ways of the Torah, which are pleasant and proper to those who understand, they hate the Jewish people to the utmost, and devise deep plots to cause the Torah to be forgotten from Israel.[103]

Perhaps most striking of all is the explanation of the statement "Gentiles outside the land of Israel are not idolators, they just follow the custom of their forefathers" (Hullin, 13b). R. Isaac writes that these Gentiles "know that the Jewish religion is the choice of all religions, but despite this, they cling to their own religion as their forefathers accustomed them to do. [Thus they] hate all who follow the Torah, for everything hates its opposite."[104] Many churchmen believed that the Jewish people recognize the truth of Christianity deep in their hearts but refuse to accede to it out of a kind of perverse obstinacy.[105] Here the doctrine is turned on its head and used against Christianity. Christian recognition of the Torah's superiority over any other law is reflected in the imitation of Jewish practices and observances. Yet since the copy cannot reach the same level as the original, the possessors of the truth are envied, hated, and oppressed.

In addition to these polemical sallies, there is one extensive passage described by the author as a record of his own disputation against a Christian scholar. It appears in the comment on the aggadah in which R. Joshua b. Levi is told by Elijah that he can find the Messiah sitting at the gate of Rome. After giving an allegorical interpretation, R. Isaac goes on to write:[106]

And now I will speak openly, following the obvious meaning of these aggadic statements, telling what I answered to one of the Christian scholars. While debating with me, he asked me why we keep silent about the messianic king who has come (according to their opinion, based on the new religion started for them). They find support in these and similar aggadot, [claiming] that the sages prophesied about their faith, and testified that the Messiah had already come and was present in the city of Rome, a great city to their God whom they worship. This man asked me, "What did they mean, and what did they want to teach us, when they said that the Messiah already existed in their time and went to Rome if not that they prophesied about the Messiah who came during their days and brought into being a new religion and faith, that of the Christians?" Therefore we wait in vain for someone else to come to lead us out of this long exile, for we have fallen through the sin of our ancestors, and we will not arise again. This was the thrust of the question he asked, and he thought it was a great one.

I answered my taunter that we await and believe in a messianic king—that a man will arise in the midst of his people inspired with God's spirit; He will stir him to gain power over his people and to rule them as king, anointed with oil, leading them out of their crushing servitude. This king will be a human being, a man whole-hearted and upright . . . He will arise from among his brothers just as Saul and David and Solomon his son arose—kings who ruled and performed God's work, chosen for this purpose, and anointed with oil by a prophet. Even so will be the messianic king. There will never again cease to be a ruler over the chosen people from his descendents, as Ezekiel the prophet taught, speaking God's words: "And David My servant shall be their prince [nasi] forever [37:25]. Thus he taught that the king [Messiah] will be from royal lineage of the Davidic family, and that the sceptre and ruler's staff will not depart from his descendents so long as the earth endures.

The passage continues explaining the title "nasi," which implies an individual endowed with abundant wisdom and great personal stature, while the ordinary king may himself be ignorant and rely totally on the counsel of advisers. R. Isaac then returns to the problem of the aggadah:

This king, about whom the prophets promised, has not yet come, but he will come in the future. Even if the wheels of his chariot tarry until now, his time is close! He will surely come, he will not delay! When the sages said that he existed, they did not intend to teach that he was actually in existence in their day. For this king, distinguished in God's sight, is a human being composed of the four elements and formed out of matter like everyone else, according to the belief of the congregation of Moses. He too will die when the time apportioned to his physical component comes to an end. He will not live forever, but his son will rule after him, and his sovereignty will be established forever, through his grandson and great-grandson and all who follow from the royal line, generation after generation. If then he existed so many years ago, as it seems from the apparent meaning of these statements of theirs, why has he remained hidden until now for a thousand years . . . ?[107] Why has he delayed in coming, so that it is not known where he is? This is all but impossible in our eyes! We do not believe in such a long life for him, but rather that he will live the same life span as others who reach old age.

If he will come to deliver the people from its enemies, why has he sinned against the people by remaining hidden and not making himself known to them? Why has God denied him glory by wasting his time to no avail? . . . Behold, we, the congregation of Moses, will not believe that he existed at that time when the sages lived, because we have not seen him, and he has tarried until now!

As for your question, what the sages intended to teach us by saying that he existed in their time, know, you who would investigate
these words carefully and discover minute details which reveal an
impoverished heart, that in these statements the sages follow the
words of the prophets, who speak about a future event in the past
tense because they have seen in a prophetic vision that it is destined
to come about. They use the past tense, testifying faithfully that it
was, in order to teach the powerful endurability of God's words,
and that His good promise cannot change, and that He will not
break His good word.[108] The sages of the Talmud followed Moses
and the other true prophets in saying here that the Messiah existed,
in that he was promised to the people by name—that a new king
would arise over them, personally summoned by God, who would
choose him to lead the people out of their long exile. Therefore they
said of him that he existed—that the promise made to them about
the Messiah is not an allegory. For His promise does not remain
unfulfilled, but it will come about whenever He desires. They said he
existed, while speaking about the future.

And do not take this matter lightly, for you have already buttressed your new religion by this manner of interpreting the prophets. You claim they prophesied that your religion would come into
being eventually, and that they prophesied about the future while
speaking in the past tense, if it is according to your words. For the
prophet said, "Behold, a young woman conceives [harah] and bears
a son" [Isa. 7:14], and according to your way of thinking, this did
not come about until a thousand years or more later. According to
you, he said "harah" to hint and prophesy about the future event.
He referred to her as "conceiving and bearing" together, even though
at that time the mother from whom the son would emerge had not
yet been born. Even so the sages spoke here, saying that the messianic king existed, but referring to the future.

This is followed by the passage quoted and discussed in chapter IV, section 3, reporting the encounter between the Messiah and the Pope in
Rome. The comment then concludes:

If it is according to your words that our Messiah came many
[years] ago and went to Rome, where he set up for himself a place to
sit by the city wall, how could the men of that generation not have
believed Elijah, who came to herald his advent? Elijah was their
prophet while alive, and he appeared to them at that time to inform
them that [the Messiah] had come to save their lost souls, and that if
they would believe him, the Messiah would come in that very day
without delay—if they would just hearken to his voice . . . [109] He
would gather in the dispersed so that all could return to their own
borders. According to the Christian position, how could the sages of
that generation not have believed the words of the prophet who

came to inform them at God's behest that this was the Lord's Mes-
iah, made captive because of their corruption, and that he would
redeem Israel so that they would not see destruction?

So this man spoke to me, and so I answered him. He was mollified
by my words and did not summon the strength or the effrontery to
raise his head.

Of particular interest as we consider the polemical nature of this report
and its historical setting are the Christian use of rabbinic aggadah to
prove that the Messiah has already come and the description of the Messiah appearing before the Pope in Rome. Both of these themes bear upon
the dating of the passage in relation to the Disputation of Barcelona.

It is often assumed that the new mode of argument, using Talmudic
aggadot to buttress the claims of Christianity, was first introduced as
part of the infamous Disputation of 1263. If this were so, then R. Isaac's
debate would have to be dated later than this, providing a *terminus a quo*
for the entire work. However, the origins of this type of argument have
recently been traced back to the twelfth-century author, Alan of Lille,
who wrote:

In Sehale [sic] Elijah said that the world will last for 6000 years, 2000
of vanity, which refers to the time before the Mosaic law, 2000 of
the Mosaic law, and the following 2000 of the Messiah. But it is clear
that more than 4000 years have passed. Therefore it is clear that the
Law has passed away, and the Messiah has come.[110]

More important, in his own account of the Disputation, Nachmanides
himself states he has heard that Fra Pablo Christiani had been traveling
through the communities of Southern France trying out this argument
based on Talmudic aggadot.[111] It is by no means impossible that the
Christian scholar with whom R. Isaac debated was Pablo himself.

There is certainly no indication in this passage that the author was
aware of the Disputation of Barcelona. Had he been writing after that
event, we might expect at least a passing reference to it or to the fact that
the great R. Moses b. Nahman had responded to the identical question.
The answer given to the Christian is totally different from Ramban's approach to the same Talmudic passage. Accepting the simple meaning of
the aggadah that the Messiah has already been born, Nachmanides is
forced to argue that the statement represents an individual opinion which
he himself does not accept, but that it is fully possible for the Messiah to
live one thousand or two thousand years or forever.[112] In contrast, R.
Isaac explicitly rejects this concept of the Messiah, insisting that his life
span will be within the natural range. He is therefore compelled to turn to
the argument based on tense. While it is possible that he already knew of
Nachmanides' response and deliberately ignored it, there is no basis for
proving that the passage was written after 1263.

The concluding statement implies that the Christian debater was thoroughly confounded by R. Isaac's answer. But if the debater was indeed Fra Pablo, we may be sure that the answer found here would not have dissuaded him from continuing on his path to Barcelona. The argument that the sages, following the style of the prophets, used the past tense while speaking about the future is supposed to explain the obvious meaning of the aggadah, but it is clearly inadequate to that task. If the description of the Messiah sitting at the gate of Rome refers to the future day when he will convince the Pope to order that the Jews of Christendom be released, how are we to understand the statement that R. Joshua b. Levi traveled to Rome, found the Messiah there, and spoke to him? R. Isaac rejects such a meeting in ancient times as impossible, but he never explains what this assertion means. Even if we are to interpret R. Joshua's encounter as having occurred in some kind of vision or dream, the argument here virtually concedes the plausibility of the Christian interpretation of Isaiah 7:14, while every Jewish commentator insisted that it could not possibly refer to the distant future. Perhaps this is why Nachmanides chose a different approach in his debate. While he too alludes to the Messiah coming before the Pope,[113] it is significant that he does not do so in the context of this particular aggadah.

The second question is whether the lines describing the confrontation between Messiah and Pope can help us date the passage. There is no obvious chronological niche in which to place the characterization of Rome and the unquestioned authority of the Pope over all the kings of Christendom. It is hard to imagine anyone writing the words "Whatever he decrees to the Gentile kings who are adherents of the faith, not one of them will disobey him, nor will they speak after he has spoken" before the death of Frederick II in 1250, while the papacy was still locked in bitter battle with the emperor.[114] It is equally difficult to imagine the words "Rome, where in his palace dwells the Pope . . . and the Cardinals, his advisers, surround him . . . ; each year, many notables and summoned leaders come there faithfully to greet him" being written before October of 1253, when Innocent IV returned to Rome for the first time since fleeing from that city in 1244.[115] Assuming that the author was even minimally aware of the events of his time, 1253 might be taken as the terminus a quo for the debate.

But these assertions do not fit the historical situation of the following years much better. Innocent IV died fourteen months after his return to Rome, having spent much of the intervening time outside Rome with the papal army.[116] The reign of Alexander IV (1254-1261) is generally regarded as politically disastrous for the papacy, as its position even in Italy was progressively weakened by the advances of Frederick's son, Manfred.[117] Under Urban IV (1261-1264) and Clement IV (1265-1268), the papacy solidified its position in Italy and recovered prestige while fighting the last of the Hohenstaufen. Yet it certainly did not command the allegiance of all Christian kings. Clement himself complained about the lack of support for his political efforts in terms that contrast strikingly with those of R. Isaac: "In England there is opposition, in Germany hardly anyone obeys, France groans and grumbles, Spain suffices not for itself, Italy gives no help but plays one false."[118] After the death of Clement, the papacy was vacant for three years. We are forced to conclude that the description of papal supremacy in the passage is just as exaggerated as is the evocation of papal impotence in the letter of Clement IV. While it is extremely unlikely that this passage stems from a time when the Pope was actually unable to live in Rome (before 1253), it could date from any time during the period 1253-68 without being intended as an accurate reflection of the historical vicissitudes of papal authority and power.

As we have seen, Nachmanides also refers to the Messiah's coming before the Pope. Comparison of that passage with R. Isaac's commentary fails to prove that either author depended upon the other. But it is important to note that Nachmanides speaks not as though he were introducing a radically new doctrine but rather as though he assumed that it would be familiar to his readers. The first time he refers to this theme, it is to explain the difference between the assertions that the Messiah was born and that the Messiah has come. After making an analogy with Moses, he continues, "Similarly the Messiah: when he comes to the Pope and says to him at God's command, 'Let my people go,' *then* he will have 'come.' "[119] He uses a given (that the Messiah will appear before the Pope) to clarify a matter of confusion (when is it proper to say that the Messiah has come). It is therefore unlikely that Nachmanides was the source of this notion. Whether or not he was aware of the passage in R. Isaac's commentary, he reflects a tradition of which this passage is the only other thirteenth-century example. All of this confirms Scholem's suspicion that Abraham Abulafia, in going to Rome and seeking an audience with the Pope, was basing his mission not merely on a few sentences in the account of the Disputation but on a messianic doctrine commonly held.[120]

VII

R. ISAAC'S ACHIEVEMENT

In reviewing the evidence garnered about R. Isaac b. Yedaiah, one can state that certain facts seem to be beyond question. We know that he wrote at least three works, two of which must have been of monumental proportions. From his Commentary on the Midrash Rabbah, the end of *Leviticus Rabbah* and the beginning of *Numbers Rabbah* are still intact, together with some other disparate passages from *Leviticus Rabbah*, and this material refers to comments on specific chapters of *Genesis Rabbah*. The Commentary on the Midrash Rabbah often refers to the author's *Hibbur ha-Talmud Bavli*, mentioning at least nine different tractates from that work. There is overwhelming evidence that part of this *Hibbur* survives as the Commentary on *Avot* and the Aggadot of the Talmud, hitherto attributed to Yedaiah Bedersi. The third work is called by various names: *Perush ha-Torah*, *Hibbur ha-Torah*, and *Ner Mitzvah*. Allusions to this work refer to the weekly *parashah: Bo el Paraoh, Be-Midbar Sinai, Ve-zot ha-Berakhah*.[1] As it is mentioned in both other works, this Torah commentary was probably the first of the three to be written. R. Isaac then turned to the commentary on the Talmud and finally to that on the Midrash Rabbah. We have no way of knowing if he wrote anything else, but given the apparent length of the two rabbinic commentaries, these three alone would have been ample harvest of a full literary career.

From these writings, certain biographical facts emerge. At age fifteen, Isaac b. Yedaiah entered the yeshiva of R. Meshullam in Beziers; this was almost certainly R. Meshullam b. Moses, author of *Sefer ha-Hashlamah*, who impressed him greatly and became his model rabbi. He was also profoundly influenced by the works of Maimonides. His own writings reveal a thorough knowledge of the rabbinic literature and a general grounding in Jewish philosophical thought; they do not reveal outstanding expertise in the subtleties of Talmudic dialectics or mastery of the full

range of technical philosophical problems. R. Isaac was related by marriage to an influential Jewish courtier associated with the royal administration in Beziers. Finally, he entered into debate, possibly as a representative of his community, with an unnamed Christian polemicist who
tried to use the aggadot of the Talmud to prove that the Messiah had already come. These are the only explicit links between R. Isaac and the
contemporary external world to be found in the extant writings.

The dates of R. Isaac must be deduced from internal evidence. R. Jacob
ibn Habib's guess that R. Isaac may have been the son of Yedaiah Bedersi,[2] which would place his mature years in the middle of the fourteenth century, is implausible; a mid-thirteenth-century date seems far
more likely. Each of the three biographical facts mentioned makes good
sense if we assume that R. Isaac was writing around the year 1260,
though each presents serious problems if we assume that he was writing
two or three generations later. The description of the school of R. Meshullam, if set in the first half of the thirteenth century, fits what is
known about R. Meshullam b. Moses. It would seem that this scholar
died sometime around the middle of the thirteenth century, and the author's reminiscences of his schooldays with the great master imply that
Meshullam's death had not occurred within the past several years. On
the other hand, if we were to assume a fourteenth-century date for Yedaiah's son, we would have to posit another outstanding mentor named
R. Meshullam, who would have been at the peak of his career around the
time of the conflict over the Rashba's *herem* and about whom we have no
other information.[3]

Secondly, the description of the Jewish courtier in Beziers fits precisely
the career of Astruguet Judaeus, who was active in his position as chief
financial officer for the royal administration in the seneschalcy of Carcassonne-Beziers during the years leading up to 1247-1248. This passage
gives the impression of having been written not long after the decease of
the courtier, for the spectacle of the funeral is still fresh in the author's
mind. Without further documentary sources, we have no way of knowing when Astruguet died, but again the material is perfectly consistent
with a date of about 1260 for CAT. A fourteenth-century date would
compel us to posit another Jewish courtier who held a position similar to
Astruguet's in the same area following the expulsion of 1322—a rather
unlikely supposition.

Finally, the debate with the Christian about the meaning of an aggadah
that speaks of the Messiah sitting at the gates of Rome fits beautifully
into the period immediately preceding the Disputation of Barcelona, held
in 1263. According to Nachmanides, Pablo Christiani had been practic-
ing his arguments among the Jewish communities of southern France before his spectacular confrontation in Barcelona, and this may well have
provided the opportunity for R. Isaac to respond to the challenge with

his own interpretation. A fourteenth-century date for the debate between R. Isaac and the Christian scholar would place R. Isaac's emphasis on the centrality of Rome in Christendom—"the stake [of Christendom] is driven in Rome, where in his palace dwells the Pope"—in the incongruous context of a period when the papacy was seated in Avignon.

To these three major arguments can be added the arguments from silence: the fact that there is no mention of any Jewish author after Maimonides (whereas we would expect a reference to the Disputation of Barcelona or the account of Nachmanides, had the author known of them) and the fact that there is no reference to any work of Aristotle. The Aristotelian corpus in its Averroistic garb was beginning to become available in Hebrew toward the end of the 1250s through the untiring efforts of translators such as Moses ibn Tibbon, so it is not surprising that in 1260, a non-Arabic-reading Jew, despite a passionate commitment to philosophy, would not yet have had access to these works. Two or three generations later, specific references to Aristotelian treatises were common even in nontechnical literature, as can be seen in the commentary on the Midrashim of Yedaiah Bedersi and the Biblical commentaries of Ralbag. The absence of such references in a work written by Yedaiah's son would be extremely surprising.

The age of the author when he wrote these commentaries can also be surmised by inference. R. Isaac viewed age forty as a watershed, when a man's intellect reaches ascendancy over his physical impulses and when he is, therefore, prepared to enter the realm of esoteric knowledge in pursuit of intellectual perfection. I have noted, for example, the interpretation of R. Eliezer's statement "The days of the Messiah for Israel are forty years" (*Sanh.*, 99a), based on the assumption that forty years is not the length of time the era will last but the age at which it may begin:

> They came to teach here that human intellect is found in man only from age forty on, at which time it grows progressively stronger to the end of his life. But up to that time, a man does not find the intellect complete and consistent with himself because of the boiling of his nature, which prevents him from achieving any measure of perfection.[4]

Similarly, the statement "two thousand years vanity, two thousand years Torah, two thousand years the days of the Messiah" (*Sanh.*, 97a-b) is interpreted in terms of the individual life cycle. The third era, beginning at age forty, is that of the intellect: "They taught that the intellect which cleaves to matter remains hidden all of these days until the body has completed forty years." Before this age, the power of the impulse toward evil, which opposes the intellect, is insuperable. Only when this impulse grows old and weak can the intellect emerge to reign in wisdom.[5]

This view is confirmed by explicit statements from the Talmud. For example, "Even Moses our teacher did not hint to Israel until after forty years . . . Rava said, 'We learn from this that one does not fully understand the teaching of his master until forty years have passed' " (AZ, 5b). Here is R. Isaac's comment:

> They came to teach that the Master of the Prophets did not want to hint to the people about any mystery or esoteric matter in the meaning of the Torah, even to those with understanding, until they reached the fortieth year. For until that time, a man's nature boils, and he is unable to apprehend anything recondite and purely intelligible owing to this boiling of his nature and the other obstacles that accompany him during this period. If Moses had transmitted to them matters relating to the intellectual vision of God, they might have envisioned Him in a destructive manner, harmful to faith, subverting the true meaning, and never escaping this error even when they reached old age . . . Therefore, the Master of the Prophets did did not transmit by hint any matter of profundity until they reached the fortieth year, for then the boiling of nature subsides, and there are no more obstacles. Then Moses transmitted to them every secret, no longer desiring to conceal from them a thing. You find this in Deuteronomy, where it says, "In the fortieth year . . . Moses took upon him to expound the Torah . . ."
> They explained this similarly in Tractate Avot, teaching that man can reach various types of perfection according to the period in his life. They divided the years of a human life into many parts . . . and said, "Forty years old for understanding," teaching that a man is then prepared and worthy of entering the "orchard," in order to apprehend his Creator . . .[6]

The entire chronology of Moses' instruction has been reinterpreted here. It is not that he waited until forty years after the Exodus before revealing the deeper content to the entire people but rather that he waited until each individual was forty years old before initiating him into the esoteric profundities of the Torah. Could these passages have been written by a man less than forty years old himself? The Commentary on the Aggadot reveals an author confident that he himself possesses the mysteries of the Torah and the rabbinic literature. It would be most odd for a man thirty or thirty-five years old, writing a book in which he reveals the philosophical truths concealed in the sacred literature of the Jews, to emphasize repeatedly that a man younger than forty is not eligible even to learn these truths. It is therefore reasonable to conclude that this commentary was written when R. Isaac was at least in his forties, with the Torah commentary preceding this and the Commentary on the Midrash Rabbah following it. If we set 1260 as the approximate year for the Commentary on the Aggadot and estimate that the author was then about forty-five years old, this would place his entrance into the school of R. Meshullam at age fifteen around 1230, when R. Meshullam would have been at the height of his career.

Anything more to be said about R. Isaac must remain in the realm of conjecture. For example, one might speculate about whether some of his more unusual statements about women, sexuality, marital life and adultery, and about disappointment in children may reflect aspects of his personal experience. But such hypothetical reconstructions, which would bring these commentaries from the rarefied atmosphere of pure ideas into the realm of the most intimate personal problems, cannot be validated by anything explicit in these texts, nor are they directly relevant to understanding the author as a historical figure. It is not impossible that R. Isaac was the father of Abraham Bedersi and the grandfather of Yedaiah Bedersi; given the evidence currently available, this possibility can be neither proven nor discounted.[7]

What was R. Isaac's achievement in the context of thirteenth-century Provençal Jewish culture? All R. Isaac's writings are commentaries. This was the genre of creativity par excellence in southern France. From the twelfth through the fourteenth centuries, commentaries on the classics of Jewish literature were produced in abundance—on the Bible, the halakhic material of the Talmud, the halakhic Midrash, Alfasi's *Halakhot*, Maimonides' *Mishneh Torah*, *Sefer Yetzirah*, the prayers of the liturgy, the *Guide for the Perplexed*, and eventually the full corpus of Aristotelian and Arabic philosophical works available in Hebrew translation.[8] This is not to minimize the importance of independent works in every area but rather to emphasize the naturalness of commentary as a matrix of creative expression for R. Isaac.

If formally R. Isaac's work fits into the widely-used genre of commentary, its content should be seen as part of the prevalent impulse toward popularization, the rendering of relatively technical and specialized material in more convenient forms to wider circles of the population. There were many manifestations of this impulse: the continued translation of philosophical works, which made them accessible to those who did not know Arabic;[9] the incorporation of philosophical material, usually of somewhat simplified nature, into Bible commentaries and sermons;[10] the systematic organization of philosophical and scientific knowledge into all-encompassing, encyclopedic works;[11] and the utilization of such material for belletristic purposes.[12] Among those who carried on the work of popularization, some were highly competent in technical philosophy, even to the point of being able to do important original work. Apparently, they felt a desire to address the general educated public as well as a select circle of specialists. Eminent examples of this group are Anatoli in the thirteenth century and Gersonides in the fourteenth.

On the other hand, there were those who were apparently not com-

petent to do technical or original work, whose mastery of philosophy
was not much more profound than what was revealed in their popular
writings. As we have already noted, R. Isaac seems to be in this second
category. The fact that he produced an extensive commentary on the
aggadic literature of the sages might have brought his philosophical
material to the attention of Jews who were unwilling or unable to im-
merse themselves in the study of the *Guide for the Perplexed.*[13] Not that
his commentaries would have taught them much philosophy, for what is
contained is reference to philosophical doctrines rather than exploration
and analysis of them. R. Isaac's commentaries are works of popularization in the sense that they propagate general philosophical themes rather
than delving into profound philosophical problems.

Furthermore, they should be seen as part of the ongoing effort to assert
and to prove not only the legitimacy but the absolute necessity of philosophy as a Jewish enterprise. The case for philosophy, focusing on the
philosophical works of Maimonides himself, had been clearly delineated
in the letters of his Provençal defenders during the *Kulturkampf* of the
early 1230s.[14] Between this time and the eruption of a new conflict at the
beginning of the fourteenth century, the philosophical approach to Judaism was not only defended on theoretical grounds but also harnessed to a
variety of purposes in works of different kinds. *Malmad ha-Talmidim* of
Anatoli, *Yikkavu ha-Mayim* of Samuel ibn Tibbon, the Biblical commentaries of Moses ibn Tibbon, *Sefer ha-Mevakesh* of Falaquera, and
Livyat Hen of Levi b. Abraham are but a few examples that could be
mentioned. When the battle lines reformed in 1303, the definition of the
issue had changed. While there were complaints about specific allegorical
interpretations of Biblical and aggadic material and against popular
preachers who disseminated their insights irresponsibly, virtually no one
questioned the validity of using philosophical concepts to express the essence of Judaism.[15]

The one exception to this generalization is R. Asher b. Yehiel, a cultural alien whose upbringing in the north left him two or three generations behind his contemporaries in the south, so that he alone maintains
what was the outspoken position of the anti-Maimonideans in the 1230s:
that the attempt to synthesize Judaism and philosophy is impossible by
definition, doomed to failure by its very nature.[16] For the rest, the question was not one of repudiating philosophy per se but of maintaining the
proper balance and perspective, and the issue resolved itself into one of
educational policy: the study, by those below a certain age, of Greek and
Arabic works which had been recently translated into Hebrew and were
therefore widely accessible. (The passages in which R. Isaac argues that
no one below age forty is ready for serious philosophical study suggest
that, at least theoretically, he might have found it hard to oppose the

Rashba's ban.) R. Isaac's commentaries should be seen in the context of all the other thirteenth-century Provençal writings that attempted to reinterpret the entirety of Judaism in a philosophical light and that were responsible for shifting the grounds of the argument between 1232 and 1303.

Finally, the work of R. Isaac must be viewed against the backdrop of a reawakening of interest in the aggadah, readily discernible in the thirteenth century, especially in southern France. Kabbalistic interpretations and Christian polemics both focused attention on the aggadah as a fertile and largely uncultivated field, and the philosophers hastened to sow their seeds and reap their harvest. Alongside the individual aggadot philosophically interpreted in the context of longer works, there were treatises, whether long or short, specifically devoted to the topic of aggadic exegesis. Most of this material remains in manuscript. A few outstanding examples might be mentioned. The fourth part of R. Meir b. Simon's *Milhemet Mitzvah* is devoted in part to a discussion of aggadot being used by Christians and Kabbalists for their own purposes.[17] Moses ibn Tibbon's *Sefer Pe'ah* contains philosophical interpretations of select problematical passages from the aggadah intended to demonstrate the proper approach to this literature.[18] Much of Levi b. Abraham's *Livyat Hen* resorts to aggadic exegesis, and the section of that work entitled *Sha'ar ha-Aggadah* is filled with fascinating interpretations and illuminating pronouncements.[19] Yedaiah Bedersi's philosophical commentary on the Midrashim elucidates passages of particular interest to him from the *Midrash Rabbah*, *Tanhuma*, *Sifrei*, *Pirkei de-R. Eliezer*, *Midrash Tehillim*, *Midrash Ruth*, and *Midrash Nehamot*.[20] Several pages inserted into a manuscript of Gersonides' *Milhamot ha-Shem* contain allegorical explications of the bizarre tales in the fifth chapter of *Baba Batra*.[21]

Other works have apparently been lost. Levi b. Abraham quotes interpretations of his uncle, Reuben b. Hayyim, whose commentary on the aggadot is mentioned by the sixteenth-century writer Azariah de-Rossi.[22] Shem Tov Falaquera refers to a book he wrote called *Sefer ha-Derush*, a philosophical exposition of aggadic passages from the Talmud, no longer extant.[23] Hillel of Verona, while coming from a different geographical setting, might be added to the list as a contemporary; in a passage from *Tagmulei ha-Nefesh* in which he discusses the various categories of aggadah, he reports that "I have dwelt at great length on these matters in the book I composed called *Ma'amar ha-Darban*." This also seems to be a lost commentary on the aggadot.[24]

All of this evidence begins to suggest the existence of a school of philosophically oriented aggadic interpretation centered in southern France, somewhat analogous to the native Provençal school of halakhic study.[25] At some future date, when the major extant texts of Provençal aggadic commentary will have been published and when the more fragmentary manuscript material of other authors and the exposition of individual aggadot in better-known works can be integrated into the picture, it may be possible to draw some firm conclusions about the existence and nature of this school.

I have tried to place the works of R. Isaac in their cultural context from various perspectives: the commitment to commentary as a means of self-expression, the impulse toward popularization of scientific and philosophical material, the broad drive to establish beyond question the centrality of philosophy to Judaism by systematically reinterpreting the sources of Judaism in philosophical terms, and the fascination with aggadah as problem and challenge. What then is the originality of R. Isaac's enterprise? There are actually two questions to be posed. First, what did he himself feel he had accomplished that had not been done before? And what can we, judging his work in retrospect, conclude about his achievement?

There are many instances in which R. Isaac boasts about the originality of a specific interpretation: "No one has anticipated me in this; I have not seen such an interpretation written anywhere until now."[26] But his evaluation of the work as a whole and his assessment of its significance would have come in the introductions to the commentaries. The introduction can be viewed as a kind of literary genre in itself, serving a specific purpose and following predictable, almost conventional patterns, regardless of the work to which it is appended. It generally explains the circumstances surrounding the composition of the work to follow, pointing to a pressing intellectual problem or an urgent cultural need, reflecting on the inadequacy of existing works and the absence of anything that fills the precise need defined, sometimes referring to pressures upon the author to perform the necessary task, often protesting out of a consciousness of personal inadequacy, and finally consenting to endeavor to meet the challenge.[27]

In the case of R. Isaac, I should like to indulge in an exercise of the imagination by reconstructing the broad outlines of a hypothetical introduction to the *Hibbur ha-Talmud Bavli*. The author would have spoken about the problem posed by the aggadah, probably in terms reminiscent of Maimonides' introduction to chapter Helek of his Mishnah Commentary: how the masses, following the literal meaning, are led astray to believe impossible things; how some sophisticates, impressed by their own intellectual enlightenment, mock and scorn the words of the sages that seem to be inconsistent with the insights of science; possibly even how Christians are exploiting aggadic statements to heap ridicule upon the ignorance of the rabbis or to buttress the arguments for their own faith. He would certainly have noted the achievement of Maimonides in pointing the way by his formulation of the proper approach to the aggadah and his interpretation of specific aggadic statements. He would have referred to Maimonides' original intention to write a full commentary on the aggadot and his subsequent decision to refrain from such an undertaking.[28] He would have maintained that the need for such a commentary still exists, as no one had attempted to write one since the Rambam's death, or he might have alluded to the attempts of certain authors to interpret the aggadot in accordance with the doctrine we now call Kabbala and attacked these attempts as falsifications of the sages' teachings. He would have said that he, R. Isaac b. Yedaiah, had therefore undertaken, in fear and trembling, to walk where the Master had declined to tread, to write the book Maimonides would have written had he not changed his mind, impelled to overlook his own unworthiness by the urgency of the need. He might have formulated some general principles of interpretative approach: when the simple meaning of a statement should be repudiated; into what categories the aggadah can be divided. And he might have given some specific indication of the audience for whom the work was intended.

Here we come to a fundamental issue underlying many philosophical commentaries. Was the author's purpose primarily to validate philosophy in the eyes of those who held every word of the aggadah to be sacred, or was it to reclaim the aggadah for those whose unalterable commitment to philosophy had entailed a refusal to take seriously the words of the sages? While R. Isaac would unquestionably have been pleased if both purposes had been accomplished, his primary goal was probably in the former direction. Most of the material in the commentaries seems to be addressed to those who were certain about the value of the aggadah and uncertain about the value of philosophy, for it makes the aggadah into a vehicle both to teach rudimentary philosophy and to propagandize on its behalf. The same is true for comments on passages of a legal nature; the commandments and the halakha are assumed to be rational and beneficial and are explained as means for attaining ethical virtues and creating an environment propitious for philosophical enlightenment. By demonstrating at such exhaustive length that the entire rabbinic literature is consistent with the world view of the moderate followers of Maimonides, and even more, by making it articulate that world view, R. Isaac hoped to wear down the opposition, to neutralize fears about the harmful effects of philosophical study, and perhaps even to whet the appetite for deeper investigation as a means to perfection and eternal life.

A modern evaluation of R. Isaac's achievement recognizes flashes of true originality, striking reinterpretations of rabbinic dicta, doctrines difficult to parallel elsewhere. But it is the all-encompassing nature of his work, the cumulative effect of hundreds of comments that do not in themselves reflect the spark of genius, which constitutes the real significance of these writings. On the whole, the commentaries are not the work of a brilliant and profoundly original thinker, the creator of a new synthesis. R. Isaac was no Maimonides, no Ralbag. He might be viewed as a rather good representative of the intellectual elite of thirteenth-century Provençal Jewry, though not one of those rare individuals on the frontiers of knowledge. The commentaries reveal an author who saw the trail blazed and the direction signaled by others, who then methodically, systematically, even somewhat pedantically set about to plot the entire territory. Where others had merely asserted that the whole corpus of the aggadah could be shown to be consistent with the insights of philosophy if properly understood, R. Isaac boldly set out to prove it in massive works of interpretation.

That a Jew passionately committed to philosophy would have devoted so great a proportion of his life to the explication of aggadic material forces us to reexamine the generalization that the philosophers regarded the aggadah as a "stumbling block rather than as a precious heritage."[29] The amount of energy devoted to systematic exposition of the aggadah by thirteenth-century Kabbalists seems almost insignificant when compared to the dimensions of R. Isaac's work on the aggadot of the Talmud, and it was he, not a Kabbalist, who produced what is probably the first full commentary of any kind on the Midrash Rabbah. That his works seem to have left such few traces in the subsequent literature of the Jewish people is more a reflection of the vagaries of history than a comment on the significance of his undertaking or the impressiveness of his accomplishment.

NOTES

INDEX OF CODE WORDS

INDEX OF PASSAGES CITED

GENERAL INDEX

ABBREVIATIONS

CAT   R. Isaac b. Yedaiah, *Commentary on the Aggadot of the Talmud*, Escorial MS G.IV. 3

CMR   R. Isaac b. Yedaiah, *Commentary on the Midrash Rabbah*, Jewish Theological Seminary of America MS 5028

EJ   *Encyclopedia Judaica*, Jerusalem, 1972

HJCS   Yitzhak Baer, *History of the Jews in Christian Spain*, 2 vols., Philadelphia, 1961, 1966

HUCA   *Hebrew Union College Annual*

JJS   *Journal of Jewish Studies*

JQR   *Jewish Quarterly Review*

MGWJ   *Monatsschrift für Geschichte und Wissenschaft des Judentums*

MTJM   Gershom Scholem, *Major Trends in Jewish Mysticism*, New York, 1941

PAAJR   *Proceedings of the American Academy of Jewish Research*

PL   *Patrologiae cursus completus, series Latina*

REJ   *Revue des études juives*

SMJHL   *Studies in Medieval Jewish History and Literature*, ed. Isadore Twersky, Cambridge, Mass., 1979

SRHJ   Salo Wittmayer Baron, *A Social and Religious History of the Jews*, 16 vols., Philadelphia and New York, 1952-1976

NOTES

1. The Aggadah: Problem and Challenge

1. "Aggadah" is best defined negatively as the nonlegal component of rabbinic discourse. Among its characteristics are the frequent use of hyperbole and other forms of figurative language, the variety of levels ranging from the profoundly intellectual to the unabashedly popular, the spectrum of tones including both high seriousness and good-natured banter, and the juxtaposition of two or more mutually incompatible opinions with no attempt to reach a definitive and binding conclusion. Recent attempts to analyze aspects of the aggadah from different perspectives include A. J. Heschel, *Torah min ha-Shamayim be-Aspaklariah shel ha-Dorot*, 2 vols. (London and New York, 1962, 1965); I. Heinemann, *Darkhei ha-Aggadah* (Jerusalem, 1970); J. Heinemann, *Aggadot ve-Toldoteihen* (Jerusalem, 1974).

2. An English translation by Leon Nemoy of the relevant material from Kirkisani's work appeared in *HUCA*, 7 (1930), 317-397; see esp. pp. 350-361. Cf. also W. Bacher, "Qirqisani, the Karaite, and His Work on Jewish Sects," in *Karaite Studies*, ed. P. Birnbaum (New York, 1971), pp. 259-283, esp. pp. 266-271; and S. Lieberman, *Sheki'in* (Jerusalem, 1970), pp. 11-26.

3. Salmon b. Yeruham, *Milhamot ha-Shem*, ed. I. Davidson (New York, 1934), esp. pp. 108-113. On the author, see Z. Ankori, *Karaites in Byzantium* (New York, 1959), p. 164, n. 298.

4. Our text of the gemara of *Berakhot*, 3a, attributes this incident to R. Yose. There is no indication of a different reading in *Dikdukei Sofrim ad loc.* However, Judah Halevi quotes the same passage with R. Ishmael as the protagonist (*Kuzari*, III, 73), and this establishes the likelihood that ibn Hazm's account was based on a text with this reading. Cf. also *Kevutzat Mikhtavim be-Inyenei ha-Mahloket al devar Sefer ha-Moreh ve-ha-Mada*, ed. S. Z. H. Halberstam, *Jeschurun* (Kobak), 8 (1875), 135.

5. I. Goldziher, "Proben muhammedänischer Polemik gegen den Talmud," *Jeschurun* (Kobak), 8 (1872), 76-104; the quotation is translated from pp. 102-104. See also H. Hirschfield, "Mohammedan Criticism of the Bible," *JQR*, o.s., 13 (1900-1901), 222-240. On the author, see M. Asín Palacios, *Abenházam de Córdoba y su historia crítica de las ideas religiosas*, 5 vols. (Madrid, 1927-1932), esp. II, 385-392.

6. Goldziher, "Proben," pp. 103-104.

7. Petrus Alfonsi, *Dialogi, PL*, ed. J.-P. Migne, CLVII (Paris, 1854), 535-

672, esp. ch. 1, cols. 541-567. On this work, see A. L. Williams, *Adversus Judaeos* (Cambridge, 1935), pp. 233-240; A. Funkenstein, "Ha-Temurot be-Vikkuah she-bein Yehudim le-Notzrim be-Me'ah ha-Sheteim Esreh," *Zion*, 33 (1968), 133-137; H. Merhavia, *Ha-Talmud be-Re'i ha-Natzrut* (Jerusalem, 1970), pp. 93-125.

8. Alfonsi, *Dialogi*, col. 551.

9. For example, a story about competition between the sons of Esau and the sons of Jacob at the burial of their respective fathers; the assertion that Korah's treasure was so vast that it took three hundred camels just to carry the leather keys to the chests; an episode involving the efforts of Og, king of Bashan, to destroy the Israelites; the account of Moses' successful attempt to convince the angels in heaven that the Torah should be given not to them but to the people of Israel; and the description of R. Joshua b. Levi's negotiations with the Angel of Death.

10. Alfonsi, *Dialogi*, cols. 566-567.

11. Petrus Venerabilis, *Tractatus adversus Judaeorum inveteratam duritem, PL*, ed. J.-P. Migne, CLXXXIX (Paris, 1854), 507-650, esp. ch. 5, "De ridiculis atque stultissimis fabulis Judaeorum," cols. 602-650. On this work, see Williams, *Adversus Judaeos*, pp. 384-394; Funkenstein, "Temurot," pp. 137-141; Lieberman, *Sheki'in*, pp. 27-42; Merhavia, *Talmud*, pp. 128-152. On the sources used by Peter the Venerable—whether he drew his material directly from Alfonsi and the "Alphabet of Ben Sira" or from a collection of translated aggadic material that Alfonsi himself had used—see Lieberman, p. 33, and Merhavia, pp. 148-151.

12. Petrus Venerabilis, *Tractatus*, cols. 614-615. Psalm 59:12 had been used as a justification for the physical toleration of the Jews since Augustine (*City of God*, XVIII, 46); it was cited by Peter's great contemporary St. Bernard in opposing the massacres being carried out in the wake of the Second Crusade. See Otto of Freising, *The Deeds of Frederick Barbarossa* (New York, 1966), p. 78, and R. Ephraim b. Jacob, *Sefer Zekhirah: Selihot ve-Kinot*, ed. A. M. Haberman (Jerusalem, 1970), p. 18.

13. Funkenstein, "Temurot," p. 141.

14. See, most recently, J. Rosenthal, "The Talmud on Trial," *JQR*, n.s., 47 (1956), 58-76, 145-169, and Merhavia, *Talmud*, pp. 227-348.

15. A list of the aggadot discussed can be reconstructed from the Latin source specifying the charges against the Talmud and from the Hebrew account of R. Yehiel, which presents a dramatic but tendentious description of the trial itself. See Rosenthal, "The Talmud on Trial," pp. 145-169, and R. Yehiel of Paris, *Vikkuah* (Thorn, 1873).

16. R. Yehiel, *Vikkuah*, p. 11; on the background of this charge, see Rosenthal, "The Talmud on Trial," p. 162, n. 130. Petrus Alfonsi had already pointed out that the Talmud contained statements insulting to the Christian faith, referring to those passages that aver that Jesus was a magician, conceived in incest, who led the people astray (Alfonsi, *Dialogi*, col. 573; cf. Williams, *Adversus Judaeos*, p. 238). But the purpose of Donin in citing such passages was obviously quite different from that of the earlier apostate.

17. Still another approach to the Talmud was used by Christians in the second half of the thirteenth century: the exploitation of the aggadah to disprove

central tenets of medieval Judaism and to support such Christian dogma as the advent of the Messiah, the Incarnation, and the Trinity. Adumbrations of this approach can be seen in earlier authors. See Funkenstein, "Temurot," p. 142, on Alan of Lille, and Alfonsi, *Dialogi*, col. 581, discussing *Sanhedrin*, 98a (The Messiah will come "today" if you will believe in His words).

18. For example, Moses Maimonides, *Mishnah im Perush ha-Rambam: Nezikin*, ed. J. Kafah (Jersualem, 1964), p. 201; *Sefer Hassidim*, ed. J. Wistenetski (Berlin, 1891), #811; Nachmanides, comment on Genesis 24:1; *Piskei R. Isaiah of Trani*, quoted in S. Asaf, *Mekorot le-Toldot ha-Hinnukh be-Yisrael* (Tel Aviv, 1931), II, 95; *Herem* of Rashba in *She'elot u-Teshuvot R. Abraham b. Adret* (B'nei B'rak, 1958), I, 153, cols. 1, 2; Joseph ibn Kaspi, "Sefer ha-Musar," in I. Abrahams, *Hebrew Ethical Wills* (Phila., 1926), I, 146; Shem-Tov ibn Shaprut, *Pardes Rimonim* (Jerusalem, 1968), p. 2a.

19. For example, the assertions that God wears tefillin, wraps himself in a prayer shawl, prays, and expresses displeasure over the destruction of the Temple by roaring like a lion, shedding tears, striking His hands together, and showing other physical expressions of grief. See *Otzar ha-Geonim: Berakhot*, ed. B. M. Levin (Haifa, 1928), "Teshuvot," pp. 12, 14-15, 131-132.

20. See, for example, the question addressed to Hai Gaon about the four who entered the *pardes* (*Hag.*, 14b); *Otzar ha-Geonim: Yom Tov, Hagigah u-Mashkin* (Jerusalem, 1931), pt. II, pp. 13-14.

21. For example, between the assertions that Adam "spawned evil spirits, devils, and night-demons" and that he "abstained from the woman" (*Erub.*, 18b); *Otzar ha-Geonim: Erubin u-Fesahim* (Jerusalem, 1931), pt. I, p. 9.

22. A questioner from Kairuwan cites the statement "Whoever asks for what he needs in Aramaic is not heeded by the ministering angels" (*Shab.*, 12b) yet points out that most of the prayers written by the geonim themselves were in Aramaic; *Otzar ha-Geonim: Shabbat* (Jerusalem, 1931), pt. I, p. 4.

23. Note the perplexity caused by the pronouncement that "it is permissible to pierce through an *am ha-aretz* on Yom Kippur that falls on the Sabbath" (*Pes.*, 49b), *Otzar ha-Geonim: Erubin u-Fesahim*, pt. II, p. 67; and R. Samuel b. Hofni's discussion of the Talmudic passage that indicates that God actually raised Samuel from the dead through the witch of Endor, *Otzar ha-Geonim: Yom Tov, Hagigah u-Mashkin*, pt. II, pp. 2-5.

24. *Sefer ha-Kuzari*, III, 73, "I will not deny, O King of the Khazars, that there are matters in the Talmud of which I am unable to give thee a satisfactory explanation, nor even bring them in connection with the whole.

25. *Mishnah im Perush ha-Rambam: Zera'im*, ed. J. Kafah (Jerusalem, 1963), p. 39.

26. *Mishnah im Perush ha-Rambam: Mo'ed* (Jerusalem, 1964), p. 177.

27. *Mishnah im Perush ha-Rambam: Nezikin*, p. 196; Moses Maimonides, *Guide for the Perplexed*, II, 26; *Guide*, III, 26; *Teshuvot ha-Rambam*, ed. J. Blau (Jerusalem, 1960), II, 715-716.

28. J. Mann, *Texts and Studies, II: Karaitica* (Philadelphia, 1935), p. 38.

29. There is no comment on the aggadic assertions that a rabbi in a ruin heard a voice saying, "Woe is me," over the destruction of the Temple, that God wrapped Himself in a talit like one who leads worship, and showed Moses the

order of prayer, that God Himself prays—aggadot that the geonim took great pains to explain in a manner consistent with their theology.

30. See the comment attributed to R. Gershom and the comments of Rashi and the Tosafot on *Ta'anit*, 31a: "In the future, the Holy One, blessed be He, will make a circle for the righteous and sit among them in the Garden of Eden"; a similar statement was held up to ridicule by both Kirkisani (*HUCA*, 8, 350-351) and Salmon b. Yeruham (*Milhamot ha-Shem*, pp. 110-111) as attributing corporeal nature to God, and it would later be used by a Christian polemicist to "prove" that God will again be seen in the human form of the Messiah, who is both God and man (Raymund Martini, *Pugio Fidei*, p. 734). Also Rashi, *Berakhot*, 7a, on R. Ishmael's strange encounter; *Tosafot BM*, 59b, *lo*; *Tos. Ber.*, 6a, *elu*; *Tos. Shab.*, 88a, *kafah*; Rashi and *Tos. Niddah*, 13b, *ad*. Cf. E. Melamed, *Mavo le-Sifrut ha-Talmud* (Jerusalem, 1970), pp. 112-113; E. Urbach, *Ba'alei ha-Tosafot* (Jerusalem, 1968), pp. 552-553.

31. Moses Taku, *Ketav Tamim*, ed. R. Kirchheim, *Otzar Nehmad*, 3 (1860), 63-64.

32. See Lieberman, *Sheki'in*, especially pp. 69-70. Evidence for the original reading "Woe to Me" can be found in Salmon b. Yeruham, ibn Hazm, Petrus Alfonsi, Peter the Venerable, the *Kuzari*, and the Munich manuscript of the Talmud, among others. By the thirteenth century, the Hebrew word for "to me" had dropped out in some texts of the Talmud, and by the fifteenth century, R. Solomon b. Simeon Duran, apparently unaware of the older reading, could accuse his Christian opponent of falsifying the text by adding "to me."

33. The epithet is cited by Kirkisani (p. 355), Salmon b. Yeruham (p. 113), and ibn Hazm (p. 103); see G. Scholem, *Kabbalah* (New York, 1974), p. 378. For an example of a later change in the Talmudic text where earlier commentators had tried to resolve the problem through interpretation, see Abraham Berger, "Captive at the Gate of Rome: A Messianic Motif," *PAAJR*, 44 (1977), 1-17, esp. pp. 10-11 on *Sanhedrin*, 98a. For R. Isaac's distinctive treatment of this aggadah, see, chapter IV, section 3.

34. A convenient summary of attitudes toward this work in the Middle Ages can be found in Alexander Altmann, "Moses Narboni's 'Epistle on Shi'ur Qoma,' " *Jewish Medieval and Renaissance Studies* (Cambridge, Mass., 1967), pp. 226-238.

35. R. Abraham b. Isaac Av-Beit-Din, *Sefer ha-Eshkol*, ed. A. Auerbach (Halberstadt, 1868), pt. II, p. 47; S. Baron, *SRHJ*, IV (New York, 1958), p. 47; Moses Taku, *Ketav Tamim*, p. 63. Maimonides reflects the prevalence of this view rejecting it: "Perhaps you will say to me, as many say, 'You call words in the Talmud "aggadah!" ' Yes! All these words and those similar to them are aggadah in their content, whether they be written in the Talmud, or in books of *derashot*, or in books of aggadah." His purpose here is to reduce the authority of Talmudic aggadah to the level of that in other works, all of which has little halakhic import. See *Teshuvot ha-Rambam*, p. 739.

36. For example, Saadia Gaon, *Commentaire sur le Sefer Yesira*, tr. M. Lambert (Paris, 1891), pp. 19-20, on the assertion that during the night, God "rides on His fleet cherub and flies through eighteen thousand worlds" (*AZ*, 3b). Moses Taku responds to the passage of Saadia as follows: "Ignoramus! Of the

words of an amora, spoken through the *ruah ha-kodesh* and the sacred tradition, he writes, 'All Israel is not in accord with this'; with his own idle chatter, who is in accord!?" (*Ketav Tamim*, p. 70.)

37. A. Marx, "The Correspondence Between the Rabbis of Southern France and Maimonides about Astrology," *HUCA*, 3 (1926), 356, tr. in *Medieval Political Philosophy: A Sourcebook*, ed. R. Lerner and M. Mahdi (Glencoe, Ill., 1963), pp. 234-235. Kirkisani mentions this defense against attacks on problematic aggadot, noting that some Jews "assert that not all of the Rabbanites hold these opinions, but only a few of them do so" (*HUCA*, 7, 360).

38. *Otzar ha-Geonim: Gittin* (Jerusalem, 1941), p. 152.

39. "Ma'amar al Odot Derashot Hazal," in *Milhamot ha-Shem*, ed. R. Margulies (Jerusalem, 1953), p. 91; cf. Maimonides, *Guide*, III, 43.

40. Hai Gaon, cited in *Sefer ha-Eshkol*, II, 47; Samuel b. Hofni, *Otzar ha-Geonim: Yom Tov, Hagigah u-Mashkin*, pt. II, p. 4.

41. *Milei ninhu:* Mann, *Texts and Studies*, I (Cincinnati, 1931), 593; cf. *Otzar ha-Geonim: Gittin*, p. 152: *milin be'alma. De'ot:* Mann, *Texts and Studies*, I, 322. *Umdanah: Sefer ha-Eshkol*, II, 47. *Ke-divrei havai: Otzar ha-Geonim: Erubin u-Fesahim*, pt. II, p. 67. *Guzma u-mashal: Otzar ha-Geonim: Berakhot*, "Teshuvot," p. 14.

42. Saadia Gaon, *Otzar ha-Geonim: Berakhot*, "Perushim," p. 91, n. 10; Sherira Gaon, *Sefer ha-Eshkol*, II, 47; Hai Gaon, *Otzar ha-Geonim: Yom Tov, Hagigah u-Mashkin*, pt. II, p. 59. See also Mann, *Texts and Studies*, I, 322; *Entziklopediah Talmudit*, I (Jerusalem, 1947), 62; Heschel, *Torah min ha-Shamayim*, I, xxv-xxvi; I. Heinemann, *Darkhei ha-Aggadah*, p. 187; B. Z. Dinur, *Yisrael ba-Golah*, I, 4 (Tel Aviv and Jerusalem, 1962), pp. 260-261.

43. Samuel ha-Nagid, *Mavo ha-Talmud*, s.v. "Haggadah"; Maimonides, in M. Lutzky, "Ve-khatav Mosheh," *Ha-Tekufah*, 30-31 (1946), 702, n. 124. The geonic statements were cited in the context of the Maimonidean controversies; see R. Meir ha-Levi Abulafia, *Ketav al-Rasail* (Paris, 1871), p. 36, and R. Samuel b. Abraham in *Kevutzat Mikhtavim*, pp. 151-152.

44. R. Yehiel of Paris, *Vikkuah*, p. 2.

45. *Kitvei Rabbenu Mosheh ben Nahman*, ed. H. D. Chavel (Jerusalem, 1963), I, 308. It is a matter of dispute among scholars whether Nachmanides actually believed what he said or whether he was forced to articulate a position in conflict with his true beliefs. Lieberman has argued that the statement reflects Nachmanides' actual view (*Sheki'in*, pp. 81-83); the preponderant opinion, however, is that Nachmanides, as a Kabbalist, believed that the aggadah held extremely important esoteric teachings and were thus fundamentally different from the sermon of a Christian bishop. See G. Scholem, *Les origines de la Kabbale* (Paris, 1960), p. 484.

46. *Kitvei Ramban*, I, 306.

47. See L. Ginzberg, "Allegorical Interpretation of Scripture," *On Jewish Law and Lore* (Cleveland, 1962), p. 127; E. Smalley, *The Study of the Bible in the Middle Ages* (New York, 1952), p. 2; E. Honig, *Dark Conceit: The Making of Allegory* (Evanston, 1959), p. 19; G. Scholem, *On the Kabbalah and Its Symbolism* (New York, 1965), p. 33.

48. For this typology with respect to the confrontation of the Bible and the

philosophical world view in antiquity, see H. Wolfson, *Philo* (Cambridge, Mass., 1962), I, 57-71 (on the Jews of first-century Alexandria as viewed by Philo). With respect to the confrontation between the Hebrew Bible and the new Christian world view, the traditionalist position is represented by the Jews, for whom the authority of the sacred text required an absolute rejection of the new doctrine; the revolutionary position by those Gnostics whose novel teaching shattered the authority of the Hebrew Bible in their eyes, and whose refusal to allegorize problematic passages in the Hebrew Bible was symptomatic of their break from this text; and the middle ground by the Church Fathers, typified by Origen, who showed the way to make peace between ancient sacred text and new dispensation. Cf. R. P. C. Hanson, *Allegory and Event* (Richmond, Va., 1959), esp. pp. 135-141.

49. This is the so-called "Averroist" double-truth doctrine. For its appearance in thirteenth-century Jewish thought, see G. Vajda, *Isaac Albalag: averroïste juif, traducteur et annotateur d'Al-Ghazâlî* (Paris, 1960), pp. 153-154, 251-266, and I. Albalag, *Sefer Tikkun ha-De'ot*, ed. Vajda (Jerusalem, 1973), pp. 43-44. Charles Touati has expressed reservations as to whether this is indeed a position that maintains two valid yet conflicting truths; see "Vérité philosophique et vérité prophetique chez Isaac Albalag," *REJ*, 71 (1962), 35-47.

50. In addition to the sources listed in n.47, see the fine characterization of the tensions that led to the formation of *Hassidut Ashkenaz:* H. Soloveitchik, "Three Themes in *Sefer Hasidim*," *AJS Review*, 1 (1976), 322-323.

51. *Otzar ha-Geonim: Berakhot*, "Teshuvot," p. 131, emphasis added. This passage too was quoted in the context of the Maimonidean controversy, although it was attributed to Rabbenu Nissim; see *Kevutzat Mikhtavim*, pp. 133-134. The principle that "the Torah spoke in the language of men" is taken from the Talmud (for example, *Berakhot*, 31b), but it is used here in a totally different context and given a new meaning as it is applied to statements about God.

52. Bahya ibn Pekudah, *Hovot ha-Levavot*, "Sha'ar ha-Yihud," ch. 10; Maimonides, *Mishnah im Perush ha-Rambam: Nezikin*, p. 211 (Introduction to Helek, *yesod* 3); and *Guide*, I, 59. See L. Jacobs, *Theology in the Responsa* (London and Boston, 1975), p. 8, n. 18, and Heschel, *Torah min ha-Shamayim*, I, 3-4.

53. Judah b. Barzilai, *Perush Sefer Yetzirah*, ed. S. Halberstam (Breslau, 1885), pp. 20-21. On Saadia's theory of the *kavod*, see A. Altmann, "Saadya's Theory of Revelation," *Saadya Studies*, ed. E. Rosenthal (Manchester, England, 1943), and C. Sirat, *Les théories des visions surnaturelles dans la pensée juive du Moyen Age* (Leiden, 1969), pp. 17-33; these deal primarily with the interpretation of Biblical passages.

54. Hananel in *Perush Sefer Yetzirah*, pp. 32-33; cf. Abraham b. Azriel, *Sefer Arugat ha-Bosem*, ed. E. Urbach (Jerusalem, 1939), I, 198; on Hananel, see Sirat, *Théories*, pp. 13, 92.

55. *Kuzari*, III, 73; for the general view of Halevi regarding Biblical visions, see Sirat, *Théories*, pp. 83-88.

56. *Guide*, II, 42; for the subsequent debate on this issue, see, inter alia, Nachmanides, Commentary on Genesis 18:2; R. Yom Tov b. Abraham Ishbili, *Sefer ha-Zikkaron*, ed. G. Cahana (Jerusalem, 1956), pp. 39 ff.; Abravanel, Commentary on *Guide ad loc.*, and Commentary on Genesis 18.

57. Saadia Gaon, *Emunot ve-De'ot*, 6:7; cf. "Iyyun Ya'akov" in *Ein Ya'akov* on *Berakhot*, 18b. Such removal of the aggadot from their simple meaning is relatively uncommon in Saadia's philosophical work.

58. *Kuzari*, III, 73. The problem raised by this aggadah was discussed by many subsequent writers, including R. Solomon b. Adret, *Hiddushei ha-Rashba al Aggadot ha-Shas*, ed. S. Weinberger (Jerusalem, 1966), pp. 83-84 on *Nedarim*, 39b; Levi b. Abraham, *Livyat Hen*, Vatican MS 192, ff. 57b-58a; Yedaiah Bedersi, *Perush ha-Midrashim*, Paris MS 738.3, ff. 276b-278a on *Tanhuma*, 1:1, and Parma MS 222 on *Pirkei de-Rabbi Eliezer*, ch. 3; Shem-Tov ibn Shaprut, *Pardes Rimonim*, pp. 38b-39a; Jacob ibn Habib, introduction to *Ein Ya'akov*. A serious problem in Halevi's discussion is his text of the Talmudic statement, according to which the Messiah was created before the world. Most versions of this statement read "the name of the Messiah."

59. *Teshuvot ha-Rambam*, II, 715-716. Cf. the passage from the "Letter on Astrology," cited above, where the conclusion states not so much the need for interpretation as the right to disregard the statement as an aberrant view. Maimonides also interprets the aggadah "All is in the hands of Heaven except the fear of Heaven" in the eighth of his *Shemonah Perakim*; see the discussion of E. Schweid, *Iyyunim ba-Shemonah Perakim le-Rambam* (Jerusalem, 1969), pp. 150-151.

60. See n. 47, and Wolfson, *Philo*, pp. 115-140.

61. See I. Heinemann, "Die Wissenschaftliche Allegoristik des Jüdischen Mittelalters," *HUCA*, 23 (1950-1951), 619.

62. It is true that there is a general definition of "allegory," based on its etymology, as that which "says one thing but means something *other* than what it says" (Heracleitus, *Quaestiones Homericae*, 22, in Hanson, *Allegory and Event*, p. 39); cf. also A. Fletcher, *Allegory: The Theory of a Symbolic Mode* (Ithaca, 1964), p. 2; Ginzberg, *Jewish Law and Lore*, p. 127; Wolfson, *Philo*, p. 134. This definition, however, is so inclusive as to blur important distinctions. The relationship of the new content (the nimshal) to the text (the mashal) must be carefully evaluated.

Coleridge's definition of allegorical writing has become classic: "The employment of one set of agents and images with actions and accompaniments correspondent, so as to convey, while in disguise, either moral qualities or conceptions of the mind that are not in themselves circumstances so that the difference is everywhere presented to the eye or imagination, while the likeness is suggested to the mind; and this connectedly, so that the parts combine to form a consistent whole" (*Mis. Crit.*, 30, quoted in Fletcher, *Allegory*, p. 19). For allegory in contemporary literary theory, see Honig, *Dark Conceit*; C. S. Lewis, *The Allegory of Love* (New York, 1958), ch. 2; N. Frye, *Fearful Symmetry* (Princeton, 1947), pp. 115-117, 120-128; idem, *Anatomy of Criticism* (Princeton, 1957), pp. 89-92; Fletcher, *Allegory*. It must be remembered that theories of allegorical writing apply to our subject of allegorical interpretation if we assume the commentator believed that the prophets and sages were writing allegory.

The important distinction between allegorical and metaphorical interpretation is emphasized by Heinemann, "Die Wissenschaftliche Allegoristik," pp. 611-612. The distinction between allegory and symbol, which began with Goethe (see

Fletcher, pp. 13-17, and Lewis, pp. 45-48), has been used by Scholem to characterize the difference between the interpretations of Jewish philosophy and those of the Kabbala (see *MTJM*, pp. 26-27, and *Les origines de la Kabbale*, pp. 430-31). We shall have occasion to note, however, that many of the interpretations of the Zohar are allegorical, not symbolic, and quite close to those of contemporary philosophers.

63. *Mishnah im Perush ha-Rambam: Nezikin*, p. 207. The interpretation of the statement "In the world to come . . . the righteous will sit with their crowns on their heads enjoying the radiance of the divine presence" (*Ber.*, 17a) as referring not to physical crowns but to the apprehension of God, which "crowns the human intellect with immortal life" (ibid., p. 205) is not an allegorical interpretation, as it is called by W. Bacher, "Die Agada in Maimunis Werken," in *Moses ben Maimon*, II (Leipzig, 1914), p. 142, but rather a metaphoric one.

64. *Les origines de la Kabbale*, pp. 97-99.

65. Cf. Nachmanides' Commentary on Genesis 24:1, where he refers to the interpretation in *Sefer ha-Bahir*. This passage is an important source for Ramban's attitude toward the aggadah.

66. *Perush ha-Aggadot le-Rabbi Azriel*, ed. I. Tishbi (Jerusalem, 1945), pp. 4-5.

67. With this symbolic interpretation, we may contrast the allegorical interpretation of the tefillin by R. Isaac, who sees the phylactery of the head as a representation of the cosmos (see, ch. V, sec. 3). The propagandistic use by the Kabbalists of suitably interpreted aggadot was recognized and denounced by R. Meir b. Simon, who wrote as follows: "They invent in their minds things that tend toward heresy, and they imagine that they bring proof for their words from the statements of aggadah which they interpret themselves in accordance with their own erroneous doctrine. Heaven forbid that the meaning of the sages who said these things was similar to what [the Kabbalists] claim!" *Milhemet Mitzvah*, Parma MS 155 (2749), f. 229a.

68. Scholem, *MTJM*, p. 31.

69. For example, his use of aggadot to support the argument that the religious ideal is a pure, disinterested service of God without any thoughts of worldly goals: *Mishnah im Perush ha-Rambam: Nezikin*, p. 199; see D. Hartman, *Maimonides: Torah and Philosophic Quest* (Philadelphia, 1976), pp. 72-73.

70. One might mention the interpretation of the angels in the heavenly court (*Guide*, II, 6) and the angels who guard the man who uses tefillin, fringes, and mezuzah (*Hil. Mezuzah*, 6:12, based on *Menahot*, 43b); the new understanding of ma'aseh bereshit and ma'aseh merkavah as Greek physics and metaphysics (*Mishnah im Perush ha-Rambam: Mo'ed*, p. 377, *Hil. Yesodei ha-Torah*, 2:11); the use of R. Haninah's rebuke of a reader who added laudatory adjectives to the fixed liturgy as exemplifying the repudiation of positive attributes for God in a philosophical context (*Guide*, I, 59, on *Ber.*, 33b); and the employment of aggadot concerning God's special creation at twilight of the sixth day and the condition made with the elements, in support of the philosophical predilection against a God whose universe is such that He must intervene and tamper with its orderly operation (*Mishnah im Perush ha-Rambam: Nezikin*, p. 456; *Guide*, II, 29).

71. The opposition to philosophical interpretation of the aggadah was, if

anything, even stronger than R. Meir b. Simon's opposition to the Kabbalists (see n. 67). In addition to the traditionalist attacks recorded in the literature of the controversies of 1232 and 1305, there is a trenchant admonition, probably directed at the followers of Maimonides, by Judah b. Solomon ha-Cohen, whose encyclopedic treatise *Midrash ha-Hokhmah* shows a broad knowledge of and commitment to the sciences: "Do not think that you can understand the mysteries [of the aggadot] on the basis of what we have set down previously from the works of Aristotle—the details from these books pertaining to physics and metaphysics, which is called "divine science." For the mysteries [of the aggadot] totally and absolutely transcend the content of these books. Whoever undertakes to understand those mysteries on the basis of the works of Aristotle, and to interpret the sacred words by means of profane ones, and thinks that by doing so he is exalting and glorifying the sacred Jewish faith, is like one who makes for a great king a crown of clay." *Midrash ha-Hokhmah*, Vatican MS 338, f. 308a, quoted by Colette Sirat, "Juda b. Salomon ha-Cohen," *Italia*, 2 (1979), 45.

72. Maimonides at one time intended to write an extensive commentary explaining "all of the *derashot* [homilies] of the Talmud and other sources" on the level appropriate to them (*Mishnah: Nezikin*, p. 209). In the introduction to the *Guide*, he explains why he gave up on this plan. See also R. Abraham b. Maimonides, "Ma'amar al Odot Derashot Hazal," p. 83; I. Abravanel, *Yeshu'ot Meshiho* (Koenigsberg, 1861), p. 5a; R. Judah Loew b. Bezalel, *Be'er ha-Golah*, in *Kol Sifrei Maharal mi-Prag* (New York, 1969), IV, 49; Bacher, "Die Agada in Maimunis Werken," pp. 131-33; Baron, *SRHJ*, VI, 179.

11. Isaac ben Yedaiah and the Sages

1. The Commentary on the Aggadot of the Talmud was attributed to Yedaiah by A. Neubauer, in "Yedaya de Beziers," *REJ*, 20 (1890), 245-248, on the basis of an ascription at the beginning of the manuscript written in a hand different from that of the scribe. All subsequent scholars have followed him in this, despite the obvious chronological problems which he himself pointed to in the article. The Commentary on the Midrash Rabbah was attributed to Yedaiah by Alexander Marx in "A New Collection of Manuscripts," *PAAJR*, 4 (1933), 145. Marx assumed that it was another copy of Yedaiah's Commentary on the Midrashim, of which manuscripts exist in several European libraries. For the detailed argument proving that these works were not written by Yedaiah but by R. Isaac, see my article "R. Isaac b. Yeda'ya: A Forgotten Commentator on the Aggadah" in *REJ*, 138 (1979), 17-45.

2. M. Kasher and Y. Blacherowitz, eds., *Perushei Rishonim le-Massekhet Avot* (Jerusalem, 1974), pp. 49-74; this edition of the Commentary on *Avot* is characterized by extreme carelessness in transcription and the omission, without explanation, of phrases and entire passages. D. Genhovsky, ed., *Otzar ha-Perushim al Massekhet Horayot* (Jerusalem, 1969), pp. 12-15, is, by contrast, a fairly accurate transcription of the comments on *Horayot*. I have published and annotated several passages from the Midrash Commentary in "The Earliest Commentary on the *Midrash Rabbah*," I. Twersky, ed. *Studies in Medieval Jewish History and Literature* (Cambridge, Mass., 1979), pp. 283-306.

3. J. Llamas, "Los manuscritos hebreos de El Escorial," *Sefarad*, 1 (1941), p. 289.

4. Jacob ibn Habib, *Ein Ya'akov* (New York, 1955), I, 86b, 108b, 109a; see my "R. Isaac b. Yeda'ya," pp. 38-42. I am grateful to Isadore Twersky for having called my attention to these passages in *Ein Ya'akov*, thereby making possible the identification of the author's name.

5. Marx, "A New Collection," p. 145.

6. See M. Benayahu, "Rabbi Shemuel Yaffeh Ashkenazi," *Tarbiz*, 42 (1973), Appendix 4: "Commentators on the Rabbot," pp. 457-460. Benayahu did not know of R. Isaac's manuscript and speaks of the commentary of Yedaiah Bedersi as the earliest commentary on the full Midrash Rabbah.

7. This is the way R. Isaac regularly refers to the work I have designated CAT. The passage appears in *Pesahim*, 111b; the commentary on *Pesahim* is not extant.

8. CMR, 84a. Cf. R. David Kimhi's comment on Psalm 91:6.

9. CMR, 88a.

10. CMR. 93b. The parallel statement in the Babylonian Talmud occurs in *Shabbat*, 99a; the dispute between Gentile sages and the "sages of Israel," apparently identified by R. Isaac as Babylonians in contrast with the "sages of the *land* of Israel," is in *Pesahim*, 94b. In his *Guide*, II, 8, Maimonides maintains it is explicitly stated in the gemara that the Gentiles "defeated" the Jewish sages. This phrase, which appears in the R. Isaac passage (and also Samuel ibn Tibbon, *Ma'amar Yikkavu ha-Mayim* [Pressburg, 1837], p. 52, and Abraham Bibago, *Derekh Emunah* [Jerusalem, 1970], p. 53b, col. 2), is not found in printed editions of the Talmud, although it is probably implied. See the discussion of the gemara in question by R. Abraham b. Maimonides, "Ma'amar al Odot Derashot Hazal," pp. 86-88 (and p. 99, n. 1), and the other sources cited by I. Twersky, "Joseph ibn Kaspi," *SMJHC*, p. 256, n. 52; also M. Friedländer, *Guide of the Perplexed*, pt. II, 44-45; and J. Even-Shemuel, *Moreh Nevukhim*, II, 1 (Jerusalem, 1959), p. 129, n. 4.

11. CAT, 51a (comparing *Sanh.*, 65b, with *Gen. R.*, 11:5: "As you will find this question in a different formulation written in *Genesis Rabbah*, chapter 11 . . ."); CMR, 88b: ("They said further here . . . while in the parallel place the Babylonians said . . . , but this and that are the same, both have the same meaning"). Many other examples could be added.

12. The classic formulation for Biblical material is that of Maimonides in his Introduction to the *Guide*. Jacob Elbaum, referring to *Guide*, III, 43, argues that Maimonides' approach to the aggadah is fundamentally different from his approach to the Bible, and that it was the innovation of Maharal of Prague to extend Maimonides' rule to the realm of rabbinic wisdom ("Rabbi Judah Loeb of Prague and his Attitude to the Aggadah," *Scripta Hierosolymitana*, 22 [1971], 33). While it is true, as we have noted, that Maimonides does not generally use the technique of allegorical interpretation for the aggadah, the assumption of two levels of meaning, with the more valuable meaning concealed, is formulated by Maimonides in his Introduction to the Commentary on the Mishnah (*Mishnah im Perush ha-Rambam: Zera'im*, p. 36) and in his Introduction to chapter Helek of *Sanhedrin* (*Mishnah im Perush ha-Rambam: Nezikin*, p. 202). These passages re-

veal an approach to the aggadah not materially different from the statement in
the Introduction to the *Guide*.

13. CMR, 16b.

14. CAT, 76b.

15. CAT, 79b; cf. CAT, 109b. Maimonides, *Guide*, Introduction: "All of
this is merely to complete the illustration of the allegory in its literal meaning;" R.
Abraham b. ha-Rambam, "Ma'amar," fourth category of *ma'aseh:* "to make the
parable realistic and to round out the content of the riddle." R. Nissim of Marseilles maintains that the sages sometimes made the mashal as strange as possible
precisely in order to conceal the true meaning (He-Halutz, 7 [1865], 129).

16. CAT, 100a-b, referring to use of Genesis 7:22 in *Sanh.*, 108a.

17. CAT, 5a. The question of whether an ignorant man who had no philosophical education could become a prophet through an act of God's will was one
that divided the philosophers not only from the masses but from many of the
Kabbalists; see Maimonides, *Guide*, II, 32, first opinion, and Jacob Anatoli, *Malmad ha-Talmidim* (Lyck, 1886), p. 150a, in contrast with the Zohar, quoted in
Baer, *HJCS*, I, 271-272.

Twice in their edition of this text, Kasher and Blacherowitz omit the key
words, expressing the idea that the sages sometimes spoke according to the erroneous belief of the masses. They give no explanation for this omission but
merely substitute three ellipsis points (. . .) to indicate that material has been de-
leted (p. 50). I am at a loss to understand this method of transcribing a manuscript.

18. CAT, 50a. For this concept of Adam's nature when he was created, see
also CAT, 36b, and CMR, 97a; cf. Bahya b. Asher on Genesis 3:5 (based largely
on *Guide*, I, 2). See also Levi b. Abraham's allegorical interpretation of this aggadah: *Livyat Hen*, Vatican MS 192, f. 42a.

19. CMR, 85a.

20. There are several Maimonidean principles of Biblical interpretation
with which these passages of R. Isaac should be compared. First is the rabbinic
phrase "The Torah spoke according to the language of human beings" (*BM*, 31b),
applied by Maimonides to the problem of anthropomorphic expressions and
positive attributes concerning God. The Torah uses expressions that can be easily
comprehended and understood by all, even though they do not express philosophical truth when read literally, so that the masses will believe in God's existence and perfection (*Guide*, I, 26). Here, as in R. Isaac's doctrine, we have a
choice of language that coincides with what the masses believe, even though
what they believe is false. But the purpose of this choice is not to conceal the
truth from the masses, as it is for R. Isaac; this language is chosen because it is the
only way to establish the belief in God's existence and perfection among the uneducated multitude. Ibn Kaspi generalizes this principle by explaining that the
Bible often speaks in a manner that expresses not the truth but the thoughts or beliefs of various individuals (*Amudei Kesef ad loc.*, *Sheloshah Kadmonei Mefarshei ha-Moreh* [Jerusalem, 1961], pt. II, 38; see the discussion by I. Twersky,
"Joseph ibn Kaspi," *SMJHL*, pp. 238-242); this formulation is closer to R. Isaac's
assumption about the aggadah.

Second, there is the psychological assumption that the masses cannot change their ways overnight. Maimonides uses this assumption as the basis for his explanation of the sacrificial cult: as the people could not immediately shift from the sacrificial service of false deities to the pure worship of the true God, the forms of the older service were retained while the object was changed so that it was no longer idolatrous, and the exercise of sacrifice was restricted so that it would be gradually replaced with a higher type of worship (Guide, III, 32). R. Isaac also recognizes that the masses could not suddenly abandon the belief in demons that was so entrenched in them, and he explains that the sages spoke about demons in the hope that the fear inspired by the demons would eventually be transferred to God. Again there is a difference: Maimonides explains the existence of a mode of worship that is not in itself false but merely a relatively low form of service, whereas R. Isaac is compelled to explain statements in which the sages appear to affirm the complete opposite of what is true.

Finally, Maimonides maintains that the Torah makes various assertions about God—for example, that He grows angry at those who rebel against Him—which, though untrue in themselves, are necessary for the establishment of a stable social order, for the masses are incapable of law-abiding behavior without such a belief (Guide, III, 28; see M. Narboni ad loc., Sheloshah Kadmonei Mefarshei ha-Moreh, pt. III, 61b). In R. Isaac's passage, the idea is not that the assertion of something false brings such obvious and immediate benefit to human affairs that it is justified but rather that the statement of the truth will simply not be tolerated by the masses.

21. CAT, 45a; cf. also 43b: "They duplicated the content using different words, for there is one meaning to them both."

22. Cf. Maimonides, Guide, I, 8: "What I say in a particular passage [of the Bible] is a key for the comprehension of all similar passages." Note that many statements about women and wives in the Talmudic and midrashic aggadah are not interpreted allegorically. For example, on the basis of Maimonides' remark about the adulterous woman in Proverbs, it would be possible to interpret the statements about the sotah as allegory. This R. Isaac does not do. Thus, no simple key can be applied automatically to all statements.

23. For relatively rare uses of this term, see CMR, 19b and 47b. The term regularly used instead of "peshat" is nigleh.

24. CAT, 4b, Kasher and Blacherowitz, p. 49. This meaning of "masar" is linked with a similar meaning of masoret as "esoteric content," with examples cited from Yoma, 21a, and Peshahim, 86b. The opening of Avot is thus understood to mean that Moses transmitted the knowledge of the incorporeal God and His angels to those select few who were prepared to comprehend it, and not to the masses.

25. CAT, 6a-b (Kasher, p. 52); CAT, 6b (Kasher, pp. 52-53); CAT, 7b (Kasher, pp. 53-54). The commentator explains why a colleague is more valuable than a master, so that a stronger verb, "acquire," is used, and wherein lies the difference between "keep far from" and "do not consort with."

26. For example, "drink their words thirstily" interpreted as alluding to the perpetual life of the soul after death: CAT, 6a (Kasher, p. 51); "silence" interpreted as avoidance of attributing positive qualities to God: CAT, 8b (Kasher, pp. 55-56); fulfilling the Torah in "wealth" interpreted as the spiritual reward of

high status in God's sight: CAT, 18a (Kasher, p. 70).

27. CAT, 120a; see F. Mistral, *Dictionnaire Provençal-Francais* (Aix-en-Provence, 1886), II, 145, col. 1. The primary listing is *iruge*, with "iroutge" listed as a variant identified as *languedocien*. With this should be compared Ralbag's comment on Proverbs 30:15, in which the vernacular translation appears as *irtugei*; this is obviously an error and should read *irutgei*. The use of vernacular by R. Isaac cannot begin to compare with the multitude of Provençal words in the commentaries of Radak; see, for example, L. Finkelstein, *The Commentary of David Kimhi on Isaiah* (New York, 1926), pp. lxxv-lxxix.

28. *El* and *elohim*, as in I Sam. 2:3 (cf. *Guide*, I, 2), applied to *Sanh.*, 92a: CAT, 67a. *Mal'akh* (cf. *Guide*, I, 14), applied to *AZ*, 5a: CAT, 115b-116a. *Lev*, as in Eccles. 10:2 (cf. *Guide*, I, 39), applied to *Sanh.*, 99a: CAT, 40b, 85b, 89b; CMR, 62b. *Panim*, as in Eccles. 8:1 and Exod. 33:11 (cf. *Guide*, I, 37), applied to *Num. R.*, 12:1 ("They knew that when Moses' complexion assumed a ruddy glow the divine communication had reached him"): CMR, 79a. *Regel*, as in Gen. 30:30 (cf. *Guide*, I, 28), applied to *Num. R.*, 12:1 (Jacob blessed Pharaoh "that the Nile should rise up *le-raglo*"): CMR, 80a. Ruah, as in Prov. 29:11 (cf. *Guide*, I, 40), applied to *Sanh.*, 89a ("the ruah of Naboth led him astray"): CAT, 61a.

29. R. Isaac seems to understand this verse in a novel way, not as parallels but as contrast: unlike the hakham, the navon may acquire wily strategems even for perversity.

30. CAT, 16a-b (Kasher, p. 67).

31. CAT, 79b-80a.

32. CMR, 16a.

33. CMR, 53b-54a; for kedeisha, cf. ibn Ezra on Deut, 23:18 and Hag., 2:12.

34. CAT, 14a (Kasher, p. 64); CAT, 21a (Kasher, p. 72). R. Jonah Gerondi and R. Menahem Meiri have similar explanations of the phrase in *Avot*, 5:10; see also Anatoli, *Malmad ha-Talmidim*, p. 18b.

35. CAT, 12a (Kasher, p. 61).

36. CAT, 91b-92a.

37. CMR, 21a.

38. CMR, 32b.

39. CAT, 44a, *ad loc.* cites the first part of this statement and says, "I have explained it," undoubtedly referring to his commentary on *Sotah*, 2a.

40. CMR, 11b-12a.

41. CMR, 12b.

42. CAT, 128b.

43. CAT, 97b-98a.

44. CAT, 95b-96a.

45. CAT, 24a-b, 40b-41a, 57b, 22b-23a.

46. CMR, 9a-b; cf. CAT, 58b on *Sanh.*, 82a, "One does not enter a place of study with weapons."

47. CAT, 112a. Moses ibn Tibbon gives a similar, yet apparently independent interpretation of this phrase in his *Sefer Pe'ah*. For him, the teaching of children means the perpetuation of the species through a new generation to replace the old. Alternatively, he suggests in an interpretation bordering on alle-

gory, it may refer to the perfection of the intellect following the weakening of the body in old age; the new, actualized intellect is depicted as a child. See Oxford Bodleian MS 939, f. 15b.

48. CAT, 66a-b; cf. the parallel interpretation of "song" in CMR, 51a-b.

49. The problem of Jewish men having sexual relations with servant women was notorious in the thirteenth century, especially in Christian Spain. See Baer, *HJCS*, I, 254-262, and especially the following sources: R. Jonah Gerondi, *Sha'arei Teshuvah* (Jerusalem, 1968), pp. 131-33; Nachmanides, *Kitvei Ramban*, I, 381-382; R. Solomon b. Adret, *She'elot u- Teshuvot ha-Rashba*, I, 1205, and IV, 314 (discussed by Baer in *HJCS*, I, 255-256 and 434, n. 13); Todros b. Judah Abulafia, in H. Schirmann, *Ha-Shirah ha-Ivrit bi-Sefarad u-vi-Provans* (Jerusalem, 1971), II, 433-434.

50. For example, Maimonides, *Hil. Teshuvah*, 8:1 and 8:5.

51. CMR, 70a-b.

52. CAT, 50b. Cf. Levi b. Abraham, *Livyat Hen*, Vatican MS 192, f. 42b-43a.

53. Note the characterization of R. Isaac's work by R. Jacob ibn Habib: "In many places he does not worry if the context of the gemara contradicts his words completely," *Ein Ya'akob* (New York, 1955), I, 86b.

54. For example, Maimonides, *Guide*, II, 6, in which he quotes the gemara under discussion.

55. CAT, 37a-b.

56. CAT, 94a. Note the interpretation of "There is no atonement for the dead" to mean that the dead themselves do not have the capacity to make atonement for themselves. The intellect is dependent upon the body for the acquisition of knowledge, and the level of its actualization is frozen when it departs from the body; if it has not been actualized by this time, it is doomed to oblivion.

57. R. Isaac's attitude toward gematria in general is not particularly positive. Cf. CAT, 91b, where he comments on the statement "In the future, the Holy One, blessed be He, will give to each and every righteous man 310 worlds, as it is said, 'That I may cause those who love me to inherit *yesh*' [Prov. 8:21]: *yesh* in *gematria* is 310" (*Sanh.*, 100a). This number, according to R. Isaac, is not intended to be taken very seriously (*lav davka*), as no one can possibly know the precise nature of the reward for the soul. The number 310 is thus given "as a poetic ornament" (*al tzad melitzat ha-shir*).

58. CMR, 62b; a similar statement is made by ibn Ezra *ad loc.*

59. CAT, 131a. This comment assumes that no miracle occurred.

60. CMR, 99a.

61. CAT, 134a.

62. CMR, 43b-44a.

63. CMR, 52b.

64. Cf. Maimonides, *Hil. Deot*, 3:3; *Guide*, III, 27.

65. CAT, 68b-69a.

66. CMR, 43a.

67. CMR, 35a.

68. CMR, 19a-b.

69. The phrase "the *shekhinah* is in the east" does not appear in the Tal-

mud; see the debate in *BB*, 25a-b, where the positions taken are "the shekhinah is in the west" (R. Joshua b. Levi) and "the shekhinah is everywhere" (several sages). The objection raised by R. Aha b. Jacob (*BB*, 25a) implies that the shekhinah may be in the east; see commentary attributed to R. Gershom *ad loc.*

70. See, however, CAT, 110b, where the expression "God sits" (*AZ*, 3b) is explained to be "human language" conveying the eternity of God vis-à-vis His changing creatures, for "sitting" is a more stable activity than standing; cf. *Guide*, I, 11.

71. For example, CAT, 103b; CAT, 112a; CMR, 32b-33a.

72. CAT, 26b-27a.

73. CAT, 108a-b.

74. CMR, 4a.

75. CMR, 65a.

76. CMR, 47b-48a; see fuller discussion in chapter V, section 3.

77. This is the text cited by R. Isaac, CAT, 81b. There is significant textual variation in this passage; some versions read "By the entrance of R. Simeon b. Yohai's burial cave" and others "By the entrance of the Garden of Eden." R. Isaac views these as two separate aggadot related in meaning, and he comments on them separately. The text used here is virtually the same as that in the original Soncino printing of the Talmud; see *Dikdukei Sofrim, Sanhedrin*, p. 292, n. 2.

78. CAT, 82a.

79. The text cited by R. Isaac for R. Joseph's response differs slightly from that of the printed versions and of the manuscripts noted in *Dikdukei Sofrim*.

80. CAT, 82b.

81. CAT, 92b, emphasis added.

82. CAT, 59a.

83. Here R. Isaac seems to be setting up a straw man; probably no one ever thought that the sages intended the meaning he repudiates. The context makes it clear that the statement was meant to assert only that the priest must wear his special vestments while performing the divine service, or else he will be considered in the category of an alien. It seems that R. Isaac deliberately misrepresents this simple meaning of the statement, identifying the "manifest content" with a literal reading that is obviously false, in order to facilitate his repudiation of it. His own interpretation of the statement is that only if the vestments are accompanied by the perfections of character that they represent is the priest a true priest of God. Otherwise, if he wears the vestments in order to appear legitimate without having the necessary personal perfections, he will be as an alien (CAT, 59a). This is, indeed, a significant reinterpretation of a statement with halakhic importance for the priesthood.

84. One of the most influential statements of exegetical methodology is that of R. Saadia Gaon, in his *Emunot ve-De'ot*, VII ("Resurrection"), 2. Applied specifically to the interpretation of the Bible, it maintains that a Biblical verse may be interpreted in a way that rejects its plain meaning only if it conflicts with (1) sense perception, (2) reason, (3) another clear verse of the Bible, and (4) authentic tradition. The first reason corresponds to what we have called "common experience," the second to part of what we have called "principles of faith" (such as the incorporeality of God), and the third reason—conflict with a clear state-

ment of the Bible—is also common to both authors. As Saadia's fourth reason—conflict with an authentic tradition—was apparently intended to apply to commandments and halakhic tradition, it is not directly relevant to the subject. Saadia would not have accepted the conflict with the laws of nature as grounds for repudiating the simple meaning of a Biblical verse, as this would have implied a denial of miracles.

It should not be assumed that the same criteria will be applied to interpretation of both Bible and aggadah. Yedaiah Bedersi, in his "Iggeret ha-Hitnatzlut" to R. Solomon Adret, holds up stricter requirements for rejecting the peshat of a Biblical verse than for rejecting the peshat of an aggadah. His conclusion is that the plain meaning of both a Biblical verse and an aggadah is to be repudiated if it contradicts the laws of reason (such as the assertion of two opposites in the same subject at the same time or the assertion that God can make Himself more than One or corporeal) but that the peshat of the aggadah is to be rejected if it conflicts with the laws of nature and has no great value for religious faith. This is not sufficient reason for rejecting the peshat of a Biblical verse (*She'elot u-Teshuvot ha-Rashba*, I, 169-170). This discussion of Yedaiah does not deal with the issues of conflict with common experience or with verses of the Bible. Furthermore, it is not at all clear that R. Isaac would have accepted Yedaiah's position that the peshat of aggadot must be maintained even when it conflicts with the laws of nature if a strengthening of faith is involved, for one of the examples given by Yedaiah is "All the statements linked with the coming of the Messiah." We have noted that R. Isaac rejects the plain meaning of the statement "In the future, women will give birth every day" because it is impossible according to natural law.

Where no generalizations are made but specific examples are given, the reason for rejecting the peshat must be carefully defined from the context. For example, Samuel ibn Tibbon states, "Even though we interpret 'when were the angels created' in a manner which is not the plain meaning that is widely understood, it is better to violate the language than to violate reality" (*Ma'amar Yikkavu ha-Mayim*, p. 17), meaning by "reality" (*ha-metzi'ut*) the assumptions of scientist-philosophers about the realms of being with respect to the order of Creation. But when Jacob Anatoli writes, "This [that whoever lives out a full year after Rosh Hashana is shown not to have been evil during the previous year] is an out-and-out lie, for reality refutes it" (*Malmad ha-Talmidim*, p. 175a), he means by "reality" (ha-metzi'ut) what I have called "common experience." Cf. also the categories in R. Abraham b. Maimonides' "Ma'amar" where the peshat is to be rejected: the second type of *derashah* and the fourth type of *ma'aseh*.

85. CAT, 18a-b.

86. CAT, 68a. Note that precisely the same kind of reinterpretation is given to the statement "There is no messiah for Israel" (*Sanh.*, 99a); see chapter IV, section 3.

87. CAT, 114a.

88. CMR, 98b-99a.

89. CAT, 44a.

90. CAT, 44b.

91. CAT, 44b.

92. CMR, 19b.

93. CMR, unnumbered folio following 99b. A further argument why this statement is not to be understood according to its plain meaning is that it is accompanied by the proof text "For thy husband is thy maker" (Isa. 54:5): "If their words were laughing jests, they would never have used as an asmakhta this most distinguished verse."

A similar argument was used by commentators to prove that the Song of Songs could not have been meant to be read according to its plain meaning: the romantic love between man and woman is simply not a subject worthy of one of the books of our sacred Scriptures; see R. Joseph ibn Aknin, *Hitgalut ha-Sodot ve-Hofa'at ha-Me'orot*, ed. Abraham Halkin (Jerusalem, 1964), pp. 3, 491. St. Augustine used the same argument of inconsistency with the dignity of Scripture to deny any literal meaning for the commandment "Thou shalt not boil a kid in its mother's milk" (Beryl Smalley, *The Study of the Bible in the Middle Ages* [New York, 1953], p. 303).

94. This is an appropriate context for some remarks on I. Heinemann's extremely important article "Die Wissenschaftliche Allegoristik des Jüdischen Mittelalters," *HUCA*, 23 (1950-1951), 611-643. Heinemann argues against the accepted view, that Jewish allegorical interpretation fulfilled the purpose of "harmonization," or reconciling the Biblical and Aristotelian world views, as did certain metaphorical interpretations, or the interpretations of events as visions occurring only in the mind. Rather, he points to specific religious motivations (demonstrating the superiority of Scripture over human writings through its double level of meaning, increasing the value of the wisdom literature, and giving religious sanction to the philosophical world view), and "scientific" motivations (in which allegorization, limited to such places as indicate deeper meaning by their content or by hints of the author, is used to express what the commentator actually believed was the true significance of the text); see pp. 612-613, 638-640.

While these conclusions may be valid for the allegorical interpretation of the Bible by certain medieval Jewish authors, my analysis of the Commentaries of R. Isaac b. Yedaiah indicates that they must be modified in important respects. We have seen that there are many instances in which the conflict between the literal meaning and other assumptions of the commentator is of the essence, and where allegorization does play the role of harmonization. In many of these cases, the literal level of the aggadah is explicitly rejected, so that Heinemann's generalization that allegorization of the Bible provides *Mehrdeutung* and not *Umdeutung* cannot be applied to the aggadah. Perhaps most interesting is the fact that allegorization in these commentaries is not restricted to a relatively small group of passages (cf. Heinemann, p. 637) but is applied to a wide range both of aggadic and of Biblical statements. Indeed, it can be said that the reluctance to use allegorical interpretation or any kind of interpretation pointing to a deeper, hidden meaning is restricted to a relatively small group of statements.

III. Cryptic Meanings in the Aggadah

1. Jacob Anatoli, *Malmad ha-Talmidim*, p. 23a; cf. Joseph ibn Aknin, *Hitgalut ha-Sodot*, p. 203, Todros Halevi Abulafia, *Otzar ha-Kavod ha-Shalem*

(Warsaw, 1879; Jerusalem, 1970), p. 5. For a contemporary statement, see C. S. Lewis, *The Allegory of Love*, p. 44: "to represent what is immaterial in picturable terms."

2. Most of the code words used by R. Isaac are not original with him. Many are taken from Maimonides, who applied them to Biblical verses, and used by R. Isaac for aggadic statements. In order to keep this chapter from reaching an unconscionable length, I have generally not discussed the history of a particular code word in the body of the text but rather relegated comparative material, including parallel interpretations found in other thirteenth-century works, to the footnotes. A thorough study of allegorical interpretations of the Bible in the Zohar and other thirteenth-century kabbalistic texts would undoubtedly reveal many more parallels than I have noted.

3. For the medieval use of the word *hash'alah*, see Moses ibn Ezra, *Sefer ha-Iyyunim ve-ha-Diyyunim* (Jerusalem, 1975), p. 229; Maimonides, *Millot ha-Higayon*, 13:4:5 (Jerusalem, 1965), p. 97. The clearest distinction in the use of this terminology applied to exegesis I have found in a medieval Hebrew writer is in R. Nissim of Marseilles. Discussing the verse "The mountains and the hills shall break forth before you into singing" (Isa. 55:12), he remarks that it can be understood either as a hash'alah (metaphor)—the hills are so covered with trees bearing every good fruit that the expression "joyous singing" is extended to apply to them—or as a mashal (allegory)—the "mountains" refer to the powerful leaders who tower over the people, and it is they who will sing, as in Targum Jonathan: *He-Halutz*, 7 (1865), 131. See also Samuel ibn Tibbon, *Perush Me-ha-Millot ha-Zarot*, s.v. "Shem meshutaf."

4. For example, the assertion that Moses found God "writing" is said to be both *"al derekh mashal"* and *"al tzad ha-hash'alah"* (CAT, 103a-b; cf. also 66b). When speaking of the representation of the supreme incorporeal Angel by fire, R. Isaac almost always uses the word "himshilu" (see, for example, CMR, 27b, 81a, 93a, 17a; CAT, 136a), but in one place, parallel to the others, he uses hish'ilu (CMR, 45a).

5. For "king" as a man who rules over his impulses, see CAT, 42b; for "husband" and "wife" as the spiritual and physical components of the human being, see CAT, 43a-44b. It is an interesting point of comparison that in R. Azriel's kabbalistic commentary on the aggadot, most of the code words are taken to refer to the realm of the sefirot, which is part of the Godhead; see *Perush ha-Aggadot*, pp. 129-135.

6. CMR, 27b; cf. CAT, 48a.

7. Exod. 3:2: CMR, 45a, 89b. Deut. 4:24: CMR, 45a. Isa. 6:6: CMR, 17a-b, 45a; CAT, 38a. II Kings 2:11: CMR, 17a-b, 81a.

8. CAT, 48a-b, and CMR, 27b-28a on *Num. R.*, 2:23. Cf. the kabbalistic interpretation, cited by R. Bahya b. Asher on Lev. 10:1, that the sin was in concentrating exclusively on the "attribute of justice" and not the "proper Name." While he cites the aggadah from *Sanh.*, 52a, he makes no attempt to link it with the kabbalistic interpretation.

9. CMR, 45a.

10. CMR, 93a; see also CMR, 81a on *Num. R.*, 12:2, "The Holy One, blessed be He, took what resembled a coin of fire . . . and showed Moses."

11. CMR, 17a-b.

12. CMR, 95b, based on *Guide*, I, 49.

13. Cf. Samuel ibn Tibbon's discussion of the dispute between R. Yohanan and R. Haninah over whether the angels were created on the second or the fifth day: R. Haninah means that the angels were not needed until the fifth day, immediately before the creation of man (*Ma'amar Yikkavu ha-Mayim*, pp. 16-17).

14. CMR, 82b on *Num. R.*, 12:3: "The Torah, which was given with the right hand of the Holy One."

15. CMR, 86b, the text of the midrash cited by R. Isaac differs from ours. See also CMR, 40b, interpreting Exodus 33:18, "Show me, I pray Thee, Thy *kavod*," as referring to the Angel.

16. CAT, 136a. In this statement, "serafim" is taken to refer to the entire realm of incorporeal beings; cf. Anatoli, *Malmad ha-Talmidim*, p. 95a.

17. CMR, 27a, 76a-b.

18. CAT, 38a, cf. 112a. Cf. the discussion of the passage in *Sanhedrin*, 38b by Meir b. Simon, *Milhemet Mitzvah*, Parma MS 155(2749), ff. 232b-233a.

19. See Ramban on Exodus 12:12, R. Bahya on Exodus 24:1; G. Scholem, *Jewish Gnosticism, Merkabah Mysticism and Talmudic Tradition* (New York, 1965), p. 43, n. 4; idem, *Kabbalah* (New York, 1974), p. 380. For the use of Metatron in kabbalistic texts, see R. Margulies, *Mal'akhei Elyon* (Jerusalem, 1964), pp. 73-108.

20. For the assimilation of Michael and Metatron, see Scholem, *Gnosticism*, p. 40; *Kabbalah*, pp. 379-380; and the quotations from *Sefer Zerubabel* and *Magen Avot* of Duran in Margulies, p. 110.

21. CAT, 139a, based on *Guide*, I, 49.

22. CMR, 40a-b.

23. *Hil. Yesodei ha-Torah* 3:1.

24. CMR, 82b.

25. CMR, 27b. In the Kabbalah, Michael is said to be on the right hand of God and Gabriel on the left; see Margulies, p. 24. Cf. Rashba's interpretation of "Gabriel" in *Hiddushei*, p. 97.

26. CAT, 72a-b.

27. Maimonides, *Guide*, II, 29, on *Gen. R.*, 5:5, and comment on *Avot*, 5:6.

28. CMR, 86b; cf. *Guide*, I, 9 (which cites both verses without distinguishing between them); Rashba, *Hiddushei*, p. 77.

29. CMR, 40b; the text of the midrash cited by R. Isaac differs from that of the printed editions.

30. CMR, 86b, cf. 40b. For the text of the *Yotzer*, see S. Baer's commentary in *Seder Avodat Yisrael*, p. 211. Other passages from the liturgy discussed in these works are the line *"Tif'eret u-gedulah serafim ve-ofanim ve-hayyot ha-kodesh"* from the same Sabbath-morning *Yotzer* (CAT, 135b), the benediction concerning the *minim* (CAT, 132b), and the penitential prayer *Makhnisei Rahamim* (CAT, 122a).

31. CMR, 10b.

32. The closest parallel I have found to the allegorical interpretation of the Jonah story as the biography of the individual soul is in the Zohar, *Va-Yakhel*,

199a-b, "Jonah descending into the ship is symbolic of man's soul that descends into this world to enter his body . . ." (Soncino Ed. [London, 1949], IV, 173-176). For the view that the story of Jonah, or at least the swallowing by the fish, is to be understood as a prophetic vision and did not actually take place, see R. Nissim of Marseilles, who finds this view in ibn Ezra (*He-Halutz*, 7 [1865], 133), and R. Zerahiah Hen in his letter to Hillel of Verona (*Otzar Nehmad*, 2 [1857], 137).

33. The interpretations of the stories of Rabba bar bar Hana (*BB*, 73a-74a) can be taken as a fine case study of varying approaches to the aggadah. See, for example, R. Yom Tov b. Abraham Ishbili (Ritba) *ad loc.* in *Ein Ya'akov* and *Hiddushei ha-Ritba al Masekhet Baba Batra*, ed. M. Y. Blau (New York, 1954), pp. 279-281; R. Shem Tov ibn Shaprut, *Pardes Rimonim* (Sabionetta, 1554; Jerusalem, 1968), p. 7b; Rashba, *Hiddushei*, pp. 87-95; the commentary in Munich MS 94, ff. 209a-212b (probably the one erroneously attributed by Solomon Duran to Ralbag: see C. Touati, *La Pensée philosophique et théologique de Gersonide* [Paris, 1973], pp. 62-63); R. Isaac Arama, *Akedat Yitzhak*, Sha'ar 24, 25; Maharal of Prague, *Be'er ha-Golah*, in *Kol Sifrei Maharal mi-Prag* (New York, 1969), IV, 88b-92a, and *Hiddushei Aggadot*, XI, 85a-102a; R. Nahman of Bratslav, *Likkutei Moharan* (New York, 1976), I, 2a-26b.

34. CMR, 10b-11a.

35. CAT, 100a; the text of the aggadah cited by R. Isaac contains material not found in the Vilna text.

36. CAT, 71b-72a; cf. ibn Ezra on Exodus 8:2.

37. CMR, 13b; cf. Rashba, *Hiddushei*, pp. 94, 96.

38. CMR, 91b-92b; cf. CAT, 145b-146a, on *Shevuot*, 47b, where the same interpretation of the rivers as the four elements is given.

39. This discussion shows the influence of Maimonides, *Guide*, II, 6: "But 'angel' means *messenger*; hence everyone that is entrusted with a certain mission is an 'angel' . . . The elements are also called 'angels.' "

40. For Gabirol and ibn Ezra, see the text published by M. Mortara, *Otzar Nehmad*, 2 (1857), 218, and discussion in D. Kaufmann, *Studien über Salomon ibn Gabirol* (Budapest, 1899), pp. 66-70; Albalag, *Sefer Tikkun ha-De'ot*, ed. G. Vajda (Jerusalem, 1973), p. 48; Levi b. Abraham, *Livyat Hen*, "Ma'aseh Bereshit," Vatican MS 192, ff. 3b-4a (this source was called to my attention by Professor Colette Sirat); R. Nissim, *He-Halutz*, 7 (1865), 114; Zohar, *Bereshit*, 27a, Soncino tr. (London, 1949), I, 103; Abravanel, *Perush al ha-Torah*, *Bereshit* (Jerusalem, 1964), p. 117, col. 2.

41. The derivation of Pishon from the word connoting largeness (*u-fashu* in Habakkuk 1:8) is found in Rashi on Genesis 2:11; explanations of Parath and Hidekel are in the gemara (*Berakhot*, 59b), although R. Isaac reads the second element of Hidekel not as *kal* but as *kol*. The explanation of Gihon seems to be original. Although not explicitly stated, the context indicates that the name is derived from Daniel 7:2, "The four winds of the heaven broke forth (*megihan*) upon the sea," which yields a word suitable for the element of air. This would seem to be a better verse than the one chosen by Levi b. Abraham: "Though the Jordan rush forth (*yagiah*) to his mouth" (Job 40:23), which refers to water. Levi follows the gemara, and not R. Isaac, in identifying the second element of Hidekel as *kal*. While his is indeed the closest passage to that of R. Isaac, there is no sign of dependence.

42. Cf. Ramban, "Derasha al Kohelet" (*Kitvei Ramban*, pp. 184-186), who states this as the theme of the first chapter of Ecclesiastes but reads 1:7, in accordance with its plain meaning, as applying only to the element of water. For the allegorical interpretation of this verse by the sages, see I. Heinemann, *Darkhei ha-Aggadah*, p. 152.

43. CMR, 41a; based on *Guide*, II, 30.

44. CAT, 99b; see also the interpretation of Judges 5:4, "The earth trembled," as referring to the elements in the material component of man, which "trembled" when the Torah was given, as it teaches man to purify his intellect from these elements until he is vouchsafed an intellectual apprehension of God (CMR, 17b).

45. CMR, 27a; cf. the doctrine found in the Zohar and *Tikkunei ha-Zohar* that each of the four archangels is appointed over a specific element (Margulies, p. 186). There are variations, but Uriel is always associated with either air or earth, never with fire.

46. CAT, 11a-b. Note also that the term "angel of death," in places such as *AZ*, 20b, and *AZ*, 35b, is defined in precisely the same manner as "Leviathan": "the privation inherent in matter" (CAT, 128a, 134b). Rashba, *Hiddushei*, pp. 91-92, also explains "Leviathan" as "joining," based on Genesis 29:34, but explaining a different aggadah (*BB*, 74b), he deals with the joining of the intellect with the soul in the body. Cf. also R. Nissim of Marseilles, *He-Halutz*, 7 (1865), 126.

47. *Mishnah im Perush ha-Rambam: Zera'im*, p. 42; Kafah's translation should read, "*u-vinyan ha-nefesh be-heres ha-guf.*" Cf. the pronouncement in the Zohar that God "smashes the body in order to give dominion to the soul" (I, 180a, quoted in I. Tishbi, *Mishnat ha-Zohar* [Jerusalem, 1961], II, 725, discussed in II, 85). This statement, however, is based on the assumption that the body is the creation of Satan, and it is used to explain the suffering of the righteous. The passage from R. Isaac merely asserts that the dissolution of the individual body, necessary for the perpetuation of the species as a whole, also benefits the individual human being by breaking down the barriers to full intellectual apprehension and thus to the attainment of eternal life. See also CMR, 69a: "The mortification of the body is vivification for the soul."

48. This is different from most other allegorical interpretations of the snake, such as ibn Ezra citing Gabirol: the power of desire (*Otzar Nehmad*, 2 [1857], 228); Radak: the material intellect ("Kimhi's Allegorical Commentary on Genesis," in *The Commentary of David Kimhi on Isaiah*, ed. Louis Finkelstein [New York, 1926], p. lx); Ralbag: the faculty of imagination (*Sefer Ralbag al ha-Torah* [Venice, 1547; New York, 1958], p. 14b, col. 2).

49. This interpretation of Proverbs was originally that of Maimonides' father; see I. Heinemann, "Die Wissenschaftliche Allegoristik," p. 626, n. 46. Joseph ibn Aknin maintains that Plato was following the model of Solomon's allegory (*Hitgalut ha-Sodot*, p. 201).

50. A few of many possible examples must suffice. Anatoli refers to Maimonides (*Malmad*, pp. 25b, 115a), and applies this to other Biblical passages, including that about Lot and his wife (p. 19a; cf. also 7b, 30a, 42b, 153a). Radak, referring to the "scientists" (*hakhmei ha-mehkar*), uses the identification of woman with matter for his allegorical interpretation of "Eve" ("Allegorical Com-

mentary," p. lix). Moses ibn Tibbon writes that it is an ancient practice of sages and prophets "to represent matter allegorically as a woman or female, and the soul as a man or male; or the soul as a woman and the human intellect as a man . . ." (*Perush la-Shir ha-Shirim* [Lyck, 1874], Introduction, p. 9). As to the reasons for this choice of allegorical representation, most are agreed that it is because matter receives various forms, as the woman passively receives the man (Anatoli, p. 115a; Radak, p. lix; Rashba, *Hiddushei*, p. 91); Anatoli also gives another reason: that the blood of the woman produces matter, while the seed of the man produces the form (p. 25b). For the use of this allegorization in Christian exegesis, see J. Ferrante, *Woman as Image in Medieval Literature* (New York, 1975), pp. 19, 33.

51. CAT, 42b-43a.

52. Rashi, *Sanh.*, 22a, "*or hashakh*," referring to *Mo'ed Katan*, 7b, "*ein ohalo ela ishto.*"

53. CAT, 43b-44a; a similar theme is expressed in CAT, 89a-b on *Sanh.*, 99b, "What is 'He who commits adultery with a woman lacks understanding'?" and CMR, unnumbered following 99b, on *Sanh.*, 22b: "A woman is a shapeless lump . . ."

54. CAT, 43a-b.

55. CAT, 44b.

56. Other examples of this interpretation of "night" can be found in CAT, 65b, 95b; CMR, 60b.

57. CAT, 68b-69a.

58. CAT, 92a-b. See also CAT, 56b, on the "leprous house" as the human body.

59. CMR, 93b-94a, emphasis added.

60. CMR, 45a; cf. CMR, 89a-b: the bush burning represents the human body when composed of matter especially appropriate for intellectual apprehension. It cleaves to the Angel, which purifies the intellect to such an extent that no physical hunger is felt (apparently reading, "The bush did not consume [*okhel*]" rather than "The bush was not consumed [*ukal*]").

61. CMR, 47a, emphasis added. The dependence on the Maimonidean theory of prophecy as requiring perfection of both the imagination and the intellect (*Guide*, II, 36 ff.) is obvious; CAT, 99a interprets Exodus 3:5 in the same way. Anatoli (*Malmad*, 45b-46a) also allegorically interprets the removal of shoes as the removal of obstacles but does not specifically relate them to imagination and intellect.

62. For Anatoli (*Malmad*, 45b, 95a), the bush is an allegorical representation of the lower realm of matter and of the Jewish people, but it is clear that the bush actually exists and was chosen in order to convey certain truths to Moses. There is a tradition of allegorical interpretation of Moses' shoes in Islamic exegesis (see I. Goldziher, *Die Richtungen der Islamischen Koranauslegung*, [Leiden, 1952], pp. 199-200, 232, 236). Of special interest in this context is al-Ghazali's forceful insistence that the literal level of the statement about the shoes must not be rejected when it is given an allegorical interpretation (pp. 236-237).

63. R. Isaac's statements about the holiness of the land of Israel never imply any metaphysical difference between this and other lands. It is holy because

its air and climate are conducive to clear intellectual apprehension of God. See especially CMR, 53b: "It has no holiness in and of itself; holiness rests upon it because of the people who dwell therein . . ."

64. CMR, 17b.

65. CMR, 81a.

66. The continuation of the comment on *Num. R.*, 12:11, explaining the rabbinic application to Elijah of Proverbs 30:4, states that Elijah's prophetic mission was fulfilled *after* his "ascent" to heaven, which could not therefore have been a unique occurrence at the end of his life. See CMR, 94a.

67. CAT, 81b.

68. Radak on II Kings 2:1; he also holds that the chariot and horses of fire were a vision of Elisha (comment on 2:1). R. Nissim of Marseilles (*He-Halutz*, 7, 129) refers to "one who interpreted" the entire episode of Elijah and the storm as a vision of Elisha; this could not refer to Radak, who holds that Elijah did actually ascend in a storm, but rather to a position similar to that implied by R. Isaac.

69. CAT, 119a; both passages follow Maimonides, *Guide*, III, 9. Cf. *Malmad ha-Talmidim*, p. 95b, on code terms for the material intellect.

70. CMR, 80a.

71. CMR, 16a.

72. CAT, 31a-b. The language seems to be deliberately ambiguous. It is unclear to me whether the commentator believes that a snake actually bit and killed the man as a punishment "measure for measure," or whether the statement is a purely figurative expression for the death of the soul caused by the effects of the impulse toward evil inherent in the body.

73. CMR, 16b. See also CAT, 49b, on *Sanh.*, 59b, in which two serpents represent competing impulses; and CMR, 56b on Isaiah 11:8, where "asp" and "basilisk" are said to be among the names used metaphorically by the prophets for the impulse toward evil.

74. CMR, 83a. Moses ibn Tibbon also rejects the simple meaning of the assertion about Jonathan b. Uzziel but interprets the "birds" as the problems solved by the rabbi's intellect; *Sefer Pe'ah*, Oxford Bodleian MS 939, ff. 34b-35a.

75. CMR, 45b.

76. Cf. Moses ibn Tibbon's interpretations of passages from ibn Ezra's Torah Commentary (London, Beit ha-Din and Beit ha-Midrash Library MS 40.3, Jerusalem Microfilm 4708), f. 35a on Genesis 12:6: "Or we could say that the word 'Canaanite' is one of the seven faculties of the body . . . for it is well known that these seven nations are, in the esoteric mode, the seven faculties of the body."

Zohar, *Shalah*, 159a-160b, interprets Numbers, ch. 13, as speaking esoterically about the study of Torah. " 'Amalek dwells in the south land'—the evil inclination, the seducer of man, is always in his body." (Anatoli also speaks of the esoteric meaning of "Amalek" as the impulse toward evil: *Malmad*, p. 82a). The famous passage from the Zohar (*Bereshit*, 25a-b) which includes the Anakim among the five categories of *erev rav* is quite different, representing not philosophical homily but social criticism.

For Christian allegorization of the seven Canaanite nations, see B. Smalley, *The Study of the Bible in the Middle Ages* (New York, 1952), p. 28, and I. Heine-

236 NOTES TO PAGES 68-70

mann, "Die Wissenschaftliche Allegoristik," p. 621.

77. CMR, 71b.

78. CAT, 34a, quoting *BB*, 16a; emphasis added.

79. Yet another allegorical representation for the body is the vineyard: just as the planter of a vineyard does not get anything without tending it for at least two years, so the body, even if prepared to attain perfection, cannot fully achieve it during the human life, for full wisdom comes only at the end (CAT, 143a, *Shev.*, 35b, on Song of Songs 8:12).

80. *De Anima*, II, 3, 414a, 31-32; Maimonides, "Eight Chapters," ch. 1, see E. Schweid, *Iyyunim ba-Shemonah Perakim le-Rambam* (Jerusalem, 1969), pp. 40-63.

81. By this is probably meant "common sense" and the estimative faculty, both of which are included by Maimonides under the general term "imagination"; see H. Wolfson, "Maimonides on the Internal Senses," in *Studies in the History of Philosophy and Religion*, I (Cambridge, Mass., 1973), pp. 344-370.

82. Cf. *Guide*, II, 37, on those (false prophets) with strong powers of imagination but weak intellects, who see "a strange mixture of true and imaginary things." As an example of the combinations made by the imagination, Maimonides gives a man with a horse's head and wings (I, 73, proposition 10).

83. CMR, 35a. The same identification of "female" with the imagination is made in CMR, 43b, on *Num. R.*, 4:20, and CMR, 77a, on *Num. R.*, 11:3.

84. CAT, 141b. Cf. CAT, 67a, on *Sanh.*, 91b-92a, where the "embryos in their mothers' bellies" are interpreted as the "faculties of the body and all the components of the soul." Anatoli interprets "brothers" as faculties of the soul, as in Psalm 133:1 (*Malmad*, p. 75a).

85. CMR, 16b; the text of the midrash cited by R. Isaac differs from that of the printed editions.

86. The problem is which of the faculties of the soul should be identified with "Satan" and the "impulse toward evil." Maimonides finds the source of the desires that lead to evil in the imagination (*Guide*, I, 2). But in II, 30, commenting on *Pirkei de R. Eliezer*, ch. 13, he seems to imply that Samael/Satan is different from the "snake," which represents the imagination. Shem Tov and Efodi understand him to mean that Samael/Satan is the appetitive faculty, while Crescas disagrees (see also Crescas on III, 22). Since R. Isaac states clearly that the imagination is needed to aid the intellect, it seems more plausible to understand the controversy here as pertaining to the role of the appetitive faculty.

87. This passage is obviously related to Maimonides' discussion of precisely the same question: why Satan is not said to "present himself before the Lord" as do the other "sons of God" (*Guide*, III, 22). Most of the commentators assume that Maimonides understands the "sons of God" as the intelligences and spheres, which control the affairs of the world, and "Satan" as the privation inherent in matter, which brings about misfortune: see Narboni, Shem Tov, Efodi, Crescas *ad loc*. Zerahiah Hen, in an extensive discussion of the passage in the *Guide*, explains the "sons of God" as the forms that give individual identity to the various beings in the world, and "Satan" as matter (*Tikvat Enosh*, ed. I. Schwarz [Berlin, 1968], I, 182-183). Ralbag interprets the "Satan" of chapter 1 as privation. Thus, none of these commentators views the scene in the first chapter of Job

as transpiring in the psychological realm, as does R. Isaac (although Crescas raises the possibility that "Satan" might be identified with the imagination, and Ralbag understands the "Satan" of chapter 2 to refer to a faculty of the soul which can have the function of serving the intellect, and thus "presents itself before God"). R. Isaac's is apparently a novel interpretation of the prologue to Job, and perhaps a novel interpretation of the Rambam.

I have translated the other faculties listed by R. Isaac as "the retentive, digestive, and excretory faculties," although the Hebrew for the first is ha-koah ha-ma'amid (34b, l. 2). This phrase does not appear in the long list of combinations with koah given by Klatzkin (Otzar ha-Munahim ha-Pilosofiim ve-Antologia Pilosofit [Berlin, 1928], pt. 2, pp. 74-77). The standard listing of the four faculties relating to nourishment are ingestion, retention (koah ha-mahazik), digestion, and excretion (see, Hovot ha-Levavot, Sha'ar ha-Behinah, 5 and Sha'ar Avodat Elohim, 9; Olam Katan, 2:2; Shemonah Perakim, 1). I have therefore taken koah ha-ma'amid in this context as an error for koah ha-mahazik.

88. CAT, 85b-86a. For a similar meaning of "redemption," see CAT, 114a; for "heart," see CAT, 40b, 89b; CMR, 62b. A similar use of "ministering angels" is in CMR, 23a on Num. R., 2:5.

89. See also CAT, 111a on AZ, 3b: during the third part of the day, God "sits and nourishes the entire world from the horns of wild oxen to the eggs of lice." The entire passage is interpreted as applying to four periods of the human life, the third part being the onset of old age, when the physical faculties grow weak. The "horns of wild oxen" represent "the other faculties, those components of the soul that are necessary for the intellect," which are "nourished and sustained" to help the intellect acquire its rational apprehensions. R. Isaac finds nothing wrong with the plain meaning of this statement about the third part of the day—that God provides sustenance for the entire world—but he rejects it because (1) this doctrine is obvious to everyone, and (2) it does not fit the context, for the other parts of the aggadah are clearly not to be understood literally. However, he concludes, "If one wants to say that the sages spoke here on both a manifest and an esoteric level, there is no harm in this."

90. CAT, 49b.

91. CAT, 31a-b.

92. CAT, 118b. The idea that age forty is a watershed, when the pursuit of intellectual perfection can begin in earnest because control of the physical impulses has been established, is common in CAT. See especially CAT, 117a, on AZ, 5b, CAT, 84b and 76b, discussed in chapter VII.

93. CAT, 49a on Sanh., 59b. The rabbis had already interpreted this verse allegorically; see I. Heinemann, Darkhei ha-Aggadah, p. 152; idem, Altjüdische Allegoristik (Breslau, 1936), p. 56. Cf. Anatoli, Malmad, p. 168a: the rabbis said that Solomon "represented talmud torah allegorically as working the soil."

94. CAT, 97a on Sanh., 104b; see also CAT, 66b.

95. CAT, 97a; the reinterpretation of the phrase "rational commandments" (mitzvot sikhliyot) is discussed in chapter V, sec. 1.

96. CAT, 69a. See also the interpretation of the following statement of R. Eliezer: "Whoever leaves broken pieces on his table is like an idolator"; this is said to refer to the man who publicly performs good deeds and observes all the

commandments but secretly is a thief, murderer, and adulterer (CAT, 69a-b).

97. For the problem of "antinomian perfectibilism" in the Christian context, see John Passmore, *The Perfectibility of Man* (New York, 1970), p. 141. R. Isaac treats the same theme in the comments on *AZ*, 17b (CAT, 123b), *Avot*, 2:2 (CAT, 10a [Kasher and Blacherowitz, p. 58]), and *Avot*, 4:1 (CAT, 17a, ibid., pp. 67-68). Note also the problem raised by Asher Crescas (in a different context and a somewhat more theoretical sense) in his comment on *Guide*, I, 2: why should abandoning ethical standards affect the intellectual accomplishments of the scholar? "Indeed, we have seen many exceedingly wise men, enlightened in every branch of learning, who are drawn after desires for food, drink, and sex, yet nevertheless their learning remains abundant, and their wisdom gushes forth from their mind to their tongue like a spring of flowing water, whenever they want."

98. "Messiah": CAT, 76a, 78a; "Days of the Messiah": CAT, 118b; "Redemption": CAT, 114a. These interpretations will be treated systematically in chapter IV, section 3. Another allegorical term for the intellect is "infant" or "child," as in Ecclesiastes 4:13 and Isaiah 11:8: CMR, 56b.

99. CMR, 16b.

100. CMR, 17a. For other examples of travel as a metaphor for the human life, see CAT, 12b, 112b; CMR, 4a.

101. CMR, 79b-80a. For the interpretation of *regel*, see *Guide*, I, 28; Rashba uses a similar interpretation for aggadic statements in *Hiddushei*, pp. 28, 111, 118.

102. CAT, 87b. This interpretation, in contrast with that of CMR, 91a-b and CAT, 145b-146a, represents the tradition in which the rivers are allegorized as teaching about psychology and epistemology. See Radak's "Allegorical Commentary": the river is "the intellect emanated from the Active Intellect," and the four heads are the four cavities of the brain containing the faculties of imagination, cogitation, and memory (in *The Commentary of David Kimhi on Isaiah*, pp. lv-lvi); Ralbag, "that which is emanated from the material intellect to the other faculties of the soul" (*Sefer Ralbag al ha-Torah*, p. 14b, col. 2); R. Isaac Arama, "the secret of the soul and its component parts" (*Akedat Yitzhak*, Sha'ar 7, pp. 57b-58a).

103. Note that it is not a matter of conflict between CAT and CMR, for CAT itself contains both interpretations (87b, 145b-146a). Other examples of the river as an allegorical representation of intellectual speculation can be found in relation to Jeremiah 31:12 (11) (CAT, 87b) and Ezekiel 1:1 (CMR, 21a and 84b). In the latter case, the name of the river, Kevar, is taken to indicate the eternal existence of God, the ultimate object of intellectual apprehension.

104. CMR, 17b.

105. CMR, 17b-18a. Cf. Anatoli, *Malmad*, p. 78a (also discussing Ps. 133:3): the Psalmist, like Hosea (14:6), "represented allegorically that effluence by dew"; also ibid., p. 50b, where the rain (in Hosea 6:3) represents metaphysics.

106. CMR, 60b-61a; the same interpretation of "Zion" is found in CMR, 41b, 99b. Again, Anatoli has a similar interpretation (*Malmad*, pp. 77b-78a). Plays on the word "Zion" were already used by the sages; for example, "*metzuyyanim be-halakha*" (*Ber.*, 8a, on Ps. 87:2), "*metzuyyanim be-mitzvot*" (*Midrash Tehillim*, 20:5), see I. Heinemann, *Altjüdische Allegoristik*, p. 30.

107. CMR, 97a. For the annotated Hebrew text of this passage, see my article "The Earliest Commentary on the *Midrash Rabbah*," *SMJHL*, pp. 297-301. Other commentators dealing with the esoteric meaning of Adam's "sacrifice" in *Hullin*, 60a treat it quite differently; see R. Todros Abulafia, *Otzar ha-Kavod ha-Shalem*, pp. 18-19; Rashba, *Hiddushei*, pp. 109-111; Moses ibn Tibbon, *Sefer Pe'ah*, Oxford Bodleian MS 939, f. 23a-b.

108. Anatoli has the same interpretation of the word "shor," but he applies it to Isaiah 1:3 (*Malmad*, p. 154b); the interpretation is attributed Michael Scot, Anatoli's colleague in translation.

109. While the doctrine of negative attributes is mentioned often, there is no full exploration of its meaning in theological terms; while component aspects of the soul are indicated, there is no attempt at a rigorous epistemology (in contrast with such allegorical commentaries as that of Moses ibn Tibbon and Gersonides on the Song of Songs); while primal matter and the elements are discovered in unlikely places, there is no detailed treatment of a single problem relating to Creation (in contrast with a work such as Samuel ibn Tibbon's *Ma'amar Yikkavu ha-Mayim*). In short, the philosophical content of these commentaries is on a grade-school level. (For explanations of why the sages might have concealed teachings that are not particularly profound, see Maimonides, Introduction to Mishnah Commentary; Rashba, *Hiddushei*, p. 58; Shem Tov ibn Shaprut, *Pardes Rimonim*, p. 2a).

There is no indication anywhere in these commentaries that there is a still deeper, technical meaning, which the author intentionally refrains from divulging, as there is in Rashba, *Hiddushei*, p. 4.

110. This is in contrast with the technique of interpretation in the aggadah itself; see Heinemann, "Wissenschaftliche Allegoristik," pp. 641-642. An example would be that the allegorical interpretation of Jonah represents not the experience of Israel in exile but the individual soul seeking knowledge of God.

111. This is the esoteric interpretation of Ezekiel 48:35; see also CMR, 87a. Elsewhere, "Jerusalem" is interpreted as the realm where the souls of the righteous dwell (in Ps. 122:2, *Mak.*, 10a; CAT, 147b); see also CMR, 23a, on Song 6:4 in *Num. R.*, 2:5. "Eretz Yisrael" is also interpreted as the realm of eternal life for the soul, CMR, 11b, on *Lev. R.*, 35:8.

For the four-fold interpretation of "Jerusalem" in Christian exegesis, see Smalley, *The Study of the Bible*, p. 28. It is somewhat ironic that a trend opposite to R. Isaac's removal of Jewish content from the aggadic material exists in contemporary Christian commentaries. St. Albert, expounding the book of Lamentations, deals with its historical subject matter; he notes that earlier commentators have explained the fourfold division of the book as referring to the four elements but asserts that "our custom is not to concern ourselves with divisions which cannot be deduced from the letter"; ibid., p. 299.

112. "Torah": CAT, 5b, 23b, 56a, 89a; "Talmud": CAT, 101b, CMR, 7b; "Israel": CAT, 86a-b.

iv. From Exegesis to Innovation

1. CAT, 16a (Kasher and Blacherowitz, p. 66); cf. CAT, 37a.

2. The closest parallel to this passage is in *Guide*, II, 11, but there is no

reference to emanation there. While Maimonides does use the term "emanation" in association with his theory of creation ex nihilo in a different context (*Guide*, II, 12), he uses it in a special sense in opposition to the neo-Platonized Aristotelian view, which seems to be maintained by R. Isaac. See H. Wolfson, *Studies in the History of Philosophy and Religion* (Cambridge, Mass., 1973), p. 233.

3. There is no attempt to deal with the problems of the other intellects or spheres, of how the material sphere is emanated from the incorporeal Angel, of how a simple, unified intellect can emanate both a sphere and another intellect, and other similar questions taken up by proponents of this theory.

4. CAT, 37a; cf. *Guide*, I, 72, Hil. *Yesodei ha-Torah*, 4:6.

5. CMR, 87a; see also CAT, 138a and *Guide*, I, 72.

6. CMR, 41a; cf. *Guide*, II, 4 and 10.

7. CMR, 86a-b.

8. CMR, 86b.

9. CAT, 53b; the context of this assertion is a denial of the existence of incorporeal demons.

10. CMR, 93a.

11. CMR, 96b. Similarly, the serafim in *AZ*, 43b, are said to represent the realm of the incorporeal angels, while a different term is used for the supreme Angel, "Of all of them the ultimate in rank and stature" (CAT, 135b-136a).

12. CMR, 45a.

13. See *Gen. R.*, 1:1. R. Menahem Meiri suggests as an alternative interpretation that the "precious instrument" refers to "that which is reached by the ultimate of human apprehension," referring to the active intellect, but this is merely a reinterpretation of the word "Torah" in the proof text in accordance with a philosophical understanding of the midrash cited; see *Beit ha-Behirah: Avot* (Jerusalem, 1964), p. 53. R. Isaac suggests a totally new meaning for the "precious instrument."

14. CAT, 16a (Kasher and Blacherowitz, p. 66). The argument that the soul is the "precious instrument through which the world was created" because it returns to the Angel and becomes part of it after separating from the body would seem to imply that the emanation of the world from the Angel is part of an eternal process, not a unique event. Here, as in other cases, it is difficult to pin down R. Isaac on a specific philosophical issue.

15. CAT, 37a; also CAT, 66b.

16. CAT, 38a.

17. CMR, 95b.

18. On the distinction between "nefesh," "ruah," and "neshamah" in kabbalistic thought and its background in philosophical theory, see G. Scholem, *Kabbalah* (New York, 1974), pp. 155-157, and I. Tishbi, *Mishnat ha-Zohar*, II, 3-67.

19. CAT, 136a.

20. CAT, 38a-b.

21. CAT, 112a. See also CMR, 88a on the disappearance of prophecy with the beginning of exile: "The Angel has not appeared in the midst of its people . . ."

22. Burning bush: CMR, 45a, 89b; ascending of mountain: CAT, 38a-b; request to see God's glory: CMR, 40b; Elijah's vision: CMR, 17a-b; Isaiah's vi-

sion: CAT, 38a, CMR, 17a-b, 45a. In one place (CAT, 112a-b) it is maintained that Moses, in contrast with the other prophets, had direct communication with God rather than through the mediation of the Angel.

23. CAT, 112a.

24. The context of this comment is interesting. It deals with the assertion, from *AZ*, 3b, that after the destruction of the Temple, when God no longer "plays with Leviathan," He teaches children. It is then asked, *"U-me-ikkarah,* who taught them?" This is universally understood as meaning: before the destruction, when God was preoccupied with Leviathan during this period of the day, who filled the function that He now assumes? R. Isaac interprets *"me-ikkarah"* as referring not to the period before the destruction but to the first three periods of the day, when God is otherwise occupied. In this way, he introduces the theme of Metatron, the supreme incorporeal Angel, as the instrument of intellectual enlightenment not only before the destruction but at present as well.

25. CAT, 48a, 97b; CMR, 17b, 27b, 80b. CMR, 40b. CAT, 133b.

26. CAT, 112a; cf. CMR, 96b, 98a.

27. For example, CAT, 88a; see also CMR, 79b.

28. CAT, 88a; CMR, 82b, 98a.

29. CMR, 52a.

30. CAT, 38a, discussing Exodus 24:1 and 24:12.

31. CMR, 45a.

32. CMR, 36b, 79b, 85b, 95b. CAT, 133b, CMR, 45a. CAT, 90b.

33. CMR, 40a.

34. CAT, 144a; CMR, 85a-b.

35. CAT, 62a, 88a.

36. CMR, 28a, 42b.

37. CAT, 38b.

38. See H. Davidson, "The Active Intellect in the *Cuzari* and Hallevi's Theory of Causality," *REJ,* 131 (1972), 354-355. The first part of this article (pp. 351-374) provides a good summary of the background of the doctrine of the active intellect in Arabic philosophy; see also Davidson's "Alfarabi and Avicenna on the Active Intellect," *Viator,* 3 (1972), 109-178.

39. *Emunah Ramah* (Frankfurt am Main, 1853), p. 64; C. Touati, *La pensée philosophique et théologique de Gersonide,* pp. 349, 351; *Sefer ha-Ikkarim,* ed. I. Husik (Philadelphia, 1929), II, 61-62.

40. *Torot ha-Nefesh,* ed. I. Broydé (Paris, 1896), p. 71; cf. J. Guttman, *Philosophies of Judaism* (Garden City, 1966), p. 125, I. Husik, *A History of Medieval Jewish Philosophy* (New York, 1966), p. 109.

41. *Keter Shem Tov,* ed. A. Jellinek, *Ginzei Hokhmat ha-Kabbalah* (Leipzig, 1853), p. 33.

42. On the background of this view concerning the motion of the sphere, see H. Wolfson, *Crescas' Critique of Aristotle* (Cambridge, Mass., 1971), pp. 77-78, 535-538.

43. See Aristotle, *De Anima,* II, 412b5; *Emunah Ramah,* p. 21.

44. See *Torot ha-Nefesh,* p. 74; Ramban on Lev. 17:11, opinion attributed to the Greeks. Attempts were made to fuse the Aristotelian definition of soul as *entelechy* (actuality or form) of the body with the view of the soul as an inde-

pendent, incorporeal substance emanated from the active intellect; see, for example, ibn Sina, described in M. Fakhry, *A History of Islamic Philosophy* (New York, 1970), p. 159; Joseph ibn Tzaddik, *Sefer ha-Olam ha-Katan*, pp. 37-40, described in Guttmann, *Philosophies*, p. 131; Hillel of Verona, *Tagmulei ha-Nefesh* (Lyck, 1874), p. 7b, described in Husik, *History*, p. 317. R. Azriel of Gerona, like R. Isaac, uses the Aristotelian definition of soul as "form of the body" without any attempt to explain the contradictions between this definition and other doctrines he holds concerning the soul: *Perush ha-Aggadot le-Rabbi Azriel*, p. 33; cf. G. Scholem, *Les origines de la Kabbale*, p. 481.

45. *Torot ha-Nefesh*, pp. 85-86.

46. *Kuzari*, V, 10, position attributed to "the philosophers": "If a man's intellect is in conjunction with [the active intellect], this is called his paradise and everlasting life"; cf. Davidson, "The Active Intellect," pp. 364-365; Hillel of Verona, *Tagmulei ha-Nefesh*, p. 10a. Ralbag, in contrast, denies the possibility of unity with the active intellect; see Touati, *La pensée philosophique*, pp. 434-438.

47. See, for example, *Guide*, I, 74, and commentators.

48. CAT, 38a.

49. Cf. Samuel ibn Tibbon, *Perush me-ha-Millot Zarot*, s.v. *sekhel ha-po'el*: "It seems to be that [the active intellect] is what the Rabbi refers to in his Composition [the *Mishneh Torah*] when he said its name was 'ishim.' " Ibn Tibbon confesses that he does not know where Maimonides found the term "ishim" in the rabbinic literature with this meaning and surmises that it must have been "in works of midrash or of some other type." See also Joseph Heller, "Mahuto ve-Tafkido shel ha-Sekhel ha-Po'el lefi Torat ha-Rambam," *Sefer Yovel li-khevod Shmuel Kalman Mirsky*, (New York, 1958), p. 40.

50. Note also Ralbag's view that the angel that appeared to Moses in the flaming bush—which R. Isaac identifies as the supreme incorporeal Angel—represents "the active intellect, which is God's emissary to save those who cleave to it/Him from the evil about to come upon them," *Sefer Ralbag al ha-Torah* (New York, 1958), p. 54b, col. a.

51. *Emunah Ramah*, pp. 64, 71; cf. *Guide*, II, 37.

52. *Guide*, II, 37; I, 2.

53. *Emunot ve-De'ot*, II, 10; cf. A. Altmann, "Saadya's Theory of Revelation," *Saadya Studies*, ed. E. Rosenthal (Manchester, England, 1943); C. Sirat, *Les théories des visions surnaturelles dans la pensée juive du moyen-age*, pp. 22 ff.

54. J. Dan, *Torat ha-Sod shel Hassidut Ashkenaz* (Jerusalem, 1968), ch. 5, esp. the summary, p. 170. For the emanation of the soul from the *Kavod*, see Judah Hasid, *Sod ha-Yihud*, cited in Dan, p. 166; for the ascent of the soul to the *Kavod*, see *Sefer ha-Hayyim*, ibid., p. 155.

55. G. Scholem, *Les origines de la Kabbale*, pp. 226-230; cf. I. Twersky, *Rabad of Posquières* (Cambridge, Mass., 1962), p. 289, n. 14, and A. Altmann, "Moses Narboni's 'Epistle on *Shi'ur Qoma*,' " *Jewish Medieval and Renaissance Studies* (Cambridge, Mass., 1967), p. 238.

56. Abraham Abulafia in Scholem, *MTJM*, p. 140, and M. Idel, "Kitvei R. Avraham Abulafia u-Mishnato," submitted to the Hebrew University, 1976, pp. 88-89. Gersonides, Commentary on Proverbs 1:8. German Pietists in Dan, *Torat ha-Sod*, p. 219.

57. It is possible, of course, that R. Isaac had access to a source unknown to us, in which the full doctrine of the supreme incorporeal Angel was already developed. One might speculate on a source conveying the idiosyncratic teachings of the ninth-century Karaite, Benjamin al-Nahawandi (see H. Wolfson, "The Pre-Existent Angel of the Magharians and al-Nahawandi," *JQR*, n.s., 51 [1961], 89-106), or even a Christian—or Catharist—source from R. Isaac's own cultural milieu. Until such a source is discovered, however, we must assume that the doctrine as described is R. Isaac's own creation.

58. CAT, 44b-45a; CMR, 19b; CAT, 9a (Kasher and Blacherowitz, p. 56); CAT, 14b (Kasher and Blacherowitz, p. 64).

59. CAT, 96b.

60. CMR, 17a.

61. For representative expressions of rabbinic antifeminism, see *Shab.*, 33b and 152a, *Ber.*, 24a, *Kid.*, 70a, *Gen. R.*, 45:5. For medieval Jewish literature, see M. Steinschneider, "Zur Frauenliteratur," *Israelitische Letterbode*, 12 (1888), pp. 49-95, and especially Judah ibn Shabtai, "Minhat Yehudah Sonei Nashim," ed. A. Ashkenazi, *Ta'am Zekenim* (1854), pp. 1-12. For views of women in contemporary high Christian culture, see Carolly Erickson, "The Vision of Women," in *The Medieval Vision: Essays in History and Perception* (New York, 1976), and J. M. Ferrante, *Woman as Image in Medieval Literature* (New York, 1975). Ferrante's generalization that "thirteenth-century literature shows the strong influence of two antifeminist views: the Aristotelian—of woman as a defective male, a creature lacking in reason, useful only to bear children; and the moralist—of woman as a threat to man's salvation" (p. 3) is beautifully exemplified by the material in this section.

62. CAT, 53b. For some reason, the text of the gemara used in this comment is not that of the Babylonian Talmud (*Sanh.*, 67a), but rather that of the Palestinian (*Sanh.*, 7:13). No variant is listed in *Dikdukei Sofrim* ad loc.

63. CMR, 43b.

64. CMR, 72a.

65. CAT, 42a.

66. CAT, 42a.

67. Aristotle's statement: see *Nicomachean Ethics*, III, 10; Maimonides cites this in *Guide*, II, 36; II, 40; III, 8; and III, 49. For a discussion of the use of this statement in medieval Hebrew literature, see D. Kaufmann, *Die Sinne* (Leipzig, 1884), pp. 188-191; on Maimonides in particular, see Leo Strauss, *Persecution and the Art of Writing* (Glencoe, Ill., 1952), pp. 75-76.

68. CAT, 141b, CMR, 62a.

69. CMR, 82a.

70. CMR, 70b on *Avot* 2:7; cf. CAT, 129b. The same theme is expressed in *Hil. De'ot*, 4:19; see also "Iggeret ha-Kodesh," in *Kitvei Ramban*, II, 326, and Shem Tov Falaquera, "Iggeret Musar," in *Kovetz al Yad*, 1 (11) (1936), 75. That emission of sperm through sexual intercourse was a primary cause of disease was maintained by Galen; cf. *The Canon of Medicine of Avicenna*, pp. 230, 417-419, 427.

71. CMR, 82b.

72. See *Hil. De'ot*, 3:3.

73. CMR, 32b.

74. CMR, 62b-63a, on *Num. R.*, 9:7, comparing Jer. 5:8 with 4:22.

75. CMR, 19b.

76. CAT, 141b, emphasis added.

77. For example, CMR, 46a and the passages cited in the following three notes. Cf. *Hil. Issurei Biah*, 21:11.

78. CMR, 32b; emphasis added.

79. CAT, 9a (Kasher and Blacherowitz, p. 56).

80. CAT, 141b.

81. *Sefer Ba'alei ha-Nefesh*, ed. J. Kafah (Jerusalem, 1964), pp. 116-118. Rabad mentions four or five acceptable thoughts during intercourse, each relating to a legitimate purpose of the sex act. First is "for the sake of being fruitful and multiplying," second is for the welfare of the child (based on the aggadah in *Niddah*, 31a, expressing the popular medical theory that intercourse during the last six months of pregnancy was beneficial to the fetus), third is to allay the desire of the wife (the obligation of onah), fourth is to restrain one's own desire and thus avoid the temptation to sin (a less meritorious motivation), and finally to promote the health of one's own body, a reason treated as an aspect of the fourth motivation. The entire discussion here is placed in a religious context, the question under consideration being, under what circumstances does the act of intercourse in marriage merit a reward for the fulfillment of a mitzvah? It is obvious that not only the conclusions but the entire approach to the subject of sexuality in Rabad's work is fundamentally different from that in R. Isaac's commentaries.

82. "Coitus is divided into three aspects: one for being fruitful and multiplying regardless of desire, the second to relieve the fulness [or the moistures] of the body, the third for desire similar to animal desire" (for the textual problem, see D. Feldman, *Marital Relations, Birth Control, and Abortion in Jewish Law* [New York, 1974], p. 95, n. 73). Ramban (*ad loc.*) repeats this word for word, introducing the comment with "We know that," and not attributing it to any author; R. Bahya (*ad loc.*) does attribute it to ibn Ezra, and he adds the single word "curative" as an explanation of the second aspect. The context of the passage explains the apparent anomaly of omitting the wife's right to onah and other motives mentioned by Rabad. Ibn Ezra is explicating the language of the verse that forbids sexual relations with a married woman other than one's wife, and the three aspects that he mentions are possible motivations for such an illicit act. Onah, benefit to the fetus, and guarding oneself against the desire to sin are clearly inapplicable. Ibn Ezra is not implying that all three are legitimate motivations for sexual intercourse in general; he is asserting that according to the verse, even the highest of the three possible motives for an act of adultery, that of procreation, cannot justify such a sin. Despite the similarity of two of the categories, this formulation is thus totally different in meaning from the R. Isaac passage.

83. This is analogous to the discussion of eating habits in the same passage, in which Maimonides uses not the religious categories of pure and impure animals, permitted or forbidden foods, but the general categories of sweet and tasty foods as compared with beneficial ones. The purpose of maintaining physical health is not so that one may engage in "Torah and prayer," as it is in a similar statement of Rabad of Posquières (*Ba'alei ha-Nefesh*, p. 126; see I. Twersky, *Rabad of Posquières*, p. 272), but so that one may rationally understand the various scientific disciplines (*hokhmot*).

84. See *Sefer ha-Mitzvot*, Negative 262; *Hil. Ishut*, ch. 14. Cf. *Kesef Mishneh* on *Hil. De'ot*, 3:2.

85. It is a function of the wife to guard her husband against forbidden relations, but this is not suggested as a legitimate motivation for sexual relations with her. Christian tradition at this time was generally more restrictive even than R. Isaac. Thomas Aquinas, a contemporary of R. Isaac, rejects the maintenance of health as a justification for sexual intercourse with one's wife; only procreation remains; see Ferrante, *Woman as Image*, p. 104, J. Noonan, *Contraception* (Cambridge, Mass., 1966), p. 242.

86. CAT, 57a-b.

87. CAT, 58a, CMR, 63a.

88. CMR, 83b.

89. CMR, 34b. Note how the halakhic concept of *hezek re'iyah* is turned on its head: it is not the damage to the person seen but the damage to the person seeing that he finds significant. See also CAT, 151a-b, on "Ten things cause difficulty for the student: passing between two women . . ." (*Horayot*, 13b), published by Genhovsky, *Otzar ha-Perushim*, p. 15, col. a. We might contrast the pietistic ideal demanded by R. Joseph Karo's Maggid: the true ascetic should be able to see a naked woman without feeling any temptation (R. J. Z. Werblowsky, *Joseph Karo: Lawyer and Mystic* [Phila., 1977], p. 161).

90. CMR, 63a, 58a.

91. CMR, 62a.

92. CMR, 83b, 62b.

93. CMR, 63b. Cf. Aquinas' teaching that a man has the right to divorce an adulterous wife (though the opposite is not true) in order to avoid committing murder (cited in Ferrante, *Woman as Image*, p. 105). The Christian teaching about incest was that it was worse than adultery; see Gratian, cited by Noonan, *Contraception*, p. 174. According to R. Isaac, the reason for the prohibition of incest is simply to repudiate the belief in the eternity of a world governed totally in accordance with nature. God commands something opposed to nature— refraining from sexual relations with females of the family—in order to assert His authority as judge and ruler of all (CMR, 63a). However, the general purpose for the prohibitions of illicit sexual relations in the Torah is stated as being "so that one will not concentrate exclusively on these matters to his detriment but will remain healthy" (CMR, 38a), a reason far closer to the author's general approach to *ta'amei ha-mitzvot*.

94. CAT, 58a.

95. CMR, 6a, bound near the end of the manuscript.

96. CMR, 62a.

97. CMR, 32b. It must be pointed out that the description of an unhappy marriage, which follows immediately after this passage, is at least as convincing as the evocation of marital bliss.

98. CAT, 131b. See also CAT, 36b, on the relationship between circumcision and the desire for Gentile women: the phrase *moshekh orlato* in *Erubin*, 19a is understood not as the disguising of one's circumcision but as allowing oneself to be drawn after sexual pleasure. The idea that circumcision weakens the sexual drive is stated classically by Maimonides, *Guide*, III, 49.

99. The phrase *u-mazra'at tehilah* is based on *Berakhot*, 60a; for the orig-

inal meaning, in association with the doctrine of female seed, see Feldman, *Marital Relations*, ch. 7. Here, however, the context clearly demands the meaning of "experience an orgasm": cf. ibid., pp. 138-139.

100. CMR, 90a-91a. The Hebrew text with annotation is published in my "Earliest Commentary on the *Midrash Rabbah*," pp. 294-97.

101. On Jewish men and Christian women in Jewish sources, see Moses of Coucy, *Sefer Mitzvot Gadol*, Negative Commandment 112; Nachmanides, *Kitvei Ramban*, I, 370; Zohar, II, 3a-b (cited in Baer, *HJCS*, I, 262), and II, 87b (cited in B. Z. Dinur, *Yisrael ba-Golah*, II, 4 [Tel Aviv, 1969], 291); *Ra'aya Mehemna*, cited ibid., p. 292; R. Judah b. Asher, *Zikhron Yehudah* (Berlin, 1846), responsa 63, 17; R. Joshua ibn Shu'eib, *Derashot*, end of *Pinhas* (cited in Dinur, p. 292); L. Epstein, *Sex Laws and Customs in Judaism* (New York, 1948), pp. 172-173.

For Christian sources on Jewish men and Christian women, see *Las Siete Partidas del Rey Don Alfonso el Sabio*, VII, 24, ix (Madrid, 1807), III, 674, and the papal complaints about the abominations committed by Jewish men with Christian nurses and servant women in their homes, S. Grayzel, *The Church and the Jews in the XIIIth Century* (New York, 1966), pp. 107, 199.

For complaints about miscegenation of both types (Jewish men with Christian women and Jewish women with Christian men), see Grayzel, ibid., pp. 157, 167, 169, 205, 207, 259, 283, 295, 309, 315.

102. CAT, 57b, emphasis added.

103. For the Christian use of aggadot to disprove the medieval Jewish doctrine of the Messiah, see A. Funkenstein, "Temurot," esp. pp. 141-144; S. W. Baron, *SRHJ*, IX, 97-134, esp. 105-110 and nn. 4, 7; S. Lieberman, *Sheki'in* (Jerusalem, 1970), pp. 43-91; and the vast literature on the Disputation of Barcelona in 1263.

104. CAT, 77b, 82, and many others. Cf. Nachmanides, "Vikuah," in *Kitvei Ramban*, I, 310, to the king of Aragon: "For the Messiah is nothing more than a king of flesh and blood, like yourself."

105. CAT, 79b-80b. For the idea that the son and grandson of the Messiah will reign after the Messiah's death, see Maimonides, Introduction to Helek, *Mishnah im Perush Rambam: Nezikin*, p. 208. Abravanel argued that the entire royal line originating with the Messiah would be called "David," just as the royal lines of Egypt were called Pharaoh or Ptolemy: *Commentary on Later Prophets*, Ezekiel 37:24.

106. CAT, 79b-80a. The same distinction between "melekh" and "nasi" is found in CAT, 136b. R. Isaac's interpretation of Ezekiel 37:25 goes against that of the gemara in *Sanhedrin*, 98b, which implies that the nasi is lower than the melekh. We do not have his interpretation of the statement "If a nasi has renounced the honor due him, that honor is officially renounced, but if a king has renounced the honor due him, that honor is not officially renounced" (*Sanh.*, 19b). In the commentary on *Sanhedrin* (CAT, 42a), he says simply, "I have interpreted it," presumably in one of the other occurrences of this statement in the Talmud. In the Midrash Commentary (CMR, 49a), he explains only the assertion about the king and does not contrast it with the situation of the nasi.

107. CAT, 84a. There is no justification in *Dikdukei Sofrim* for the reversal

of these statements; one wonders whether R. Isaac had a different text, or whether he reversed the order intentionally to fit his interpretation.

108. CAT, 84a-b. The superiority of Moses to the Messiah was not maintained by all Jewish philosophers. Ralbag, for example, argues that the Messiah will be as great as, or greater than Moses: see C. Touati, *La pensée philosophique*, pp. 468, 535, and the critique of this view by Abraham Bibago, *Derekh Emunah*, p. 98d.

109. CAT, 81a-b.

110. For this type of apocalyptic messianic literature, see especially J. Even-Shemuel, *Midreshei Ge'ulah* (Jerusalem, 1968).

111. An interesting example of the confrontation with these problematics can be seen in Joseph ibn Kaspi's *Tam ha-Kesef* (London, 1913; Jerusalem, 1970), pp. 44-45. Writing in the first decades of the fourteenth century, Kaspi indicates that there are various possibilities for the fulfillment of the messianic mission to return the land of Israel to Jewish hands: (1) the Messiah will negotiate with the rulers of the Mamelukes and the Mongols, (2) a great king, perhaps that of the Mongols, will conquer the Mamelukes (who then controlled Palestine), (3) the king of France will launch a new Crusade, (4) God will simply put it into the heart of the ruling authority to give the land of Israel to the Jews and allow the Jews from all over the world to gather there. Cf. S. Pines, "Ha-Tekumah me-Hadash shel Medinah Yehudit lefi Yosef ibn Kaspi u-lefi Spinoza," *Iyyun*, 14-15 (1963-1964), 301-302.

It is interesting that Kaspi does *not* mention the Pope as a party to any of these eventualities; this undoubtedly reflects the decline in the position of the papacy in the early fourteenth century. By the end of the fifteenth century, Abravanel could write, "As for the Pope today, he does not have total authority, as did ancient Rome, for according to their religion, he is leader only with regard to matters of the soul" (*Yeshu'ot Meshiho*, p. 23b).

112. *Kitvei Ramban*, I, 312; cf. also the other passage, ibid., I, 306, cited by Scholem, *MTJM*, p. 128: "When the time of the end will have come, the Messiah will, at God's command, come to the Pope and say to him, 'Let my people go that they may serve me,' and only then will the Messiah be considered really to have come, but not before that."

The same tradition appears in Ralbag's *Commentary on Daniel* (Rome, before 1480; copy in library of Jewish Theological Seminary of America). On Daniel 7:13, he writes, "It seems that at first he will be like any ordinary man, without any especially exalted status. He will come before the Aged One, who is today in authority over the kingdom of Rome, to supplicate before him on behalf of his people, just as Moses came to the king of Egypt. At the conclusion of the matter, this authority to rule will be granted to him." The term *ha-yashish*, used for the Pope, is Ralbag's translation of *atik yomin* in Daniel 7:13. This brief, general description, whether or not based directly on the Ramban, certainly does not show familiarity with the passage of R. Isaac. Note that Ralbag, in contrast with both R. Isaac and Ramban, does not say that the Messiah will come to Rome, for the seat of the papacy was in Avignon at time he was writing.

113. CAT, 80a.

114. CAT, 119b.

115. CMR, 74a.
116. CAT, 82b.
117. CMR, 44a.
118. CMR, 99a.
119. See Y. Baer, *HJCS*, I, 273-277.
120. CAT, 107a. For other statements about the loss of prophecy coinciding with the exile of the Jewish people, see CAT, 83b, 99b, CMR, 88a.
121. CAT. 82b.
122. CAT, 73b, 77b, 85a.
123. CAT, 77b.
124. CAT, 61a-b. A similar distinction between "Israel," referring to an elite group among the Jews, and "House of Jacob," referring to the rest of the Jewish people, is made by the sixteenth-century Kabbalist R. Solomon Turiel in his "Derush al ha-Ge'ulah," published by G. Scholem, *Sefunot*, I (1957), 76. Here, however, the elite includes not philosophers but Kabbalists. The author develops the idea that this elite, who concern themselves with the mysteries of the inner content of the Torah, will not be subject to the messianic king as will the Talmudists, who are concerned exclusively with halakha, but will live in the terrestrial Garden of Eden and study Torah directly from God. There is an interesting parallel with R. Isaac's idea that the philosophers have no need for the Messiah, although the contrast should be noted. For R. Isaac, the Messiah will enable the masses to achieve what the philosophers can achieve at present; for R. Solomon Turiel, the masses, and even the outstanding Talmudists, will still be of lower status than the Kabbalists even in the messianic age. I am grateful to Prof. Y. Yerushalmi for directing me to this source.
125. CAT, 85a-b. In quoting the statement of R. Hillel, R. Isaac omits the phrase, "For they have already consumed it in the days of Hezekiah," which would not fit his interpretation. The phrase in question is missing also in the Munich manuscript of the Talmud (*Dikdukei Sofrim ad loc.*, p. 294), and it seems likely that it was not in the text used by R. Isaac. Cf. the interpretation of Ecclesiastes 9:11, CAT, 68a.
126. CAT, 85a, 77b.
127. CAT, 85b.
128. The doctrine *extra ecclesiam nulla salus* was formulated first by Origen and repeated by many of the Latin Fathers, especially Jerome and Augustine. On the problem of salvation for those before the Incarnation or outside the Church, see L. Caperan, *Le Problème du salut des infidèles* (Toulouse, 1934), and J. Daniélou, *The Salvation of the Nations* (New York, 1962).

Later Jewish writers referred to the Christian doctrine that before Jesus no one had a chance for salvation in an entirely different context, that of the polemic against Jewish philosophers, who seemed to make the same claim about Aristotle: see R. Solomon Alami, *Iggeret Musar* (Jerusalem, 1946), p. 42; R. Joseph Yabetz, *Or ha-Hayyim* (Lublin, 1912), p. 15a.
129. See *Hil. Teshuvah*, ch. 8.
130. *Sanh.*, 97b-98a (position of R. Eliezer), *Shab.*, 118b.
131. CAT, 85b.
132. CAT, 76b.

133. CAT, 97b.

134. CAT, 74a.

135. CAT, 78a.

136. CAT, 82b.

137. CAT, 83a.

138. CAT, 72b; see also 85a.

139. CAT, 85b.

140. CAT, 104b.

141. CAT, 104b-105b.

142. R. Isaac's interpretation of this statement apparently appeared in his commentary on *Rosh Hashanah*, which is no longer extant. The statement also occurs in *Sanhedrin*, 97a, but there he writes simply, "I have interpreted it" (CAT, 75a).

143. CAT, 118b, also CAT, 76a-b. This is the only instance in the extant Talmud commentary in which a statement occurring in two different places (*Sanh.*, 97a-b and *AZ*, 9a) is given two full comments. Though not literally identical, both follow the same general lines. A similar interpretation of these statements is found in Moses ibn Tibbon's explications of ibn Ezra's commentary on Genesis (London Beit ha-Din and Beit ha-Midrash Library MS 40.3). The "secret" mentioned by ibn Ezra on Genesis 1:5 is said to be that each thousand years refers to a decade of human life. Unfortunately, only the first two and the seventh millennia are explained, and there is no reference to the "days of the Messiah" (f. 33a).

144. CAT, 72b-74b. R. Isaac's text of Abaye's statement at the end differs from the printed version; there is no support for his reading in *Dikdukei Sofrim*.

145. CAT, 84b-85a.

146. For attempts by other commentators to interpret this aggadah so as to eliminate the reference to the actual city of Rome, see A. Berger, "Captive at the Gate of Rome: A Messianic Motif," *PAAJR*, 44 (1977), 10-11.

147. CAT, 78a-79b. The text describing the Messiah's bandages ("While he does not untie one until he has rebandaged one") differs from the printed versions; missing from R. Isaac's text is the explanation "Perhaps I will be needed, and I must not be delayed."

148. In his *Sefer Pe'ah*, ibn Tibbon interprets an aggadic discussion about the destruction of the Temple in allegorical terms relating to the human life span. He refers to the postdestruction, premessianic period as that in which "the intellect—which is the servant of the Lord and His anointed [Messiah]—has not become actualized." The final period of a man's life is that in which "the physical forces begin to weaken, the three stages have passed, the 'days of the Messiah' are completed, and he reaches the 'one of destruction,' when he cleaves to the separate intellect" (Oxford Bodleian MS 939, f. 15b). This implies an understanding of the aggadic seven-thousand-year cycle including the "days of the Messiah" (*AZ*, 9a, *RH*, 31a) as referring to the seventy-year cycle of life, which is precisely the interpretation suggested in the explications of ibn Ezra's commentary on Genesis (see n. 143).

149. *Livyat Hen*, Vatican MS 192, ff. 34b-35a. On the nature of this work, see, most recently, A. S. Halkin, "Why Was Levi ben Hayyim Hounded,"

PAAJR, 34 (1966), 65-76, and C. Sirat, "Les différentes versions du Liwyat Hen," *REJ*, 122 (1963), 167-177.

150. *Ha-Kabbalah shel Sefer Temunah ve-shel Avraham Abulafia* (Jerusalem, 1973), p. 112; see also pp. 115, 159, 165.

151. Idel, "Kitvei R. Avraham Abulafia u-Mishnato," p. 396, citing *Sefer ha-Melitz*, Munich MS 285, f. 13a.

152. *Sefer ha-Ot*, ed. A. Jellinek, *Ginzei Hokhmat ha-Kabbalah* (Jerusalem, 1969), p. 23; the passage is actually from *Sefer Hayyei ha-Olam ha-Ba*. It is interesting that in two later paraphrases of this idea, by Judah Albottini in *Sulam ha-Aliyah*, ed. G. Scholem, *Kitvei Yad be-Kabbalah* (Jerusalem, 1930), p. 228, and by Johanan Alemanno, in *Sha'ar ha-Heshek* (Halberstadt, c. 1862), pp. 30b-31a, the most extreme phrase "And he will be the anointed [Messiah] of the Lord," is omitted. For similar allegorization of the Messiah by the Kabbalist Isaac of Acre, see Idel, p. 398, and E. Gottlieb, *Mehkarim be-Sifrut ha-Kabbalah*, ed. J. Hacker (Tel Aviv, 1976), pp. 241-242.

153. Cf. R. Joseph Soloveitchik, *Al ha-Teshuvah* (Jerusalem, 1975), p. 236: "*The sinner who returns in teshuvah becomes his own messianic king, and redeems himself from the pit-of-captivity of sin*" (emphasis in the original); p. 252: "He is himself the redeemer, and he is himself the messianic king who comes to redeem him from the darkness of his exile to the light of his redemption." These passages were presumably not written under the influence of Abraham Abulafia, and they show how Abulafia's own formulation need not have been influenced by anyone. They also illustrate the perils of judging isolated quotations from Abulafia—or anyone else—outside the context of the entire work in which they appear.

v. Torah, Mitzvot, and Halakha

1. For the relationship of *din shamayim* to *din torah* in German Pietism, see Y. Baer, "Ha-Megamah ha-Datit ha-Hevratit shel Sefer Hasidim," *Zion*, 3 (1938), esp. 12-14, and H. Soloveitchik, "Three Themes in the *Sefer Hasidim*," pp. 311-325. For the doctrine of the mitzvah as a test see J. Dan, *Torat ha-Sod shel Hassidut Ashkenaz*, pp. 238-239; Dan, *Sifrut ha-Musar ve-ha-Derush*, pp. 62-65; and the passages from *Sefer Rokeah* quoted in J. Hacker, *Olamah ha-Hevrati ve-ha-Ruhani shel Hassidut Ashkenaz* (Jerusalem, 1970), pp. 97-99.

2. See especially I. Tishbi, *Mishnat ha-Zohar*, II, 429-578, and G. Scholem, "The Meaning of the Torah in Jewish Mysticism," in *On the Kabbalah and its Symbolism* (New York, 1965), pp. 32-86.

3. For the doctrine of Saadia and Maimonides, see the discussion in the following pages.

4. An exception to this generalization that the philosophers following Saadia and Maimonides added little to the doctrine of Torah, mitzvot, and halakha is R. Levi b. Gershom's attempt to link the halakha directly with the Biblical text, rejecting the rabbinic use of asmakhta and the thirteen hermeneutical principles. See his *Commentary on the Torah*, Introduction, p. 2b, and Touati, *La pensée philosophique*, pp. 506ff.

5. CAT, 4b (Kasher and Blacherowitz, p. 49).

6. CAT, 82b-83a.

7. CAT, 61a-b.

8. CAT, 4a, 10a, 89a, 106a, 114a, 127a.

9. CAT, 129a.

10. CAT, 106a. Note that here the commandments that affect only the soul are of a higher status than those that affect body and soul. Cf. *Derashot ha-Ran*, ed. A. L. Feldman (Jerusalem, 1974), p. 72.

11. CAT, 10a (Kasher and Blacherowitz, p. 57).

12. CAT, 97a. Examples of rational commandments are those in Exod. 20: 2, 3, Deut. 6:4, and the commandment of prayer (CAT, 11a).

13. CMR, 69b; see also CMR, 41b, top.

14. *Emunot ve-De'ot*, 3:1. See, most recently, M. Fox, "On the Rational Commandments in Saadia's Philosophy," *Proceedings of the Sixth World Congress of Jewish Studies* (Jerusalem, 1977), III, 33-44, and the literature cited p. 33, n. 1.

15. *The Eight Chapters of Maimonides' Ethics*, ed. J. Gorfinkel (New York, 1966), Hebrew text, p. 36, English text, p. 77, and n. 3; cf. E. Schweid, *Iyyunim ba-Shemonah Perakim la-Rambam* (Jerusalem, 1969), pp. 108-109.

16. *The Eight Chapters*, Hebrew text, pp. 12-13, English text, pp. 43-44; see p. 44, n. 2, for a bibliography on this subject. The expression "practical commandments" is used by Anatoli while discussing the role of the practical intellect (*Malmad*, p. 73b); cf. *Derashot ha-Ran*, p. 72.

17. Note that Maimonides later shifts to a threefold classification of the commandments by isolating the two elements of "well-being of the body." Thus the purpose of all commandments must be (1) to teach some true doctrine, (2) to develop desirable ethical dispositions, or (3) to establish proper social behavior (III, 31; cf. III, 28). R. Isaac does not accept this threefold division, except possibly in the passage referred to in n. 10.

18. CAT, 131b.

19. CAT, 91a, 29a.

20. CAT, 135a, 152a; in this respect, the Torah is contrasted with the Christian faith.

21. CAT, 21a (Kasher and Blacherowitz, p. 72).

22. CAT, 10a-b (Kasher and Blacherowitz, p. 58). This seems to be a novel interpretation of the passage.

23. CAT, 21a (Kasher and Blacherowitz, p. 72).

24. CAT, 48b.

25. CAT, 151a, bottom.

26. CAT, 151a, top.

27. CAT, 123a.

28. Cf. Bahya ibn Pakuda, *Hovot ha-Levavot*, tr. M. Hyamson (Jerusalem, 1965), I, 26-31. The question whether R. Isaac's division of the commandments was at all influenced by Bahya's distinction between the "duties of the heart" and the "duties of the limbs" (*hovot ha-eivarim*) would appear to be answered in the negative. While all the duties of the heart are rational, the duties of the limbs are divided by Bahya on the basis of Saadia's distinction between rational and traditional (pp. 16-19); this is clearly opposed to the theory of R.

Isaac. Furthermore, the duties of the limbs are said to be 613 in number, which means that Bahya identifies them with all the commandments of the Torah (pp. 26-27), whereas for R. Isaac, the practical commandments are the majority but not all the mitzvot in the Torah. When we add to this the total difference in terminology, we may conclude that no influence is apparent.

29. CAT, 151a, 114b, 108a.

30. CMR, 69a-b.

31. CMR, 7a. Denunciations of those who perform the commandments mechanically and without kavvanah are legion in the thirteenth century; for a parallel to this passage, see Anatoli, *Malmad*, p. 73b (specifically on prayer) and 177b (on the commandments in general).

32. CAT, 88a-b.

33. CAT, 114b, 129a.

34. For the commandments as a source of knowledge about God, see Maimonides, *Sefer ha-Mitzvot*, Positive Commandment 3, and the parallel between science and the reason for the sacrificial commandments in *Guide*, III, 32.

35. CAT, 139b.

36. *Guide*, III, 26-49; cf. C. Neuberger, *Das Wesen des Gesetzes in der Philosophie des Maimonides* (Danzig, 1933), and I. Heinemann, *Ta'amei ha-Mitzvot be-Sifrut Yisrael* (Jerusalem, 1954), I, 79-97. Note also the general statements of Maimonides in the *Mishneh Torah* for examples, Hil. Me'ilah, 8:8; Hil. Temurah, 4:13; Hil. Mikva'ot, 11:12), and I. Twersky, "Some Non-Halakic Aspects of the Mishneh Torah," *Jewish Medieval and Renaissance Studies*, pp. 104-106.

37. CMR, 89b.

38. CAT, 138a, 38a; cf. *Guide*, III, 48.

39. CAT, 51b. The formulation of the first benefit differs from that of Maimonides, who emphasized the well-being of the body in a weekly day of rest. R. Isaac's explanation is closer to that of ibn Ezra on Exodus 20:8 and Psalm 92:5; see also Nachmanides on Exodus 20:8 and Gersonides, *Sefer Ralbag al ha-Torah*, p. 79d bottom. The purpose of the sabbatical year is explained in a manner similar to that of the weekly Sabbath in CAT, 75a-b.

The philosophical discussion of the Sabbath is spiced with several folkloristic motifs, not at all common in R. Isaac's commentaries. There is a reference to the river Sambatyon, which prevents the ten exiled tribes of Israel from returning to their brothers (see *Eldad ha-Dani*, ed. A. Epstein [Pressburg, 1901], pp. 5-6, and nn. 11 and 12 on pp. 13-17 on the development of this legend), and mention of the tradition that the souls of sinners are not punished on the Sabbath (see J. Trachtenberg, *Jewish Magic and Superstition* [New York, 1974], pp. 66, 285, n. 9), a belief in obvious conflict with R. Isaac's philosophical position that there is no punishment for the souls of the wicked except for annihilation and failure to achieve the rewards of eternal life. Perhaps most interesting is the reference to a fish called *dag yehudi*, which rests on the Sabbath and will not attempt to escape the nets of fishermen on that day. This tradition appears in the Hebrew translation of Razi's zoological work known as *De Proprietatibus membrorum . . . animalium*, Paris MS 1122, f. 26a (cf. M. Steinschneider, *Die hebraeischen Uebersetzungen*, pp. 728-729). It is mentioned by R. David Kimhi in his comment on

Genesis 2:3 and discussed by Levi b. Abraham (*Livyat Hen*, Vatican MS 192, f. 129b), who adds, "I have seen it."

40. CMR, 65a.

41. This argument is made by a Christian persona in a polemical chapter of *Sefer ha-Ikkarim*, ed. I. Husik (Phila., 1930), III, 25, p. 473.

42. CAT, 41a-b. Unlike R. Isaac, Moses ibn Tibbon dismissed Maimonides' explanation (*ein ta'am la-ta'am*) and gave a different one of his own (*Sefer Pe'ah*, f. 39b).

43. CMR, 71a-b, 72b.

44. CMR, 73a. Another example of a commandment for which the reason given by Maimonides is greatly expanded by R. Isaac is circumcision; see chapter IV, section 2.

45. CAT, 139b.

46. CAT, 139b. Cf. Maimonides, *Hil. Avot ha-Tum'ot*; 3:1 ff. The Rambam makes no attempt to give an explanation for this "decree of Scripture."

47. CAT, 136b; cf. the interpretation of *nitma le-metim* (Num. 9:10) in CAT, 86b, discussed below. A similar approach is taken to the statement "Ten things are hard for the student . . . looking at the face of dead man" (*Hor.*, 13b); this is explained by the fact that confrontation with the death of a person frightens a man and distracts him from study. God prevented priest, prophet, and nazirite from contact with the dead in order to protect them from the resulting sorrow (CAT, 161b).

48. See also CAT, 63b, where "impurity" (*tum'ah*) is said to be used as a metaphor for a false belief or a bad ethical quality. This approach may have been inspired by Maimonides, *Hil. Mikva'ot*, 11:12.

49. CMR, 64b. Gersonides reveals a similar approach to the symbolism of the red cow, although no direct influence is detectable; see *Sefer Ralbag al-ha-Torah*, pp. 193b-194a, and C. Touati, *La pensée philosophique*, p. 499. Cf. also Anatoli, *Malmad*, pp. 89b-90b.

50. CAT, 60b-61a.

51. CMR, 38b-39a. The granting of a double portion to the first-born is not usually counted as one of the 613 commandments. Maimonides, for example, includes this in the general category of "laws of inheritance," based on Numbers 27:8-11 (*Sefer ha-Mitzvot*, Positive Commandment 248). R. Isaac, by referring several times to God's *commanding* that the first-born receive a double share, follows the position of Ramban (*Commentary on the Torah*, Deut. 21:16; *Hasagot on Sefer ha-Mitzvot*, "Negative Commandments which the Rabbi Forgot, according to the Ramban," 12).

52. The assertion that the first-born lives to one hundred while the others die as young men is obviously exaggerated, but there seems to be a point of some demographic importance here. To what extent this generalization is based on personal observation and to what extent on medieval medical theory is not clear from the passage.

53. Maimonides, *Hil. De'ot*, 3:3, 4:1; *Guide*, III, 27. Cf. CAT, 44b: "For one cannot perfect his soul if he wants for bread."

54. See especially *Guide*, I, 34.

55. See esp. Maimonides, Introduction to *Mishnah Commentary* (*Mishnah*

im Perush Rambam: Zera'im), pp. 43-44. This doctrine is to be distinguished from the ideological justification of Christian monasticism, according to which society was divided into those who work, those who fight, and those who pray. Here too, the work necessary to provide food was done by others, but the prevailing belief was that the spiritual activity of the monks benefited not only their own souls but the society as a whole, to which they contributed in their special way; see R. W. Southern, *Western Society and the Church in the Middle Ages* (Aylesbury, England, 1970), pp. 224-225.

56. CAT, 151b-152a.

57. Maimonides (*Sefer ha-Mitzvot*, Positive Commandment 198, *Hil. Malveh ve-Loveh*, 5:1), Gersonides (*Torah Commentary* on Deut. 23:21), and *Sefer ha-Hinukh* (ed. H. D. Chavel [Jerusalem, 1961]) count this as a commandment. For the majority who disagree, see Rabad, *Hasagot ad loc.*; other commentators on this passage in the *Mishneh Torah* citing Ramban and Rashba; Meiri, *Beit ha-Behirah: Baba Metzia* (Jerusalem, 1959), p. 266.

58. That the Jewish moneylender might spend too much time among his Gentile debtors trying to recover his debts and thus come to learn about and imitate a non-Jewish life style. The scholar class excluded itself from this restriction, claiming that the reason behind their decree did not apply to them: *BM*, 70b, 71a; Meiri, *Beit ha-Behirah: Baba Metzia*, p. 266.

59. Rashi, *Makkot*, 24a, *ve-afilu le-ovdei kokhavim*. It is interesting that R. Nissim of Marseilles, writing around 1300, accuses his contemporary coreligionists of precisely this: by taking interest from the Gentiles, they have developed bad ethical dispositions, which have become so firmly entrenched in their souls that they actually do take interest from other Jews (*He-Halutz*, 7 [1965], 143). R. Isaac's treatment of usury as a symptom of an ethical imperfection differs from the contemporary Christian discussion of this theme as well as from the Talmudic explanation cited in n. 58. Medieval Christian authors tended to treat usury not as a manifestation of the sin of avarice, which would have required merely internal sorrow for atonement, but as a kind of robbery and sin against justice, which required restitution of the ill-gotten profits (J. T. Noonan, *The Scholastic Analysis of Usury* [Cambridge, Mass., 1957], pp. 17, 30; J. W. Baldwin *Masters, Princes, and Merchants* [Princeton, 1970], pp. 302-307). It would seem that the themes of usury as a mode of gain unnatural in itself and naturally hated by men, and of the ethical disposition that leads some to want to accumulate unlimited money as an end in itself may show the influence of the discussion of this subject in Aristotle's *Politics* (1257b-1258b), which became the object of considerable study in thirteenth-century Europe.

60. At least three different explanations were given. One line of thought argued that exigencies of Jewish life under Christian rulers, especially the overwhelming burden of taxes levied against the Jews by kings and nobles, made all income from moneylending fit the category of that which is necessary for subsistence and therefore permitted even by Talmudic law; nothing could be considered pure profit, as any profit could be taken by the ruler at whim (Rashi cited in *Maggid Mishneh* to *Hil. Malveh ve-Loveh*, 5:2; R. Tam in *Tos. BM*, 70b, *tashikh*; Meiri, *Beit ha-Behirah: Baba Metzia*, p. 266). Another argument focused on the reason given for the Talmudic restriction, stating that Jews now had so

many contacts with Gentiles in affairs other than moneylending that the contact of creditor with debtor no longer posed a special threat that the Jew would be influenced by the Christian (R. Tam, *Tos. BM,* 70b, *tashikh*). Still a third seized on the exception made for scholars and sages: nowadays, everyone considers himself to be in this category and thus immune to the danger of learning the ways of the Gentile (Ramban cited in *Maggid Mishneh* to *Hil. Malveh ve-Loveh,* 5:2). For an overview of this issue, see Judah Rosenthal, "Ribbit min ha-Nokhri," *Talpiyyot,* 5 (1952), 475-492; 6 (1953), 130-152; and Siegfried Stein, "The Development of the Jewish Law of Interest from the Biblical Period to the Expulsion of the Jews from England," *Historia Judaica,* 17 (1955), 3-40.

61. Baron, unaware of this passage, wrote that the earliest formulation of the idea that money lending left Jews free for cultural enterprise dates from the fifteenth century and is attributed to R. Shalom b. Isaac Sekel (*SRHJ* IV, 223-224; XII, 132, 196). Cf. H. H. Ben Sasson, *Perakim be-Toldot ha-Yehudim bimei ha-Beinayim* (Tel Aviv, 1969), p. 193.

62. CMR, 41a, bottom.

63. CAT, 45a-b.

64. CMR, 51b. Cf. CMR 7a-b, where R. Isaac criticizes the masses for their limited awareness of the obvious reasons for the commandments and the philosophically ignorant Talmudists for their failure to be cognizant of "the hidden meaning of each commandment."

65. CMR, 52a, emphasis added.

66. Cf. the homiletical application of the laws relating to the purification of the leper in Anatoli's *Malmad,* end of *parashat Tazriah* (p. 102a). For Christian allegorization of Biblical leprosy, see S. N. Brody, *The Disease of the Soul* (Ithaca, 1974), esp. pp. 124-134.

67. CAT, 86b; cf. CMR, 37a-b.

68. For accusations of neglect of the commandments resulting from their philosophical reinterpretation, see E. Urbach, *Ba'alei ha-Tosafot* (Jerusalem, 1968), p. 116; *Minhat Kena'ot* (Pressburg, 1838), pp. 60, 94; *She'elot u-Teshuvot ha-Rashba,* I, 153, col. 2, bottom; G. Scholem, *MTJM,* pp. 397-398, n. 154. All of these passages indicate an ideological rejection of the peshat of the commandments on rationalistic grounds. Excoriations of the laxity in observance are legion, but many of the other sources do not make it clear to what extent this was a result of carelessness and indifference, to what extent a result of a developed ideology; see R. Moses of Coucy, *Sefer Mitzvot Gadol,* Positive Commandment 3, Negative Commandment 112, 148 (and Urbach, pp. 386-387); R. Jonah Gerondi, *Sha'arei Teshuvah,* III, 8, 76, 96; 75, 99; 13, 47, 61, 79; idem, "Iggeret ha-Teshuvah"; *Minhat Kena'ot,* p. 46; B. Z. Dinur, *Toldot Yisrael: Yisrael ba-Golah,* II, 4, pp. 283-289.

69. See for example, A. S. Halkin, "Why Was Levi ben Hayyim Hounded," *PAAJR,* XXXIV (1966), 65-76.

70. R. Menaham ha-Meiri, *Beit ha-Behirah: Avot* (Jerusalem, 1964), pp. 64-66.

71. See, for example, St. Augustine's denial that the prohibition against seething a kid in its mother's milk had any literal meaning and his insistence that it was pure allegory (Smalley, *The Study of the Bible in the Middle Ages,* p. 303).

R. Meir b. Simon's contemporary (mid-thirteenth-century) dispute on money-lending begins with an attack on Christian exegesis of the commandments: "You have opened your mouth wide without measure on the subject of moneylending on interest. Now stand up and I shall enter into judgment with you about it. What greater crime have you found in it than in the eating of ritually forbidden animals, carcasses, or fish without fins and scales, since you reduce everything to its metaphorical meaning [le-mashal], which is called figura. Why do you not interpret the law on interest figuratively like the other prohibitions and thus allow (following your own exegesis) the lending on interest even to your own people?" (S. Stein, "A Disputation on Moneylending between Jews and Gentiles in Me'ir b. Simeon's Milhemeth Miswah (Narbonne, Thirteenth Century)," JJS, 10 [1959], p. 51).

72. For example, the aggadah commentaries of R. Azriel, Moses ibn Tibbon, Todros Abulafia, Rashba, and Shem Tov ibn Shaprut, and the commentary on the Midrashim of Yedaiah Bedersi. Note the apology of R. Jacob ibn Habib for including a few halakhic passages in his work and his self-justification that he found in them "a fine principle pertaining to faith" (Ein Ya'akov [New York, 1955], Shabbat, p. 51a).

73. Unlike the term "ta'amei ha-mitzvot," "ta'amei ha-halakhot" is not an expression with wide currency in the discussion of the philosophical approach to Jewish law. Here too, the central figure is Maimonides, although in this case the crucial work is not the Guide but the Mishneh Torah. He states in one of his responsa that "my purpose in this entire composition [the Mishneh Torah] is to show the rationality of the laws" (le-hakriv ha-dinim el ha-sekhel). The term "ta'amei ha-halakhot" itself is used by Chaim Tchernowitz in relation to the Mishneh Torah (Toldot ha-Poskim [New York, 1946], I, 205, 286; indeed, he goes so far as to say that "the Rambam did not leave a single halakha in the Mishneh Torah without some kind of rational reason or explanation" (ibid., 286). Tchernowitz uses the term "ta'amei ha-halakhot" to mean two different things. First, it is the demonstration of how the halakha necessarily follows from the logic of the verse or principle in the Torah which is its basis (see esp. pp. 286-287; the anti-Karaite purpose of such an approach is stressed, pp. 202-206). Second, it is the demonstration that a specific halakha is inherently rational or logical, independent of its source in the Torah. It is primarily this second meaning that concerns us here. For examples of Maimonides' rationalization of the halakha in this sense, see Tchernowitz, esp. p. 201, n. 13, and pp. 287-289, nn. 87-88. Cf. also I. Twersky, A Maimonides Reader (New York, 1972), p. 19: "While not too many laws are actually rationalized, the mandate to engage in rationalization, to penetrate to their essence and their real motive powers . . . is clearly issued in the Mishneh Torah."

74. CAT, 42b. The identification of "woman" or "wife" with the physical component of the individual is commonplace in these commentaries; see chapter III, section 2. For similar interpretations of "king" in nonhalakhic contexts, see Rashba, Hiddushei, p. 78, Anatoli, Malmad, p. 21b, bottom.

75. Mishneh Torah, Hilkhot Melakhim, 1:11.

76. CAT, 156b-157a. For other similar interpretations of the "spring" or "flowing water" in aggadic statements, see chapter III, section 2.

77. Cf. *Guide*, I, 38, end.

78. CMR, 47b-48a; the full text with annotation can be found in my article "The Earliest Commentary on the *Midrash Rabbah*," pp. 290-292.

79. For example, R. Mordecai (cited by Alfasi as below and many others as part of the gemara in *Yoma*, 53b; cf. Rashba as below, Responsum 436). R. Amram, *Seder Rav Amram Gaon* (Warsaw, 1865), pp. 9b-10a. R. Nahshon (cited in *Otzar ha-Geonim*, ed. B. M. Levin [Jerusalem, 1934], VI [*Yoma* and *Sukkah*], p. 24). *Halakhot Gedolot*, ed. E. Hildesheimer, I (Jerusalem, 1971), pp. 4, 5, and esp. 34. R. Saadia, *Siddur Rav Saadia Gaon*, ed. I. Davidson et al., (Jerusalem, 1941), p. 20. R. Sherira (cited in *Otzar ha-Geonim*, VI, 23). R. Hai (cited ibid., p. 24). R. Nissim b. Jacob, *Sefer ha-Mafteah le-Man'ulei ha Talmud* (cited in *Sefer ha-Me'orot*, as below, p. 109). R. Isaac Alfasi, *Halakhot, Berakhot*, end ch. 5. R. Isaac ibn Giat (cited in *Orhot Hayim*, as below, p. 16a, #44). R. Moses b. Maimon, *Hilkhot Tefilah*, 5:10. R. Yom Tov b. Abraham (Ritba), *Hiddushei ha-Ritba al Masekhet Yoma* (Jerusalem, 1967), p. 62. R. Solomon b. Adret (Rashba), *She'elot u-Teshuvot*, I, responsa 381, 436 (and cf. 675). R. Asher b. Yehiel (Rosh), *Rabbenu Asher on Berakhot*, end ch. 5; cf. *Tur*, as below. R. Jacob b. Asher, *Tur Orah Hayim*, section 123. R. Abraham b. Isaac, *Sefer ha-Eshkol*, ed. A. Auerbach (Halberstadt, 1868), I, 26. R. Meir b. Simon, *Sefer ha-Me'orot: Berakhot, Pesahim*, ed. M. Blau (New York, 1964), p. 109. R. Aaron ha-Cohen of Lunel, *Orhot Hayim* (Florence, 1750), I, 15a, 16a. R. Abraham of Montpellier, *Perush Rabbenu Avraham min ha-Har al Masekhtot . . . Yoma* (New York, 1975), pp. 219-220. R. Menahem Meiri, *Beit ha-Behirah: Yoma* (Jerusalem, 1970), p. 130. See also R. Isaiah di-Trani (Rid), *Piskei Rid, Yoma* (Jerusalem, 1966), p. 424, and *Mahzor Vitry*, ed. S. Hurwitz (Berlin, 1893), p. 18. Baron discusses this custom, *SRHJ*, VII (Philadelphia, 1958), pp. 77, 251.

80. R. Meir b. Simon, *Sefer ha-Me'orot: Berakhot, Pesahim*, p. 59.

81. Anatoli, *Malmad*, p. 159a.

82. The passage appears in the section of *Milhemet Mitzvah* devoted to an interpretation of Deut. 6:4, published by M. Blau in *Sefer ha-Me'orot ve-Sefer ha-Hashlamah: Berakhot, Pesahim*, p. 36.

83. See, for example, Maimonides, *Hil. Yesodei ha-Torah*, 6:2, 5.

84. CAT, 142b-143a. The terms "great," "mighty," and "awesome" were identified as positive attributes by Maimonides in a different context, with regard to a different Talmudic passage (*Guide*, I, 59). For the meaning of "el" and "elohim," see also *Guide*, II, 2, and CAT, 67a.

85. It is not entirely clear whether R. Isaac, ignoring the legal tradition, denies the simple halakhic meaning of the statement and considers his own interpretation to be the primary meaning of the passage, or whether he accepts the halakha as formulated in the *Mishneh Torah* and then goes on to give a deeper meaning relevant to theological doctrine.

86. See, for example, *Tos. AZ*, 36b, *mi-shum*, end; *Tos. Sanh.*, 52b, *perat le-eshet aherim*; *Tos. Kidd.*, 21b, *eshet*; *Tos. Sotah*, 26b, *yatzah Kuti*.

87. CAT, 58a-b. Cf. *Guide*, III, 8: "Men in truth, and not beasts having only the appearance and shapes of men." The statement in the *Guide*, however, does not distinguish between Jews and non-Jews; it is applicable to all human beings. On the interpretation of the word "ishut," see CMR, 58a: *ein ishut la-teva*,

meaning that nature does not recognize any distinctively human quality and therefore does not repudiate incest in human beings any more than it does in beasts; also CMR, 63a.

88. CAT, 47a. The contrast between the man who accepts the authority of the law but sins because of natural inclination and the man who denies all the basic principles of revealed religion is common in these commentaries; see, for example, the discussion of the categories of meshummad (CAT, 30a-b).

89. Again it is not clear here or in the previous example that R. Isaac rejects the simple meaning of the statements as usually understood. It is obvious that he does not consider this to be particularly important.

90. Maimonides, *Hil. Sanhedrin*, 2:1, 6.

91. CAT, 26b-27a.

92. R. Isaac states that he has also discussed this area of Jewish law in his commentary on Tractate *Sotah* of the Babylonian Talmud, but this is not extant (CMR, 66b).

93. CMR, 66b.

94. CMR, 68b.

95. CMR, 67a.

96. It is instructive to compare this approach to that of Ralbag. Both R. Isaac and Gersonides explicitly or implicitly reject as inadequate the rabbinic derivation of halakhot through the traditional hermeneutical principles. For both, by implication, the verse used by the sages is more an asmakhta than the true foundation of the law. But Ralbag, writing a commentary on the Torah, attempts to show how the halakha can be deduced from Biblical verses through the more rational tools of Aristotelian dialectic and rhetoric (see the Introduction to his Torah Commentary, and Touati, *La pensée philosophique*, pp. 506-513). He is thus concerned with the rationalization of the halakha in the first sense noted above (note 73). R. Isaac, in contrast, explores the implications of the halakha on its own terms, explaining how it is rational in the context of its purpose, without concern for the rigorous derivation of halakha from Scripture.

97. CMR, 67a-b; the full text with annotation can be found in my article "The Earliest Commentary on the *Midrash Rabbah*," pp. 292-294. For the phrase translated "stimulate themselves with phallic forms," see the annotation to *meshamshot be-tzalmei zakhar*.

98. The classical statement of this principle is in *Guide*, III, 34.

99. CAT, 55a-b. Cf. *Hil. Mamrim*, 7:11, and Meiri, *Beit ha-Behirah: Sanhedrin* (Jerusalem, 1965), p. 197. Meiri also gives a reason for certain cases excluded from the general rule: "Even though they are tradition, all of these matters are plausible in some respects." His approach is similar to that of R. Isaac, although his specific explanations show no dependence.

100. CAT, 56b.

101. CMR, 64b-65a.

102. Rashi, commenting on *Sotah*, 8a, construes the case differently, as he must explain the reason given by the gemara: if both women are given the oath at the same time, and the first woman, who is innocent, refuses to confess, then the second woman, who is guilty, may likewise refuse to confess out of pride. See also Meiri, *Beit ha-Behirah: Sotah* (Jerusalem, 1967), p. 24.

103. As I have noted, this explanation of the heifer is somewhat strange in that it does not explicitly deal with the issue of tum'at meit.

104. This explanation of the neck-breaking ritual is based on *Guide*, III, 40.

105. Cf. *Guide*, III, 17, near end; CMR, 83b.

106. CAT, 47b. The description of death by stoning does not fit the method indicated by the Mishnah (*Sanh.*, 45a) of pushing the person from a height and then letting a heavy stone fall on him; cf. *Hil. Sanhedrin*, 15:1.

107. CMR, 72a-b.

108. CAT, 60b-61a. Cf. Rashba, *Hiddushei*, pp. 20-21 on *Berakhot*, 7a; there too the tefillin of the head together with strap signify God's relationship to the universe He created, but no interpretation of the four cases is given. R. Bahya b. Asher on Deut. 28:10 gives a totally different reason for the four compartments: they represent the four animals of the throne and the four cavities of the brain.

109. As in so many cases, R. Isaac ignores the reason given in the gemara for the disqualification of the dice player (that he is not engaged in a constructive activity beneficial to society; this is accepted over Rami bar Hama's reason that gambling involves a form of asmakhta, which does not convey legal title to the winnings [*Sanh.*, 24b]) and gives an independent reason of his own, as if there were no halakhic literature between the statement of the Mishnah and his own work.

110. CAT, 20a-b. Another example of explaining the latent reasoning behind both sides of a controversy is CAT, 46a-b on *Sanh.*, 46b: "Is the eulogy honor to the living or honor to the deceased?"

111. CAT, 22b.

112. See Maimonides, *Hil. Sanhedrin*, 22:4.

113. See, for example, J. Fraenkel, *Darko shel Rashi be-Ferusho la-Talmud ha-Bavli* (Jerusalem, 1975), p. 303.

114. See also CAT, 60a-b, on *Sanh.*, 88a: "If he says, 'so it seems to me,' and they say 'It is a tradition,' he is killed." Here, however, the statement explained is consistent with the halakha; it simply is not as extreme as the ultimate halakhic formulation R. Isaac ignores.

115. CMR, 66a-b, emphasis added.

116. The mishnah of *Sotah*, ch. 4, states that "wives may be warned with regard to all forbidden sexual unions, except for that with a minor and with one who is not a man." The gemara of *Sotah*, 26b, considers the possibility that the phrase "one who is not a man" in the mishnah refers to the gentile idolator but rejects it on the basis of an authoritative statement of Rav Hamnuna, "Warning may be made with regard to an idolator." It then goes on to explain why Rav Hamnuna's statement was necessary at all, why it is not obvious, showing the reasoning that might have led to the erroneous conclusion that in the case of warning and subsequent seclusion with an idolator, the woman is *not* "defiled" for her husband—a conclusion forestalled by Rav Hamnuna (see the paraphrase of this argument by R. Asher: *Rosh* on *Ketubot*, 3b, *ve-liderosh*, end). Maimonides, reflecting the discussion in *Sotah*, 26b, states that the warning may apply to any man, "even if he is her father or her brother or an idolator." If after proper warning, the wife is secluded with the man named, "she is forbidden to her hus-

band until she drinks the bitter waters and the matter is investigated. Now that there is no ritual of the water for the suspected adulteress, she is forbidden to him [her husband] forever, and she must leave him without payment of her *ketubah*" (*Hil. Sotah*, 1:1-2).

Other passages in the gemara also show it is assumed that a woman who voluntarily has sexual relations with a non-Jew may not return to her husband; see *Ketubot*, 3b, on the *jus primae noctis* (especially Rashi *ad loc.*, *ikah perutzot*, and *Ketubot*, 26b, on the woman imprisoned by gentiles (especially Rashi *ad loc.*, *asurah le-va'alah*).

117. This position is problematic in itself; see Tosafot to *Yebamot*, 61a, *ve-ein*.

118. See Maimonides, *Hil. Sotah*, 1:1.

119. See *Hil. Issurei Bi'ah*, 15:3.

120. Tosafot *Ketubot*, 3b, *ve-liderosh*. Note that in Tosafot Sens to *Sotah*, 26b, exactly the opposite position is attributed to Rabbenu Tam.

121. Rabbenu Asher on *Ketubot*, 3b, *ve-liderosh*; emphasis added.

122. *Tur, Even ha-Ezer* section 178, near end; emphasis added.

123. *Bayit Hadash* to *Tur, Even ha-Ezer*, beginning of section 178; emphasis added.

124. *Beit Yosef* to *Tur, Even ha-Ezer* section 178, near end.

125. See, for example, *Hiddushei R. David Luria*, and Moshe Aryeh Mirkin *ad loc.*

126. See for example, *Tiferet Tzion* of Isaac Yadler.

127. CAT, 146a-b. Maimonides (*Hil. Edut*, 20:2) states that once the falsely accused man is executed, the false witnesses may not be put to death *min ha-din* ("on the basis of Torah law," or possibly, in accordance with the language of the gemara, "because of an *a fortiore* argument"; see *Kesef Mishneh* ad loc.). The implication, as understood by Radbaz, is that they may be punished according to the discretion of the court. There is no agreement among the commentators as to the problem that Rabad found in Maimonides' formulation of the halakha. An attempt to justify the halakha can be found in the *Kesef Mishneh ad loc.*, end.

128. This ending, after what has come before, calls to mind certain texts from a totally different genre and intellectual milieu, texts described by scholars as belonging to a school of Latin Averroism, which flourished in Paris and Italy in the thirteenth and fourteenth centuries. Representatives of this school discussed philosophical positions—relating to necessity, Creation, God's knowledge, the soul, and other matters—which conflicted with the official teaching of the Church. They argued that the position of Aristotle or Averroes is philosophically true and cannot be refuted by any rational proofs, and that the position of faith cannot be proven rationally and can be refuted on philosophical grounds. Nevertheless, they conclude, the teaching of Aristotle or Averroes is erroneous, because of the authority of the Church in its interpretation of Scripture. I do not mean to imply the existence of any direct connection or any lines of influence between R. Isaac and the Averroists but merely a parallelism in the structure of the argument. That R. Isaac's argument is in the realm of halakha and that of the Averroists in the realm of theology exemplifies the areas in which the Jewish and Christian communities of the Middle Ages chose to exercise authority.

On Latin Averroism, see E. Gilson, *History of Christian Philosophy in the Middle Ages* (New York, 1955), pp. 387-402 and 521-527 (a working definition is given on p. 388); P. Mandonnet, *Siger de Brabant et L'Averroisme latin au XIIIme siècle* (Fribourg, 1899), esp. ch. 7; F. Van Steenberghen, *Aristotle in the West* (Louvain, 1970), esp. ch. 8; C. J. Ermatinger, "Averroism in Early Fourteenth Century Bologna," *Medieval Studies*, 16 (1954), pp. 35-56; A Maier, "Ein Beitrag zur Geschichte des italienischen Averroismus," *Quellen und Forschungen aus italienischen Archiven und Bibliotheken*, 33 (1944), pp.136-157. The sincerity of the concluding statement proclaiming acceptance of the traditional teaching is still disputed by scholars, and it is almost impossible to prove, as it rests on an evaluation of tone, irony, humor, and so forth; see, for example, Gilson, p. 524, on John of Jandun.

vi. The Historical Setting

1. The Hebrew text of the entire passage has been published as part of *Perushei Rishonim le-Masekhet Avot*, ed. M. Kasher and Y. Y. Blacherowitz (Jerusalem, 1973). Unfortunately, the manuscript has been transcribed and edited with little concern for accuracy in reproducing the text. Even phrases from Biblical verses used by the author are mangled by the editors so as to become unrecognizable. For technical reasons, it is impossible to list all the errors here. One outstanding example, which could skew the proper understanding of the entire passage, is the omission of *ha-melekh* from the phrase *mi-ta'am ha-melekh adonei ha-aretz* (p. 54, line 21; cf. Jon. 3:7 and Gen. 42:30).

2. The argument that court life leads one to ignore all that is truly important and to concentrate exclusively on serving the king is made by Maimonides in his comment on this statement from *Avot* and is repeated by R. Menahem Meiri (*Beit ha-Behirah* on *Avot*, [Jerusalem, 1964], p. 18). The accusation that courtiers were lax in the observance of the mitzvot was made by Nachmanides in the thirteenth century (*Kevutzat Mikhtavim*, p. 123, *Kitvei Ramban*, I, 366), and by R. Menahem b. Zerah, from a different perspective, in the fourteenth century (*Tzeidah la-Derekh*, Introduction). Abravanel, commenting on this statement from *Avot*, states that all of the first five commandments may be interpreted specifically as warning against the sins of court life (*Nahlat Avot*, [New York, 1953], p. 71).

3. On Jehosef ibn Negrela, see *The Book of Tradition by Abraham ibn Daud*, ed. Gerson Cohen (Phila., 1967), p. 76. The fortunes of the thirteenth-century courtier are exemplified by the Alconstantini family in Aragon (Baer, *HJCS*, I, 105-106, based on the letter of Nachmanides cited in n. 2), and by Don Çag de la Maleha in Castile (Baer, "Todros b. Yehuda Ha-Levi u-Zemano," *Zion*, 2 (1937), 19-55; *HJCS*, I, 120-130. Cf. the statement of R. Asher b. Yehiel that reverence for a courtier, in contrast with reverence due to the Babylonian Exilarch, is not obligatory, "for the man's power will not last forever" (quoted Baer, *HJCS*, I, 319).

4. See, for example, R. Asher b. Yehiel's reservations about Jews adjudicating capital matters in general in Spain and his approval of a death sentence meted out against a Jewish informer by the Jewish judges of Seville ("Now the

Jews have been granted authority by the crown to try him in secret and, if found guilty, to execute him. . . They did well in sentencing him to hang" (quoted in Baer, *HJCS*, I, 324).

5. It may well be this mention of Beziers, coming near the beginning of the manuscript, which led to the original—and erroneous—identification of the author as Yedaiah Bedersi.

6. Robert Fawtier, *The Capetian Kings of France* (London, 1960), p. 122.

7. C. De Vic and J. Vaissete, *Histoire générale de Languedoc*, VI (Toulouse, 1879), 658-659.

8. See Auguste Molinier, "Sur l'expédition de Trenceval et le siège de Carcassonne," ibid., VII, 448-461.

9. The position was therefore fundamentally different from that of Jews used in the administration of Philip the Fair to collect taxes owed by the Jewish community. See Gustave Saige, *Les Juifs du Languedoc antérieurement au XIVe siècle* (Paris, 1881), pp. 90, 115, 217-218.

10. *Histoire générale*, VII, 499-500. Baron apparently refers to this in *SRHJ*, X (New York, 1965), 339, but his reference is to III, 300, clearly an error. See also Gérard Nahon, "Pour une géographie administrative des Juifs dans la France de Saint Louis," *Revue historique*, 264, 2 (1975), 324-325.

11. For a discussion of these documents as historical sources, see Molinier, *Histoire générale*, VII, 464-466, where the royal Inquisition as an institution is also analyzed.

12. Ibid., pt. 2, col. 6.

13. There is even a correlation in the use of terminology for the geographical-political region. The Latin source says *qui recepit pro domino Rege justicias et emendas istius terre*, using the word "terra" to refer to the seneschalcy of Carcassonne-Beziers. When the Hebrew source uses the phrase *ve'al piv yi-shak kol amei ha-aretz* (cf. Gen. 41:40), the word "aretz" may be assumed to have the same meaning.

14. Baer, *HJCS*, I, 241; I. Twersky, "Aspects of the Social and Cultural History of Provençal Jewry," *Jewish Society Through the Ages*, ed. H. H. Ben Sasson and S. Ettinger (London, 1971), p. 189.

15. British Museum, Hebrew Manuscript 930.1 (see G. Margoliouth, *Catalogue of the Hebrew and Samaritan manuscripts in the British Museum* [London, 1899-1935], p. 246), the elegy in the manuscript begins f. 44a; Vienna, Oesterreichische Nationalbibliothek, Hebrew Manuscript 111, beginning f. 223b. This collection of poems was analyzed by H. Schirmann, "Iyyunim ba-Kovetz ha-Shirim ve-ha-Melitzot shel Avraham ha-Bedersi," *Sefer ha-Yovel le-Yitzhak Baer* (Jerusalem, 1961), pp. 154-173, but he fails to take note of this long elegy despite its historic importance. Cf. Gross, *Gallia Judaica*, pp. 103-104.

16. The relevant material can be found in the Vienna manuscript, ff. 228b, 229b, 230a, 233a. Among the subjects of study mentioned, in addition to *ha-hokhmot ha-hitzonot* and *hokhmot ha-dikduk* are all six orders of the Mishnah and gemara, including *Seder Taharot*, as well as "*Sifra, Sifrei, Tosefta*, and the entire Talmud."

17. Molinier, *Histoire générale*, VII, 500.

18. The language of this passage seems to fit especially the political realities

of the emperor. See, for example, the negotiations of Frederick II with the German princes to gain acceptance of his son Henry as King of the Romans in 1219-1220 and of his son Conrad as "King of the Romans and future Emperor" in 1236 (Ernst Kantorowicz, *Frederick the Second, 1194-1250*, [New York, 1957], pp. 99-100, 432-433.

19. CMR, 29a-b; the Hebrew text of entire comment with annotation can be found in my article "The Earliest Commentary on the *Midrash Rabbah*," *SMJHL*, pp. 288-290.

20. See Jacob Mann, *The Jews in Egypt and in Palestine under the Fatimid Caliphs* (New York, 1970), esp. I, 172-174, 252-254, 271, and S. D. Goitein, *A Mediterranean Society*, II: *The Community* (Berkeley, 1971), esp. 19, 23, 32.

21. Goitein, ibid., pp. 318, 353.

22. For such honors, expressing allegiance to the authority of the nasi, see ibid., pp. 19-20.

23. Mann, *Jews in Egypt*, I, 248, II, 326.

24. Abraham Maimonides, *Responsa*, ed. A. Freimann (Jerusalem, 1938), pp. 19-22. Cf. the caustic remarks of his father, the Rambam, concerning the use of unmerited titles such as *rosh yeshiva* and *av-beit-din* in the land of Israel and in Spain (comment on Mishnah *Bekhorot*, 4:4, *Mishnah im Perush Rambam: Kodashim* (Jerusalem, 1967), p. 245.

25. *Kevutzat Mikhtavim*, pp. 120-124; *Kitvei Ramban*, I, 364-366; Baer, *HJCS*, I, 105-106; idem, *Devir*, 2 (1924), 316-317.

In his article "Ma'avak al Shilton Tziburi be-Vartzelona be-Tekufat ha-Pulmus al Sifrei ha-Rambam" (*Tarbiz*, 42 [1973], 389-400), Bernard (Dov) Septimus interprets a letter complaining about an uprising against the nesi'im of Barcelona as pertaining to the opposition of Nachmanides and his circle. In this reconstruction, the nesi'im, especially the ibn Hasdai family, represented the rationalist position in the controversy over Maimonides' works. Their opponents, including R. Solomon of Montpellier, R. Jonah Gerondi, R. David b. Saul, and Nachmanides, were attacking both the works of Maimonides and the hereditary position of the nasi. Therefore, the supporters of the nesi'im struck back by questioning the purity of lineage of R. Jonah and his family, challenging the orthodoxy of belief of their Kabbalist opponents, and excoriating the effrontery of those who rise up against established authority.

If indeed the letter published by Septimus does belong to the conflict of Nachmanides and not to the uprising of Samuel Benveniste, our source shows that Septimus' identification of rationalist Maimonideans with supporters of the nesi'ut and Kabbalist anti-Maimonideans with opponents of the nesi'ut is overly simplistic. Here is a vehement attack on the hereditary transmission of the nesi'ut, corresponding to the position stated by Nachmanides, by a fervent Maimonidean rationalist (see his praise of Maimonides and the *Guide* in CMR, 34a and 21a).

26. A. Neubauer, "Ergänzungen und Verbesserungen zu Abba Maris Minhat Kenaot," *Israelitische Letterbode*, 4 (1878-1879), 162-168. Septimus' analysis of this source in "Piety and Power in Thirteenth-Century Catalonia," *SMJHL*, esp. pp. 197-201, appeared too late for me to make use of it.

27. Ibid., p. 163. James I of Aragon was the direct overlord of Montpellier.

28. For the accusations against the anti-Nasi faction, see ibid., pp. 162-163;

for the terms of the ban against the "rebel" group, see pp. 165-166.

29. For example, it was the practice in Babylonia to carry the Torah scroll to the Exilarch, while all other Jews walked to the Torah to read from it: Yerushalmi *Sotah*, ch. 7, 22a (see Moses Beer, *Rashut ha-Golah be-Bavel bi-mei ha-Mishnah ve-ha-Talmud* (Tel Aviv, 1970), pp. 171-178).

30. CAT, 80a; the same distinction between "melekh" and "nasi" is found in CAT, 136b. See chapter IV, n. 106.

31. *Israelitische Letterbode*, 4, 165.

32. See Arthur Zuckerman, *A Jewish Princedom in Feudal France, 768-900* (New York, 1972); Jeremy Cohen, "The Nasi of Narbonne: A Problem in Medieval Historiography," *AJS Review*, 2 (1977), 45-76; Aryeh Grabois, "Ha-Hevrah ha-Yehudit be-Tzorfat ha-Deromit . . . al pi ha-Keronikah shel Almoni me-Narbonah," *Proceedings of the Sixth World Congress of Jewish Studies* (Jerusalem, 1975), II, 75-86.

33. *Sefer Masa'ot shel R. Benjamin*, ed. M. Adler (London, 1970), p. 3.

34. Saige, *Les Juifs du Languedoc*, p. 43; Zuckerman, *A Jewish Princedom*, p. 168.

35. Zuckerman, pp. 169-171.

36. *Kevutzat Mikhtavim*, pp. 104-105, 89.

37. The text of the gemara quoted here differs from both the Vilna text and the alternate version of some manuscripts.

38. CAT, 98b.

39. The dependence on Maimonides' theory of prophecy is clear (*Guide*, II, 36 ff.). See also CMR, 47a.

40. See, for example, R. Hai Gaon, responsum cited in *Sefer ha-Eshkol*, ed. Abraham Auerbach (Halberstadt, 1868), pt. 2, p. 49; Rashi *ad loc.*; Ritba citing Ramban, quoted in turn by R. Jacob ibn Habib (*Ein Ya'akov* on Hagigah, 10a); *Anaf Yosef* to *Ein Ya'akov* on this statement in *Sanhedrin*, which expresses horror at the interpretation that the word "talmud" means the Babylonian Talmud as a literary work.

41. CAT, 28a-b. Yedaiah Bedersi also discusses this statement from the Talmud. Commenting on a passage in his version of *Tanhuma Noah*, " 'The people who walk in darkness' [Isa. 9:1]—these are the masters of talmud," he points out that this follows the statement " 'He has made me to dwell in dark places'—this is the Babylonian talmud"; the reason for the darkness is "the disputes and the confusing doubts which require tremendous effort to resolve." But the rest of his comment shows that he did not understand this in the way R. Isaac did. The midrash continues, " 'Have seen a great light'—the light created on the first day." This "light created on the first day" is taken by Yedaiah to be a metaphor for the teaching of proper conduct and the correct ordering of society, which is the primary concern of the Talmud and which is necessary for the elite to achieve immortality for their souls (Commentary on the Midrashim, Escorial MS G,III,8, ff. 77a-b, Paris MS 783/3, f. 281b). He does not understand the disputes of the Talmud to be an obstacle to the achievement of true knowledge, as does R. Isaac; rather the "darkness" of these disputes is dispelled by the "light" of true teaching about proper conduct that emerges from them.

42. Bahya ibn Pakuda, *Hovot ha-Levavot*, Introduction, (tr. Moses

Hyamson [Jerusalem, 1965], p. 29). *Guide for the Perplexed*, III, 51. Shem-Tov Falaquera, *Sefer ha-Mevakesh* (Warsaw, 1924), pp. 91-99. Joseph ibn Kaspi, "Sefer ha-Musar" (*Tzava'ah*), chs. 11-14, *Hebrew Ethical Wills*, ed. Israel Abrahams, (Philadelphia, 1926), pp. 148-152. Cf. also Jacob Anatoli, *Malmad ha-Talmidim*, end of Introduction. Many other examples could be given. For a general discussion of this theme, see I. Twersky, "Religion and Law," *Religion in a Religious Age*, ed. S. D. Goitein, (Cambridge, Mass., 1974), pp. 69-77.

43. CAT, 98a.

44. CAT, 160b; Genhovsky (*Otzar ha-Perushim*), p. 15a, col. 1.

45. B. Z. Dinur, *Toldot Yisrael: Yisrael ba-Golah*, II, 4 (Tel Aviv, 1969), pp. 305, 304; cf. S. M. Stern, "Rationalists and Kabbalists in Medieval Allegory," *JJS*, 6 (1955), 73-86. Kalonymos b. Kalonymos, *Even Bohan* (Tel Aviv, 1956), pp. 55-57.

46. This was the first passage from the Aggadot Commentary to be published. See A. Neubauer, "Yedaya de Béziers," *REJ*, 20 (1890), 244-248.

47. G. Scholem, *Les origines de la Kabbale*, p. 420. R. Meir states that the antikabbalistic section of his *Milhemet Mitzvah* was written with the endorsement of R. Meshullam: Parma MS 155 (2749), ff. 232a-b.

48. *Hilkhot Yesodei ha-Torah*, 2:11; *Mishnah im Perush ha-Rambam: Mo'ed*, p. 377. For the philosophical understanding of the *ofan*, see *Guide*, beginning of Book III.

49. See, for example, his commentary on *Avot*, 4:5.

50. R. Menahem b. Zerah, *Tzeida la-Derekh*, quoted in S. Asaf, *Mekorot le-Toldot ha-Hinukh be-Yisrael*, II (Tel Aviv, 1931), 58. See also Asaf, pp. 52, 60-62, 67, for problems relating to the hiring and salaries of rabbis and teachers of Torah.

51. An interesting basis for comparison is provided by a somewhat earlier Christian source, the description of the school of Bernard of Chartres and his method of teaching, as recorded by John of Salisbury, *Metalogicon*, I, 24, tr. and ed. Daniel McGarry (Berkeley and Los Angeles, 1955) pp. 67-71. This passage also ends with a complaint about a precipitous decline following the death of the master.

52. Cf. Nachmanides' praise of the French rabbis in his letter to R. Meshullam, *Kitvei Ramban*, 362: *nelekh Tsorfatah* . . .

53. This theme is expressed by the proverb "Whatever wisdom does not enter with its possessor to the bathhouse is not true wisdom"; see Asaf, *Mekorot*, II, 47-48 (Falaquera's *Sefer ha-Mevakesh*), 69 (Profiat Duran's Introduction to *Ma'aseh Efod*). Note also the criticism of those who have not internalized the material they studied as being compelled to "rely on the skins of dead animals" (for example, *Muserei ha-Pilosophim* I, 1, attributed to Socrates; Shem-Tov Falaquera, "Iggeret ha-Musar," *Kovetz al-Yad*, I (XI) [1936], 58; Kalonymos b. Kalonymos, "Iggeret Musar," ibid., p. 108).

54. Nachmanides, writing to R. Meshullam b. Moses in 1232, addresses him as he would an elder scholar (*Kitvei Ramban*, I, 360, 364), so Meshullam could have been born no later than about 1190. The author of this passage states that he entered R. Meshullam's academy at age fifteen. Yedaiah apparently reached this age around 1285 or 1290, when Meshullam would have been ninety-

five or one hundred years old. But nothing in the passage indicates that the teacher was of such an extraordinary age. On the contrary, the author's lament, "Because of the sin of the disciples and of all the generation, this righteous man was lost to them and was gathered to his people," strongly implies the opposite— that Meshullam did not live to a particularly advanced age (cf. Haim Brody, Introduction to Sefer ha-Hashlamah on Berakhot [Berlin, 1893], p. xiii). Placing the birth date of Yedaiah, and therefore of his father, Abraham Bedersi, a generation earlier than had been generally thought created more problems than it solved; but assuming that the passage is about a different R. Meshullam merely substituted an unknown for a known.

55. See chapter VII.

56. My dating makes R. Isaac a contemporary of R. Meir b. Simon of Narbonne, a leading Talmudist, polemicist, opponent of the early Kabbalah, and public figure. R. Meir was the nephew of R. Meshullam b. Moses, whose teachings pervade the younger scholar's Talmudic writings, and it is entirely possible that he and R. Isaac studied with R. Meshullam at the same time and knew each other. On Meir b. Simon, see H. Gross, "Meir ben Simon and seine Schrift Milchemeth Mizwa," *MGWJ*, 30 (1881), 295-305, 444-452, 554-569; M. Blau, introduction to *Sefer ha-Me'orot* on *Berakhot* and *Pesahim* (New York, 1964); S. Stein, "A Disputation on Moneylending," *JJS*, 10 (1959), 45-61; and H. Merhaviah, "Li-zemano shel ha-Hibbur Milhemet Mitzvah," *Tarbiz*, 45 (1976), 296-302.

57. Neubauer, "Yedaya de Béziers," p. 245.

58. On the sack of Béziers in 1209, see *Histoire générale de Languedoc*, V, 288-289, and recently, Zoe Oldenbourg, *Massacre at Montségur* (New York, 1961), esp. pp. 110-121; Joseph Strayer, *The Albigensian Crusades*, (New York, 1971), pp. 61-64; Philippe Wolff, *Documents de l'histoire du Languedoc* (Toulouse, 1969), pp. 106-114. The estimate of twenty thousand indiscriminately massacred was first made by Arnald-Amalric, Abbot of Citeaux and commander of the Catholic forces, in a letter to Innocent III written the day after the event (Oldenbourg, pp. 183-184). It should be noted that according to a contemporary chronicle, the Jews of Beziers left the city with the Viscount Raymond-Roger Trenceval and were not included in the massacre (ibid., p. 111).

59. See R. Chazan, *Medieval Jewry in Northern France* (Baltimore, 1973), pp. 100-153, on Louis IX and his policy toward the Jews.

60. *Sanh.*, 101a, on Prov. 15:3.

61. CAT, 92b.

62. Jacob Anatoli, Introduction to *Malmad ha-Talmidim*. See also pp. 6b, 121b, 159a for other references to those who opposed his preaching. Anatoli himself laments the fact that there are no preachers in his day with courage to stand up to the powerful leaders of the Jewish community and reproach the people (p. 151a). On Anatoli's sermons, see I. Bettan, *Studies in Jewish Preaching* (Cincinnati, 1939), pp. 49-88; J. Dan, *Sifrut ha-Musar ve-ha-Derush*, pp. 82-91.

63. An analysis of Anatoli's use of aggadah would require an extensive study of the entire work. For one representative example, see his discussion of the aggadah about Samael and Yom Kippur, which includes some important general statements (pp. 162b-164b).

64. These attacks rise in a crescendo at the beginning of the fourteenth century and become a dominant motif in the controversy culminating in the Rashba's ban. For eyewitness accounts of sermons, see *Minhat Kena'ot*, pp. 48, 106, 139; *Hoshen Mishpat*, ed. D. Kaufmann, *Tiferet Seivah* in honor of Zunz, p. 147. For hostile reports apparently based on hearsay, see *Minhat Kena'ot*, pp. 3, 31, 48, 58, 59, 118, 123, 175. Even opponents to the ban concede that there are a few preachers guilty of excess: *Minhat Kena'ot*, pp. 68, 90; Menahem Meiri, *Hoshen Mishpat*, pp. 166-167; Yedaiah ha-Penini, *She'elot u-Teshuvot ha-Rashba*, I, 157, col. 1.

65. *Commentary on the Mishnah*, Introduction to Helek, translation from I. Twersky, *A Maimonides Reader* (New York, 1972), p. 408.

66. See chapter I, n. 18.

67. Hillel of Verona, *Tagmulei ha-Nefesh* (Lyck, 1874), p. 26a.

68. See chapter II, esp. with regard to statements such as "A woman is unformed matter and her husband makes her a vessel" (*Sanh.*, 22b).

69. On the role of entertainment in more philosophical sermons delivered at wedding feasts, see I. Heinemann, "Die Wissenschaftliche Allegoristik," pp. 640-641.

70. For example, CAT, 30a-b, 141b-132a; see chapter V.

71. CMR, 7a-b. This interpretation follows Maimonides' understanding of the terms "Scripture," "Mishnah," and "Talmud" in *Kiddushin*, 30a: *Hil. Talmud Torah*, 1:11-12. See the discussion by I. Twersky, "Some Non-Halakic Aspects of the Mishneh Torah," *Jewish Medieval and Renaissance Studies* (Cambridge, Mass., 1967), pp. 106-111.

72. CMR, 41b-42a. Perhaps the reference is to Moses Taku's *Ketav Tamim*.

73. CMR, 36b-37a.

74. See Joshua Trachtenberg, *Jewish Magic and Superstition* (New York, 1974), based on the literature of Germanic Jewry from the eleventh to sixteenth centuries (p. viii).

75. J. Shatzmiller, "Li-temunat ha-Mahloket ha-Rishonah al Kitvei ha-Rambam," *Zion*, 34 (1969), pp. 136-137, 143-144. The title of this article is a surprising misnomer for two reasons: it denies the existence of a conflict over the works of Maimonides before the 1230s, and it implies that the conflict of 1302-05 should be called the "second conflict over the works of Maimonides," while actually this later dispute did not deal with Maimonides at all. A similar picture of southern attitudes is revealed in Nachmanides' letter to the French rabbis. Ramban says he has heard that some of the rabbis attacked the *Sefer ha-Mada* because of its statement that God has no form or image (see *Hil. Yesodei ha-Torah*, 1:9). He therefore feels compelled to launch into a protracted defense of the total incorporeality of God and the consequent need to interpret Biblical verses and aggadot that seem to imply the opposite, citing authorities such as Saadia, R. Hananel, R. Nissim, and even R. Eleazar b. Judah of Worms to substantiate his position. The length and force of his argument against corporealist conceptions of God show that he believed these notions were strongly entrenched among many of the French rabbis and all the more so among the masses (*Teshuvot ha-Rambam ve-Iggerotav*, III, 9d-10a, *Kitvei Ramban*, pp. 345-347.

76. CMR, 100b. Cf. the characterization of the Capetian dynasty of French

kings by R. Nissim of Marseilles, writing around 1300. He attributes the great success of this dynasty to the practice of each king, upon ascending the throne, of executing one or more leading nobles with little cause in order to strike fear into the hearts of the people. This practice is related to Leviticus 10:3 (*He-Halutz*, 7 [1865], 136).

77. *Sefer ha-Me'orot ve-Sefer ha-Hashlamah: Berakhot, Pesahim,* ed. M. blau, pp. 16-18; see also R. Chazan, "A Jewish Plaint to St. Louis," *HUCA*, 45 (1974), 287-305.

78. CAT, 131b-133a.

79. Cf. Menahem Meiri, *Beit ha-Behirah: Avodah Zarah,* p. 60.

80. Cf. Jacob Katz, *Exclusiveness and Tolerance* (New York, 1962), p. 70.

81. *Hil. Teshuvah,* 3:7, 3:9.

82. *Gittin,* 45b; cf. *Hil. Tefillin,* 1:13, and Meiri. There is some confusion over the terminology in the sources. My statement of the halakha, in contrast with the position of R. Isaac, is based on the Bodleian Codex of the Mishneh Torah; see *Sefer Ahavah, The Book of Adoration,* ed. Moses Hyamson (Jerusalem, 1965), p. 120b.

83. Of thirteenth-century apostates who hounded their former coreligionists, Nicholas Donin and Pablo Christiani are especially notorious. Subsequent apostate polemicists are listed by Baron, *SRHJ,* IX, 292, n. 6. Note also the challenge posed by a bishop to Meir b. Simon: "In the past, those who abandoned your faith were scoundrels . . . but now that learned scholars have repudiated Judaism, you should understand from them that they have found the pomegranate and want to throw away the husk and eat what is inside"; *Milhemet Mitzvah,* ff. 226b-227a.

84. *Vikkuah R. Yehiel mi-Paris,* p. 11; A. Lewin, "Die Religionsdisputation des R. Yechiel von Paris, 1240," *MGWJ,* 18 (1869), 200, n. 4.

85. CAT, 148b-150a.

86. For the ceremony involving the newly elected popes, see Baron, *The Jewish Community* (Philadelphia, 1942), I, 217 and note; F. Gregorovius, *The Ghetto and the Jews of Rome* (New York, 1966), pp. 53-58; A. Castro, *The Spaniards* (Berkeley, 1971), p. 91. For secular rulers, see the account of the entrance of the kings of Castile and Portugal into Seville in the middle of the fourteenth century: "And the Moorish people made great rejoicing, the Jews with their Torahs received these kings well" (Castro, p. 90). Among the contemporary illustrations depicting the Italian campaign of the Emperor Henry VII from 1310 to 1313, there is one that shows the newly crowned emperor on horseback with his retinue facing a group of Jews on foot. The emperor holds a sceptre in his left hand, the end of a scroll in his right; on the scroll are lines representing the artist's conception of Hebrew writing. The other end of the scroll is held by the bearded and hooknosed leader of the Roman Jewish community. The caption beneath the picture reads, *"Imp[er]ator redit dans Judeis lege[m] Moysi[s] i[n] rotulo"* ("The emperor returns, giving to the Jews the Law of Moses on a scroll"). Note that while R. Isaac claims that the king and every member of his retinue always descend to the ground to honor the Torah, here the entire imperial party, except for two dignitaries leading the emperor's horse, remains mounted (*Die Romfahrt Kaiser Henrichs VII im Bildercyklus Balduini Trevirensis,* ed. Georg Irmer [Berlin, 1881], plate XXIVa ff. p. 80).

87. *Shulhan Kesef*, MS Turin f. 165a-b, quoted by Barry Mesch, *Studies in Joseph ibn Caspi* (Leiden, 1975), p. 57.

88. CMR, 47b-48a.

89. CAT, 121a-122b.

90. This criticism appears already in the anti-Talmudic tract of the Karaite al-Kirkisani (see chapter I), *HUCA*, 7 (1930), pp. 332-333. For an overview of the problem of prayer to beings other than God in the *Selihot*, see *Seder Selihot*, ed. D. Goldschmidt (Jerusalem, 1965), pp. 11-12, and S. Y. Agnon, *Days of Awe* (New York, 1965), pp. 35-36.

91. *Malmad ha-Talmidim*, p. 68a.

92. *Milhemet Mitzvah*, ff. 234b-235a. See also Maimonides, *Hil. Yesodei ha-Torah*, 2:1, and *Mishnah im Perush ha-Rambam: Nezikin*, p. 212, *yesod* 5; Nachmanides, *Kitvei Ramban*, I, 171.

93. *Ketav Tamim*, pp. 74-75; G. Scholem, *Les origines de la Kabbale*, pp. 422-423; *She'elot u-Teshuvot ha-Ribash* (New York, 1954), #157, p. 34a; '*Alilot Devarim*, in *Otzar Nehmad*, IV (1863), 184.

94. *Malmad ha-Talmidim*, p. 173b. See also the clear definition of heretical dualism in R. Meir b. Simon's *Milhemet Mitzvah*: "Who believe in two Gods, one good, one bad, and say that all that we see through the sense of sight is *not* the creation of the one good God"; quoted by G. Scholem, *Sefer Bialik* (Tel Aviv, 1934), p. 152. Elsewhere R. Isaac defines dualism as the belief in a High God who created the eternal beings and a second god who created the realm of change, including man. He does not explicitly say that this second god is evil, but he associates with this belief the verse "The earth is given into the power of an evil one" (Job 9:24), thus apparently referring to the Gnostic faith (CAT, 32a, 48a).

95. Note also that Ribash reports that the non-Kabbalists think the Kabbalists "believe in dualism" for addressing their prayers to the sefirot and quotes a "philosophizer" as saying, "The Christians believe in the Trinity, the Kabbalists in the Decimity" (*She'elot u-Teshuvot ha-Ribash*).

96. Cf. J. Trachtenberg, *Jewish Magic and Superstition*, p. 64 and nn. pp. 284-285. For a Jewish account of the Christian belief in the intercessory powers of the dead, see Joseph Kimhi, *Sefer ha-Berit* (Jerusalem, 1974), pp. 54-55; also Abraham Bibago, *Derekh Emunah* (Constantinople, 1522; Jerusalem, 1970), p. 96a.

97. On this question in the rabbis and Church fathers, see Israel Levi, "*Si les morts ont conscience de ce qui se passe ici bas*," *REJ*, 26 (1893), 69-74. R. Meir b. Simon, who discusses this question in light of the view that Jews go to the cemetery on a day of public fast "so that the dead will ask for mercy upon us" (*Ta'anit*, 16a) is willing to concede that the dead have knowledge of the living, that they sorrow in their sorrow and rejoice in their joy. But even the sage who believes that the dead may ask for mercy does not hold it is proper for the living to request them to do so. See *Milhemet Mitzvah*, ff. 236b-237a.

98. CAT, 27a.

99. Jewish polemical works against Christianity utilizing a knowledge of Latin to attack the New Testament include Jacob b. Reuben's *Milhamot ha-Shem* (ed. J. Rosenthal [Jerusalem, 1963]); R. Joseph b. Nathan Official's *Sefer Yosef Ha-Mekanne* (ed. J. Rosenthal [Jerusalem, 1970]); and *Sefer Nitzahon Yashan* (in J. Wagenseil, *Tela Ignea Satanae* [1681, reprinted Jerusalem, 1968]). Cf. Rosen-

thal, "Bikoret Yehudit shel ha-Berit ha-Hadashah min ha-Me'ah ha-Shelosh Esreh," in *Studies in Jewish Bibliography, History and Literature in Honor of I. Edward Kiev* (New York, 1972); also E. Urbach, *Ba'alei ha-Tosafot* (Jerusalem, 1968), p. 116 (on R. Joseph Bekhor-Shor). The Disputation of Paris in 1240 may have been conducted in Latin, making knowledge of that language extremely important; see A. Lewin, "Religionsdisputation," p. 151, A. Kisch, "Die Anklageartikel gegen den Talmud," *MGWJ*, 23 (1874), 129.

100. CAT, 135a, and esp. 152a, which compares the two faiths with regard to fasts: we Jews fast once a year (sic), while the Christians fast day after day.

101. CAT, 38b, 104a.

102. CAT, 126b.

103. CAT, 78b; cf. 29b, where he writes about the nations who made up laws and religions, rules and regulations, in order to imitate the Jews because of their jealousy of the perfect religion given to the people of Israel; also 152a. Cf. *Malmad ha-Talmidim*, pp. 15b, 45b, 98b, 150a, 180a, all of which passages contain the theme of the nations, especially the Christians, imitating the Jews and their Torah.

104. CAT, 96a.

105. James Parkes, *The Conflict of Church and Synagogue* (Cleveland, 1961), pp. 102, 298; S. Grayzel, *The Church and the Jews in the XIIIth Century* (New York, 1966), p. 92, n. 2, on *perfidia*; ibid., pp. 252-253, on attempts of Jews to keep their children ignorant of the Law and prophets because of their fear of the truth. The accusations that Jews make their Christian nursemaids empty their milk into the latrine for three days after the Easter communion (ibid., pp. 114-115) and that they attempt to "torture" the host (see R. Chazan, *Medieval Jewry in Northern France*, pp. 181-182) imply belief in the doctrine of transubstantiation.

106. CAT, 79b-81b.

107. Omitted are the Hebrew words *"pa'amim va-yihyu be-eineinu ke-yamim ahadim,"* which make no sense to me in this context.

108. Cf. the statements of David Kimhi, cited by Talmadge, *David Kimhi*, p. 140: "Past instead of future, and there are many instances of this. It is frequent in prophecy. Even though the prophecy refers to the future, it is as if it were already fulfilled." "Past instead of future . . . for the word of the prophet is as certain as if it had already been fulfilled." Abravanel also understands this aggadah as referring to a date in the future: see *Yeshu'ot Meshiho*, p. 23a.

109. Omitted are the Hebrew words *"le-ha'amin ba-shilush,"* which make no sense to me in this context.

110. A. Funkenstein, "Temurot," pp. 141-142; see his n. 62 for conjectures about the word *"Sehale."*

111. *Kitvei Ramban*, I, 303. For a summary of the source material relating to Pablo Christiani, see E. Renan, *Les Rabbins français de commencement du XIVe siècle* (Paris, 1877), pp. 563-571. The author concludes that Pablo engaged in disputations in Provence and Catalonia from 1260-1273 (ibid., p. 569).

112. *Kitvei Ramban*, I, 307-309.

113. Ibid., pp. 306, 312.

114. Contrast the assertion in R. Meir b. Simon's *Milhemet Mitzvah*: "For

we see great wars among you between your pope and your emperor, the two heads of the Gentiles and of your faith" (H. Merhavia, "Li-zemano shel ha-Hibbur Milhemet Mitzvah," p. 298).

115. Horace K. Mann, *The Lives of the Popes in the Middle Ages*, XIV, *Innocent IV*, 48 (his flight from Rome in 1244), 140 (his return in 1253).

116. Ibid., pp. 140-147.

117. Mann, *Lives of the Popes*, XV, *Alexander IV-Gregory X*, 16-45. Of his six and a half years as Pope, a total of only one and a half were spent in Rome (ibid., p. 46).

118. Ibid., p. 242. Urban IV never went to Rome during his entire pontificate, spending most of his time at Orvieto (p. 154).

119. *Kitvei Ramban*, I, 306.

120. *Ha-Kabbalah shel Sefer ha-Temunah ve-shel Avraham Abulafia* (Jerusalem, 1973), p. 113. For Abulafia's journey to Rome and his attempt to see the Pope, see also Idel, pp. 396, 405-406.

vii. R. Isaac's Achievement

1. CAT, 66a, 129b; CMR, 15a, 21a. It is possible that we are dealing with two separate books, a commentary on the Torah (*Hibbur* or *Perush ha-Torah*, cited in CAT) and a homiletical work similar to Anatoli's *Malmad ha-Talmidim* (*Ner Mitzvah*, cited in CMR), but this is not very likely. A homily on the pericope *Mas'ei*, identified as coming from a book entitled *Ner Mitzvah*, is inserted into the middle of a manuscript containing the Torah text and *masorah* (Paris MS 1328-29, ff. 103a-106b). This homily gives an interesting interpretation of the Israelite journeys as allegorical representations of the human life beginning from birth. But the reference to "*ha-Rav Penei David*," the citation of the Zohar, and the use of gematria, all foreign to the commentary on the aggadot and the commentary on the Midrash Rabbah, together with the absence of any distinctive signs of R. Isaac, make it all but certain that this is the work of a different author.

2. *Ein Ya'akov* (New York, 1955), I, 108b, col. 2.

3. It is true that R. Menahem Meiri mentions a R. Meshullam [b.] R. Gershom of Beziers as author of a halakhic work called *Shalman*; see *Beit ha-Behirah: Avot*, p. 56. But this is an extremely problematic passage, and the attempt to reconcile it with conflicting information in other works is mind-boggling (see S. Buber's n. 535 on R. Isaac ibn Lattes, *Sha'arei Tzion* [Jaroslau, 1884], p. 44). The Meiri text cannot be said to establish for certain the existence of a second, later R. Meshullam, let alone establish his candidacy as the outstanding Provençal scholar of his generation, as he appears in our passage.

4. CAT, 84b.

5. CAT, 76b.

6. CAT, 117a. For age forty as a turning point when the intellect first becomes evident, see also Levi b. Abraham in A. S. Halkin, "Why Was Levi ben Hayyim Hounded," PAAJR, 34 (1966), 69.

7. Abraham Bedersi indicates that his father, whose name was Isaac, was a man of some stature (see "Herev ha-Mithapekhet," line 98, and his *Diwan*, Vienna MS 111, f. 234a). If Yedaiah's grandfather wrote his commentaries in the

1260s, it is conceivable that by the beginning of the following century, when Yedaiah was writing his own commentary on the Midrashim, the monumental work of his grandfather may not have been available to him.

8. Bible: the commentaries of David Kimhi, Samuel and Moses ibn Tibbon, Menahem Meiri, Joseph ibn Kaspi, Levi b. Gershom; see I. Twersky, "Aspects of the Social and Cultural History of Provencal Jewry," p. 187, n. 9. Talmud: Rabad of Posquières, Jonathan of Lunel, Abraham of Montpellier, Menahem Meiri. Halakhic Midrash: Rabad on Sifra (see Twersky, *Rabad of Posquières*, pp. 97-106). Alfasi: Rabad's Hassagot, Zerahiah ha-Levi's *Sefer ha-Ma'or*, the commentary of Jonathan ha-Cohen of Lunel. *Mishneh Torah:* Rabad, Jonathan of Lunel, Moses of Lunel (see Twersky, "Aspects," p. 193, and "The Beginning of *Mishneh Torah* Criticism," *Biblical and Other Studies* [Cambridge, Mass., 1962], pp. 161-183). *Sefer Yetzirah:* Isaac the Blind and R. Azriel (see Scholem, *Les origines de la Kabbale*, pp. 262-265 and 394). Liturgy: R. Azriel (ibid., pp. 394-395), and R. Reuben b. Hayyim's *Sefer ha-Tamid* (in *Otzar ha-Hayyim*, 11 [1935], 1-38). *Guide:* Shem Tov Falaquera, Joseph ibn Kaspi, Moses Narboni. Aristotle: especially those of Gersonides and Narboni (see Steinschneider, *Die hebraeischen Uebersetzungen*).

9. Ibid. As Harry Wolfson has pointed out, the popularity of these works can be seen in the number of extant manuscripts: 20 of the Epitome of the *Physics*, 18 of the Epitome of *De Caelo*, 25 of the Epitome of *Parva Naturalia*, 36 of the Middle Commentary on *De Caelo*; see "Plan for the Publication of a *Corpus Commentariorum Averrois in Aristotelem*," *Studies in the History of Philosophy and Religion*, I (Cambridge, Mass., 1973), 431. By the beginning of the fourteenth century, Yedaiah Bedersi, writing his own commentary on ibn Rushd's Epitome of the *Physics* (Parma MS 1399), had enough manuscripts of this work available to him to compare textual readings just as Talmudic scholars had been doing: "This is the reading you find in a few manuscripts, but it is not what you find in most" (f. 159b; see also ff. 94b and 144a).

10. See esp. F. Talmadge, "David Kimhi and the Rationalist Tradition," *HUCA*, 39 (1968), 177-218, and "David Kimhi and the Rationalist Tradition II: Literary Sources," *Studies in Jewish Bibliography, History and Literature in Honor of I. Edward Kiev* (New York, 1972), pp. 453-478. Samuel ibn Tibbon appended selected translations of passages from Averroes' treatises on the intellect to his commentary on Ecclesiastes, prior to the earliest dated translation of a full work by Averroes (1232); a generation later, his son, Moses, was citing extensive passages from Alfarabi and Averroes in the introduction to his commentary on the Song of Songs; by the time Gersonides wrote his own commentaries, he was including references to specific works of Aristotle and Averroes on almost every page.

11. Especially *Sha'ar ha-Shamayim* of Gershom b. Solomon, and *Battei ha-Nefesh ve-ha-Lehashim* and *Livyat Hen* of Levi b. Abraham.

12. For example, Joseph ibn Zabara's *Sefer Sha'ashu'im*, Shem Tov Falaquera's *Sefer ha-Mevakesh*, Isaac ibn Sahula's *Meshal ha-Kadmoni*. For the relationship of the scientific material in *Sefer Sha'ashu'im* to that in *Sha'ar ha-Shamayim*, see I. Davidson's introduction to *Sefer Sha'ashu'im of Joseph ibn Zabara* (New York, 1914), pp. lxviii, lxxii, lxxxvii. While the three works mentioned

were actually composed in Christian Spain, they were apparently just as popular across the Pyrenees.

13. An indication of this purpose and of the relatively wide audience for which this work was intended can be seen in R. Isaac's characterization of himself as "explaining ancient texts for a multitude of people (*be-rov am*) . . . to enlighten their minds in this matter" (CMR, 47b).

14. In particular, men such as David Kimhi, Samuel b. Abraham, Asher b. Gershom. See *Kovetz Teshuvot ha-Rambam ve-Iggerotav*, III, 1-4; *Kevutzat Mikhtavim* in *Jeschurun*, VIII, 125-155; J. Shatzmiller, "Iggarto shel R. Asher ben R. Gershom," *Mehkarim le-Zekher Tzvi Avneri* (Haifa, 1970), pp. 129-140.

15. Rashba's novellae on the aggadot are filled with philosophical concepts and philosophical interpretations; the work as a whole reveals the influence of philosophy at least as much as the influence of Kabbala. Even in the letters written within the context of the conflict, Rashba recognizes in principle that philosophy contains truths as well as falsehood; he opposes the indiscriminate dissemination to those who are too young to distinguish what should be kept from what should be rejected (*Minhat Kena'ot*, pp. 22, 27). Abba Mari of Lunel, the spearhead of the "antiphilosophical" effort in southern France, accepts the ideological position of the philosophers that philosophy was a native Jewish enterprise introduced to the world by Abraham; he has a relatively positive attitude toward Aristotle, and he affirms the intrinsic value of the sciences (*Minhat Kena'ot*, pp. 15, 123-127).

16. For the position of R. Asher, see *Minhat Kena'ot*, p. 178, and *She'elot u-Teshuvot Rabbenu Asher* (New York, 1954), #55, p. 53a. For the analogous position in the controversy of the 1230s, see Judah Alfakhar in *Kovetz Teshuvot ha-Rambam*, p. 1, col. 1, middle.

17. Parma MS 155(2749), ff. 179b-240a. The first part of this section is a response to aggadot cited by Christian opponents for various purposes. The following statement may serve as an example of R. Meir's approach: "Sir! you know, as does every wise man, that one takes the words of a sage literally if they are rational and sensible. But if they are not rational and sensible when taken literally, then we must take them figuratively" (f. 215b, quoted by Talmadge, *David Kimhi*, p. 81). When asked by a Christian why the sages spoke in such an arcane manner rather than making their message clear to all, he replied that the Christian Gospels contain at least one incident (the cursing of the fig tree in Matthew 21:18-19 and Mark 11:12-14) that Christian commentators interpret allegorically because the simple meaning is abhorrent (f. 220a-b). This is in defense of his allegorical interpretation of a statement concerning twenty-four toilets (*Nedarim*, 49b) as referring to the need for self-scrutiny and confession throughout the twenty-four hours of the day. R. Meir interprets aggadot that had troubled the geonim (God's using tefillin and talit, ff. 221a-222a), aggadot that had been exploited by Petrus Alfonsi and Peter the Venerable (Korah's wealth, Og's size, ff. 220b-221a, 222b-223a), passages concerning Jewish-Gentile relations that caused trouble in the Disputation of Paris (ff. 214b-215a, 225a-226b), and statements used to "prove" Christian doctrines such as the changing of the law in messianic times (f. 224a-b). In his polemic against the incipient Kabbala, there is an extensive and important analysis of "Metatron, whose name is like the name of

his Master" (ff. 233a-234a).

18. Oxford Bodleian MS 939; this work is being prepared for publication by Colette Sirat, who graciously made available to me a transcription. The introduction is extremely valuable, defining the problem (Gentile scholars mocking the aggadah, Jewish "philosophizers" not knowing how to penetrate beyond the simple meaning) and suggesting the proper approach to various types of rabbinic discourse. The longest comment in this work, on God's activities during the twelve hours of the day (*AZ*, 3b, ff. 14a-16b), bears careful comparison with R. Isaac's comment on this passage, although there is no sign of direct influence.

19. Vatican MS 192. The *Sha'ar ha-Aggadah* contains the following general statement: "It is known that some of the aggadot are intended for the masses, some for those of average intelligence, some for the wise, and some for everyone. These last have both a manifest and an esoteric content. Sometimes philosophical matters are mixed together with other things as allegory in order to conceal them . . . , for the Talmud was written for all . . . When the sages saw that men of true wisdom were lacking, that there was a decline from generation to generation, that sufferings increased and spread, and that those who attained the peak of true philosophical insight were few indeed, they realized it would be better to lock the gates of theoretical philosophy and let tradition suffice until a true teacher would arise. They contented themselves with leaving a few allusions for those with the capacity to understand them" (f. 123b). In addition to the allegorical interpretations of messianic statements already noted (ff. 34b-35a; see chapter IV, section 3), Levi gives noteworthy explications of the stories about Og and Moses (ff. 68b-71a) and about the "oven of Akhnai" (ff. 125b-127a).

20. *Perush ha-Midrashim*; for a comparison of this work with R. Isaac's commentaries, see my "R. Isaac b. Yeda'yah," *REJ*, 1979. The well-known discussion of the aggadah in Yedaiah's *Iggeret ha-Hitnatzlut* may be supplemented by his comment on the statement "Do you desire to know the One who brought the world into being through His word? Study aggadah." Yedaiah writes: "They meant by this that because the books of the various branches of knowledge were lost from our nation, and our understanding disappeared, the sages of our tradition in all the generations of the exile were wise enough to find a strategem through which they could preserve the truths [of the sciences] by their own authority, so that masses and elite alike would not despise these truths. They did this by alluding to such doctrines in the homilies and nonlegal utterances that are interspersed among the laws of the Torah and the rules for conduct. Whoever did not have comprehension adequate to the understanding of these truths would take the statements entirely according to their obvious, simple meaning and would not despise them . . . But when they would reach those select few who do not wrong their own souls but who have perhaps already had a whiff of some theoretical axioms, such people would begin to react to the hidden meaning of those allegories and extract from them true insights relating to the secrets of the Torah and the roots of belief and the secrets of the realm of being, which are called *sitrei torah*. From these can be known and apprehended all that is possible to know of God, and this is how one draws near to Him insofar as is possible" (Parma MS 222 on *Sifrei, Ekev*, 49).

21. Munich MS 94, ff. 209a-212b; cf. Touati, *La pensée philosophique*, pp.

62-63. The hidden content of the stories, revealed by the allegorical interpretation, is defined as "the ways of apprehending the intelligibles of the lower and upper realms" (f. 210a). For example, the seven seas surrounding the land of Israel, mentioned by R. Yohanan in *Baba Batra,* 74b are the seven books of Aristotle, which are necessary for the actualization of the human intellect, and the "land of Israel" itself refers to philosophical wisdom (f. 212b).

22. *Livyat Hen,* f. 134b; de-Rossi, *Me'or Einayim* (Vilna, 1866), p. 336.

23. *Moreh ha-Moreh* (Pressburg, 1837), p. 114; cf. *Falaquera's Book of the Seeker,* ed. M. H. Levine (New York, 1976), p. xliv.

24. *Tagmulei ha-Nefesh* (Lyck, 1874), p. 26b; cf. I. Barzilay, *Between Reason and Faith* (The Hague, 1967), p. 45.

25. See I. Twersky, *Rabad of Posquières,* pp. 62-64.

26. For example, CMR, 47b, 52b, 97b. Such emphasis on originality is not common among medieval writers, but it is certainly not unique. A kindred spirit was Joseph ibn Kaspi: "Most of it contradicts everything that has been set down by earlier commentators"; "I will solve the difficulty in a manner I have neither heard nor seen in any previous writer" (Barry Mesch, *Studies in Joseph ibn Caspi,* pp. 31, 37). Of course, such proclamations cannot be taken as evidence of originality; some medieval authors were not above making similar claims when they had indeed borrowed from other sources. Each case must be investigated separately.

27. This generalization would be validated by comparison of the following introductions, representing works of different genres: Zerahiah ha-Levi to *Sefer ha-Ma'or,* Abraham b. Nathan to *Sefer ha-Manhig,* Menahem Meiri to *Magen Avot* and to *Beit ha-Behirah,* Joseph Kimhi to *Sefer ha-Galui,* Jacob Anatoli to *Malmad ha-Talmidim,* Moses ibn Tibbon to *Sefer Pe'ah,* Levi b. Gershom to *Perush Shir ha-Shirim,* Joseph ibn Kaspi to *Sefer ha-Sod,* Judah ibn Tibbon to tr. of *Hovot ha-Levavot,* Samuel ibn Tibbon to tr. of *Moreh Nevukhim,* Jacob Anatoli to tr. of ibn Rushd's commentary on Aristotle's *Organon* (cited Dinur, *Yisrael be-Golah,* II, 4, 153-154), Levi b. Abraham to *Battei ha-Nefesh ve-ha-Lehashim* (ed. I. Davidson in *REJ,* 105 [1939], 80-94).

28. For Maimonides' intention to write a commentary on the aggadot that seem to conflict with science and philosophy, and his subsequent decision to abandon this task, see chapter I, n. 72.

29. Scholem, *MTJM,* p. 31.

Index of Code Words

Index of Passages Cited

BIBLE

278

General Index

HARVARD JUDAIC MONOGRAPHS